Essentials of Operations Management

Essentials of Operations Management

Second Edition

Nigel Slack

Alistair Brandon-Jones

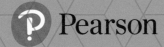

Harlow, England • London • New York • Boston • San Francisco • Toronto • Sydney • Dubai • Singapore • Hong Kong
Tokyo • Seoul • Taipei • New Delhi • Cape Town • São Paulo • Mexico City • Madrid • Amsterdam • Munich • Paris • Milan

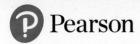

Pearson Education Limited

KAO Two
KAO Park
Harlow
CM17 9NA
United Kingdom
Tel: +44 (0)1279 623623
Web: www.pearson.com/uk

First published 2011 (print)
Second edition published 2018 (print and electronic)

ISBN: 978-1-292-23884-5 (print)
     978-1-292-23890-6 (PDF)
     978-1-292-23888-3 (ePub)

British Library Cataloguing-in-Publication Data
A catalogue record for the print edition is available from the British Library.

Library of Congress Cataloging-in-Publication Data
Essentials of Operations Management
Library of Congress Cataloging in Publication Control Number: 2018019814

10 9 8 7 6 5 4 3 2 1
22 21 20 19 18

Front cover photo: Taiwan Taoyuan International Airport by Kiwihug on Unsplash

Design by Design Deluxe, Bath

Print edition typeset in 9.75/13pt Avenir LT Pro by SPi Global.
Print edition printed and bound in Slovakia by Neografia.

NOTE THAT ANY PAGE CROSS REFERENCES REFER TO THE PRINT EDITION

Brief contents

Contents

Operations management and performance

2

Operations strategy

3

Product and service innovation

Process design – resources

Process design – analysis

6

Supply chain management

7

Capacity management

8

Inventory management

9

Resource planning and control

10

Lean operations

In fact, most operations produce both services and products. Figure 1.2 shows a number of operations positioned in a spectrum, from 'pure' products to 'pure' service. Crude oil producers are concerned almost exclusively with the product from their oil wells. Aluminium smelters are similar, but might also deliver some 'facilitating' services, such as technical advice. To an even greater extent, machine tool manufacturers deliver facilitating services such as technical advice and applications engineering. The restaurant is both a manufacturer of meals and a provider of service. An information systems provider may create software 'products', but primarily provides a service to its customers. Certainly, a management consultancy, although it produces reports and documents, is primarily a service provider. Finally, some pure services solely create and deliver services – a psychotherapy clinic, for example.

Increasingly, the distinction between services and products is difficult to define and not particularly useful. Software has moved from being primarily a product (sold on a disk) to an intangible download when sold over the internet, to an even less tangible rental or subscription service based 'in the cloud'. Indeed, one could argue that all operations are service providers that may create and deliver products as part of the offering to their customers.

operations principle
Whether an operation produces tangible products or intangible services is becoming increasingly irrelevant. In a sense, all operations produce service for their customers.

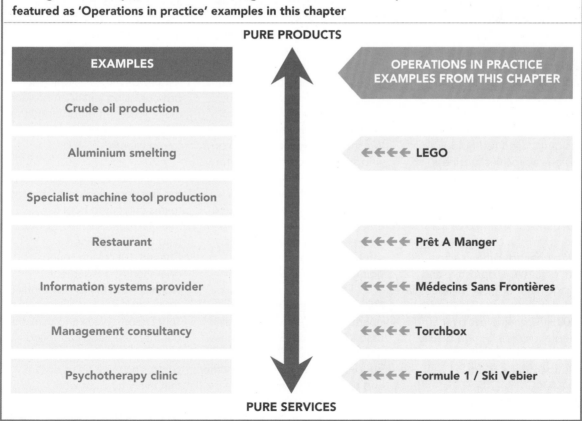

FIGURE 1.2   **Most operations produce a mixture of products and services. Some general examples are shown here, together with some of the operations featured as 'Operations in practice' examples in this chapter**

PURE PRODUCTS

EXAMPLES	OPERATIONS IN PRACTICE EXAMPLES FROM THIS CHAPTER
Crude oil production	
Aluminium smelting	⇐⇐⇐⇐ LEGO
Specialist machine tool production	
Restaurant	⇐⇐⇐⇐ Prêt A Manger
Information systems provider	⇐⇐⇐⇐ Médecins Sans Frontières
Management consultancy	⇐⇐⇐⇐ Torchbox
Psychotherapy clinic	⇐⇐⇐⇐ Formule 1 / Ski Vebier

PURE SERVICES

Operations improvement

11

Quality management

Project management

Guide to 'Operations in practice' examples

Chapter	Location	Company/ example	Region	Sector/ activity	Company size
Chapter 5 Process design – analysis	p.133	Changi Airport	Singapore	Air travel	Large
	p.137	Fast food	General	Restaurants	Large
	p.143	Sainsbury's line of visibility	UK	Retail	Large
	p.155	Shouldice Hospital	Canada	Healthcare	Small
Chapter 6 Supply chain management	p.166	Ocado	UK	Retail	Medium
	p.168	Managing Apple's supply network	Global	Technology	Large
	p.170	The North Face of sustainable purchasing	Global	Retail	Medium
	p.181	The tsunami effect	Global	All	N/A
Chapter 7 Capacity management	p.203	Heart surgery and shipping	India/ global	Healthcare/ transport	Large
	p.209	Panettone	Italy	Food production	Large
	p.217	Annualized hours at Lowaters	UK	Retail	Small
Chapter 8 Inventory management	p.237	An inventory of energy	Global	Energy	Large
	p.244	Treasury Wine's hangover	Australasia	Retail	Large
	p.254	Inventory management at Flame Electrical	South Africa	Wholesale	Medium
	p.261	Amazon's 'anticipatory shipping'	Global	Retail	Large
Chapter 9 Resource planning and control	p.277	BMW scheduling	UK	Motor service	Medium
	p.288	Can airline passengers be sequenced?	General	Air transport	N/A
	p.294	The life and times of a chicken sandwich	General	Food production	N/A

Supporting resources

Visit **www.pearsoned.co.uk/slack** to find valuable online resources

MyLab Operations Management

For students

- Interactive tutorial exercises with immediate feedback
- A personalized study plan with a range of self-assessment questions
- Excel spreadsheets designed to help support your understanding of key concepts
- An online glossary to explain key terms
- Flashcards to test your understanding of key terms

For instructors

- Operations management simulations allow students to apply key theory to real business scenarios
- A homework and assignment manager, allowing you to assign exercises for your students
- A Gradebook which tracks students' performance on sample tests as well as assessments of your own design

The **Companion Website** provides suggested model answers to the first question in the 'problems and applications' section of each chapter.

For more information please contact your local Pearson Education sales representative or visit www.pearsoned.co.uk/slack

Preface

INTRODUCTION – OPERATIONS MAY NOT RUN THE WORLD, BUT IT MAKES THE WORLD RUN.

Operations management is *important*. It is concerned with creating the services and products upon which we all depend. All organizations produce some mixture of services and products, whether that organization is large or small, manufacturing or service, for profit or not for profit, public or private. Thankfully, most companies have now come to understand the importance of operations. This is because they have realized that effective operations management gives the potential to improve both customer service and efficiency simultaneously. But more than this, operations management is *everywhere*; it is not confined to the operations function. All managers, whether they are called Operations or Marketing or Human Resources or Finance, or whatever, manage processes and serve customers (internal or external). This makes at least part of their activities 'operations'.

Operations management is also *exciting*. It is at the centre of so many of the changes affecting the business world – changes in customer preference, changes in supply networks brought about by internet-based technologies, changes in what we want to do at work, how we want to work, where we want to work and so on. There has rarely been a time when operations management was more topical or more at the heart of business and cultural shifts.

Operations management is also *challenging*. Promoting the creativity that will allow organizations to respond to so many changes is becoming the prime task of operations managers. It is they who must find the solutions to technological and environmental challenges, the pressures to be socially responsible, the increasing globalization of markets and the difficult-to-define areas of knowledge management.

THE AIM OF THIS BOOK

This book provides a clear, authoritative, well-structured and interesting treatment of operations management as it applies to a variety of businesses and organizations. The text provides both a logical path through the activities of operations management and an understanding of their strategic context.

More specifically, this text is:

 strategic in its perspective – it is unambiguous in treating the operations function as being central to competitiveness

 conceptual in the way it explains the reasons why operations managers need to take decisions

 comprehensive in its coverage of the significant ideas and issues that are relevant to most types of operation

 practical in that the issues and challenges of making operations management decisions in practice are discussed (the 'Operations in practice' examples that feature in every chapter explore the approaches taken by operations managers in practice)

 global in the examples that are used, with descriptions of operations practice from all over the world, and in the treatment of core OM ideas

 balanced in its treatment, in that it accurately reflects the balance of economic activity between service and manufacturing operations.

WHO SHOULD USE THIS BOOK?

This book is for anyone who is interested in how services and products are created:

 Undergraduates on business studies, technical or joint degrees should find it sufficiently structured to provide an understandable route through the subject (no prior knowledge of the area is assumed).

 MBA students should find that its practical discussions of operations management activities enhance their own experiences.

 Postgraduate students on other specialist Master's degrees should find that it provides them with a well-grounded and, at times, critical approach to the subject.

DISTINCTIVE FEATURES

Clear structure

The structure of the book uses the '4 Ds' model of operations management that distinguishes between the strategic decisions that govern the *direction* of the operation, the *design* of the processes and operations that create products and services, planning and control of the *delivery* of products and services, and the *development*, or improvement, of operations.

Illustrations-based

Operations management is a practical subject and cannot be taught satisfactorily in a purely theoretical manner. Because of this we have used examples and short 'operations in practice' examples that explain some of the issues faced by real operations.

Summary answers to key questions

Each chapter is summarized in the form of a list of bullet points. These extract the essential points that answer the key questions posed at the beginning of each chapter.

Problems and applications

Every chapter includes a set of problem-type exercises. These can be used to check your understanding of the concepts illustrated in the worked examples. There are also activities that support the learning objectives of the chapter, which can be undertaken individually or in groups.

Want to know more?

Every chapter ends with a short list of further reading that takes the topics covered in the chapter further, or treats some important, related issues. The nature of each further reading is also explained.

To the instructor

THE *ESSENTIALS* SECOND EDITION

When we created the first edition of *Essentials* we hoped that we were keeping up with the requirements and preferences of our book users. We were responding to what we thought was a demand from both lecturers and students for a text aimed at shorter, more introductory courses in operations management. We believed that there was a demand for an authoritative but not necessarily fully comprehensive text. It appears we were right. The first edition of *Essentials,* based on the approach that has made both *Operations Management* and *Operations and Process Management* market-leading texts, was particularly well received – hence this second edition.

 We have retained the concept of a text that is shorter than its companion texts, with coverage focused on what extensive research indicates are key topics. In some cases, this has involved incorporating content from more than one chapter of our longer texts. For example, in this edition we have combined operations management and operations performance content to free up space for an additional chapter on project management that wasn't in the first edition.

 We have also retained many learning features, including 'Operations in practice' examples, 'Key questions', 'Worked examples', 'Test your knowledge', 'Problems and applications', and the 'Want to know more?' features.

 What is new to this edition, in addition to many new examples and increased coverage of some topics, is that for the first time we offer model answers to the 'Problems and applications' exercises at the end of each chapter. Answers to the first question are included in the companion student website to this text. Answers to the other questions are available to bona fide lecturers and tutors in order to support their teaching.

To the student

All academic texts in business management are, to some extent, simplifications of the messy reality that is actual organizational life. Any book has to separate topics in order to study them, which in reality are closely related. For example, operations strategy impacts on process design, which in turn impacts on approach to quality management; yet, for simplicity, we are obliged to treat these topics individually. The first hint, therefore, in using this text effectively is to look out for all the links between the individual topics. Similarly, with the sequence of topics, although the chapters follow a logical structure, they need not be studied in this order. Every chapter is, more or less, self-contained. Therefore, study the chapters in whatever sequence is appropriate to your course or your individual interests. The same applies to revision – study the introductory passages and 'Test your knowledge' sections.

The text makes full use of the many practical examples and illustrations that can be found in all operations. Many of these were provided by our contacts in companies, but many also come from journals, magazines and newspapers. So, if you want to understand the importance of operations management in everyday business life, look for examples and illustrations of operations management decisions and activities in newspapers and magazines. There are also examples that you can observe every day. Whenever you use a shop, eat a meal in a restaurant, access music via your phone or ride on public transport, consider the operations management issues of all the operations for which you are a customer.

The 'Problems and applications' exercises are there to provide an opportunity for you to think further about the ideas discussed in the chapters. They can be used to test out your understanding of the specific points and issues discussed in the chapter and to discuss them as a group, if you choose. If you cannot answer these you should revisit the relevant parts of the chapter. When you have done this individually, try to discuss your analysis with other course members. Most important of all, every time you analyze one of the case exercises (or any other case or example in operations management), start off your analysis with these two fundamental questions:

 How is this organization trying to compete (or satisfy its strategic objectives if a not-for-profit organization)?

 What can the operation do to help the organization compete more effectively?

Ten steps to getting a better grade in operations management

We could say that the best rule for getting a better grade is to be good. We mean really, really good! But, there are plenty of us who, while fairly good, don't get as good a grade as we really deserve. So, if you are studying operations management, and you want a really good grade, try following these simple steps:

1 ➜ **Practice, practice, practice.** Use the 'Test your knowledge' and the 'Problems and applications' features to check your understanding. Use the 'Study plan' feature in MyLabOM and practice to master the topics that you find difficult.

2 ➜ Remember a few **key models,** and apply them wherever you can. Use the diagrams and models to describe some of the examples that are contained within each chapter. You can also use the revision podcasts on MyLabOM.

3 ➜ Remember to use both **quantitative and qualitative** analysis. You'll get more credit for mixing your methods appropriately: use a quantitative model to answer a quantitative question and vice versa, but qualify this with a few well-chosen sentences. Both the chapters of the text and the exercises on MyLabOM incorporate qualitative and quantitative material.

4 ➜ There's always a strategic **objective** behind any operational issue. Ask yourself, 'Would a similar operation with a different strategy do things differently?'. Look at the 'Operations in practice' pieces in the text.

5 ➜ **Research** widely around the topic. Use websites that you trust – we've listed some good websites in the 'Notes' section at the end of the text and on MyOMLab. You'll get more credit for using references that come from genuine academic sources.

6 ➜ **Use your own experience.** Every day, you're experiencing an opportunity to apply the principles of operations management. Why is the queue at the airport check-in desk so long? What goes on 'behind the scenes' to deliver you the latest tech gadget? Use the clips on MyLabOM to look further at operations in practice.

7

➔ **Always answer the question.** Think 'what is really being asked here?'. 'What topic or topics does this question cover?' Find the relevant chapter or chapters, and search the 'Key questions' at the beginning of each chapter and the 'Test your knowledge' at the end of each chapter to get you started.

8

➔ Take account of the **three tiers of accumulating marks** for your answers:

a) First, demonstrate your knowledge and understanding. Make full use of the text and MyLabOM to find out where you need to improve.

b) Second, show that you know how to illustrate and apply the topic. The 'Operations in practice' sections, combined with those on MyLabOM, give you hundreds of different examples.

c) Third, show that you can discuss and analyze the issues critically. Where appropriate, consider alternative viewpoints.

Generally, if you can do (a) you will pass; if you can do (a) and (b) you will pass well; and if you can do all three, you will pass with flying colours!

9

➔ Remember not only **what** the issue is about, but also understand **why**! Read the text and apply your knowledge until you really understand why the concepts and techniques of operations management are important, and what they contribute to an organization's success. Your new-found knowledge will stick in your memory, allow you to develop ideas and enable you to get better grades.

10

➔ **Start now!** Don't wait until two weeks before an assignment is due or an exam is about to take place. Read on, log on (www.myomlab.com) and GOOD LUCK!

Nigel Slack and Alistair Brandon-Jones

About the authors

Nigel Slack

Nigel Slack is an Emeritus Professor of Operations Management and Strategy at Warwick University, an Honorary Professor at Bath University and an Associate Fellow of Said Business School, Oxford University. Previously he has been Professor of Service Engineering at Cambridge University, Professor of Manufacturing Strategy at Brunel University, a University Lecturer in Management Studies at Oxford University and Fellow in Operations Management at Templeton College, Oxford. He worked initially as an industrial apprentice in the hand-tool industry and then as a production engineer and production manager in light engineering. He holds a Bachelor's degree in Engineering and Master's and Doctor's degrees in Management, and is a Chartered Engineer. He is the author of many books in Operations Management, including *Operations Management* (with Alistair Brandon-Jones and Robert Johnston), the eighth edition published in 2016, *Operations and Process Management* (with Alistair Brandon-Jones), the fifth edition published in 2018, *Operations Strategy* (with Michael Lewis), the fourth edition published in 2014, *The Manufacturing Advantage,* published in 1991, *Making Management Decisions* (with Steve Cooke) published in 1991, *Service Superiority* (with Robert Johnston), published in 1993, *The Blackwell Encyclopedic Dictionary of Operations* Management, published in 1997, and *Perspectives in Operations Management* (with Michael Lewis), published in 2003. Nigel has authored numerous academic papers and chapters in books. He also acts as a consultant to many international companies around the world in many sectors, especially financial services, transport, leisure and manufacturing. His research is in the operations and manufacturing flexibility and operations strategy areas.

Alistair Brandon-Jones

Alistair Brandon-Jones is a Full Chaired Professor in Operations and Supply Management at the University of Bath, and an Adjunct Professor at Hult International Business School. He was formerly a Reader at Manchester Business School, an Assistant and Associate Professor at Bath University and a Teaching Fellow at Warwick Business School, where he also completed his PhD. In addition to *Essentials of Operations Management,* his other books include *Operations and Process Management* (with Nigel Slack), the fifth edition published in 2018, *Operations Management* (with Nigel Slack and Robert Johnston), the eighth edition published in 2016 and *Quantitative Analysis in Operations Management* (with Nigel Slack), published in 2008. Alistair is an active empirical researcher, focusing on e-enabled operations and supply management, professional services and healthcare operations. He has published this research extensively in world-leading journals including *Journal of Operations Management, International Journal of Operations and Production Management, International Journal of Production Economics* and *International Journal of Production Research.* He has also disseminated his research through various practitioner publications, conferences, workshops and white papers. Alistair has consulting and executive development experience with organizations around the world, in various sectors including petrochemicals, health, financial services, manufacturing, defence and government. In addition, he has won numerous prizes for teaching excellence and contributions to pedagogy, including from Times Higher Education, Association of MBAs (AMBA), Production Operations Management Society (POMS), University of Bath, University of Manchester and University of Warwick.

Acknowledgements

During the preparation of our portfolio of books, we have received an immense amount of help from friends and colleagues in the operations management community. In particular, everybody who has attended one of the regular 'faculty workshops' deserves thanks for their many useful comments. The generous sharing of ideas from these sessions has influenced this and all the other OM books that we prepare. It is, to some extent, invidious to single out individuals – but we are going to. We thank: Pär Åhlström of Stockholm School of Economics; James Aitken of the University Of Surrey; Professor Sven Åke Hörte of Lulea University of Technology; Eamonn Ambrose of University College, Dublin; Andrea Benn of the University of Brighton; Yongmei Bentley of the University of Bedfordshire; Helen Benton of Anglia Ruskin University; Ran Bhamra of Loughborough University; Mattia Bianchi of the Stockholm School of Economics; Tony Birch of Birmingham City University; Emma Brandon-Jones of Bath University; John K. Christiansen of Copenhagen Business School; Philippa Collins of Heriot-Watt University; Henrique Correa of Rollins College, Florida; Paul Coughlan of Trinity College Dublin; Simon Croom of the University of San Diego; Doug Davies of University of Technology, Sydney; Stephen Disney of Cardiff University; Carsten Dittrich of the University of Southern Denmark; Tony Dromgoole of the Irish Management Institute; David Evans of Middlesex University; Ian Evans of Sunderland University; Paul Forrester of Keele University; Abhijeet Ghadge of Heriot Watt University; Ian Graham of Edinburgh University; J.A.C. de Haan of Tilburg University; Alan Harle of Sunderland University; Norma Harrison of Macquarie University; Catherine Hart of Loughborough Business School; Steve Hickman of University of Exeter; Chris Hillam of Sunderland University; Ian Holden of Bristol Business School; Matthias Holweg of Oxford University; Mickey Howard of Exeter University; Kim Hua Tan of the University Of Nottingham; Stavros Karamperidis of Heriot Watt University; Tom Kegan of Bell College of Technology, Hamilton; Denis Kehoe of Liverpool University; Mike Lewis of Bath University; Xiaohong Li of Sheffield Hallam University; Bart McCarthy of Nottingham University; Peter McCullen of University of Brighton; John Maguire of the University of Sunderland; Charles Marais of the University of Pretoria; Roger Maull of Exeter University; Harvey Maylor of Cranfield University; John Meredith Smith of EAP, Oxford; Michael Milgate of Macquarie University; Keith Moreton of Staffordshire University; Chris Morgan of Cranfield University; Adrian Morris of Sunderland University; Andy Neely of Cambridge University; Steve New of Oxford University; John Pal of Manchester Metropolitan University; Sofia Salgado Pinto of the Católica Porto Business School; Gary Priddis of University of Brighton; Carrie Queenan of the University of South Carolina; Peter Race of Henley College, Reading

University; Jawwad Raja, Copenhagen Business School; Gary Ramsden of University of Lincoln; Steve Robinson of Southampton Solent University; Frank Rowbotham of University of Birmingham; James Rowell of University of Buckingham; Ian Sadler of Victoria University; Hamid Salimian of University of Brighton; Sarah Schiffling of University of Lincoln; Alex Skedd of Northumbria Business School; Andi Smart of Exeter University; Amrik Sohal of Monash University; Dr Ebrahim Soltani of the University of Kent; Rui Soucasaux Sousa of the Católica Porto Business School; Nigel Spinks of the University of Reading; Martin Spring of Lancaster University; R. Stratton of Nottingham Trent University; Dr. Nelson Tang of the University of Leicester; David Twigg of Sussex University; Arvind Upadhyay of University of Brighton; Helen Valentine of the University of the West of England; Professor Roland van Dierdonck of the University of Ghent; Dirk Pieter van Donk of the University of Groningen; Nick Wake, Hult International Business School; Vessela Warren of the University of Worcester; Bill Wright of Bpp Professional; Ying Xie of Anglia Ruskin University; Maggie Zeng of Gloucestershire University; and Li Zhou of the University of Greenwich.

Our academic colleagues in the Operations Management Group at Warwick and Bath also helped, both by contributing ideas and by creating a lively and stimulating work environment. At Warwick, thanks go to Vikki Abusidualghoul, Haley Beer, Nicola Burgess, Mehmet Chakkol, Max Finne, Emily Jamieson, Mark Johnson, Pietro Micheli, Giovanni Radaelli, Ross Ritchie, Rhian Silvestro, and Chris Voss. At Bath, thanks go to Maria Battarra, Emma Brandon-Jones, Jie Chen, Günes Erdogan, Emmanuel Fragniere, Vaggelis Giannikas, Andrew Graves, Yufei Huang, Jooyoung Jeon, Adam Joinson, Richard Kamm, Mike Lewis, Sheik Meeran, Ibrahim Muter, Fotios Petropoulos, Lukasz Piwek, Tony Roath, Jens Roehrich, Brian Squire, Kate Sugar, Christos Vasilakis, Xingjie Wei, Emma Williams, and Baris Yalabik.

We were lucky to receive continuing professional and friendly assistance from a great publishing team at Pearson. Especial thanks to Natalia Jaszczuk, Catherine Yates, Carole Drummond, Akshay Samson, Shweta Sharma and Emma Marchant.

Finally, to our families, who both supported and tolerated our nerdish obsession. Thanks are inadequate, but thanks anyway to Angela and Kathy, and Emma and Noah.

Nigel Slack and Alistair Brandon-Jones

Publisher's acknowledgements

We are grateful to the following for permission to reproduce copyright material:

Figures

Figure 7.5 Adapted from What is the right supply chain for your product?, Harvard Business Review, March–April, pp. 105 –16 (Fisher, M.C. 1997); **Figure 12.1** From from The EFQM Website, www.efqm.org; **Figure 12.4** Adapted from A conceptual model of service quality and implications for future research, Journal of Marketing, 49, Fall, pp. 41–50 (Parasuraman, A. et al. 1985).

Text

p. 41 From Cookson C (2015) Guildford's SSTL leads world in small satellite supply, Financial Times, June 12; **p. 48** From Ron Johnson (2011) What I Learned Building the Apple Store, HBR Blog network, November 21 https://hbr.org/2011/11/what-i-learned-building-the-ap; **p. 54** From http://searchcio.techtarget.com/definition/outsourcing; **p. 57** from Marty Lariviere (2011) How Apple spends on operations, The Operations Room, November 16; **p. 66** from Definition from techtarget.com, searchdatacenter.techtarget.com/; **p. 73** from https://www.merriam-webster.com/dictionary/innovation; **p. 75** from (2012) iPhone was almost scrapped, says Apple design guru, The Times, July 30; **p. 388** from The EFQM Website, www.efqm.org; **p. 401** from The EFQM Website, www.efqm.org.

In some instances we have been unable to trace the owners of copyright material, and we would appreciate any information that would enable us to do so.

Photographs

(Key: b-bottom; c-centre; l-left; r-right; t-top)

123RF.com: Brent Hofacker 209, Cathy Yeulet 254, Cihan Demirok 6, Deskcube 12, Dmitriy Shironosov 107, Guruxox 106, Kirill Cherezov 12, Oleksii Nikolaiev 6, Sarah Maher 50, Wavebreak Media Ltd 106; **Alamy Stock Photo:** Agnieszka Olek/Caia Image 288, Allsorts Stock Photo 273, Ammentorp Photography ixl, BJ Warnick/Newscom 317, Bstar Images 26, Chris Gascoigne-View 129, Dpa picture alliance xl, Equinox Imagery 23, Food Collection viiir, Ian Dagnall 28, Ivan Vdovin 424, J. W. Alker/imageBROKE 133,

Operations management and performance

1

Introduction

Operations management is about how organizations create and deliver services and products. Everything you wear, eat, sit on, use, read or knock about on the sports field, and every treatment you receive at the hospital, every service you expect in the shops and every lecture you attend at university has been created by 'operations'. While the people who supervised their creation and delivery may not always be called operations managers, that is what they really are. And that is what this book is concerned with – the activities and decisions of those operations managers who have made the services and products on which we all depend. It is a hugely important activity for any type of organization. As well as impacting the quality, cost and delivery of the services and products that we consume, operations management can help or hinder how an organization achieves its strategic ambitions, and how it fulfills its environmental responsibilities. In this introductory chapter, we will examine what we mean by 'operations management', why it is important, how operations processes are all similar yet different and what it is that operations managers do. Figure 1.1 shows the model of operations management that is developed in the chapter.

Key questions

What is operations management?

What is the input–transformation–output process?

Why is operations management important to an organization's performance?

What is the processes hierarchy?

How do operations and processes differ?

What do operations managers do?

What is operations management?

Operations management is the activity of managing the resources that create and deliver services and products. The operations function is the part of the organization that is responsible for this activity. Every organization has an operations function because every organization creates services and/or products. Operations managers are the people who have particular responsibility for managing some, or all, of the resources and processes within the operations function. However, not all types of organization will necessarily call the operations function by this name. (Note that we also use the shorter terms 'the operation' or 'operations' interchangeably with the 'operations function'.) Similarly, the operations manager could be called by some other name. For example, he or she might be called the 'fleet manager' in a distribution company, the 'administrative manager' in a hospital, or the 'store manager' in a supermarket.

The Prêt A Manger example illustrates how important the operations function is for any company whose reputation depends on producing safe, high-quality, sustainable and profitable services or products. Its customers could choose to go to its competitors if Prêt's operations failed to deliver excellent levels of service or to produce attractive products, which is why it is

operations principle
All organizations have 'operations' that produce some mix of services and products.

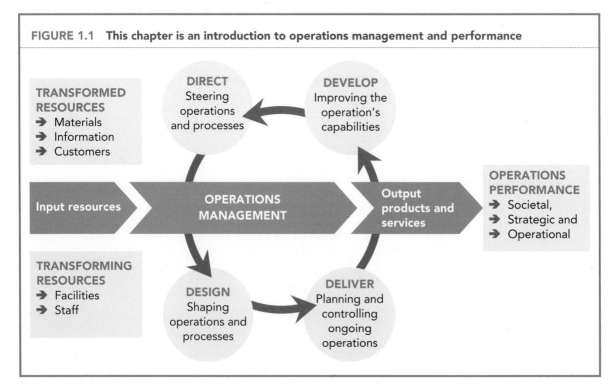

FIGURE 1.1   **This chapter is an introduction to operations management and performance**

Operations in practice

Customer service at Prêt A Manger[1]

Prêt A Manger is proud of its customer service. 'We'd like to think we react to our customers' feelings (the good, the bad, the ugly) with haste and absolute sincerity', its directors say. 'Prêt customers have the right to be heard. Do call or email. Our UK managing director is available if you would like to discuss Prêt with him. Alternatively, our CEO hasn't got much to do; hassle him!'

Prêt A Manger opened its first shop in London and now has over 350 shops spread across the UK, Paris, the USA, Hong Kong and Shanghai. It says that its secret is to focus continually on the quality of both its food and its service. It avoids the chemicals and preservatives common in most 'fast' food. 'Many food retailers focus on extending the shelf-life of their food, but that's of no interest to us. At the end of the day, we give whatever we haven't sold to charity.' Prêt A Manger shops have their own kitchen where fresh ingredients are delivered every morning, with food prepared throughout the day. The team members serving on the tills at lunchtime will have been making sandwiches in the kitchen that morning. 'We are determined never to forget that our hardworking people make all the difference. When they care, our business is sound. If they cease to care, our business goes down the drain. In a retail sector where high staff turnover is normal, we're pleased to say our people are much more likely to stay around! We work hard at building great teams. We take our reward schemes and career opportunities very seriously.'

Examining customers' comments for improvement ideas is a key part of weekly management meetings, and of the daily team briefs in each shop. Moreover, staff at Prêt collect bonuses for delivering outstanding customer service. Every week, each Prêt outlet is visited by a secret shopper who scores the shop on such performance measures as speed of service, product availability and cleanliness. In addition, the mystery shopper rates the 'engagement level' of the staff; questions include, 'did servers connect with eye contact, a smile and some polite remarks'? Above a certain score, every team member receives an extra payment for every hour worked; and if an individual is mentioned by the mystery shopper for providing outstanding service, they get an extra payment. ● ● ●

meticulous about monitoring its quality and ensuring that its processes operate to precise standards. Of course, exactly what is involved in producing products and services will depend to some extent on the type of organization of which the operations function is a part. Table 1.1 shows some of the activities of the operations function for various types of organization.

TABLE 1.1   Some activities of the operations function in various organizations

Internet service provider	Fast food chain	International aid charity	Furniture manufacturer
▶ Maintain and update hardware	▶ Locate potential sites for restaurants	▶ Provide aid and development projects for recipients	▶ Procure appropriate raw materials and components
▶ Update software and content	▶ Provide processes and equipment to produce burgers, etc.	▶ Provide fast emergency response when needed	▶ Make sub-assemblies
▶ Respond to customer queries	▶ Maintain service quality	▶ Procure and store emergency supplies	▶ Assemble finished products
▶ Implement new services	▶ Develop, install and maintain equipment	▶ Be sensitive to local cultural norms	▶ Deliver products to customers
▶ Ensure security of customer data	▶ Reduce impact on local area, and reduce packaging waste		▶ Reduce environmental impact of products and processes

Operations can produce both services and products

There is a common misperception that operations management is concerned largely with producing physical products. Not so. In all developed economies, services generate a far higher proportion of wealth than manufacturing. Of the four organizations in Table 1.1, the furniture manufacturer produces tangible products. The fast food chain produces food but also serves it to its customers. The international aid charity does not directly produce products but does distribute them and coordinate aid. The internet service provider has no tangible product as such – it provides intangible services. Yet they are all operations with (as we shall see later) similar activities and objectives. Of course, there are some differences between products and services. Products are usually tangible, whereas services are activities or processes. Also, while most products can be stored, at least for a short time, service only happens when it is consumed or used. So, accommodation in a hotel room, for example, will perish if it is not sold that night; a restaurant table will remain empty unless someone uses it that evening.

operations principle
Most operations produce a mixture of tangible products and intangible services.

Operations in practice

Torchbox: award-winning web designers[2]

We may take it for granted, yet browsing websites as part of your studies, your job or your leisure is an activity that we all do, probably every day, probably many times each day. All organizations need a web presence if they want to sell products and services, interact with their customers or promote their cause. And, not surprisingly, there is a whole industry devoted to designing websites so that they have the right type of impact. It has been one of the fastest-growing industries in the world. But it's also a tough business. Not every web design company thrives, or even survives beyond a couple of years. To succeed, web designers need technology skills, design capabilities, business awareness and operational professionalism. One that has succeeded is Torchbox, an independently-owned digital agency for the charity, non-profit and higher education sectors, with offices in Oxfordshire and Bristol in the UK and Philadelphia in the USA. Founded back in 2000, it now employs over 50 people, providing 'high-quality, cost-effective and ethical solutions for its clients'.

Co-founder and technical director Tom Dyson has been responsible for its technical development. 'There are a number of advantages about being a relatively small operation', he says. 'We can be hugely flexible and agile, in what is still a dynamic market. But at the same time, we have the resources and skills to provide a creative and professional service. Any senior manager in a firm of our size cannot afford to be too specialised. All of us here have their own specific responsibilities; however, every one of us shares the overall responsibility for the firm's general development. We can also be clear and focused on what type of work we want to do. Our ethos is important to us. We set out to work with clients who share our commitment to environmental sustainability and responsible, ethical business practice; we take our work, and that of our clients, seriously. If you're an arms dealer, you can safely assume that we're not going to be interested.'

Nevertheless, straightforward operational effectiveness is also essential to Torchbox's business. 'We know how to make sure that our projects run not only on time and to budget', says Olly Willans, also a co-founder and the firm's creative director, 'but we also like to think that we provide an enjoyable and stimulating experience – both for our customers' development teams and for our staff too. High standards of product and service are important to us: our clients want accessibility, usability, performance and security embedded in their web designs, and of course they want things delivered on time and on budget. We are in a creative industry that depends on fast-moving technologies, but that doesn't mean that we can't also be efficient. We back everything we do with a robust feature-driven development process using a kanban project management methodology that helps us manage our obligations to our clients.'

The 'kanban' approach used by the Torchbox web development teams originated from car manufacturers such as Toyota (and is fully explained in Chapter 10). 'Using sound operations management techniques helps us constantly to deliver value to our clients', says Tom Dyson. 'We like to think that our measured and controlled approach to handling and controlling work helps ensure that every hour we work produces an hour's worth of value for our clients and for us.' ● ● ●

Operations in practice

MSF operations provide medical aid to people in danger[3]

Médecins Sans Frontières (MSF) is an independent humanitarian organization providing medical aid where it is most needed and raising awareness of the plight of the people it helps around the world. Its core work takes place in crisis situations – armed conflicts, epidemics, famines and natural disasters. It delivers both medical aid and material aid (including food, shelter, blankets, etc.). Each year, MSF sends doctors, nurses, logisticians, water-and-sanitation experts, administrators and other professionals to work alongside around thousands of locally hired staff. It is one of the most admired and effective relief organisations in the world. But no amount of fine intentions can translate into effective action without superior operations management. As MSF says, it must be able to react to any crisis with 'fast response, efficient logistics systems and efficient project management'.

MSF response procedures are continuously being developed to ensure that they reach those most in need as quickly as possible. The process has five phases: proposal, assessment, initiation, running the project and closing. The information that prompts a possible mission can come from governments, the international community, humanitarian organizations or MSF teams already present in the region. Once the information has been checked, MSF experts carry out a quick evaluation and send a proposal back to the MSF office. After approval, MSF select personnel, organize resources and secure funds. Initiation involves sending equipment and resources to the area. Thanks to their pre-planned processes, specialized kits and the emergency stores, MSF can distribute material and equipment within 48 hours, ready for the response team to start work as soon as it arrives. Once the critical medical needs have been met, MSF begins to close the project with a gradual withdrawal of staff and equipment. All of which depends on an efficient logistics system working from MSF's four logistical centres based in Europe and East Africa, plus stores of emergency materials in Central America and East Asia where they purchase, test and store equipment. ● ● ●

Operations management in not-for-profit organizations

Terms such as 'business', 'competitiveness' and 'markets', which are used in this text, are usually associated with companies in the for-profit sector. Yet operations management is also relevant to organizations whose purpose is not primarily to earn profits. Managing the operations in an animal welfare charity, hospital, research organization or government department is essentially the same as in commercial organizations. These operations have to create and deliver service and products, invest in technology, contract out some of their activities, devise performance measures, improve their operations performance and so on. However, the objectives of not-for-profit organizations may be more complex, involving a mixture of political, economic, social or environmental objectives. Nevertheless, the vast majority of the topics covered in this text are relevant, even if some terms may have to be adapted.

What is the input– transformation–output process?

All operations create and deliver service and products by changing *inputs* into *outputs* using an 'input–transformation–output' process. Figure 1.3 shows this general transformation process model. Put simply, operations are processes that take in a set of input resources that are used to transform something, or are transformed themselves, into outputs of services and products. And although all operations conform to this general model, they differ in the nature of their specific inputs and outputs. So, if you stand far enough away from a hospital or a car plant, they might look very similar, but move closer and clear

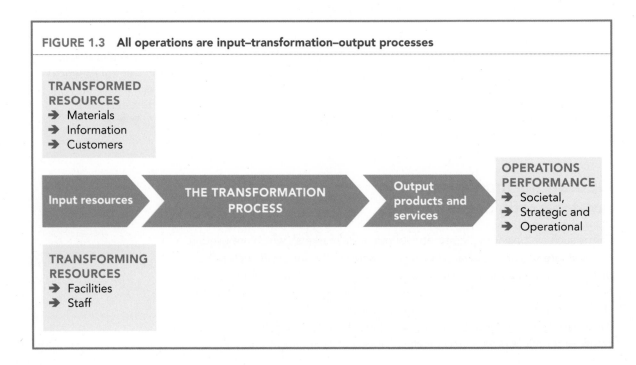

FIGURE 1.3   **All operations are input–transformation–output processes**

TRANSFORMED RESOURCES
➜ Materials
➜ Information
➜ Customers

Input resources ➜ THE TRANSFORMATION PROCESS ➜ Output products and services ➜ OPERATIONS PERFORMANCE
➜ Societal,
➜ Strategic and
➜ Operational

TRANSFORMING RESOURCES
➜ Facilities
➜ Staff

differences do start to emerge. One is a service operation delivering 'services' that change the physiological or psychological condition of patients, the other is a manufacturing operation creating and delivering 'products'. What is inside each operation will also be different. The hospital contains diagnostic, care and therapeutic processes, whereas the motor vehicle plant contains metal-forming machinery and assembly processes. Perhaps the most important difference between the two operations, however, is the nature of their inputs. The hospital transforms the customers themselves. The patients form part of the input to, and the output from, the operation. The vehicle plant transforms steel, plastic, cloth, tyres and other materials into vehicles.

operations principle
All processes have inputs of transforming and transformed resources that they use to create products and services.

Inputs to the process

One set of inputs to any operation's processes is the transformed resources. These are the resources that are treated, transformed or converted in the process. They are usually a mixture of the following:

 Materials   Operations that process materials could do so to transform the materials' *physical properties* (shape or composition, for example). Most manufacturing operations are like this. Other operations process materials to change their *location* (parcel delivery companies, for example). Some, like retail operations, do so to change the *possession* of the materials. Finally, some operations *store* materials, such as warehouses.

 Information   Operations that process information could do so to transform the *informational properties* (that is, the purpose or form of the information); accountants do this. Some change the *possession* of the information – for example, market research companies sell information. Some *store* the information, such as archives and libraries. Finally, some operations, such as telecommunication companies, change the *location* of the information.

★ **Customers**   Operations that process customers might change their *physical properties*: for example, hairdressers or cosmetic surgeons. Some, like hotels, *store* (or more politely *accommodate*) customers. Airlines and mass rapid transport systems transform the *location* of their customers, while hospitals transform their *physiological state*. Some are concerned with transforming their *psychological state* – for example, entertainment services such as television, radio and theme parks. But customers are not always simple 'passive' items to be processed. They can also play a more active part in many operations and processes. For example, they create the atmosphere in a restaurant; they provide the stimulating environment in learning groups in education. When customers play this role, it is usually referred to as 'co-production' because the customer plays a vital part in the provision of the product/service offering.

operations principle
Transformed resource inputs to a process can be materials, information or customers.

Some operations have inputs of materials *and* information *and* customers, but usually one of these is dominant. For example, a bank devotes part of its energies to producing printed statements by processing inputs of material, but no one would claim that a bank is a printer. The bank also is concerned with processing inputs of customers at its branches and contact centres. However, most of the bank's activities are concerned with processing inputs of information about its customers' financial affairs. As customers, we may be unhappy with badly printed statements and we may be unhappy if we are not treated appropriately in the bank. But if the bank makes errors in our financial transactions, we suffer in a far more fundamental way. Table 1.2 gives examples of operations, with their dominant transformed resources.

The other set of inputs to any operations process is the transforming resources. These are the resources that act upon the transformed resources. There are two types that form the 'building blocks' of all operations:

 facilities the buildings, equipment, plant and process technology of the operation;

 staff the people who operate, maintain, plan and manage the operation. (Note we use the term 'staff' to describe all the people in the operation, at any level.)

The exact nature of both facilities and staff will differ between operations. To a five-star hotel, its facilities consist mainly of 'low-tech' buildings, furniture and fittings. To a nuclear-powered aircraft carrier, its facilities are

TABLE 1.2   Dominant transformed resource inputs of various operations

Predominantly processing inputs of materials	Predominantly processing inputs of information	Predominantly processing inputs of customer
All manufacturing operations	Accountants	Hairdressers
Mining companies	Bank headquarters	Hotels
Retail operations	Market research companies	Hospitals
Warehouses	Social media operations	Mass rapid transports
Postal services	News services	Theatres
Container shipping lines	University research units	Theme parks
Trucking companies	Telecoms companies	Dentists

'high-tech' nuclear generators and sophisticated electronic equipment. Staff will also differ between operations. Most staff employed in a factory assembling domestic refrigerators may not need a very high level of technical skill. In contrast, most staff employed by an accounting company are, hopefully, highly skilled in their own particular 'technical' skill (accounting). Yet, although skills vary, all staff can make a contribution. An assembly worker who consistently misassembles refrigerators will dissatisfy customers and increase costs just as surely as an accountant who cannot add up. The balance between facilities and staff also varies. Microchip manufacturers, such as Samsung or Intel, will have significant investment in physical facilities. A single chip fabrication plant can cost in excess of $5 billion, so operations managers will spend a lot of their time managing their facilities. Conversely, a management consultancy firm depends largely on the quality of its staff. Here, operations management is largely concerned with the development and deployment of consultant skills and knowledge.

operations principle
All processes have transforming resources of facilities (equipment, technology, etc.) and people.

CUSTOMERS

Customers may be an input to many operations, but they are also the reason for their existence. Without customers, there would be no operation. So, it is critical that operations managers are aware of customers' current and potential needs. It is also why most operations put considerable effort into assessing how customers view their offerings and bringing what is sometimes known as the 'voice of the customer' into their operation.

Why is operations management important to an organization's performance?

It is no exaggeration to view operations management as being able to either 'make or break' any business. The operations function is large and, in most businesses, represents the bulk of its assets and the majority of its people. But, more than this, the operations function gives any organization the ability to compete by providing the ability to respond to customers and by developing the capabilities that will keep it ahead of its competitors in the future. When things go wrong in operations, whether it be the recall of a faulty product, a customer being injured on a theme park ride or the failure to protect against a cyber-attack, the financial and reputational damage can last for years.

Performance at three levels

The idea of operations 'performance' is not a straightforward or simple concept. Several measures are always needed to convey a realistic overview of the various aspects of performance. Also, performance can be assessed at different levels. Here we will look at how operations can judge their performance at three levels:

 the broad, societal level, using the idea of the 'triple bottom line';

 the strategic level – how an operation can contribute to the organization's overall strategy;

 the operational level, using the five operations 'performance objectives'.

These three levels of operations performance are illustrated in Figure 1.4.

OPERATIONS PERFORMANCE AT A SOCIETAL LEVEL

No operation exists, or performs, in isolation. Its decisions affect a whole variety of 'stakeholders'. (Stakeholders are the people and groups who have

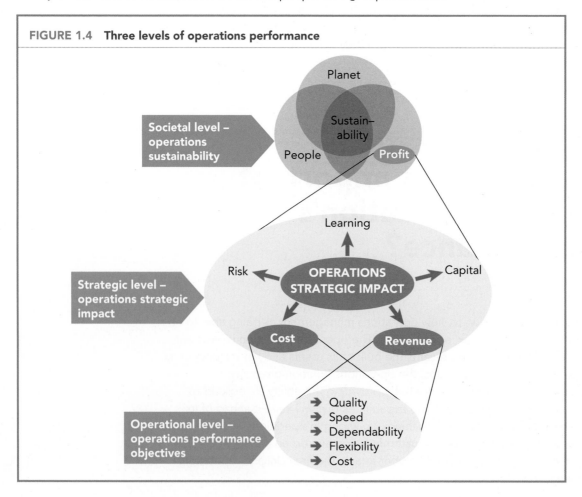

FIGURE 1.4   **Three levels of operations performance**

a legitimate interest in the operation's activities.) Some stakeholders are internal – for example, the operation's employees; others are external – for example, customers, society or community groups and a company's shareholders. And although different stakeholders will be interested in different aspects of operations performance, if one is to judge operations at a broad societal level, one must judge the impact it has on all its stakeholders.

Corporate social responsibility (CSR) and the triple bottom line (TBL)
This idea that operations should take into account their impact on a broad mix of stakeholders is often termed 'corporate social responsibility' (CSR). According to the UK Government's definition: 'CSR is essentially about how business takes account of its economic, social and environmental impacts in the way it operates – maximizing the benefits and minimizing the downsides.' A common term that tries to capture this idea is the 'triple bottom line'[4] (TBL), also known as 'people, plant and profit'. The idea is simply that organizations should measure themselves not just on the traditional economic profit that they generate for their owners, but also on the impact their operations have on society and their ecological impact on the environment.

The social bottom line (people) is measured by the impact of the operation on the quality of people's lives – for example, by assessing factors such as customer safety from products and services, employment impact of an operation's location, implications of outsourcing, staff safety and workplace stress, non-exploitation of developing country suppliers, etc.

The environmental bottom line (planet) is measured by the environmental impact of the operation – for example, by assessing factors such as recyclability of materials, energy consumption, waste material generation, transport-related energy, pollution, and the environmental impact of process failures.

The economic bottom line (profit) is measured by profitability, return on assets and other conventional financial measures of the operation.

The combination of these three factors indicates a business' 'sustainability'. A sustainable business is one that creates an acceptable profit for its owners, but minimizes the damage to the environment and enhances the existence of the people with whom it has contact. In other words, it balances economic, environmental and societal interests. The assumption underlying the triple bottom line (which is not universally accepted) is that a sustainable business is more likely to remain successful in the long term than one that focuses on economic goals alone.

OPERATIONS PERFORMANCE AT A STRATEGIC LEVEL

Many (though not all) of the activities of operations managers are operational – they deal with relatively immediate, detailed and local issues. However, operations decisions can also have a significant strategic 'impact' (see the next chapter). So, it makes sense to ask how they impact on the organization's strategic 'economic' position:

operations principle
All operations decisions should reflect the interests of stakeholder groups.

operations principle
Operations should judge themselves on the triple-bottom-line principle of 'people, plant and profit'.

Cost   Almost all the activities that operations managers regularly perform (and all the topics that are described in this text) have an effect on cost. And for many operations managers it is *the* most important aspect of how they judge their performance. Indeed, there cannot be many, if any, organizations that are indifferent to their costs.

Revenue   Cost is not necessarily always the most important strategic objective for operations managers. Their activities also can have a huge effect on revenue. High-quality, error-free products and services, delivered fast and on time, where the operation has the flexibility to adapt to customers' needs, are likely to command a higher price and sell more than those with lower levels of quality, delivery and flexibility.

Required level of investment   How an operation manages the physical resources (such as buildings and equipment) that are necessary to produce its products and services will also have a strategic effect. If, for example, an operation increases its efficiency so that it can produce, say, 10 per cent more output, then it will not need to spend investment (sometimes called capital employed) to produce 10 per cent more output. Producing more output with the same resources (or producing the same output with fewer resources) affects the required level of investment.

Risk of operational failure   Well-designed and well-run operations should be less likely to fail. That is, they are more likely to operate at a predictable and acceptable rate without either letting customers down or incurring excess costs. And if they ever do suffer failures, well-run operations should be able to recover faster and with less disruption (this is called resilience).

Building the capabilities for future innovation   Operations managers have a unique opportunity to learn from their experience of operating their processes in order to understand more about those processes. It is this learning that can build into the skills, knowledge and experience that allows the business to improve over time. But more than that, it can build into what are known as the 'capabilities' that allow the business to innovate in the future (an idea we explore in the next chapter).

> **operations principle**
> All operations should be expected to contribute to their business at a strategic level by controlling costs, increasing revenue, making investment more effective, reducing risks and growing long-term capabilities.

OPERATIONS PERFORMANCE AT AN OPERATIONAL LEVEL

Societal-level performance and strategic-level performance, while clearly important, particularly in the longer term, tend to form the backdrop to operations decision making. Running operations at an operational day-to-day level requires a more tightly defined set of objectives. These are called operations 'performance objectives'. There are five of them and they apply to all types of operation. They are: quality, speed, dependability, flexibility and cost.

Why is quality important?

Quality means producing services and products consistently to specification. (We shall look further at how quality can be defined in Chapter 12.) All operations regard service and product quality as a particularly important objective. It is the most visible part of what an operation does, and it is something that a customer

> **operations principle**
> Quality can give the potential for better services and products and a saving of costs.

finds relatively easy to judge. Is the product or service right or is it wrong? There is something fundamental about quality. Because of this, it is clearly a major influence on customer satisfaction or dissatisfaction. Customer perception of high quality means customers are more likely to consume services or products again. Quality can also reduce costs. The fewer mistakes made within the operation, the less time will be needed to correct the mistakes.

Why is speed important?

Speed means the elapsed time between customers requesting services or products and their receiving them. The main external benefit of speedy delivery is that the faster customers can have the service or product, the more likely they are to buy it, or the more they will pay for it. Speed can also reduce costs. The faster materials, information or customers flow through an operation, the less it costs to store, care for and keep track of them. (This is an important idea that will be explored in Chapter 10 on lean operations.)

operations principle
Speed can give the potential for faster delivery of services and products and a saving of costs.

Why is dependability important?

Dependability means doing things in time so customers can receive services or products exactly when they are needed, or at least when they were promised. Customers can only judge the dependability of an operation after the service or product has been delivered, yet, over time, dependability can override all other criteria. No matter how cheap or good quality is a delivery service, if it is always late (or unpredictably early), then potential customers will never be able to rely on it. It is the same inside an operation. A lack of dependability results in an ineffective use of time, which translates into extra cost.

operations principle
Dependability can give the potential for more reliable delivery of services and products and a saving of costs.

Why is flexibility important?

Flexibility means being able to change the operation in some way. This may mean changing so that the operation can produce new or modified services or products, being able to produce a wide range of services or products, being able to change its level of output or activity to produce different quantities of services or products, or the ability to change the timing of the delivery of its services or products. And all of these types of flexibility can give value to customers. But, once again, there are internal advantages to having operational flexibility. Flexible operations can switch between activities without wasting time and money; they can keep on schedule when unexpected events disrupt the operation's plans, which, in turn can also save costs.

operations principle
Flexibility can give the potential to create new, wider-variety, differing volumes and differing delivery dates of services and products and a saving of costs.

Why is cost important?

To the companies that compete directly on price, cost will clearly be their major operations objective. The lower the cost of producing their goods and services, the lower can be the price to their customers. Even those companies that do not compete on price will be interested in keeping costs low. Every euro, pound or dollar removed from an operation's cost base is a further euro, pound or dollar added to its profits. Not surprisingly, low cost is a universally attractive objective. However, the ways in which operations management can influence cost will depend largely on where the operation costs are incurred. Some operations (such as advertising agencies) will spend most of their money on staff, some (such as semiconductor chip makers) spend vast amounts on facilities, technology and equipment and others (for example, supermarkets) spend large amounts on the 'bought-in' goods that they sell on to their customers.

Quality, speed, dependability and flexibility can all save costs

Looking back at the benefits of quality, speed, dependability and flexibility, it is important to note how cost reduction can be achieved through internal effectiveness. Each of the performance objectives has the internal potential to reduce costs. High-quality operations do not waste time or effort having to re-do things. Fast operations reduce the level of internal inventory, as well as reducing administrative overheads. Dependable operations can be relied on to deliver exactly as planned, which eliminates wasteful disruption. Finally, flexible operations adapt to changing circumstances quickly and without disrupting the rest of the operation and can change between tasks without wasting time and capacity. So, one important way to improve cost performance is to improve the performance of the other operations objectives (see Figure 1.5).

operations principle
Cost is always an important objective for operations management, even if the organization does not compete directly on price.

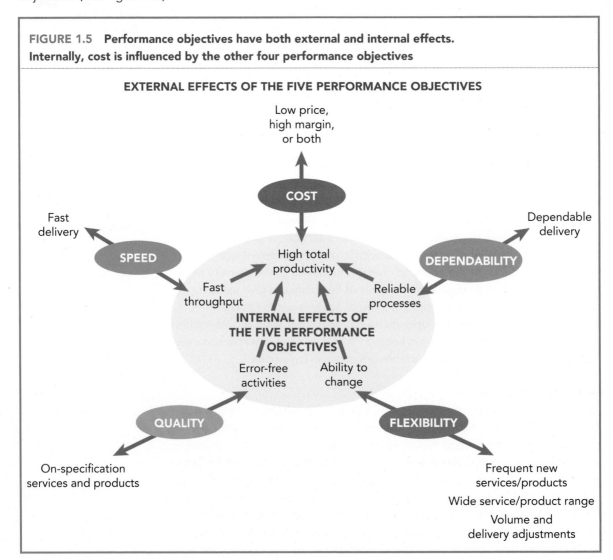

FIGURE 1.5 **Performance objectives have both external and internal effects. Internally, cost is influenced by the other four performance objectives**

LEGO: building a creative experience[5]

The toy business is one of the world's trickiest. It is difficult to forecast, unfailingly subject to fickle kids' latest fads and subject to constant technological innovation. Yet The LEGO Group, with headquarters in Billund, Denmark, has become one of the most reputable manufacturers of play materials in the world. Its success founded on a deceptively simple idea. A single LEGO brick is unremarkable, but put one or two together and possibilities start to emerge. After that, numbers rise exponentially. With the approximately 4,200 different elements in the LEGO range and 58 different colours, together with various decorations, the total number of active combinations is huge. (And your pieces will always fit together perfectly.) All of the basic LEGO elements have studs on top that are slightly bigger than the tubes on the inside. Pressing the bricks together produces a temporary joint without the use of an additional fastener. But this principle does depend on the elements being made to very high levels of precision and quality, which explains the company's motto: 'Only the best is good enough'.

LEGO 'elements' are manufactured at the group's factories in Denmark, Hungary, The Czech Republic and Mexico, together with new factories built in Hungary and China. Locations that have been chosen to be near key markets. The aim is to 'build a stable manufacturing base around the world'. But it is the company's operations processes that are central to maintaining its reputation for quality, and its ability to produce millions of elements profitably and sustainably. The plastic moulding stage is particularly important, because every LEGO piece must be made with tolerances as small as 10 micrometres. Robots travel between the machines, picking up boxes and leaving empty ones, automation that means few people are required for the process. The robots transport the boxes to conveyors, which move them into the storage area where robotic cranes stack them until they are needed. From there some pieces go to the 'decoration' stage, where they are individually painted. Decoration is the most expensive part of the LEGO process. Other pieces go straight to packing, where the LEGO sets take their final form. The automatic movement system knows exactly how much each box of LEGO should weigh, and at any stage high-precision scales monitor its weight. Any deviation, even of a few micrograms, sets off an alarm.

Quality assurance staff perform frequent inspections and tests to make sure the toys are robust and safe. Only about 18 of every million LEGO elements, (that's 0.00002 per cent) fail to pass the tests. In addition, throughout the process, the company tries to achieve high levels of environmental sustainability. Plastic is extensively recycled in the factory. All scrap is ground up and put back into the production process. ● ● ●

What is the processes hierarchy?

So far, we have discussed operations management and the input–transformation–output model at the level of 'the operation'. For example, we have described 'the website designer', 'the bank', 'the sandwich shop', 'the disaster relief operation' and so on. But look inside any of these operations and one will see that all operations consist of a collection of processes (though these processes may be called 'units' or 'departments'), interconnecting with each other to form a network. Each of these processes acts as a smaller version of the whole operation of which they form a part, with transformed resources flowing in between them. These processes are the mechanisms that actually transform inputs into outputs within any operation. In fact, the formal definition of a 'process' is an arrangement of resources and activities that transform inputs into outputs in order to satisfy (internal or external) customer needs. They are the 'building blocks' of all operations, and they form an 'internal network' within an operation. Each process is, at the same time, an internal supplier and an internal customer for other processes. This idea of processes being 'internal customers' provides a model to analyse the internal activities of an operation. It is also a useful reminder that, by treating internal customers with the same care as external customers, the effectiveness of the whole operation can be improved.

The idea of a network can also be used to describe what happens within processes, because a process is a network of individual units of resource, such as individual people and individual items of process technology (machines, computers, storage facilities, etc.). Again, transformed resources flow between each unit of transforming resource. So, any business, or operation, is made up of a network of processes and any process is made up of a network of resources.

operations principle
The idea of interconnected networks can be used at three levels: the level of the supply network; the level of the operation itself; and the level of individual processes.

Moreover, taking a wider perspective, any business or operation can itself be viewed as part of a greater network of businesses or operations. It will have other operations that supply it with the services and products it needs, and unless it deals directly with the end consumer, it will supply customers who themselves may go on to supply their own customers. Moreover, any operation could have several suppliers, several customers and may be in competition with other operations creating similar services or products to itself. This network of operations is called the supply network.

This idea is sometimes called 'the hierarchy of operations'. It allows the input–transformation–output model to be used at a number of different 'levels of analysis'. Here we have used three levels – the process, the operation and the supply network. But one could define many different 'levels of analysis', moving upwards from small to larger processes, right up to the huge supply network that describes a whole industry. Figure 1.6 illustrates the idea for a business that makes television programmes and videos. It has inputs of creative and administrative staff, various technical hardware and software, and so on, which it transforms into finished programmes and promotional videos. At a more macro level, the business itself is part of a whole supply network, acquiring services from creative agencies, casting agencies and studios, liaising with promotion agencies and serving its broadcasting company customers. At a more micro level there are many individual processes: workshops, marketing, maintenance and repair, production units and so on. Each of these individual processes can be represented as a network of yet smaller processes, or even individual units of resource. So, for example, the set construction process comprises four smaller processes: set design, set construction, props acquisition and set finishing.

Operations management is relevant to all parts of the business

The example in Figure 1.6 demonstrates that it is not just the operations function that manages processes; all parts of an organization do. For

FIGURE 1.6 **Operations and process management requires analysis at three levels – the supply network, the operation and the process**

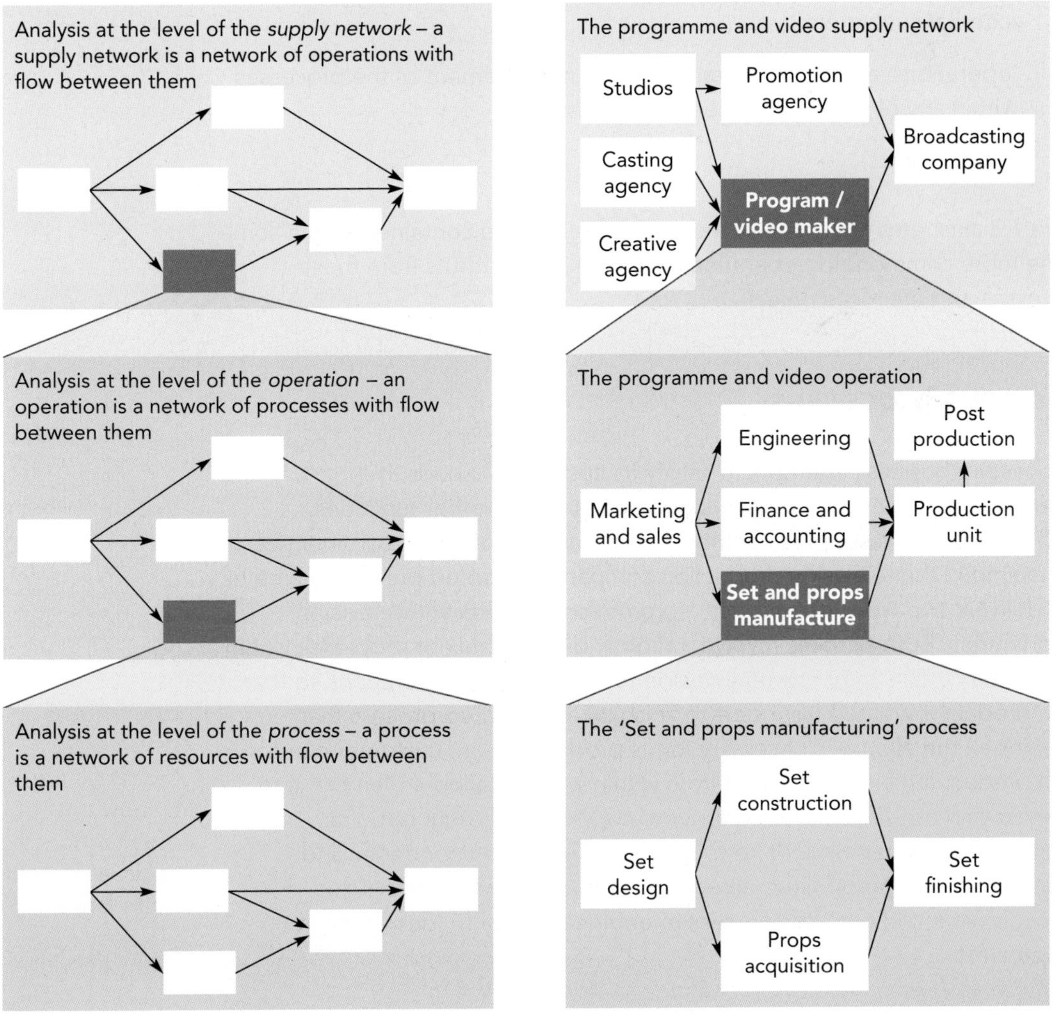

Analysis at the level of the *supply network* – a supply network is a network of operations with flow between them

The programme and video supply network

Studios → Promotion agency → Broadcasting company
Casting agency
Creative agency
Program / video maker

Analysis at the level of the *operation* – an operation is a network of processes with flow between them

The programme and video operation

Engineering
Post production
Marketing and sales → Finance and accounting → Production unit
Set and props manufacture

Analysis at the level of the *process* – a process is a network of resources with flow between them

The 'Set and props manufacturing' process

Set construction
Set design
Props acquisition
Set finishing

example, the marketing function will have processes that create demand forecasts, processes that create advertising campaigns and processes that create marketing plans. These processes in the other functions also need managing using similar principles to those within the operations function. Each function will have its 'technical' knowledge. In marketing, this is the expertise in designing and shaping marketing plans; in finance, it is the technical knowledge of financial reporting. Yet each will also have a 'process management' role of producing plans, policies, reports and services. The implications of this are very important. Because all managers have some responsibility for managing processes, they are, to some extent, operations managers. They all should want to give good service to their (often internal) customers, and they all will want to do this efficiently. So, operations management is relevant for all functions, and all managers should have something to learn from the principles, concepts, approaches and techniques of operations management. It also means that we must distinguish between two meanings of 'operations':

 'operations' as a function, meaning the part of the organization that creates and delivers services and products for the organization's external customers;

 'operations' as an activity, meaning the management of the processes within any of the organization's functions.

operations principle
All parts of the business manage processes, so all parts of the business have an operations role and need to understand operations management principles.

Table 1.3 illustrates just some of the processes that are contained within some of the more common non-operations functions, the outputs from these processes and their 'customers'.

Business processes

Whenever a business attempts to satisfy its customers' needs, it will use many processes, both in its operations and its other functions. Each of these processes will contribute some part to fulfilling customer needs. For example, the television production company described previously creates and delivers two types of 'product' – promotional videos and television programmes. Both of these involve a slightly different mix of processes within the company. The company may decide to reorganize its operations so that each product is created from start to finish by a dedicated process that contains all the elements necessary for its production. So, customer needs for each product are entirely fulfilled from within what is called an **'end-to-end'** business process. These often cut across conventional organizational boundaries. Reorganizing (or 're-engineering') process boundaries and organizational responsibilities around these business processes is the philosophy behind business process re-engineering (BPR) (described in Chapter 11).

operations principle
Processes are defined by how the organization chooses to draw process boundaries.

TABLE 1.3 Some examples of processes in non-operations functions

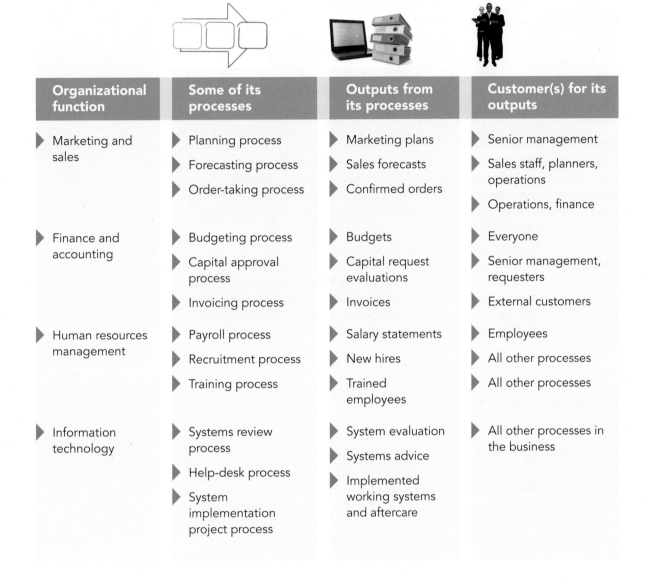

Organizational function	Some of its processes	Outputs from its processes	Customer(s) for its outputs
▶ Marketing and sales	▶ Planning process ▶ Forecasting process ▶ Order-taking process	▶ Marketing plans ▶ Sales forecasts ▶ Confirmed orders	▶ Senior management ▶ Sales staff, planners, operations ▶ Operations, finance
▶ Finance and accounting	▶ Budgeting process ▶ Capital approval process ▶ Invoicing process	▶ Budgets ▶ Capital request evaluations ▶ Invoices	▶ Everyone ▶ Senior management, requesters ▶ External customers
▶ Human resources management	▶ Payroll process ▶ Recruitment process ▶ Training process	▶ Salary statements ▶ New hires ▶ Trained employees	▶ Employees ▶ All other processes ▶ All other processes
▶ Information technology	▶ Systems review process ▶ Help-desk process ▶ System implementation project process	▶ System evaluation ▶ Systems advice ▶ Implemented working systems and aftercare	▶ All other processes in the business

How do operations and processes differ?

Although all operations and processes are similar in that they all transform inputs into outputs, they do differ in a number of ways, four of which, known as the four Vs, are particularly important:

the *volume* of their output;

 the *variety* of their output;

 the *variation* in the demand for their output;

 the degree of *visibility* that customers have of the creation of their output.

The volume dimension

Let us take a familiar example. The epitome of high-volume hamburger production is McDonald's, which serves millions of burgers around the world every day. Volume has important implications for the way McDonald's operations are organized. The first thing you notice is the repeatability of the tasks people are doing and the systemization of the work, where standard procedures are set down specifying how each part of the job should be carried out. Also, because tasks are systematized and repeated, it is worthwhile developing specialized fryers and ovens. All this gives *low unit costs*. Now consider a small local cafeteria serving a few 'short order' dishes. The range of items on the menu may be similar to the larger operation, but the volume will be far lower, so the repetition will also be far lower and the number of staff will be lower (possibly only one person) and therefore individual staff are likely to perform a wider range of tasks. This may be more rewarding for the staff, but less open to systemization. Also, it is less feasible to invest in specialized equipment. So, the cost per burger served is likely to be higher (even if the price is comparable).

The variety dimension

A taxi company offers a relatively high-variety service. It is prepared to pick you up from almost anywhere and drop you off almost anywhere. To offer this variety it must be relatively *flexible*. Drivers must have a good knowledge of the area, and communication between the base and the taxis must be effective. However, the cost per kilometre travelled will be higher for a taxi than for a less customized form of transport, such as a bus service. Although both provide the same basic service (transportation), the taxi service has a higher variety of routes and times to offer its customers, while the bus service has a few well-defined routes, with a set schedule. If all goes to schedule, little, if any, flexibility is required from the bus operation. All is standardized and regular, which results in relatively low costs compared with using a taxi for the same journey.

The variation dimension

Consider the demand pattern for a successful summer holiday resort hotel. Not surprisingly, more customers want to stay in summer vacation times than in the middle of winter. At the height of 'the season' the hotel could be full to its capacity. Off-season demand, however, could be a small fraction of its capacity. Such a marked variation in demand means that the operation must change its capacity in some way – for example, by hiring extra staff for the summer. The hotel must try to predict the likely level of demand. If it gets this wrong, it could result in too much or too little capacity. Also, recruitment costs, overtime costs and under-utilization of its rooms all have the effect of increasing the hotel's costs operation compared with a hotel of a similar standard with more level demand. By contrast, a hotel with relatively level demand can plan its activities well in advance. Staff can be scheduled, food can be bought and rooms can be cleaned in a *routine* and *predictable* manner. This results in a high utilization of resources and lower costs than a hotel with highly variable demand.

The visibility dimension

'Visibility' means how much of the operation's activities are experienced by customers, or how much the operation is exposed to its customers. Generally, customer-processing operations are more exposed to their customers than material- or information-processing systems. But even customer-processing operations have some choice as to how visible they wish to be. For example, a retailer could operate as a high-visibility 'bricks and mortar', or a lower visibility web-based operation. In the 'bricks and mortar', high-visibility operation, customers will experience directly most of its 'value-adding' activities. Customers will have a relatively *short waiting tolerance,* and may walk out if not served in a reasonable time. Customers' perceptions, rather than objective criteria, will also be important. If they perceive that a member of the operation's staff is discourteous to them, they are likely to be dissatisfied, so high-visibility operations require staff with good customer contact skills. Customers could also request services or products that clearly would not be sold in such a shop, but because the customers are actually within the operation they can ask what they like. This is called 'high received variety'. This makes it difficult for high-visibility operations to achieve high productivity of resources, so they tend to be relatively high-cost operations. Conversely, a web-based retailer, while not a pure low-contact operation, has far lower visibility. Behind its website, it can be more 'factory-like'. The *time lag* between the order being placed and the items ordered by the customer being retrieved and dispatched does not have to be minutes, as in the shop, but can be hours or even days. This allows the tasks of finding the items, packing and dispatching them to be *standardized* by staff who need few customer contact skills. Also, there can be relatively *high staff utilization*. The web-based organization can also centralize its operation on one (physical) site, whereas the 'bricks and mortar' shop needs many shops close to centres of demand. All of which means that low-visibility web-based operations have lower costs than a high-visibility shop.

operations principle
The way in which processes need to be managed is influenced by volume, variety, variation and visibility.

MIXED HIGH- AND LOW-VISIBILITY PROCESSES

Some operations have both high- and low-visibility processes within the same operation. In an airport, for example, some activities are totally 'visible' to the customers – such as information desks answering people's queries. The staff here operate in what is termed a 'front-office' environment. Other parts of the

Two very different hospitality operations

Ski Verbier Exclusive
Ski Verbier Exclusive Ltd is a provider of 'up-market' ski holidays in the Swiss winter sports resort of Verbier. It looks after luxury properties in the resort that are rented from their owners for letting to Ski Verbier Exclusive's clients. The properties vary in size and the configuration of their rooms, but the flexibility to reconfigure the rooms to cater for the varying requirements of clients is important. 'We are very careful to cultivate as good a relationship with the owners as we are with our clients that use our holiday service', says Tom Avery, joint founder and director of the company. 'We have built the business on developing these personal relationships, which is why 40 to 50 per cent of clients come back to us year after year. We pride ourselves on the personal service that we give, from the moment clients begin planning their ski holiday, to the journey home. What counts is our ability to customise client experience.' And client requests can be anything from organizing a special mountain picnic, to providing an ice sculpture of Kermit the Frog for a kids' party. The company's specialist staff have all lived and worked in Verbier and take care of all details of the trip well in advance, from organizing airport transfers to booking a private ski instructor, from arranging private jet or helicopter flights to Verbier's local airport, to making lunch reservations in the best mountain restaurants. 'We cater for a small, but discerning market', says Tom. 'Other

airport have little, if any, customer 'visibility', such as the baggage handlers. These rarely-seen staff perform the vital but low-contact tasks, in the 'back-office' part of the operation.

The implications of the four Vs of operations processes

All four dimensions have implications for the cost of creating and delivering services and products. Put simply, high volume, low variety, low variation and low customer contact all help to keep processing costs down. Conversely, low volume, high variety, high variation and high customer contact generally carry some kind of cost penalty for the operation. This is why the volume dimension is drawn with its 'low' end at the left, unlike the other dimensions, to keep all the 'low cost' implications on the right. To some extent, the position of an operation in the four dimensions is determined by the demand of the market it is serving. However, most operations have some discretion in moving themselves on the dimensions. Figure 1.7 summarizes the implications of such positioning.

operations principle
Operations and processes can, all things being equal, reduce costs by increasing volume, reducing variety, reducing variation and reducing visibility.

companies may be bigger, but with us it's our personal service that clients remember.' The company's busiest period is the mid-December to mid-April snow season, when all the properties are full. The rest of the year is not so busy, but the company do offer bespoke summer vacations in some of their properties. 'We adapt to clients' requirements', says Tom. 'That is why the quality of our staff is so important. They have to be good at working with clients, be able to judge the type of relationship that is appropriate and be committed to providing what makes a great holiday.'

Formule 1

Hotels are high-contact operations – they are staff-intensive and have to cope with a range of customers, each with a variety of needs and expectations. So, how can a highly successful chain of affordable hotels avoid the crippling costs of high customer contact? Formule 1, a subsidiary of the French Accor group, manages to offer outstanding value by adopting two principles not always associated with hotel operations – standardization and an innovative use of technology. Formule 1 hotels are usually located close to roads, junctions and cities, which makes them visible and accessible to prospective customers. The hotels themselves are made from state-of-the-art volumetric prefabrications. The prefabricated units are arranged in various configurations to suit the characteristics of each individual site. All rooms are nine square metres in area, and are designed to be attractive, functional, comfortable and soundproof. Most important, they are designed to be easy to clean and maintain. All have the same fittings, including a double bed, an additional bunk-type bed, a wash basin, a storage area, a working table with seat, a wardrobe and a television set. The reception of a Formule 1 hotel is staffed only from 6.30 am to 10.00 am and from 5.00 pm to 10.00 pm. Outside these times an automatic machine sells rooms to credit card users, provides access to the hotel, dispenses a security code for the room and even prints a receipt. Technology is also evident in the washrooms. Showers and toilets are automatically cleaned after each use by using nozzles and heating elements to spray the room with a disinfectant solution and dry it before it is used again. To keep things even simpler, Formule 1 hotels do not include a restaurant, as they are usually located near existing ones. However, a continental breakfast is available, usually between 6.30 am and 10.00 am, and of course on a 'self-service' basis! ● ● ●

What do operations managers do?

The exact details of what operations managers do will, to some extent, depend on the way an organization defines the boundaries of the function. Yet there are some general classes of activities that apply to all types of operation, irrespective of whether it is service, manufacturing, private or public sector, and no matter how the operations function is defined. We classify these activities under the four headings direct, design, deliver and develop:

Worked example

Figure 1.8 illustrates the different positions on the dimensions of the Ski Verbier Exclusive operation and the Formule 1 hotel chain (see the 'Operations in practice' example). At the most basic level, both accommodate people, yet they are very different. Ski Verbier Exclusive provides luxurious and bespoke vacations for a relatively small segment of the ski-holiday market. Its variety of services is almost infinite – customers can make individual requests in terms of food and entertainment. Variation is high, with four months of 100 per cent occupancy, followed by a far quieter period. Customer contact, and therefore visibility, is also very high (in order to ascertain and provide customers' requirements). All of which is very different from Formule 1 hotels, where customers usually stay just one night, the variety of services is strictly limited and business and holiday customers use the hotel at different times, which reduces variation. Most notably, though, customer contact is kept to a minimum. Ski Verbier Exclusive has very high levels of service, which means it has relatively high costs. Its prices, therefore, are not cheap. Certainly not as cheap as Formule 1, which has arranged its operation in such a way as to provide a highly standardized service at low cost. ● ● ●

FIGURE 1.7 A typology of operations

IMPLICATIONS   **IMPLICATIONS**

→ Low repetition → Each staff member performs more of each task → Less systemization → High unit costs	Low **VOLUME** High	→ High repeatability → Specialization → Capital intensive → Low unit costs

→ Flexible → Complex → Match customer needs → High unit costs	High **VARIETY** Low	→ Well-defined → Routine → Standardized → Regular → Low unit costs

→ Changing capacity → Anticipation → Flexibility → In touch with demand → High unit costs	High **VARIATION IN DEMAND** Low	→ Stable → Routine → Predictable → High utilization → Low unit costs

→ Short waiting tolerance → Satisfaction governed by customer perception → Customer contact skills needed → Received variety is high → High unit costs	High **VISIBILITY** Low	→ Time lag between production and consumption → Standardization → Low contact skills → High staff utilization → Centralization → Low unit costs

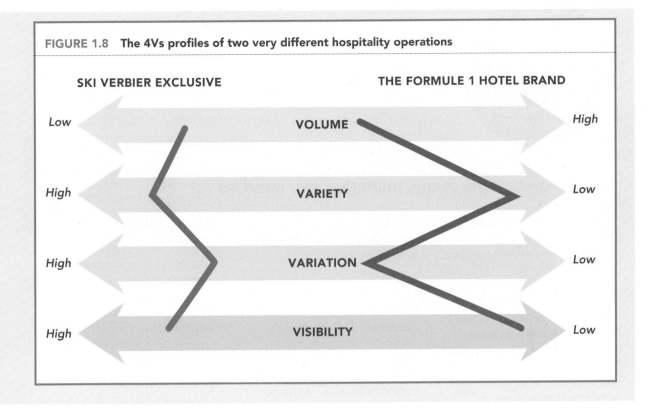

FIGURE 1.8   The 4Vs profiles of two very different hospitality operations

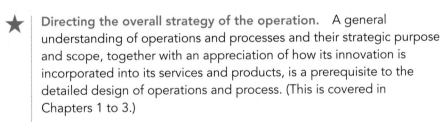

★ **Directing the overall strategy of the operation.**   A general understanding of operations and processes and their strategic purpose and scope, together with an appreciation of how its innovation is incorporated into its services and products, is a prerequisite to the detailed design of operations and process. (This is covered in Chapters 1 to 3.)

★ **Designing the operation's processes.**   Design is the activity of determining the physical form, shape and composition of operations and processes. (This is covered in Chapters 4 and 5.)

★ **Planning and control process delivery.**   After being designed, the delivery of services and products from suppliers, through the total operation to customers must be planned and controlled. (This is covered in Chapters 6 to 10.)

★ **Developing process performance.**   Increasingly, it is recognized that operations, or process managers, cannot simply routinely deliver services and products in the same way that they always have done. They have a responsibility to develop the capabilities of their processes to improve process performance. (This is treated in Chapters 11 to 13.)

Critical commentary

To be a great operations manager you need to ...[6]

So, you are considering a career in operations management and you want to know, 'is it for you?'. What skills and personal qualities will you need to make a success of the job as well as enjoying yourself as you progress in the profession? Well, the first thing to recognize is that there are many different roles encompassed within the general category of 'operations management'. Someone who makes a great risk-control system designer in an investment bank may not thrive as a site manager in a copper mine. A video game project manager has a different set of day-to-day tasks when compared with a purchasing manager for a hospital. So, the first skill you need is to understand the range of operations-related responsibilities that exist in various industries; and there is no better way to do this than by reading this text! However, there are also some generic skills that an effective operations manager must possess. Here are some of them. How many of them do you share?

Enjoys getting things done
Operations management is about doing things. It takes energy and/or commitment to finish tasks. It means hitting deadlines and not letting down customers, whether they are internal or external.

Understands customer needs
Operations management is about adding value for customers. This means fully understanding what 'value' means for customers. It means 'putting yourself in the customer's place' – knowing what it is like to be the customer, and knowing how to ensure that your services or products make the customer's life better.

Communicates and motivates
Operations management is about directing resources to produce services or products in an efficient and effective manner. This means articulating what is required and persuading people to do it. Interpersonal skills are vital. Operations managers must be 'people people'.

Learns all the time
Every time an operations manager initiates an action (of any kind) there is an opportunity to learn from the result. Operations management is about learning, because without learning there can be no improvement, and improvement is an imperative for all operations.

Committed to innovation
Operations management is always seeking to do things better. This means creating new ways of doing things, being creative, imaginative and (sometimes) unconventional.

Knows their contribution
Operations management may be the central function in any organization, but it is not the only one. It is important that operations managers know how they can contribute to the effective working of other functions.

Capable of analysis
Operations management is about making decisions. Each decision needs to be evaluated (sometimes with very little time). This involves looking both at the quantitative and the qualitative aspects of the decision. Operations managers do not necessarily have to be mathematical geniuses, but they should not be afraid of numbers!

Keeps cool under pressure
Operations managers often work in pressured situations. They need to be able to remain calm, no matter what problems occur. ● ● ●

The model of operations management

We can now combine two ideas to develop the model of operations management that will be used throughout this text. The first is the idea of transformation systems that take in inputs and use process resources to transform them into outputs. The second idea is that the resources, both in an organization's operations as a whole and in its individual processes, need to be managed in terms of how they are *directed*, how they are *designed*, how *delivery* is planned and controlled and how they are *developed* and improved. Figure 1.9 shows how these two ideas go together. This text will use this model to examine the more important decisions that should be of interest to all managers of operations and processes.

operations principle
Operations management activities can be grouped into four broad categories: directing the overall strategy of the operation; designing the operation's products, services and processes; planning and controlling delivery; and developing performance.

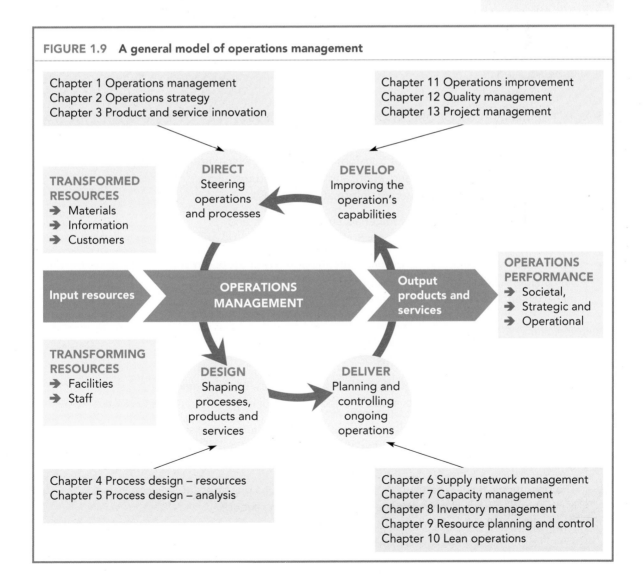

FIGURE 1.9   **A general model of operations management**

Summary answers to key questions

Each chapter has a 'Summary answers to key questions' section. Use it to check your understanding of the issues covered in the chapter.

WHAT IS OPERATIONS MANAGEMENT?

★ Operations management is the activity of managing the resources that are devoted to the creation and delivery of services and products. It is one of the core functions of any business, although it may not be called operations management in some industries.

★ Operations can produce both services and products, but most create and deliver a combination of services and products.

★ Operations management is not just for commercial businesses – it is just as relevant for not-for-profit organizations, even if terminology has to be adjusted.

WHAT IS THE INPUT–TRANSFORMATION–OUTPUT PROCESS?

★ All operations can be modelled as input–transformation–output processes. They all have inputs of transforming resources, which are usually divided into 'facilities' and 'staff', and transformed resources, which are some mixture of materials, information and customers.

★ Some operations have inputs of materials *and* information *and* customers, but usually one of these is dominant.

★ Operations management is concerned with managing processes. And all management functions also have processes. Therefore, operations management has relevance for all managers.

WHY IS OPERATIONS MANAGEMENT IMPORTANT TO AN ORGANIZATION'S PERFORMANCE?

★ Operations management can 'make or break' any business. It is large and usually represents the bulk of its assets and the majority of its people.

★ Operations management affects performance at three different levels: the broad societal level (using the idea of the triple bottom line); the strategic level; and the operational level.

★ The operational level is particularly relevant to operations managers. It is measured using five 'performance objectives': quality, speed, dependability, flexibility and cost.

WHAT IS THE PROCESS HIERARCHY?

★ All operations are part of a larger supply network that, through the individual contributions of each operation, satisfies end customer requirements.

★ All operations are made up of processes that form a network of internal customer–supplier relationships within the operation.

★ End-to-end business processes that satisfy customer needs often cut across functionally based processes.

HOW DO OPERATIONS AND PROCESSES DIFFER?

★ Operations and processes differ in terms of the volume of their outputs, the variety of outputs, the variation in demand for their outputs and the degree of 'visibility' they have.

★ High volume, low variety, low variation and low customer 'visibility' are usually associated with low cost.

WHAT DO OPERATIONS MANAGERS DO?

★ Responsibilities can be classed in four categories – direct, design, deliver and develop.

★ Direct includes understanding relevant performance objectives, setting an operations strategy and the scope of operations activities, together with how innovation is incorporated into its products and services.

★ Design includes choosing the resources to be used by processes and analyzing their detailed design.

★ Delivery includes the planning and controlling of the activities of the operation.

★ Develop includes the improvement of the operation over time, the management of quality and managing improvement projects.

Problems and applications

All chapters have problems and application questions that will help you practice analyzing operations. They can be answered by reading the chapter. Model answers for the first question can be found on the companion website for this text.

1   ➜ Quentin Cakes makes about 20,000 cakes per year in two sizes, both based on the same recipe. Sales peak at Christmas time when demand is about 50 per cent higher than in the quieter summer period. Its customers (the stores who stock its products) order its cakes in advance through a simple internet-based ordering system. Knowing that it has some surplus capacity, one of its customers has approached it with two potential new orders.

The custom cake option – this would involve making cakes in different sizes, where consumers could specify a message or greeting to be 'iced' on top of the cake. The consumer would give the inscription to the store, who would email it through to the factory. The customer thought that demand would be around 1,000 cakes per year, mostly at celebration times such as Valentine's Day and Christmas.

The individual cake option – this option involves Quentin Cakes introducing a new line of about 10 to 15 types of very small cakes intended for individual consumption. Demand for this individual-sized cake was forecast to be around 4,000 per year, with demand likely to be more evenly distributed throughout the year than its existing products.

The total revenue from both options is likely to be roughly the same and the company has only capacity to adopt one of the ideas. But which one should it be?

2   ➜ Read the 'Operations in practice' case on Prêt A Manger.

a)   Do you think Prêt A Manger fully understand the importance of their operations management?

b)   What evidence is there for this?

c)   What kind of operations management activities at Prêt A Manger might come under the four headings of direct, design, deliver and develop?

3 ➡ Visit an IKEA superstore and a smaller furniture store. Observe how the shop operates – for example, where customers go, how staff interact with them, how big it is, how the shop has chosen to use its space, what variety of products it offers and so on. Talk with the staff and managers if you can. Think about how the two shops differ from each other. Then consider the question, 'What implications do the differences between IKEA and the smaller shop have for their operations management?'

4 ➡ Write down five services that you have 'consumed' in the last week. Try and make these as varied as possible. Examples could include public transport, a bank, any shop or supermarket, attendance at an education course, a cinema, a restaurant, etc.

For each of these services, ask yourself the following questions:

- Did the service meet your expectations? If so, what did the management of the service have to do well in order to satisfy your expectations? If not, where did they fail? Why might they have failed?
- If you were in charge of managing the delivery of these services, what would you do to improve the service?
- If they wanted to, how could the service be delivered at a lower cost so that the service could reduce its prices?
- How do you think that the service copes when something goes wrong (such as a piece of technology breaking down)?
- Which other organizations might supply the service with products and services? (In other words, they are your 'supplier', but who are *their* suppliers)?
- How do you think the service copes with fluctuation of demand over the day, week, month or year?

These questions are just some of the issues that the operations managers in these services have to deal with. Think about the other issues they will have to manage in order to deliver the service effectively.

Want to know more?

Anupindi, R. and Chopra, S. (2013) *Managing Business Process Flows*, 3rd edition, Harlow, UK: Pearson.

➜ Takes a 'process' view of operations; it's mathematical but rewarding.

Barnes, D. (2007) *Operations Management: An international Perspective*, Boston, MA: Cengage Learning.

➜ A text that is similar in outlook to this *Essentials* one, but with more of a (useful) international perspective.

Hall, J.M. and Johnson, M.E. (2009) 'When should a process be art, not science?', *Harvard Business Review,* March.

➜ One of the few articles that looks at the boundaries of conventional process theory.

Johnston, R., Clark, E. and Shulver, M. (2012) *Service Operations Management*, 4th edition, Harlow, UK: Pearson.

➜ A great treatment of service operations from the same stable as this text.

Slack, N. (2017) *The Operations Advantage*, London: Kogan Page.

➜ Similar coverage to this text, but with more of a practical perspective.

Slack, N. and Lewis, M.A. (eds) (2005) *The Blackwell Encyclopedic Dictionary of Operations Management*, 2nd edition, Oxford: Blackwell Business.

➜ For those who like technical descriptions and definitions.

Does a restaurant produce products or services? Like most operations, it produces both. Its food and the way it serves it must be created to high standards of quality, speed dependability, flexibility and cost.

Operations strategy

2

Introduction

There is a common misapprehension that operations management is concerned only with the day-to-day and detailed aspects of running operations. But that is far from the truth. There is (or should be) a strong connection between an organization's operations management and its strategy. This is because organizations cannot plan every detail of their future actions; there is just too much uncertainty about what conditions will exist in the future. There will always have to be some adjustment to whatever plans have been made. Yet simply reacting to every short-term event can lead to constant changes in direction and the operation becoming volatile and unstable. Which is why all organizations need the 'backdrop' of a well-understood operations strategy, so they know (at least, roughly) where they are heading and how they could get there. However, the concept of 'strategy' itself is not straightforward; and neither is operations strategy. This chapter considers four perspectives that shape operations strategy, how it can form the basis for operations improvement and how an operations strategy can be formulated. Figure 2.1 shows the position of the ideas described in this chapter in the general model of operations management.

Key questions

What is strategy and what is operations strategy?

What is the difference between a 'top-down' and 'bottom-up' view of operations strategy?

What is the difference between a 'market requirements' and 'operations resources' view of operations strategy?

How can operations strategy form the basis for operations improvement?

What is the 'process' of operations strategy?

FIGURE 2.1   **This chapter examines operations strategy**

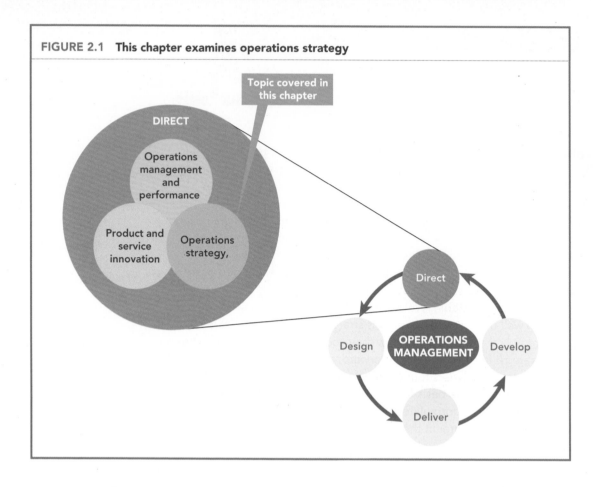

What is strategy and what is operations strategy?

Linguistically, the word 'strategy' derives from the Greek word *strategos*, meaning 'leading an army'. And although there is no direct historical link between Greek military practice and modern ideas of strategy, both military and business strategy can be described as setting broad objectives or goals, planning the path (in general, rather than specific terms) that will achieve these goals in the long term rather than short term, dealing with the total picture rather than stressing individual activities and being above the distractions of day-to-day activities. Here, strategic decisions are taken to mean those that are widespread in their effect on the organization, define its position relative to its environment and move it closer to its long-term goals. But 'strategy' is more than a single decision; it is the *total pattern of the decisions* and actions that influence the long-term direction of the business. Thinking about strategy in this way helps us to discuss *actual* rather than *intended* strategic behaviour

Operations in practice

SSTL: changing the economics of space exploration[1]

Space satellites can be expensive – very expensive. And in the early days of space missions, this meant that only superpowers could afford to develop and launch them. The conventional wisdom was that space was such a hostile environment that satellites would have to be constructed using only specially developed components that could endure such severe conditions. Yet this assumption was challenged by Sir Martin Sweeting, who was studying for his PhD at the University of Surrey in the UK, when the aerospace research team there built its first satellite (called UoSAT-1) using commercial off-the-shelf components. It was about as big as two microwave ovens, weighing in at 72 kg. By contrast, some of the huge satellites being launched by government space agencies were as large as a London double-decker bus. It was launched in 1981 with the help of NASA, who had been persuaded to provide a free launch piggybacking on the back of a mission to put a large scientific satellite into orbit. The team followed this up with a second satellite (UoSAT-2) that they built in just six months and launched in 1984. A year later, Surrey Satellite Technology Limited (SSTL) was formed to transfer the results of the team's research into a commercial enterprise. The strategy was to pioneer the use of small and relatively cheap, but reliable, satellites built from readily available off-the-shelf components. It was then a revolutionary idea that was operationalized by exploiting advances in technologies and challenging conventions to bring affordable space exploration to international customers. The company, now within the Airbus Defence and Space group, has launched over 40 satellites and employs more than 500 staff in Southeast England.

SSTL has always been innovative in finding ways of keeping the cost of building satellites down to a minimum. It pioneered the low-cost, low-risk approach to delivering operational satellite missions within short development timescales and with the capability that potential customers wanted. When the first microcomputers became commercially available, Sir Martin Sweeting speculated that it may be possible to use programmable technology to build small satellites that were 'intelligent' when compared with large hard-wired satellites, allowing satellites to be reprogrammed from the ground. Particularly important was the company's use of commercial off-the-shelf technology. Combined with a determination to learn something from each new project, a pragmatic approach to manufacture and low-cost operations, it enabled SSTL to keep costs as low as realistically possible. In effect, using industry-standard parts meant exploiting the, often enormous, investments by consumer-electronics companies, auto-part manufacturers and others who had developed complex components for their products.

Although individual components and systems are often bought off the shelf, SSTL does most of its operations activities itself so it can provide a complete in-house design, manufacture, launch, operation and consultancy service. "What distinguishes us is our vertically integrated capability, from design and research to manufacturing and operations", says Sir Martin. "We don't have to rely on suppliers, although of course we buy-in components when that is advantageous." And innovation? It's still as important as it was at the company's start. Surrey University has retained a 1 per cent stake in the company because "we wanted to cement the very close relationship between company and university", says Sir Martin. "We work together on a number of research projects and staff flow back and forth between us." ●●●

Operations strategy

Operations strategy concerns the pattern of strategic decisions and actions that set the role, objectives and activities of the operation. The term 'operations strategy' sounds at first like a contradiction. How can 'operations', a subject that is generally concerned with the day-to-day creation and delivery of goods and services, be strategic? 'Strategy' is usually regarded as the opposite of those day-to-day routine activities. But *operations* is not the same as *operational*. 'Operations' are the resources that create products and services. 'Operational' is the opposite of strategic, meaning day-to-day and detailed. So, one can examine both the operational *and* the strategic aspects of operations. It is also conventional to distinguish between the 'content' and the 'process' of operations strategy. The content of operations strategy is the specific decisions and actions that set the operations role, objectives and activities. The process of operations strategy is the method that is used to make those specific 'content' decisions.

operations principle
'Operations' is not the same as 'operational' – it does have a strategic role.

Hayes and Wheelwright's four stages of operations contribution

Most businesses expect their operations strategy to improve operations performance over time. In doing this they should be progressing from a state where strategy contributes very little to the competitive success of the business through to the point where it is directly responsible for its competitive success. Professors Hayes and Wheelwright of Harvard University[2] developed a four-stage model, which can be used to evaluate the role and contribution of the operations function. The model traces the progression of the operations function from what is the largely negative role of stage 1 operations to it becoming the central element of competitive strategy in excellent stage 4 operations. Figure 2.2 illustrates the four stages.

Stage 1: Internal neutrality   This is the very poorest level of contribution by the operations function. It is holding the company back from competing effectively. It is inward-looking and, at best, reactive, with very little positive to contribute towards competitive success. Paradoxically, its goal is 'to be ignored' (or, 'internally neutral'). At least then it isn't holding the company back in any way. It attempts to improve by 'avoiding making mistakes'.

Stage 2: External neutrality   The first step of breaking out of stage 1 is for the operations function to begin comparing itself with similar companies or organizations in the outside market (being 'externally neutral'). This may not immediately take it to the 'first division' of companies in the market, but at least it is measuring itself against its competitors' performance and trying to implement 'best practice'.

Stage 3: Internally supportive   Stage 3 operations are among the best in their market. Yet, stage 3 operations still aspire to be clearly and unambiguously the very best in the market. They achieve this by gaining a clear view of the company's competitive or strategic goals and supporting it by developing appropriate operations resources. The operation is trying to be 'internally supportive' by providing a credible operations strategy.

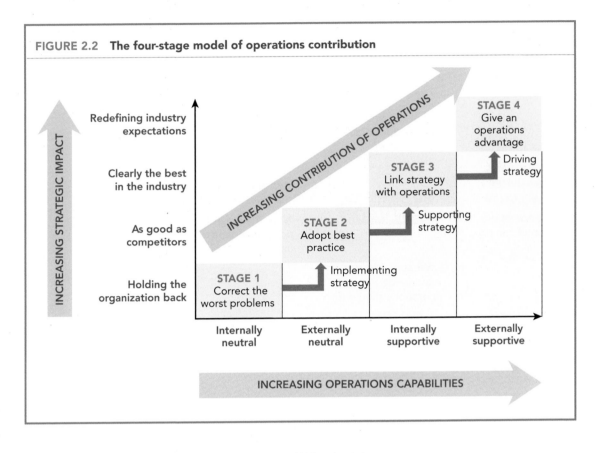

FIGURE 2.2 The four-stage model of operations contribution

Stage 4: Externally supportive Hayes and Wheelwright suggest a further stage – stage 4 – where the company views the operations function as providing the foundation for its competitive success. Operations looks to the long term. It forecasts likely changes in markets and supply, and it develops the operations-based capabilities that will be required to compete in future market conditions. Stage 4 operations are innovative, creative and proactive and are driving the company's strategy by being 'one step ahead' of competitors – what Hayes and Wheelwright call being 'externally supportive'.

Perspectives on operations strategy

Different authors have slightly different views and definitions of operations strategy. Between them, four 'perspectives' emerge:[3]

 Operations strategy is a top-down reflection of what the whole group or business wants to do.

 Operations strategy is a bottom-up activity where operations improvements cumulatively build strategy.

 Operations strategy involves translating market requirements into operations decisions (sometimes called the 'outside-in' perspective).

 Operations strategy involves exploiting the capabilities of operations resources in chosen markets (sometimes called the 'inside-out' perspective).

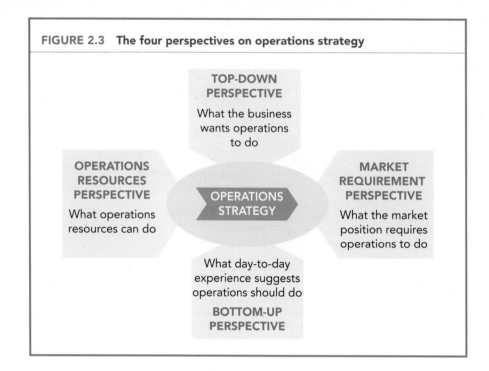

FIGURE 2.3   The four perspectives on operations strategy

None of these four perspectives alone gives the full picture of what operations strategy is, but they do provide some idea of the pressures that go to form the content of an operations strategy. First, we will treat the top-down and bottom-up perspectives together, then the market requirements and operations resource perspectives together (see Figure 2.3).

What is the difference between a 'top-down' and 'bottom-up' view of operations strategy?

'Top-down' strategies

A large corporation will need a strategy to position itself in its global, economic, political and social environment. This will consist of decisions about what types of business the group wants to be in, what markets it wants to operate in, how to allocate cash between its various businesses and so on. These decisions form the corporate or group strategy of the corporation. Similarly, within the corporate group, each business unit will also need to put together its own business strategy which sets out its individual mission and objectives. This business strategy guides the business in relation to its customers, markets and competitors, and also in relation to the strategy of the corporate group of which it is a part. Similarly, within the business, functional strategies need to consider what part each function should play in contributing to the strategic objectives of the business.

So, one perspective on operations strategy is that it should take its place in this hierarchy of strategies. Its main influence, therefore, will be whatever the business sees as its strategic direction. For example, a printing services group has a company that prints packaging for consumer products. The group's management believes that, in the long term, only companies with significant market share will achieve substantial profitability. Its corporate objectives therefore stress market dominance. The consumer packaging company decides to achieve volume growth, even above short-term profitability or return on investment. The implication for operations strategy is that it needs to expand rapidly, investing in extra capacity (factories, equipment and labour), even if it means some excess capacity in some areas. The important point here is that different business objectives would probably result in a very different operations strategy. The role of operations is therefore largely one of implementing or 'operationalizing' business strategy. Figure 2.4 illustrates this strategic hierarchy, with some of the decisions at each level and the main influences on the strategic decisions.

operations principle
Operations strategies should reflect top-down corporate and/or business objectives.

'Bottom-up' strategies

The 'top-down' perspective provides an orthodox view of how functional strategies *should* be put together. But, in fact, the relationship between the levels in the strategy hierarchy is more complex than this. When any group is reviewing its corporate strategy, it will also take into account the circumstances, experiences and capabilities of the various businesses that form the group. Similarly, businesses, when reviewing their strategies, will consult the individual functions within the business about their constraints and capabilities. They may also incorporate the ideas that come from each function's day-to-day experience. Therefore, an alternative view to the top-down perspective is that many strategic ideas emerge over time from operational experience. Sometimes companies move in a particular strategic direction because the ongoing experience of providing products and services to customers at an operational level convinces them that it is the right thing to do. There may be no high-level decisions examining alternative strategic options and choosing the one that provides the best way forward. Instead, a general consensus emerges from the operational level of the organization.

FIGURE 2.4   The top-down perspective of operations strategy and its application to the printing services group

CORPORATE STRATEGY DECISIONS
➔ What businesses to be in?
➔ Allocation of cash to businesses?
➔ How to manage the relationships between different businesses?

BUSINESS STRATEGY DECISIONS
➔ Defining the mission of the business e.g.
  – growth targets
  – return on investment
  – profitability targets
  – cash generation
➔ Setting competitive objectives

FUNCTIONAL STRATEGY DECISIONS
➔ The role of the function
➔ Translating business objectives into functional objectives
➔ Allocation of resources so as to achieve functional objectives
➔ Performance improvement priorities

PRINTING SERVICES GROUP CORPORATE STRATEGY
➔ Specialize in packaging businesses
➔ Become a major player in all its markets

CONSUMER PACKAGING BUSINESS STRATEGY
➔ Rapid volume growth
➔ Fast service
➔ Economies of scale

OPERATIONS STRATEGY
➔ Capacity expansion
➔ Tolerate some over-capacity in the short term
➔ New locations established

Suppose the printing services company described previously succeeds in its expansion plans. However, in doing so it finds that having surplus capacity and a distributed network of factories allows it to offer an exceptionally fast service to customers. It also finds that some customers are willing to pay considerably higher prices for such a responsive service. Its experiences lead the company to set up a separate division dedicated to providing fast, high-margin printing services to those customers willing to pay. The strategic objectives of this new division are not concerned with high-volume growth but high profitability.

operations principle
Operations strategy should reflect the bottom-up experience of operational reality.

This idea of strategy being shaped by operational level experience over time is sometimes called the concept of emergent strategies[4] (see Figure 2.5). This view of operations strategy is perhaps more descriptive of how things really happen. Yet while emergent strategies are less easy to categorize, the principle governing a bottom-up perspective is clear: shape the operation's objectives and action, at least partly, by the knowledge it gains from its day-to-day activities. The key virtues required for shaping strategy from the bottom up are an ability to learn from experience and a philosophy of continual and incremental improvement.

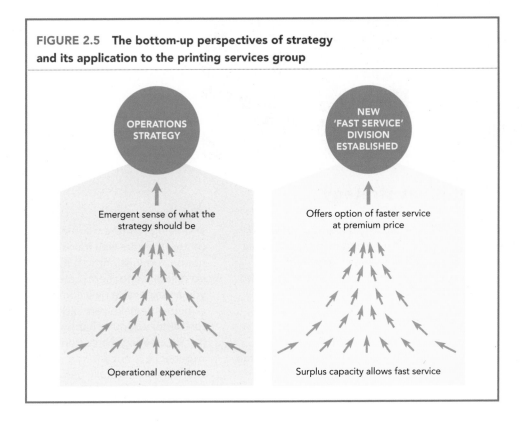

FIGURE 2.5   The bottom-up perspectives of strategy and its application to the printing services group

OPERATIONS STRATEGY

Emergent sense of what the strategy should be

Operational experience

NEW 'FAST SERVICE' DIVISION ESTABLISHED

Offers option of faster service at premium price

Surplus capacity allows fast service

What is the difference between a market requirements and operations resources view of operations strategy?

Market requirements-based strategies

No operation that continually fails to serve its markets adequately is likely to survive in the long term. Without an understanding of what markets require, it is impossible to ensure that the operations is achieving the right priority among its performance objectives (quality, speed, dependability, flexibility and cost).

THE MARKET INFLUENCE ON PERFORMANCE OBJECTIVES

Operations seeks to satisfy customers through developing the five performance objectives. For example, if customers particularly value low-priced products or services, the operation will place emphasis on its cost performance. Alternatively, a customer emphasis on fast delivery will make

Operations in practice

Apple's retail operations strategy[5]

The way Apple designs and runs its retail operations is a good example of how what operations does 'on the ground' should be aligned with what a business is trying to achieve in its market. It was back in 1990 when the late Steve Jobs, then Apple's boss, decided to build Apple stores because conventional computer retailers were reluctant to stock its products. They said that the Apple brand was too weak (which, at the time it was). The original Apple stores were heavily influenced by GAP (the clothing retailer), and so many GAP employees moved to work for Apple that they joked about working for 'Gapple'. Yet, even with the experienced GAP retailers, Apple wanted to develop its own ideas. Consequently, it built a 'prototype store' near its

Californian headquarters and after testing its retail concepts for a year, it came to the conclusion that there were two key issues for its retail operations strategy.

The first was store location: Apple has stores in some of the highest-profile locations on earth. This is expensive, but it means that its sales productivity (sales per square metre) is above most luxury goods retailers. The second was the customers' in-store experience. According to Ron Johnson, who built up Apple's shop network, "People come to the Apple store for the experience, and they're willing to pay a premium for that. There are lots of components to that experience, but maybe the most important is that the staff isn't focused on selling stuff, it's focused on building relationships

and trying to make people's lives better. They are well trained, and not on commission, so it makes no difference to them if they sell you an expensive new computer or help you make your old one run better so you're happy with it." Yet creating the customer experience is not a matter of chance – it is carefully designed into Apple's strategy. For example, staff have been told never to correct a customer's mispronunciation of a product in case it is seen as patronizing. Of course, Apple's products are attractive and Apple customers are famously passionate about the brand, but if Apple products were the only reason for the stores' success, it's difficult to explain why customers flock to the stores to buy Apple products at full price when discount retailers sell them cheaper. ● ● ●

speed important to the operation. When it is important that products or services are delivered exactly when they are promised, the performance objective of dependability will be essential for the operation. When customers value products or services that have been adapted or designed specifically for them, flexibility will be vital, and so on. This list is not exhaustive; the key point is that whatever competitive factors are important to customers should influence the priority of each performance objective.

operations principle
Operations strategy should reflect the requirements of the business' markets.

ORDER-WINNING AND QUALIFYING FACTORS

A particularly useful way of determining the relative importance of competitive factors is to distinguish between 'order-winning' and 'qualifying' factors.[6] Order-winning factors are those things that directly and significantly contribute to winning business. They are regarded by customers as key reasons for purchasing the product or service. Raising performance in an order-winning factor will either result in more business or at least improve the chances of gaining more business. Qualifying factors may not be the major competitive determinants of success, but are important in another way. They are those aspects of competitiveness where the operation's performance has to be above a particular level just to be considered by the customer. Performance below this 'qualifying' level of performance will possibly disqualify the company from being considered by many customers. But any further improvement above the qualifying level is unlikely to gain the company much competitive benefit. To order-winning and qualifying factors can be added less important factors that are neither order-winning nor qualifying. They do not influence customers in any significant way. They are worth mentioning here only because they may be of importance in other parts of the operation's activities.

Figure 2.6 shows the difference between order-winning, qualifying and less important factors in terms of their utility or worth to the competitiveness of the organization. The curves illustrate the relative amount of competitiveness (or attractiveness to customers) as the operation's performance at the factor varies. Order-winning factors show a steady and significant increase in their contribution to competitiveness as the operation gets better at providing them. Qualifying factors are 'givens'; they are expected by customers and can severely disadvantage the competitive position of the operation if it cannot raise its performance above the qualifying level. Less important objectives have little impact on customers, no matter how well the operation performs in them.

operations principle
Competitive factors can be classified as order winners or qualifiers.

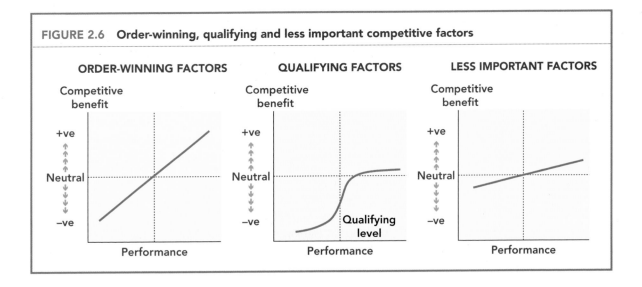

FIGURE 2.6   Order-winning, qualifying and less important competitive factors

TABLE 2.1   Different banking services require different performance objectives

	Retail banking	Corporate banking
Products	Personal financial services such as loans and credit cards	Special services for corporate customers
Customers	Individuals	Businesses
Range of services offered	Medium but standardized, little need for special terms	Very wide range, many need to be customized
Changes to service design	Occasional	Continual
Delivery	Fast decisions	Dependable service
Quality	Means error-free transactions	Means close relationships
Volume per service type	Most services are high volume	Most services are low volume
Profit margins	Most are low to medium, some high	Medium to high
Competitive factors		
Order winners	Price	Customization
	Accessibility	Quality of service
	Ease of transaction	Reliability/trust
Qualifiers	Quality	Ease of transaction
	Range	Price
Less important		Accessibility
Internal performance objectives	Cost	Flexibility
	Speed	Quality
	Quality	Dependability

DIFFERENT CUSTOMER NEEDS IMPLY DIFFERENT OBJECTIVES

If, as is likely, an operation produces goods or services for more than one customer group, it will need to determine the order-winning, qualifying and less important competitive factors for each group. For example, Table 2.1 shows two 'product' groups in the banking industry. Here, the distinction is drawn between the customers who are looking for banking services for their private and domestic needs (current accounts, overdraft facilities, savings accounts, etc.) and those corporate customers who need banking services for their organizations (letters of credit, cash transfer services, etc.).

THE SERVICE/PRODUCT LIFE CYCLE INFLUENCE ON PERFORMANCE OBJECTIVES

One way of generalizing the behaviour of both customers and competitors is to link it to the life cycle of the products or services that the operation is producing. The exact form of product/service life cycles will vary, but generally they are shown as the sales volume passing through four stages – introduction, growth, maturity and decline. The implication of this for operations management is that products and services will require different operations strategies at each stage of their life cycle (see Figure 2.7).

Introduction stage When a product or service is first introduced, it is likely to be offering something new in terms of its design or performance, with few competitors offering the same product or service. The needs of customers are unlikely to be well understood, so operations management needs to develop the flexibility to cope with any changes and be able to give the quality to maintain product/service performance.

Growth stage As volume grows, competitors may enter the growing market. Keeping up with demand could prove to be the main operations preoccupation. Rapid and dependable response to demand will help to keep demand buoyant, while quality levels must ensure that the company keeps its share of the market as competition starts to increase.

FIGURE 2.7 The effects of the product/service life cycle on operations performance objectives

Sales volume	Introduction Into market	Growth in Market Acceptance	Maturity of Market, sales Level off	Decline as Market Becomes Saturated
Customers	Innovators	Early adopters	Bulk of market	Laggards
Competitors	Few/none	Increasing numbers	Stable numbers	Declining number
Likely order winners	Product/service specification	Availability	Low price Dependable supply	Low price
Likely qualifiers	Quality Range	Price Range	Range Quality	Dependable supply
Dominant operations performance objectives	Flexibility Quality	Speed Dependability Quality	Cost Dependability	Cost

Maturity stage   Demand starts to level off. Some early competitors may have left the market and the industry will probably be dominated by a few larger companies. So, operations will be expected to get the costs down in order to maintain profits or to allow price cutting, or both. Because of this, cost and productivity issues, together with dependable supply, are likely to be the operation's main concerns.

Decline stage   After time, sales will decline, with more competitors dropping out of the market. There might be a residual market, but unless a shortage of capacity develops, the market will continue to be dominated by price competition. Operations objectives continue to be dominated by cost.

> **operations principle**
> Operations strategy objectives will change depending on the stage of the business' services and products.

The operations resources perspective

The fourth and final perspective we shall take on operations strategy is based on a particularly influential theory of business strategy – the resource-based view (RBV) of the firm.[7] Put simply, the RBV holds that firms with an 'above average' strategic performance are likely to have gained their sustainable competitive advantage because of the core competences (or capabilities) of their resources. In other words, the way an operation inherits, or acquires, or develops its resources will, over the long term, have a significant impact on its strategic success. Furthermore, the benefits that it gets from its 'operations resources' capabilities will be at least as great, if not greater, than that which it gets from its market position. So, understanding and developing the capabilities of operations resources is a particularly important perspective on operations strategy.

RESOURCE CONSTRAINTS AND CAPABILITIES

No organization can merely choose which part of the market it wants to be in without considering its ability to produce services and products in a way that will satisfy that market. In other words, the constraints imposed by its operations must be taken into account. For example, a small translation company offers general translation services to a wide range of customers who wish documents such as sales brochures to be translated into another language. A small company, it operates an informal network of part-time translators who enable the company to offer translation into or from most of the major languages in the world. Some of the company's largest customers want to purchase their sales brochures on a 'one-stop shop' basis and have asked the translation company whether it is willing to offer a full service, organizing the design and production, as well as the translation, of export brochures. This is a very profitable market opportunity. However, the company does not have the resources, financial or physical, to take it up. From a market perspective, it is good business; but from an operations resources perspective, it is not feasible.

However, the operations resources perspective is not always so negative. This perspective may identify *constraints* to satisfying some markets, but it can also identify *capabilities* that can be exploited in other markets. For example, the same translation company has recently employed two new translators who have translation software skills, so now the company can offer a new 'fast response' service that has been designed specifically to exploit the capabilities within the operations resources. Here, the company has chosen to be driven by its resource capabilities rather than the obvious market opportunities.

INTANGIBLE RESOURCES

An operations resources perspective must start with an understanding of two simple questions: what do we have, and what can we do? However, merely listing the type of resources an operation has does not give a complete picture of what it can do. Trying to understand an operation by listing its resources alone is like trying to understand an automobile by listing its component parts. To describe it more fully, we need to describe how the component parts form the internal mechanisms of the motor car. Within the operation, the equivalent of these mechanisms is its *processes*. Yet, even for an automobile, a technical explanation of its mechanisms still does not convey everything about its style or 'personality'. Something more is needed to describe these. In the same way, an operation is not just the sum of its processes. In addition, the operation has some intangible resources. An operation's intangible resources include such things as its relationship with suppliers, the reputation it has with its customers, its knowledge of its process technologies and the way its staff can work together in new product and service development. These intangible resources may not always be obvious within the operation, but they are important and have real value. It is these intangible resources, as well as its tangible ones, that an operation needs to satisfy its markets.

STRATEGIC RESOURCES AND SUSTAINABLE COMPETITIVE ADVANTAGE

The 'resources-based' explanation of why some companies manage to gain sustainable competitive advantage is that they have better or more appropriate resources. Put simply, 'above average' competitive performance is likely to be the result of the core capabilities (or competences) inherent in a firm's resources. And resources can have a particularly influential impact on strategic success if they exhibit some or all of the following properties:[8]

They are scarce   Some resources are available to almost any firm that wants them – standard 'off-the-shelf' technology, or people with 'easily acquired' skills, for example. Other resources are more difficult to acquire because they are limited – for example, landing slots at a busy airport, or people with specific technical skills such as experience with a novel application software. The scarcer the resource, the more strategically important it is likely to be, if only because competitors can't get hold of it.

They are not very mobile   Some resources are difficult to move out of a firm. For example, if a new process is developed in a company's Stockholm site and is based on the knowledge and experience of the Stockholm staff, the process will be difficult (although not totally impossible) to sell to another company based elsewhere in Europe (or even Sweden if the staff do not want to move).

They are difficult to imitate or substitute for   It is not enough only to have resources that are scarce and immobile. If a competitor can copy these resources, or replace them with alternative resources, then the original company will lose their strategic significance. That is why intangible resources (such as unique technical knowledge) are so valuable; they are particularly difficult for competitors to understand and to copy.

> **operations principle**
> The long-term objective of operations strategy is to build operations-based capabilities that are scarce, not mobile and difficult to imitate or substitute for.

STRATEGIC OPERATIONS DECISIONS

To some extent, all operations decisions can have an impact on a firm's strategy. Yet some decisions are more obviously strategic in the sense that they have a profound and long-term impact on the firm. Three sets of decisions, in particular, set the terms of what any operation has to do and how it can do it. These are: the range and type of services and products that it produces; the scope of its activities in its supply network; and where it is to be located. (The whole of the next chapter is devoted to the first issue – how services and products are developed – and Chapter 6 treats the more operational aspects of managing the supply network.) It is worth considering at this point how the scope and location of an operation's activities can have strategic implications.

OPERATIONS SCOPE

In the previous chapter we described how the input–transformation–output model can be used to describe networks of resources, processes or operations, and the most strategic of these networks was the 'supply network'. An operation's supply network will include its suppliers and customers. It will also include suppliers' suppliers and customers' customers, and so on. The 'scope' of an operation is the extent that it does things itself, as opposed to relying on other operations in the supply network to do things for it. This is often referred to as 'vertical integration' when it is the ownership of whole operations that are being decided, or 'outsourcing' when individual activities are being considered. It is an issue that will shape the fundamental nature of any business because it shapes how the operation interacts with other operations, with its markets, with its suppliers, in fact with the world in general.

Theoretically, 'vertical integration' and 'outsourcing' are the same thing. Vertical integration is 'the extent to which an organization owns the network of which it is a part'. Outsourcing is, 'an arrangement in which one company provides services for another company that could also be, or usually have been, provided in-house'.[9] It is based on the idea that no single business does everything that is required to produce its products and services. Bakers do not grow wheat. Banks do not usually do their own credit checking – they retain

Operations in practice

Contrasting strategies: ARM versus Intel[10]

Nothing better illustrates the idea that there is more than one approach to competing in the same market than the contrasting business models of ARM and Intel in the microchip business. At one point, ARM's chip designs were to be found in almost 99 per cent of mobile devices in the world, while Intel dominates the PC and server markets. Yet ARM and Intel are very different companies, with different approaches to the scope of their operations. Intel is vertically integrated, both designing and manufacturing its own chips, while ARM is essentially a chip designer, developing intellectual property. It then licenses its processor designs to manufacturers such as Samsung, who in turn rely on sub-contracting 'chip foundry' companies to do the actual manufacturing (ironically, including Intel).

Intel's integrated supply network monitors and controls all stages of production, from the original design concept right through to manufacturing. It is Intel's near-monopoly (therefore high volume) of the server and PC markets that helps it to keep its unit prices high, which in turn gives them the ability to finance the construction of the latest semiconductor manufacturing equipment before its competitors. And having the latest manufacturing technology is important – it can mean faster, smaller and cheaper chips with lower power consumption. Everyone else, including all the ARM licensees, have to make do with shared manufacturing, mainstream technology and less-aggressive physics. By contrast, ARM's supply network strategy was a direct result of its early lack of cash. It did not have the money to invest in in its own manufacturing facilities (or to take the risk of subcontracting manufacturing), so it focused on licensing its 'reference designs'. Reference designs provide the 'technical blueprint' of a microprocessor that third parties can enhance or modify as required. This means that partners can take ARM reference designs and integrate them flexibly to produce different final designs. ● ● ●

the services of specialist agencies that have the expertise to do it better. Outsourcing has become an important issue for most businesses.

This is because, although most companies have always outsourced some of their activities, a larger proportion of direct activities are now being bought from suppliers. Also, many indirect and administrative processes are now being outsourced. This is often referred to as 'business process outsourcing' (BPO). Financial service companies, in particular, are outsourcing some of their more routine back-office processes. The reason for doing this is often primarily to reduce cost. However, there can sometimes also be significant gains in the quality and flexibility of service offered. However, there is a counter-argument to outsourcing. Some believe that the only reason that outsourcing companies can do the job at lower cost is that they either reduce salaries, reduce working conditions, or both. Furthermore, they say, flexibility is only achieved by reducing job security. Employees who were once part of a large and secure corporation could find themselves as far less secure employees of a less benevolent employer with a philosophy of permanent cost cutting.

The final point to make here is that scope decisions are undeniably strategic. The 'operations in practice' example on ARM and Intel shows how their (very different) approaches to the scope of their operations have totally defined how each company does business in essentially similar markets.

OPERATIONS LOCATION

The location of each operation in a supply network is a key element in defining its performance. If an operation gets the location wrong, it can have a significant impact on the operation's costs as well as its ability to serve its customers (and therefore its revenues). Also, location decisions, once taken, are difficult to undo. The costs of moving an operation can be hugely expensive, and the risks of inconveniencing customers very high. No operation wants to move very often. But when it does change its location, its aim is usually to achieve an appropriate balance between three related objectives:

 The spatially variable costs of the operation (spatially variable means that something changes with geographical location): these are factors such as labour, land, energy and transportation costs, and the suitability of the site itself, together with so-called 'community factors' (the social, political and economic environment of its site).

 The service the operation is able to provide to its customers: for example, how far is an emergency response centre from the communities that it serves?

 The revenue potential of the operation: this could be such factors as the image of the location – some locations are firmly associated in customers' minds with a particular image (advanced technology in Silicon Valley, fashion-design houses in Milan and financial services in the City of London). More obviously, the convenience for customers is often the most important factor when service is important to customers. Locating a general hospital, for instance, in the middle of the countryside may have many advantages for its staff, but it clearly would be very inconvenient to its customers (patients).

In making decisions about where to locate an operation, operations managers are concerned with minimizing spatially variable costs and maximizing revenue/customer service. Location affects both of these, but not always equally. For example, customers may not care very much where some products are made, so location is unlikely to affect revenues significantly. However, the costs could be very greatly affected by location. Services, on the other hand, often have both costs and revenues affected by location.

Operations in practice

Apple's supply operations strategy[11]

Earlier in this chapter we looked at Apple's retail operations strategy. Here we move on to how Apple supplies its retail outlets, and others.

Behind the impressive corporate façade of Apple's Silicon Valley headquarters there are no factories churning out the millions of products that Apple sells every year. Apple, like most of its competitors, outsources its production to supplier operations around the world – mainly in the manufacturing powerhouses of Southeast Asia. So, does this mean that Apple's operations strategy is also outsourced, along with its manufacturing? Not at all. What it does mean is that operations strategy for Apple is concerned with 'supply'. In other words, making sure that current products are always supplied fast enough to meet demand and new products always meet their launch dates. Over the years, Apple has put together a remarkable supply network that is recognised as one of the most efficient in the world and, what is more important, gives them significant competitive advantage. The company's (outsourced) manufacturing, purchasing and supply logistics gives it the ability to accomplish substantial new product launches without having to build up huge and expensive pre-launch stocks. In the words of Tim Cook, who has developed Apple's operations strategy, "nobody wants to buy sour milk".

The way that Apple beats its competitors is to use its cash to secure exclusive deals on new component technologies (touch-screens, chips, LED displays, etc.). When a new component first comes out, it is usually very expensive to produce, and constructing a factory that can produce it in high volume is even more expensive. Combine this with the relatively small profit margin of many components and it becomes difficult for suppliers to make enough profit to guarantee that they can make an acceptable return on their investment. But, thanks to its successful stream of products, Apple can afford to pay for some or all of a supplier's construction cost of the new factory. In exchange, the supplier gives exclusive rights to Apple for the new component over an agreed period. This has two advantages for Apple. First, it gives Apple access to new component technology months (or even years) before its rivals, allowing it to launch radical new products that are literally impossible for competitors to duplicate. Second, even when the exclusive agreement expires, Apple will often have negotiated a discounted price. So, it can source the component at a lower cost from the supplier that is now the most-experienced and skilled provider of those parts.

In summary, according to Marty Lariviere at Stanford University, [Apple's operations strategy is to] "bet big on technology that lets them have distinctive products. With their limited product line and high volume, they can make commitments that other tech firms may shy away from. It also means that (if they are right) other firms are going to be hard pressed to catch up if Apple has locked up a large amount of supplier capacity." ● ● ●

How can operations strategy form the basis for operations improvement?

An operations strategy is not just about checking that a business' resources and processes are consistent with its overall strategy. As our earlier discussion of operations capabilities implied, it also can provide the foundation for improvement. And the objective of improvement is obvious. One way of thinking about this is to use the market requirements and operations capabilities perspectives that we discussed earlier to examine the concept of the 'line of fit'.

The 'line of fit' between market requirements and operations capabilities

At a strategic level, there should be a degree of fit between what an operation is trying to achieve in its markets (market requirements) and what it is good at doing (operations capabilities). Figure 2.8 (a) illustrates this idea. The vertical dimension represents the level of market requirements that reflect the intrinsic needs of customers or their expectations. Moving along this dimension indicates a broadly enhanced level of market performance. The horizontal scale represents the level of the organization's operations capabilities. Moving along the dimension indicates a broadly enhanced level of operations capabilities and therefore operations performance. Be careful, however, in using this diagrammatic representation. It is a conceptual model rather than a practical tool. It is intended merely to illustrate some ideas around the concept of strategic improvement. In terms of this framework, improvement means three things:

1   **Achieving 'alignment'**   This means achieving an approximate balance between 'required market performance' and 'actual operations performance'. The diagonal line in Figure 2.8 (a) therefore represents a 'line of fit', with market requirements and operations capabilities in balance.

2   **Achieving 'sustainable' alignment**   It is not enough to achieve alignment at one point in time. Equally important is whether operations processes could adapt to the new market conditions.

3   **Improving overall performance**   If the requirements of the market are undemanding, then the required level of operations capabilities will not need to be high. A more demanding level of market requirements will need a greater level of operations capabilities. But most firms would see their overall strategic objectives as achieving alignment at a level that

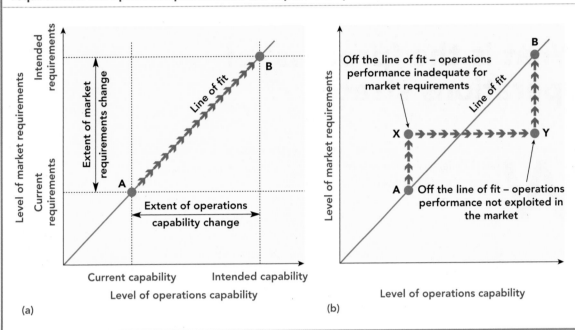

FIGURE 2.8 In operations, improvement should achieve 'fit' between market requirements and operations performance, but deviation from the 'line of fit' between market requirements and operations performance can expose the operation to risk

implies long-term competitive success – in other words, moving up from point A to point B in Figure 2.8 (a) – the assumption being that point B is more desirable because it is more likely to represent a financially successful position.

DEVIATING FROM THE LINE OF FIT

However, it may not be possible always to maintain the balance between market requirements and operations performance. Sometimes the market may expect something that the operation cannot (temporarily) deliver. Sometimes operations may have capabilities that cannot be exploited in the market. At a strategic level, there are risks deriving from any deviation from the 'line of fit'. For example, delays in the improvement to a new website could mean that customers do not receive the level of service they were promised. This is shown as position 'X' in Figure 2.8 (b). The risk to the organization is that its reputation (or brand) will suffer because market expectations exceed the operation's capability to perform appropriately. At other times, the operation may make improvements before they could be fully exploited in the market. For example, the same online retailer may have improved its website so that it can offer extra services, such as the ability to customize products, before those products have been stocked in its distribution centre. This means that, although an improvement to its ordering processes has been made, problems elsewhere in the company prevent the improvement from giving value to the

operations principle
Operations strategy should aim for alignment or 'fit' between an operation's performance and the requirements of its markets.

company. This is represented by point 'Y' on Figure 2.8 (b). In both instances, improvement activity needs to move the operation back to the line of fit.

What is the 'process' of operations strategy?

What is called the 'process' of strategy is concerned with 'how' strategies are put together. So, the 'process of operations strategy' means the method that is used to determine what an operations strategy should be. It is not a simple task. Putting an operations strategy together and making it happen is a complex and difficult thing to achieve. Even the most sophisticated organizations do not always get it right. And although any simple step-by-step model of how to 'do' operations strategy will inevitably be a simplification of a messy reality, we shall use a four-stage model to illustrate some of the elements of 'process'. This model is shown in Figure 2.9. It divides the process of operations strategy into the four stages of formulation, implementation, monitoring and control,[12] shown in Figure 2.9 as a cycle. This is because, in practice, strategies may be revisited depending on the experience gained from trying to make them happen.

> **operations principle**
> The process of operations strategy involves formulation, implementation, monitoring and control.

Operation strategy formulation

The formulation of operations strategy is the process of clarifying the various objectives and decisions that make up the strategy, and the links between

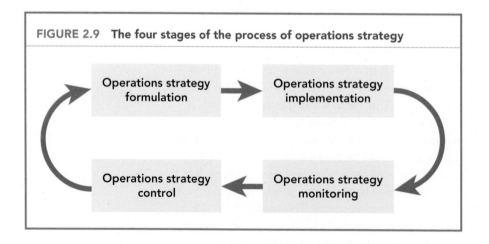

FIGURE 2.9   The four stages of the process of operations strategy

Operations strategy formulation → Operations strategy implementation → Operations strategy monitoring → Operations strategy control →

them. Unlike day-to-day operations management, formulating an operations strategy is likely to be only an occasional activity. Some firms will have a regular (e.g. annual) planning cycle, and operations strategy consideration may form part of this, but the 'complete' process of formulating an entirely new operations strategy will be a relatively infrequent event. There are many 'formulation processes' that are, or can be, used to formulate operations strategies. Most consultancy companies have developed their own frameworks, as have several academics. Most of these try to provide a set of actions that provide the 'best' outcome for an organization. But, even if we cannot assess the 'goodness' of a strategy in advance, one can ask some basic questions of any operations strategy.

Is operations strategy comprehensive?

In other words, does it include all important issues? Business history is littered with companies that simply failed to notice the potential impact of, for instance, new process technology, or emerging changes in their supply network.

Is operations strategy coherent?

As a strategy evolves over time, tensions can emerge that threaten to pull the overall strategy in different directions. This can result in a loss of coherence. Coherence is when the choices made in each decision area all direct the operation in the same strategic direction, with all strategic decisions complementing and reinforcing each other in the promotion of performance objectives. For example, if new internet-based remote diagnostic technology for heating systems is introduced that allows service engineers to customize their service advice to individual clients' needs, it would be 'incoherent' not to devise a new operating process that enabled service staff to exploit the technology's potential – for example, by emailing customers with service options before the service engineer visits.

Does operations strategy have correspondence?

The strategies pursued in each part of the strategy should correspond to the true priority of each performance objective. So, for example, if cost reduction is the main objective for an operation then its process technology investment decisions might err towards the purchase of 'off-the-shelf' (as opposed to customized) equipment that would reduce the capital cost of the technology and may also imply lower maintenance and running costs. However, it is unlikely to be as flexible. Implicitly, the strategy is accepting that cost is more important than flexibility. So, we would expect all other decisions to correspond with the same prioritization of objectives – for example, capacity strategies that exploit natural economies of scale, supply network strategies that reduce purchasing costs, performance measurement systems that stress efficiency and productivity, continuous improvement strategies that emphasize continual cost reduction and so on.

Does operations strategy identify critical issues?

The more critical the decision, the more attention it deserves. Although no strategic decision is unimportant, in practical terms some decisions are more critical than others. The judgment over exactly which decisions are particularly critical is very much a pragmatic one, which must be based on the particular circumstances of an individual firm's operations strategy. But they must be identified.

Operations strategy implementation

Operations strategy implementation is the way that strategies are operationalized or executed. It means attempting to make sure that intended strategies are actually achieved. Three issues are often mentioned by strategy practitioners as being important in achieving successful implementation:

Clarity of strategic decisions There is a strong relationship between the formulation stage and the implementation stage of operations strategy. The crucial attribute of the formulation stage is clarity. If a strategy is ambiguous it is difficult to translate strategic intent into specific actions. With clarity, however, it should be easier to define the intent behind the strategy, the few important issues that need to be developed to deliver the intent, the way that projects should be led and resourced, who will be responsible for each task and so on.

Motivational leadership Leadership that motivates, encourages and provides support is a huge advantage in dealing with the complexity of implementation. Leadership is needed to bring sense and meaning to strategic aspirations, maintain a sense of purpose over the implementation period and, when necessary, modify the implementation plan in the light of experience.

Project management Implementation means breaking a complex plan into a set of relatively distinct activities. Fortunately, there is a well-understood collection of ideas of how to do this – it is called 'project management' (and Chapter 13 is devoted to this subject).

Operations strategy monitoring

In times when things are changing rapidly, as during strategic change, organizations often want to track ongoing performance to make sure that the changes are proceeding as planned. Monitoring should be capable of providing early indications (or a 'warning bell', as some call it) by diagnosing data and triggering appropriate changes in how the operations strategy is being implemented. Having created a plan for the implementation, each part of it has to be monitored to ensure that planned activities are indeed

operations principle
Operations strategies should be comprehensive, coherent, correspond to stated objectives and identify the critical issues.

Operations in practice

Sometimes any plan is better than no plan[13]

There is a famous story that illustrates the importance of having some kind of plan, even if hindsight proves it to be the wrong plan. During manoeuvres in the Alps, a detachment of Hungarian soldiers got lost. The weather was severe and the snow was deep. In these freezing conditions, after two days of wandering, the soldiers gave up hope and became reconciled to a frozen death on the mountains. Then, to their delight, one of the soldiers discovered a map in his pocket. Much cheered by this discovery, the soldiers were able to escape from the mountains. When they were safe back at their headquarters, they discovered that the map was not of the Alps at all, but of the Pyrenees. And what is the moral of the story? It is that a plan (or a map) may not be perfect, but it gives a sense of purpose and a sense of direction. If the soldiers had waited for the right map they would have frozen to death. Yet their renewed confidence motivated them to get up and create opportunities. ● ● ●

happening. Any deviation from what should be happening (that is, the planned activities) can then be rectified through some kind of intervention in the operation.

Operations strategy control

Strategic control involves the evaluation of the results from monitoring the implementation. Activities, plans and performance are assessed, with the intention of correcting future action if that is required. In some ways, this strategic view of control is similar to how it works operationally (which is discussed in Chapter 10), but there are differences. At a strategic level, control can be difficult because strategic objectives are not always clear and unambiguous. Ask any experienced managers; they will acknowledge that it is not always possible to articulate every aspect of a strategic decision in detail. Many strategies are just too complex for that. So, rather than adhering dogmatically to a predetermined plan, it may be better to adapt as circumstances change. And, the more uncertain the environment, the more an operation needs to emphasize this form of strategic flexibility and develop its ability to learn from events.

Summary answers
to key questions

Each chapter has a 'Summary answers to key questions' section. Use it to check your understanding of the issues covered in the chapter.

WHAT IS STRATEGY AND WHAT IS OPERATIONS STRATEGY?

★ Strategy is the total pattern of decisions and actions that position the organization in its environment and that are intended to achieve its long-term goals.

★ Operations strategy concerns the pattern of strategic decisions and actions that set the role, objectives and activities of the operation.

★ Operations strategy has content and process. The content concerns the specific decisions that are taken to achieve specific objectives. The process is the procedure that is used within a business to formulate its strategy.

WHAT IS THE DIFFERENCE BETWEEN A 'TOP-DOWN' AND 'BOTTOM-UP' VIEW OF OPERATIONS STRATEGY?

★ The 'top-down' perspective views strategic decisions at a number of levels. Corporate strategy sets the objectives for the different businesses that make up a group. Business strategy sets the objectives for each individual business and how it positions itself in its marketplace. Functional strategies set the objectives for each function's contribution to its business strategy.

★ The 'bottom-up' view of operations strategy sees overall strategy as emerging from day-to-day operational experience.

WHAT IS THE DIFFERENCE BETWEEN A 'MARKET REQUIREMENTS' AND 'OPERATIONS RESOURCES' VIEW OF OPERATIONS STRATEGY?

★ A 'market requirements' perspective of operations strategy sees the main role of operations as satisfying markets. Operations performance objectives and operations decisions should be influenced primarily by a combination of customers' needs and competitors' actions. Both of these may be summarized in terms of the product/service life cycle.

★ The 'operations resources' perspective of operations strategy is based on the resource-based view (RBV) of the firm and sees the operation's core competences (or capabilities) as being the main influence on operations strategy. Operations capabilities are developed partly through the strategic decisions taken by the operation. All decisions can have a strategic impact, but the scope and the location of operations resources are particularly important.

HOW CAN OPERATIONS STRATEGY FORM THE BASIS FOR OPERATIONS IMPROVEMENT?

 An operations strategy can provide the foundation for improvement by achieving a fit between an operation's market requirements and its operations capabilities.

 During improvement, it may not be possible to maintain a balance between market requirements and operations performance. When markets expect something that the operation cannot deliver, or when operations have capabilities that cannot be exploited in the market, there are strategic risks deriving from the deviation from the 'line of fit'.

WHAT IS THE 'PROCESS' OF OPERATIONS STRATEGY?

 Putting an operations strategy together is called 'the process' of operations strategy. It has four stages, which can be viewed as a cycle: formulation, implementation, monitoring and control.

Problems and applications

All chapters have problems and application questions that will help you practice analyzing operations. They can be answered by reading the chapter. Model answers for the first question can be found on the companion website for this text.

➔ The environmental services department of a city has two recycling services – newspaper collection (NC) and general recycling (GR). The NC service is a door-to-door collection service that, at a fixed time every week, collects old newspapers that householders have placed in reusable plastic bags at their gate. An empty bag is left for the householders to use for the next collection. The value of the newspapers collected is relatively small, the service is offered mainly for reasons of environmental responsibility. By contrast, the GR service is more commercial. Companies and private individuals can request a collection of materials to be disposed of, either using the telephone or the internet. The GR service guarantees to collect the material within 24 hours unless the customer prefers to specify a more convenient time. Any kind of material can be collected and a charge is made depending on the volume of material. This service makes a small profit because the revenue both from customer charges and from some of the more valuable recycled materials exceeds the operation's running costs. How would you describe the differences between the performance objectives of the two services?

➔ A data centre is 'a facility composed of networked computers and storage that businesses or other organizations use to organize, process, store and disseminate large amounts of data. A business typically relies heavily upon the applications, services and data contained within a data centre, making it a focal point and critical asset for everyday operations.'[14] These facilities can contain network equipment, servers, data storage and back-up facilities, software applications for large companies and more. Very few businesses (or people) do not rely on them. And determining their location is a crucial decision for those operations running them. In fact, such businesses usually have a set method for choosing data centre location.

Visit the websites of the type of business that run data centres (such as Intel, Cisco or SAP) and devise a set of criteria that could be used to evaluate potential sites.

➔ DSD designs makes medical equipment for hospitals. It has a research culture and 50 per cent of manufacturing is done in-house. Its products are highly priced, but customers are willing to pay for technical excellence and customization (70 per cent of orders involve customization). Manufacturing can take three months from order to completion, but customers were more interested in on-time delivery. According to their CEO, "manufacturing is really a large laboratory. That helps us to maintain our superiority in technology and customization. However, I'm not sure how we will deal with the new products which we are getting into." These new devices could be attached to patients, or implanted. They used sophisticated electronics and could be promoted directly to consumers as well as to hospitals. "Although expensive, we have to persuade health insurance companies to encourage these new devices. We are moving towards being a consumer company, making and delivering a higher volume of more standardized products where the underlying technology is changing fast. We must become faster in our product development. And we will need some kind of logistics capability. I'm not sure whether we should outsource this. The same with manufacturing, it is important to maintain control of quality and reliability, but investing in the process technology to make the products will be very expensive. There are subcontractors who could manufacture for us, but could they maintain high quality? We will also have to deliver products at short notice. Nor are we sure of how demand might grow – probably quickly."

What new capabilities will DSD have to develop if they are to take advantage of this new product?

4 ➔ Consider the music business as a supply network. How do music downloads and streaming affect the operations in the music business, such as more traditional record shops?

Want to know more?

Boyer, K.K., Swink, M. and Rosenzweig, E.D. (2006) 'Operations strategy research', *POMS Journal, Production and Operations Management*, **14**(4).

➜ A survey of recent research in the area.

Braithwaite, A. and Christopher, M. (2015) *Business Operations Models: Becoming a Disruptive Competitor*, London: Kogan Page.

➜ Aimed at practitioners, but authoritative and interesting.

Hayes, R.H., Pisano, G.P., Upton, D.M. and Wheelwright, S.C. (2005) *Pursuing The Competitive Edge*, London: Wiley.

➜ The gospel according to the Harvard school of operations strategy. Articulate, interesting and informative.

Hill, A. and Hill, T. (2009) *Manufacturing Operations Strategy: Texts and Cases*, Basingstoke, UK: Palgrave Macmillan.

➜ Biased towards manufacturing, but well-structured and readable.

Slack, N. and Lewis, M. (2017) *Operations Strategy*, 5th edition, Harlow, UK: Pearson Education.

➜ What can we say – just brilliant, it will change your life!

Only a few years ago Nokia was the king of the mobile phone business but their operations strategy didn't allocate sufficient resources to the software and apps that became as important as the phones themselves. Nokia saw itself primarily as a hardware company rather than a software company. Its engineers were experienced at designing and producing hardware, but not the programs that drive the devices.

Product and service innovation

3

Introduction

Innovation is the act of introducing new ideas; design is about making those ideas practical. This is why the activity of product and service innovation and the activity of design are so closely linked. While operations managers may not always have full responsibility for service and product innovation, they're always involved in some way, if only to provide the information and advice upon which successful service or product development depends. However, increasingly, operations managers are expected to take a greater and more active part in product and service innovation. Unless a product, however well designed, can be produced to a high standard, and unless a service, however well conceived, can be implemented, it will never generate full benefits. Figure 3.1 shows the position of the ideas described in this chapter in the general model of operations management.

Key questions

What is product and service innovation?

What is the strategic role of product and service innovation?

What are the stages of product and service innovation?

What are the benefits of interactive product and service innovation?

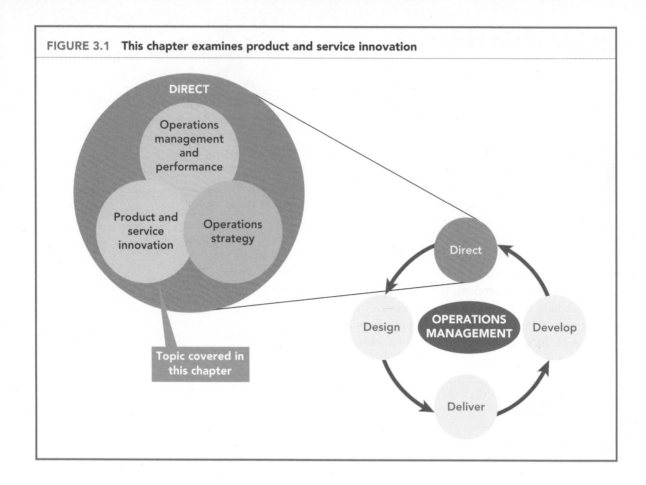

FIGURE 3.1   **This chapter examines product and service innovation**

What is product and service innovation?

There are a number of terms that we shall use in this chapter that have similar meanings, and are defined by different authorities in different ways, or overlap to some extent and are related to each other. Specifically, we explore the three related terms of creativity, innovation and design.

Innovation, creativity and design

'Creativity' is the ability to move beyond conventional ideas, rules or assumptions in order to generate significant new ideas. It is a vital ingredient in innovation. It is seen as essential, not just in product and service innovation but also in the design and management of operations processes more generally. Partly because of the fast-changing nature of many industries, a lack of creativity (and consequently of innovation) is seen as a major risk.

The term 'innovation' is notoriously ambiguous and lacks either a single definition or measure. It is. . . 'a new method, idea, product, etc.' (*Oxford English Dictionary*), "change that creates a new dimension of performance" (Peter Drucker, a well-known management writer), 'the act of introducing something new' (*American Heritage Dictionary*), or 'a new idea, method or device' (*Webster Online Dictionary*). What runs through all these definitions is the idea of novelty and change. Innovation goes further than 'creativity' or 'invention' as it implies the process of transforming ideas into something that is not simply novel, but also has the potential to be practical and provide a commercial return.

'Design' is the process that transforms innovative ideas into something more concrete. Innovation creates the novel idea; design makes it work in practice. A design must deliver a solution that will work in practice and is an activity that can be approached at different levels of detail. Figure 3.2 illustrates the relationship between creativity, innovation and design as we use the terms here. These concepts are intimately related, which is why we treat them in the same chapter. First, we will look at some of the basic ideas that help to understand innovation.

> **operations principle**
> The innovation activity is an important part of service and product design.

Incremental or radical innovation

An obvious difference between how the pattern of new ideas emerges in different operations or industries is the rate and scale of innovation. Some industries, such as telecommunications, enjoy frequent and often significant innovations. Others, such as house building, do have innovations, but they are usually less dramatic. So some innovation is radical, resulting in discontinuous, 'breakthrough' change, while other innovations are more incremental, leading to smaller, continuous changes. Radical innovation often includes large technological advancements that may require completely new knowledge and/or resources, making existing services and

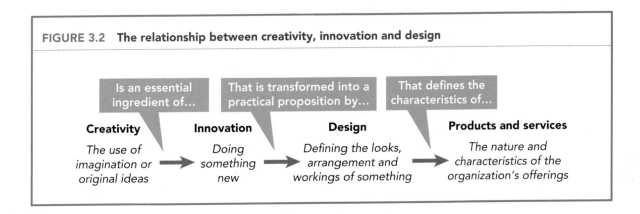

FIGURE 3.2   **The relationship between creativity, innovation and design**

Is an essential ingredient of...   That is transformed into a practical proposition by...   That defines the characteristics of...

Creativity   **Innovation**   **Design**   **Products and services**

The use of imagination or original ideas → *Doing something new* → *Defining the looks, arrangement and workings of something* → *The nature and characteristics of the organization's offerings*

Operations in practice

How the iPhone disrupted the smartphone market[1]

When Apple introduced the original iPhone, the world of smartphones was changed forever. It was arguably one of the most influential products ever to be launched in the consumer technology market and set the benchmark for smartphones that came after it. It sold millions worldwide and helped to make Apple into the world's most valuable company. However, the way that Apple managed the innovation process remained something of a secret for years after the product's launch. Originally visualized as a tablet computer, work on the iPhone was initiated partly because of the success of the firm's earlier product, the iPod music player. It was the profound effect that the iPod had on the music industry that encouraged Apple to consider what other markets it could challenge. Yet, it was a technological breakthrough, a multi-touch display, which allowed the company to change course. As Steve Jobs said later, "I had this idea about having a glass display, a multi-touch display you could type on. I asked our people about it. And six months later they came back with this amazing display. [When] we got inertial scrolling working and some other things, I thought, 'my god, we can build a phone with this' and we put the tablet aside, and we went to work on the phone." But making the multi-touch display a working proposition was challenging for Apple's engineering team. They had to create an entirely new way in which users could interact with their phones. There were many novel unsolved problems to overcome. Every single part of the design had to be rethought to adapt to touch. For example, engineers had to make scrolling work on the iPhone not only when a user's finger moved up and down, but also when a user's thumb moved in an arc across the screen. And there were many other obstacles to overcome, some which seemed almost insurmountable. Sir Jonathan Ive, senior vice-president of design at Apple, has admitted that issues with the touchscreen were so difficult that it brought the

products obsolete and therefore non-competitive. Incremental innovation, by contrast, is more likely to involve relatively modest technological changes, built upon existing knowledge and/or resources, so existing services and products are not fundamentally changed. This is why established companies may favour incremental innovation – because they have the experience to have built up a significant pool of knowledge (on which incremental innovation is based). In addition, established companies are more likely to have a mindset that emphasises continuity; perhaps not even recognising potential innovative opportunities. New entrants to markets, however, have no established position to lose, nor do they have a vast pool of experience. As such, they may be more likely to try for more radical innovation.

project to the brink of being aborted. "There were multiple times when we nearly shelved it because there were fundamental problems that we couldn't solve", said Sir Jonathan. "I would put the phone to my ear and my ear dialled a number. The challenge is that you have to then detect all sorts of ear shapes, chin shapes, skin colour and hairdos. We had to develop technology, basically a number of sensors, to inform the phone that 'this is now going up to an ear, please deactivate the touchscreen'."

Security during development was obsessively tight. For example, the senior Apple executive in charge of developing what would later become known as the iOS operating system was told that he could choose anyone he wanted from within Apple to join the embryonic iPhone team, but he was not allowed to hire anybody from outside the company. He could not even convey to potential team members exactly what they would be working on, just that it was a new and exciting project and that they would have

to 'work hard, give up nights, and work weekends for years'. When the development team formed, they were located on a separate and secured floor on Apple's campus. The development area was 'locked down' with extensive use of badge readers and cameras. Team members might have to show their badges five or six times to gain access.

The aesthetics of the iPhone were treated as being just as important as the iPhone technology. This was the responsibility of Apple's secretive industrial design group. Apple designer Christopher Stringer said that their objective was to create a "new, original, and beautiful object [that was] so wonderful that you couldn't imagine how you'd follow it". The design group, Stringer explained, was comprised of 16 'maniacal' individuals who shared one singular purpose – to "imagine products that don't exist and guide them to life". They worked closely together, often gathering around a 'kitchen table' where team members exchanged ideas,

often in a 'brutally honest' way. To the designers, even the tiniest of details were important. They often would create up to 50 designs of a single component before moving on to computer-aided design modelling and the creation of physical mock-ups.

The fact that the Apple designers overcame several technology and production bugs during development is partly a testament to the design team's belief, both in their technological skills and in their understanding of what people would buy. Apple avoids conducting market research when designing its products, a policy introduced by Steve Jobs, its late chief executive. "We absolutely don't do focus groups", says Ive. "That's designers and leaders abdicating responsibility. That's them looking for an insurance policy, so if something goes wrong, they can say, well this focus group says that only 30 per cent of people are offended by this and, look, 40 per cent think it's OK. What a focus group does is that it will guarantee mediocrity." ● ● ●

What is the strategic role of product and service innovation?

I nnovation is a risky business. Not every idea is transformed, or is capable of being incorporated into the design of a successful product or service. Sometimes this is because an innovative idea is just too challenging, at least with realistically available technology, or under prevailing market conditions. Sometimes the development cost is out of the reach of the business that had the original idea. Ideas may be abundant, but resources are limited. Yet despite the obstacles to successful innovation, almost all firms strive to be innovative. The reason is that there is overwhelming evidence that innovation can generate significant payback for the organizations that manage the incorporation of innovative ideas in the design of their products and services. What matters is the ability to identify the innovations and manage their transformation into effective designs so that they can sustain competitive advantage and/or generate social payback. As such, good design takes innovative ideas and makes them practical. So, the design activity has one overriding objective: to provide products, services and processes that will satisfy the operation's customers. Product designers try to achieve aesthetically pleasing designs that meet or exceed customers' expectations. They also try to design a product that performs well and is reliable during its lifetime. Further, they should design the product so that it can be manufactured easily and quickly. Similarly, service designers try to put together a service that meets or exceeds customer expectations. Yet at the same time the service must be within the capabilities of the operation and be delivered at reasonable cost.

The process of design

Producing design innovations for services and products is itself a process that conforms to the input–transformation–output model described in Chapter 1. Although organizations will have their own particular ways of managing innovation and design, the design process itself is essentially very similar across a whole range of industries. In general, the better the design process is managed, the better the service and product offering. Figure 3.3 illustrates the design activity as an input–transformation–output diagram. The transformed resource inputs will consist mainly of information in the form of market forecasts, market preferences, technical data and potential design ideas. It is these ideas and information that will be transformed in the design process into the final design. Transforming resource inputs includes the operations and design managers who manage the process, together with specialist technical staff with the specific knowledge necessary to solve design problems. They also may include suppliers, other collaborators and even especially interested customer groups (sometimes called 'lead users'), who are brought in to provide their expertise. Transforming resources may also include computer-aided design (CAD) equipment and software.

> **operations principle**
> The design activity is a process that can be managed using the same principles as other processes.

Design process objectives

The performance of the design process can be assessed in much the same way as we would consider the products and services that result from it, namely in terms of quality, speed, dependability, flexibility and cost. Because product and service design has such an influence on sustainability, we include it alongside our normal operational level objectives.

> **operations principle**
> Innovation processes can be judged in terms of their levels of quality, speed, dependability, flexibility, cost and sustainability.

FIGURE 3.3 The product and service design innovation activity as a process

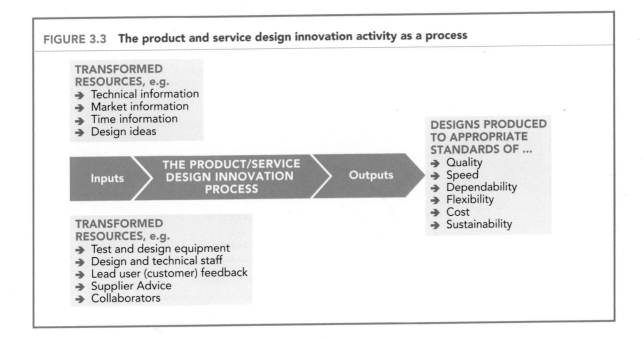

WHAT DOES QUALITY MEAN FOR THE DESIGN PROCESS?

Design quality is not always easy to define precisely, especially if customers are relatively satisfied with existing service and product offerings. Nevertheless, it is possible to distinguish high- and low-quality designs (although this is easier to do in hindsight) by judging them in terms of their ability to meet market requirements. In doing this, the distinction between the specification quality and the conformance quality of designs is important. No business would want a design process that was indifferent to 'errors' in its designs, yet some are more tolerant than others. For example, in pharmaceutical development the potential for harm is particularly high because drugs directly affect our health. This is why the authorities insist on such a prolonged and thorough 'design' process (more usually called 'development' in that industry). Although withdrawing a drug from the market is unusual, it does occasionally occur. Far more frequent are the 'product recalls' that are relatively common in, for example, the automotive industry. Many of these are design related and the result of 'conformance' failures in the design process. The 'specification' quality of design is different. It means the degree of functionality, or experience, or aesthetics, or whatever the product or service is primarily competing on.

WHAT DOES SPEED MEAN FOR THE DESIGN PROCESS?

The speed of design matters more to some industries than others. For example, design innovation in construction and aerospace happens at a much slower pace than in clothing or microelectronics. However, rapid design innovation or 'time-based competition' has become the norm for an increasing number of industries. Sometimes this is the result of fast-changing consumer fashion. Sometimes a rapidly changing technology base forces it. In addition,

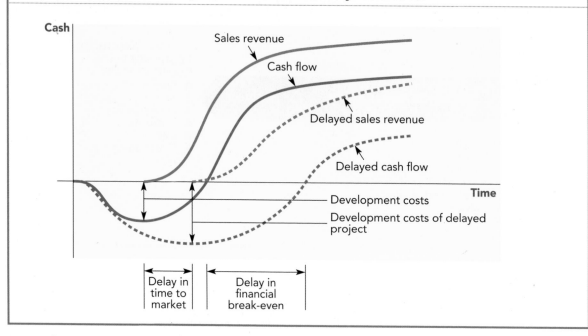

FIGURE 3.4   Delay in time to market of new innovations not only reduces and delays revenues, it also increases the costs of development. The combination of both of these effects usually delays the financial break-even point far more than the delay in the launch

delays in the speed of the design result in both more expenditure on the design and delayed (and probably reduced) revenue. The combination of these effects usually means that the financial break-even point for a new offering is delayed far more than the original delay in its launch (see Figure 3.4).

WHAT DOES DEPENDABILITY MEAN FOR THE DESIGN PROCESS?

Design schedule slippage can extend design times (speed), but, worse, a lack of dependability adds to the uncertainty surrounding the innovation process. Conversely, processes that are dependable minimize design uncertainty. Unexpected technical difficulties, such as suppliers who themselves do not deliver solutions on time, customers or markets that change during the innovation process itself and so on, all contribute to an uncertain and ambiguous design environment. Professional project management (see Chapter 13) of the innovation process can help to reduce uncertainty and prevent (or give early warning of) missed deadlines, process bottlenecks and resource shortages. Disturbances to the innovation process may also be minimized through close liaison with suppliers, as well as market or environmental monitoring.

WHAT DOES FLEXIBILITY MEAN FOR THE DESIGN PROCESS?

Flexibility in the innovation process is the ability to cope with external or internal change. The most common reason for external change is because markets, or specific customers, change their requirements. Although flexibility may not be needed in relatively predictable markets, it is clearly valuable in more fast-moving and volatile markets, where one's own customers and markets change, or where the designs of competitors' offerings dictate a matching or leapfrogging move.

Operations in practice

IKEA's slow development process[2]

Most companies are obsessed with reducing the time to market (TTM) of their design process. Short TTM means lower development costs and more opportunities to hit the market with new designs. Some auto companies have reduced the design time for their products to less than three years, while a new smartphone (a far more dynamic market) can be developed in as little as six months. So why does IKEA, the most successful homeware retailer ever, take five years to design its kitchens? Because, with the huge volumes that IKEA sells, development costs are small compared with the savings that can result from product designs that bring down the final price in their stores.

"It's five years of work into finding ways to engineer cost out of the system, to improve the functionality", IKEA said of the company's 'Metod' kitchen (which means 'method' in English). Metod is a complex product. It has over a thousand different components. The kitchen is a product of IKEA's 'democratic design' process that ensures designs that will work in homes anywhere in the world – an important consideration when you sell about one million kitchens a year. Also, unlike some big-ticket purchases, consumer taste in home furnishing does not shift rapidly. "We still hang paintings above the sofa and tend to have a TV in the corner", says IKEA Creative Director Mia Lundström. But even if trends do not materialize overnight, it is still important to spot emerging consumer preferences. A research team visits thousands of homes annually and compiles reports that look as far as a decade into the future. So without the imperative to change its designs too frequently, product cost becomes a key driver. Rather than buy prefabricated components from outside sources, IKEA will develop its own if it will keep costs down. ● ● ●

Internal changes include the emergence of superior technical solutions. In addition, the increasing complexity and interconnectedness of service and product components in an offering may require flexibility. One way of measuring innovation flexibility is to compare the cost of modifying a design in response to such changes against the consequences to profitability if no changes are made. The lower the cost of modifying an offering in response to a given change, the higher is the level of flexibility.

WHAT DOES COST MEAN FOR THE DESIGN PROCESS?
The cost of innovation is usually analyzed in a similar way to the ongoing cost of delivering offerings to customers. These cost factors are split up into three categories: the cost of buying the inputs to the process; the cost of providing the labour in the process; and the other general overhead costs of running the process. In most in-house innovation processes, the latter two costs outweigh the former.

WHAT DOES SUSTAINABILITY MEAN FOR THE DESIGN PROCESS?

The sustainability of a design innovation is the extent to which it benefits the 'triple bottom line' – people, planet and profit. The design innovation process is particularly important in ultimately impacting on the ethical, environmental and economic wellbeing of stakeholders. Organizations increasingly consider sustainability in the design process. For example, some innovation activity is particularly focused on the ethical dimension of sustainability. Banks have moved to offer customers ethical investments that seek to maximize social benefit as well as financial returns. Such investments tend to avoid businesses involved in weaponry, gambling, alcohol and tobacco, for example, and favour those promoting worker education, environmental stewardship and consumer protection. Other examples of ethically focused innovations include the development of 'fair-trade' products. Similarly, garment manufacturers may establish ethical trading initiatives with suppliers, supermarkets may ensure animal welfare for meat and dairy products and online companies may institute customer complaint charters.

Design innovation may also focus on the environmental dimension of sustainability. Critically examining the components of products towards a change of materials in the design could significantly reduce the environmental burden. Examples include: the use of organic cotton or bamboo in clothing; wood or paper from managed forests used in garden furniture, stationery and flooring; recycled materials for carrier bags; and natural dyes in clothing, curtains and upholstery. Other innovations may be more focused on the 'use' stage of an offering. The MacBook Air, for example, introduced an advanced power management system that reduced its power requirements. In the detergent industry, Unilever and Proctor and Gamble have developed products that allow clothes to be washed at much lower temperatures. Architecture firms are increasingly designing houses that can operate with minimal energy or use sustainable sources of energy such as solar panels. Some innovations focus on making product components within an offering easier to recycle or re-manufacture once they have reached the end of their life. For example, some food packaging has been designed to break down easily when disposed of, allowing its conversion into high-quality compost. Mobile phones are often designed to be taken apart at the end of their life, so valuable raw materials can be re-used. In the automotive industry, over 75 percent of materials are now recycled.

Design innovation is not just confined to the initial conception of a product; it also applies to the end of its life. This idea is often called 'designing for the circular economy'. The 'circular economy' is proposed as an alternative to the traditional linear economy (or make–use–dispose as it is termed). The idea is to keep products in use for as long as possible, extract the maximum value from them while in use and then recover and regenerate products and materials at the end of their service life. But the circular economy is much more than a concern for recycling as opposed to disposal. The circular economy examines what can be done right along the supply-and-use chain, so that as few resources as possible are used and products are recovered and regenerated at the end of their conventional life. This means designing products for longevity, reparability, ease of dismantling and recycling.

Product innovation for the circular economy[3]

Typical of the companies that have adopted the idea of the circular economy is Newlife Paints, based in the UK. It 'remanufactures' waste water-based paint back into a premium-grade emulsion. All products in their paint range guarantee a minimum 50 percent recycled content, made up from waste paint diverted from landfill or incineration. The idea for the company began to take root in the mind of industrial chemist, Keith Harrison. His garage was becoming a little unruly, after many years of do-it-yourself projects. Encouraged by his wife to clear out the mess, he realized that the stacked-up tins of paint represented a shocking waste. It was then that his search began for a sensible and environmentally responsible solution for waste paint. "I kept thinking I could do something with it; the paint had an intrinsic value. It would have been a huge waste just to throw it away." Keith thought somebody must be recycling it, but no one was, and he set about finding a way to reprocess waste paint back to a superior-grade emulsion. After two years of research, Keith successfully developed his technology, which involves removing leftover paint from tins and blending and filtering them to produce colour-matched new paints. The company has also launched a premium brand, aimed at affluent customers with a green conscience, called Reborn Paints, the development of which was partly funded by Akzo Nobel, maker of Dulux Paints. Although Keith started small (in his garage) he now licenses his technology to companies such as the giant waste company Veolia. "By licensing we can have more impact and spread internationally", he says. ●●●

What are the stages of product and service innovation?

Fully specified designs rarely spring, fully formed, from a designer's imagination. The design activity will generally pass through several key stages. These form the sequence shown in Figure 3.5, although in practice designers will often recycle or backtrack through the stages. Nor is this sequence of stages descriptive of the stages used by all companies, yet most will use some stage model similar to this one. It moves

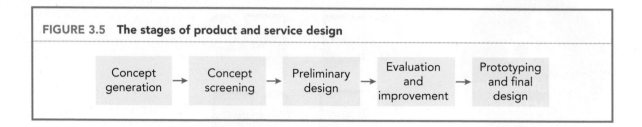

FIGURE 3.5   **The stages of product and service design**

Concept generation → Concept screening → Preliminary design → Evaluation and improvement → Prototyping and final design

from the concept generation stage, to a screening stage, to a preliminary design stage that produces a design to be evaluated and prototyped before reaching the final design.

Concept generation

This is where innovative ideas become the inspiration for new service or product concepts. And innovation can come from many different sources:

Ideas from research and development   Many organizations have a formal research and development (R&D) function. As its name implies, its role is twofold. Research develops new knowledge and ideas in order to solve a particular problem or to grasp an opportunity. Development utilizes and operationalizes the ideas that come from research. And although 'development' may not sound as exciting as 'research', it often requires as much creativity and even more persistence.

Ideas from customers   Marketing, the function generally responsible for identifying new service or product opportunities, may use market research tools for gathering data from customers in a structured way to test out ideas or check services or products against predetermined criteria. Ideas may also come from customers on a day-to-day basis, from complaints, or from everyday transactions. Organizations are increasingly developing mechanisms to facilitate the collection of this form of information. At a group level, crowdsourcing is the process of getting work or funding, or ideas (usually online) from a crowd of people. Although in essence it is not a totally new idea, it has become a valuable source of ideas largely through the use of the internet and social networking. For example, Procter & Gamble, the consumer products company, asked amateur scientists to explore ideas for a detergent dye whose colour changed when enough has been added to dishwater. Other uses of the idea involve government agencies asking citizens to prioritize spending projects.

Ideas from staff   The contact staff in a service organization or the salesperson in a product-orientated organization could meet customers every day. These staff may have good ideas about what customers like and do not like. They may have gathered suggestions from customers or have ideas of their own. One well-known example – which may be urban myth – is that an employee at Swan Vestas, the matchmaker, suggested having one instead of two sandpaper strips on the matchbox. It saved a fortune!

Ideas from competitor activity Most organizations follow the activities of their competitors. A new idea from a competitor may be worth imitating or, better still, improved upon. Taking apart a competitor's service or product to explore potential new ideas is called 'reverse engineering'. Some aspects of services may be difficult to reverse engineer (especially 'back-office' services) as they are less transparent to competitors.

OPEN SOURCING – USING A DEVELOPMENT COMMUNITY

Not all 'products' or services are created by professional, employed designers for commercial purposes. Many of the software applications that we all use, for example, are developed by an open community, including the people who use the products. If you use Google, Wikipedia or Amazon then you are using open-source software. The basic concept of open-source software is simple. Large communities of people around the world, who have the ability to write software code, come together and produce a software product. The finished product is not only available to be used by anyone or any organization for free, but is regularly updated to ensure it keeps pace with the necessary improvements. The production of open-source software is very well organized and, like its commercial equivalent, is continuously supported and maintained. However, unlike its commercial equivalent, it is absolutely free to use. Over the last decade, the growth of open source has been phenomenal, with many organizations transitioning over to using this stable, robust and secure software.

Concept screening

Not all concepts that are generated will necessarily be capable of further development into services and products. Designers need to be selective as to which concepts they progress to the next design stage. The purpose of the concept-screening stage is to evaluate concepts by assessing the worth or value of design options. This involves assessing each concept or option against a number of design criteria. While the criteria used in any particular design exercise will depend on the nature and circumstances of the exercise, it is useful to think in terms of three broad categories of design criteria:

 The feasibility of the design option – can we do it?
- Do we have the skills (quality of resources)?
- Do we have the organizational capacity (quantity of resources)?
- Do we have the financial resources to cope with this option?

 The acceptability of the design option – do we want to do it?
- Does the option satisfy the performance criteria that the design is trying to achieve? (These will differ for different designs.)
- Will our customers want it?
- Does the option give a satisfactory financial return?

The vulnerability of each design option – do we want to take the risk?
- Do we understand the full consequences of adopting the option?
- Being pessimistic, what could go wrong if we adopt the option? What would be the consequences of everything going wrong? (This is called the 'downside risk' of an option.)

operations principle
The screening of designs should include feasibility, acceptability and vulnerability criteria.

THE DESIGN 'FUNNEL'

Applying these evaluation criteria progressively reduces the number of options that will be available further along in the design activity. For example, deciding to make the outside casing of a camera case from aluminium rather than plastic limits later decisions, such as the overall size and shape of the case. This means that the uncertainty surrounding the design reduces as the number of alternative designs being considered decreases. Figure 3.6 shows what is sometimes called the design funnel, depicting the progressive reduction of design options from many to one. But reducing design uncertainty also impacts on the cost of changing one's mind on some detail of the design. In most stages of design, the cost of changing a decision is bound to incur some sort of rethinking and recalculation of costs. Early on in the design activity, before too many fundamental decisions have been made, the costs of change are relatively low. However, as the design progresses the interrelated and cumulative decisions already made become increasingly expensive to change.

Not everyone agrees with the concept of the design funnel. For some it is just too neat and ordered an idea to reflect accurately the creativity, arguments and chaos that sometimes characterize the design activity. First,

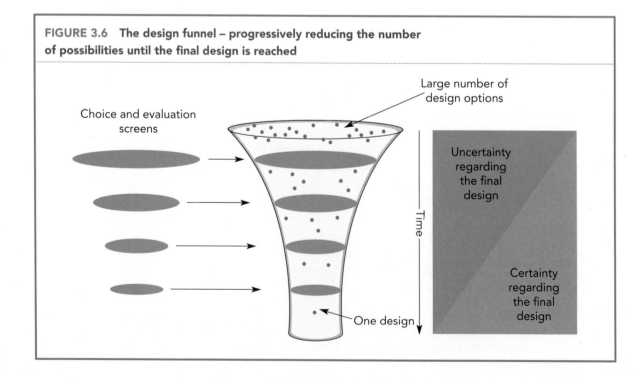

FIGURE 3.6   The design funnel – progressively reducing the number of possibilities until the final design is reached

they argue, managers do not start out with an infinite number of options. Second, the number of options being considered often *increases* as time goes by. This may actually be a good thing, especially if the activity was unimaginatively specified in the first place. Third, the real process of design often involves cycling back, often many times, as potential design solutions raise fresh questions or become dead ends.

Preliminary design

Having generated an acceptable, feasible and viable service or product concept, the next stage is to create a preliminary design. The objective of this stage is to have a first attempt at specifying the individual components or elements of the products and services, and the relationship between them, which will constitute the final offering. Initially, this will require the collection of information about such things as the constituent component parts that make up the service or product package and the component structure, the order in which the component parts of the package have to be put together. For example, the components for a remote 'presentation' mouse may include the presentation mouse itself, a receiver unit and packaging. All three items are made up of components, which are, in turn, made up of other components and so on. A 'component structure' is the diagram that shows how these components all fit together to make the final product (see Figure 3.7).

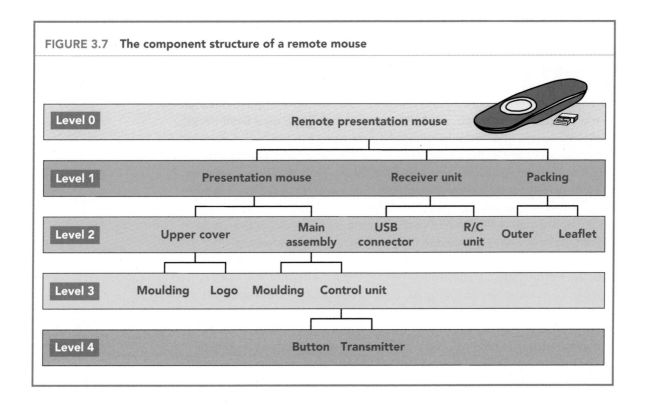

FIGURE 3.7 **The component structure of a remote mouse**

Reducing design complexity

Simplicity is usually seen as a virtue among designers of services and products. The most elegant design solutions are often the simplest. However, when an operation produces a variety of services or products (as most do), the range of services and products considered as a whole can become complex, which, in turn, increases costs. Designers adopt a number of approaches to reduce the inherent complexity in the design of their service or product range. Here we describe three common approaches to complexity reduction – standardization, commonality and modularization.

operations principle
A key design objective should be the simplification of the design through standardization, commonality, modularization and mass customization.

STANDARDIZATION

Operations sometimes attempt to overcome the cost penalties of high variety by standardizing their products, services or processes. Often it is the operation's outputs that are standardized. Examples of this are fast-food restaurants, discount supermarkets or telephone-based insurance companies. Perhaps the most common example of standardization is the clothes that most us of buy. Although everybody's body shape is different, garment manufacturers produce clothes in only a limited number of sizes. The range of sizes is chosen to give a reasonable fit for most body shapes. Many organizations have significantly improved their profitability by careful variety reduction, aimed at offering choice only where it is really valued by the end customer.

COMMONALITY

Using common elements within a service or product can also simplify design complexity. Standardizing the format of information inputs to a process can be achieved by using appropriately designed forms or screen formats. The more different services and products can be based on common components, the less complex it is to produce them. For example, the European aircraft maker, Airbus, has designed its aircraft with a high degree of commonality. This means that ten aircraft models, ranging from the 100-seat A318 through to the world's largest aircraft, the A380, feature virtually identical flight decks, common systems and similar handling characteristics. In some cases, such as the entire A320 family, the aircraft even share the same 'pilot-type rating', which enables pilots with a single license to fly any of them. The advantages of commonality for the airline operators include a much shorter training time for pilots and engineers when they move from one aircraft to another. In addition, when up to 90 per cent of all parts are common within a range of aircraft, there is a reduced need to carry a wide range of spare parts.

MODULARIZATION

The use of modular design principles, seen in computers for example, involves designing standardized 'sub-components' of a service or product, which can be put together in different ways. These standardized modules, or sub-assemblies, can be produced in higher volume, thereby reducing their cost. The package holiday industry can assemble holidays to meet a specific customer requirement, from pre-designed and purchased air travel, accommodation, insurance and so on. Similarly, in education there is an

Operations in practice

Art Attack!

A major challenge facing global programme makers is achieving economies of scale, which come as a result of high volume production while allowing customization of programmes to suit different markets. *Art Attack!*, which was made for the Disney Channel (a children's TV channel shown around the world), used the concept of mass customization to meet this challenge. Typically, over two hundred episodes of the show were made in six different languages. About 60 per cent of each show is common across all versions. Shots without speaking or where the presenter's face is not visible are shot separately. For example, if a simple cardboard model is being made, all versions will share the scenes where the presenter's hands only are visible. Commentary in the appropriate language is over-dubbed onto the scenes, which are edited seamlessly with other shots of the appropriate presenter. The final product has the head and shoulders of Brazilian, British, French, Italian, German or Spanish presenters, flawlessly mixed with the same pair of hands constructing the model. Local viewers in each market see what appears to be a highly customized show, yet the cost of making each episode is about one third of producing truly separate programmes for each market. ● ● ●

increasing use of modular courses, which allow 'customers' choice but ensure each module has economical student volumes.

Design evaluation and improvement

The purpose of this stage in the design innovation activity is to take the preliminary design and subject it to a series of evaluations, to see if it can be improved before the service or product is tested in the market. There are a number of techniques that can be employed at this stage to evaluate and improve the preliminary design. Perhaps the best known is quality function deployment (QFD).

QUALITY FUNCTION DEPLOYMENT

The key purpose of QFD is to try to ensure that the eventual innovation actually meets the needs of its customers. It is a technique that was developed in Japan at Mitsubishi's Kobe shipyard and used extensively by Toyota and its suppliers. It is also known as the 'house of quality' (because of its shape) and the 'voice of the customer' (because of its purpose). The technique tries to capture what the customer needs and how it might be achieved. Figure 3.8 shows a simple QFD matrix used in the design of a promotional USB data

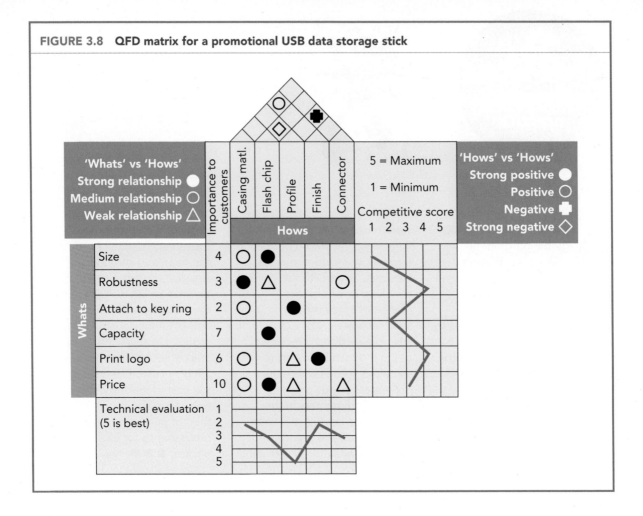

FIGURE 3.8   QFD matrix for a promotional USB data storage stick

storage pen. The QFD matrix is a formal articulation of how the company sees the relationship between the requirements of the customer (the *whats*) and the design characteristics of the new product (the *hows*):

 The *whats*, or 'customer requirements', are the list of competitive factors that customers find significant. Their relative importance is scored, in this case on a 10-point scale, with *price* scoring the highest.

 The competitive scores indicate the relative performance of the product, in this case on a 1 to 5 scale. Also indicated are the performances of two competitor products.

 The *hows*, or 'design characteristics' of the product, are the various 'dimensions' of the design, which will operationalize customer requirements within the service or product.

 The central matrix (sometimes called the relationship matrix) represents a view of the interrelationship between the *whats* and the *hows*. This is often based on value judgments made by the design team. The symbols indicate the strength of the relationship. All the relationships are studied, but in many cases where the cell of the matrix is blank, there is none.

 The bottom box of the matrix is a technical assessment of the product. This contains the absolute importance of each design characteristic.

 The triangular 'roof' of the 'house' captures any information the team has about the correlations (positive or negative) between the various design characteristics.

Prototyping and final design

At around this stage in the design activity it is necessary to turn the improved design into a prototype so that it can be tested. It may be too risky to launch a product or service before testing it out, so it is usually more appropriate to create a 'prototype' (in the case of a product) or 'trial' (in the case of a service). Product prototypes include everything from clay models and CAD systems to advanced computer simulations. Service trials may also include computer simulations, but also the actual implementation of the service on a pilot basis. Many retailing organizations pilot new services in a small number of stores, in order to test customers' reactions to them. Virtual reality-based simulations allow businesses to test new services and products as well as visualize and plan the processes that will produce them. Individual component parts can be positioned together virtually and tested for fit or interference. Even virtual workers can be introduced into the prototyping system to check for ease of assembly or operation.

ALPHA AND BETA TESTING

A distinction that originated in the software development industry, but has spread into other areas, is between the alpha and beta testing of a product or service. Most software products include both alpha and beta test phases, both of which are intended to uncover 'bugs' (errors) in the product. Alpha testing is essentially an *internal* process, where the developers or manufacturers (or sometimes an outside agency that has been commissioned) examine the product for errors. Generally, it is also a private process, not open to the market or potential customers. Although it is intended to look for errors that otherwise would emerge when the product is in use, it is, in effect, performed in a virtual or simulated environment, rather than in 'the real world'. After alpha testing, the product is released for beta testing. Beta testing is when the product is released for testing by selected customers. It is an *external* 'pilot test' that takes place in the 'real world' (or near-real world, because it is still a relatively small, and short, sample) before commercial production. By the time a product gets to the beta stage, most of the worst defects should have been removed, but the product may still have some minor problems that may only become evident with user participation. Beta testing is also sometimes called field testing, pre-release testing, customer validation, customer acceptance testing or user acceptance testing.

What are the benefits of interactive product and service innovation?

Treating each stage of design innovation as totally separate and sequential activities (as we have just done) is a little misleading. As we said earlier, it is common for companies to cycle back through stages, sometimes several times. Also, it is increasingly common to break down the once-ridged boundaries between each stage in the design process. This applies especially to the boundary between the design of the product or service and the design of the process that will produce it.

It is generally considered a mistake to separate service and product design from process design. Operations managers should have some involvement, from the initial evaluation of the concept right through to the production of the service or product and its introduction to the market. Merging the stages of the design innovation process is sometimes called 'interactive design'. The main benefit of merging stages is a reduction in the elapsed time for the whole design innovation activity, often called the time to market (TTM). Three factors in particular have been suggested that can significantly reduce time to market for a service or product:

 simultaneous development of the various stages in the overall process;

 an early resolution of design conflict and uncertainty;

 an organizational structure that reflects the development project.

Simultaneous development

We described the design innovation process as essentially a set of individual, predetermined stages, each with a clear starting and ending point – the implicit assumption being that one stage is completed before the next one commences. Indeed, this step-by-step, or sequential, approach has traditionally been the typical form of product/service development.
It has some advantages. The process is easy to manage and control because each stage is clearly defined. In addition, each stage is completed before the next stage is begun, so each stage can focus its skills and expertise on a limited set of tasks. However, the main problem of the sequential approach is that it is both time-consuming and costly. When each stage is separate, with a clearly defined set of tasks, any difficulties encountered during the design at one stage might necessitate the design being halted while responsibility moves back to the previous stage. This sequential approach is shown in Figure 3.9 (a).

Yet often there is really little need to wait until the absolute finalization of one stage before starting the next. For example, perhaps while generating the concept, the evaluation activity of screening and selection could be started. It is likely that some concepts could be judged as 'non-starters' relatively early on in the process of idea generation. Similarly, during the screening stage it is likely that some aspects of the design will become obvious before the phase is finally complete. Therefore, the preliminary work on these parts of the design could be commenced at that point. This principle can be taken right through all the stages, one stage commencing before the previous one has finished, so there is simultaneous or concurrent work on the stages (see Figure 3.9 (b)). (Note that simultaneous development is often called simultaneous or concurrent engineering in manufacturing operations.)

> **operations principle**
> Effective simultaneous development reduces time to market.

Early conflict resolution

Characterizing the design innovation activity as a whole series of decisions is a useful way of thinking about design. In some cases, changing designs makes sense – for example, as new information emerges suggesting better alternatives. However, there are other, more avoidable, reasons for designers

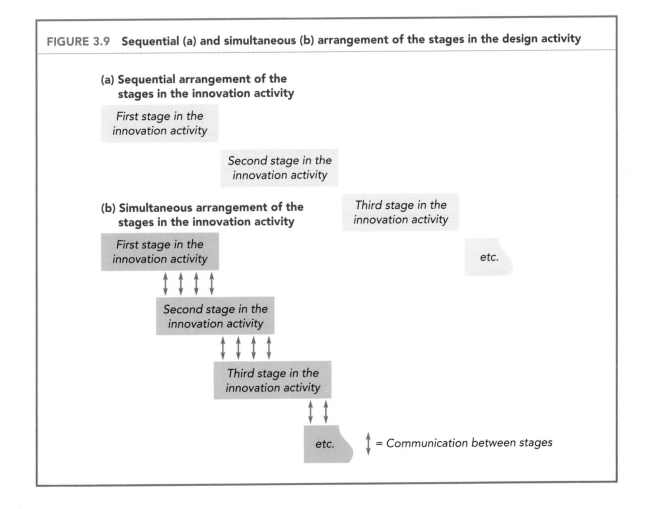

FIGURE 3.9   Sequential (a) and simultaneous (b) arrangement of the stages in the design activity

changing their minds during the design activity. Perhaps one of the initial design decisions was made without sufficient discussion among those in the organization who have a valid contribution to make. It may even be that when the decision was made, there was insufficient agreement to formalize it, and the design team decided to carry on without formally making the decision. For example, suppose the company could not agree on the correct size of electric motor to put into its vacuum cleaner. It might well carry on with the rest of the design work while further discussions and investigations take place on what kind of electric motor to incorporate in the design. Yet much of the rest of the product's design is likely to depend on the choice of the electric motor. The plastic housings, the bearings, the sizes of various apertures and so on, could all be affected by this decision. Failure to resolve these conflicts and/or decisions early on in the process can prolong the degree of uncertainty in the total design activity. In addition, if a decision is made (even implicitly) and then changed later on in the process, the costs of that change can be very large. Conversely, if the design team manages to resolve conflict early in the design activity, this will reduce the degree of uncertainty within the project and reduce the extra cost and, most significantly, time associated with either managing this uncertainty or changing decisions already made. Figure 3.10 illustrates two patterns of design changes through the life of the total design, which imply different time-to-market performances.

operations principle
The design process requires strategic attention early, when there is most potential to affect design decisions.

Project-based organizational structures

The total process of developing concepts through to market will almost certainly involve personnel from several different areas of the organization. Different functions will all have some part to play in making the decisions that will shape the final design. Yet any design project will also have an existence of its own. It will have a project name, an individual manager or group of staff who are championing the project, a budget and, hopefully, a clear strategic purpose in the organization. The organizational question is which of these two

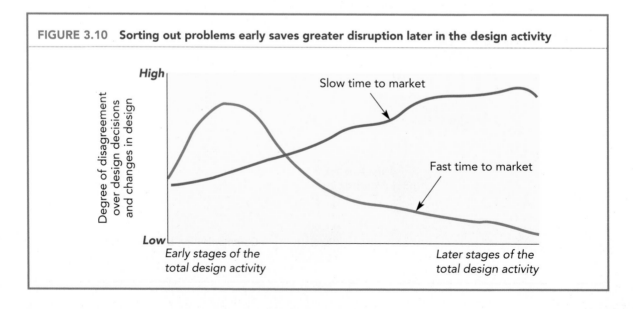

FIGURE 3.10   **Sorting out problems early saves greater disruption later in the design activity**

elements – the various organizational functions that contribute to the design, or the design project itself – should dominate the way in which the design activity is managed?

Before answering this, it is useful to look at the range of organizational structures that are available – from pure functional to pure project forms. In a pure functional organization, all staff associated with the design project are based unambiguously in their functional groups. There is no project-based group at all. They may be working full-time on the project, but all communication and liaison is carried out through their functional manager. The project exists because of agreement between these functional managers. At the other extreme, all the individual members of staff from each function who are involved in the project could be moved out of their functions and perhaps even physically relocated to a task force dedicated solely to the project. The task force could be led by a project manager who might hold the entire budget allocated to the design project. Not all members of the task force necessarily have to stay in the team throughout the development period, but a substantial core might see the project through from start to finish. Some members of a design team may even be from other companies. In between these two extremes there are various types of matrix organization,

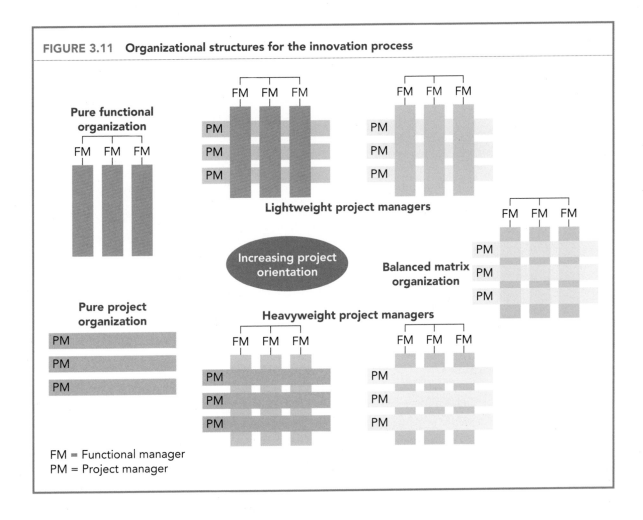

FIGURE 3.11   Organizational structures for the innovation process

Pure functional organization

FM FM FM

Lightweight project managers

FM FM FM
PM
PM
PM

FM FM FM
PM
PM
PM

Increasing project orientation

Balanced matrix organization

FM FM FM
PM
PM
PM

Pure project organization

PM
PM
PM

Heavyweight project managers

FM FM FM
PM
PM
PM

FM FM FM
PM
PM
PM

FM = Functional manager
PM = Project manager

with varying emphasis on these two aspects of the organization (see Figure 3.11). Although the 'task force' type of organization, especially for small projects, can sometimes be a little cumbersome, it seems to be generally agreed that, for substantial projects at least, it is more effective at reducing overall time to market.

SKUNKWORKS

Encouraging creativity in design, while at the same time recognizing the constraints of everyday business life, has always been one of the great challenges of industrial design. One well-known organization structure that is claimed to release the design and development creativity of a group has been called a 'skunkworks'. It is usually taken to mean a small team who are taken out of their normal work environment and granted the freedom from their normal management activities and constraints – what we have called in this text a pure 'project-based' structure. It was an idea that originated in the Lockheed aircraft company in the 1940s, where designers were set up outside the normal organizational structure and given the task of designing a high-speed fighter plane. The experiment was so successful that the company continued with it to develop other innovative products. Since that time, many other companies have used a similar approach, although 'Skunk Works' is a registered trademark of Lockheed Martin Corporation.

Summary answers to key questions

Each chapter has a 'Summary answers to key questions' section. Use it to check your understanding of the issues covered in the chapter.

WHAT IS PRODUCT AND SERVICE INNOVATION?

★ In this chapter, we explore the three related terms of 'creativity', 'innovation' and 'design'.

★ 'Creativity' is the ability to move beyond conventional ideas, rules or assumptions, in order to generate significant new ideas.

★ 'Innovation' is the act of introducing something new with the potential to be practical and give commercial return.

★ 'Design' is the process that transforms innovative ideas into something more concrete. A design delivers a solution that will work in practice.

★ Incremental and radical innovations differ in how they use knowledge. Radical innovation often requires completely new knowledge and/or resources, making existing services and products obsolete. Incremental innovation builds upon existing knowledge and/or resources.

WHAT IS THE STRATEGIC ROLE OF PRODUCT AND SERVICE INNOVATION?

★ Good design takes innovative ideas and makes them practical.

★ There is an increasingly common acceptance that design can add very significant value to all types of organization.

★ Producing design innovations for services and products is itself a process that conforms to the input–transformation–output model.

★ The performance of the design process can be assessed in the same way as any process – namely in terms of quality, speed, dependability, flexibility, cost and, more broadly, sustainability.

WHAT ARE THE STAGES OF PRODUCT AND SERVICE INNOVATION?

★ Concept generation transforms an idea for a service or product into a concept that captures the nature of the service or product and provides an overall specification for its design.

★ Screening the concept involves examining its feasibility, acceptability and vulnerability in broad terms to ensure that it is a sensible addition to the company's service or product portfolio.

Preliminary design involves the identification of all the component parts of the service or product and the way they fit together. Typical tools used during this phase include component structures and flow charts.

 Design evaluation and improvement involves re-examining the design to see if it can be done in a better way, more cheaply or more easily. The best-known tool for this is quality function deployment (QFD).

 Prototyping and final design involves providing the final details that allow the service or product to be produced. The outcome of this stage is a fully developed specification for the package of services and products, as well as a specification for the processes that will make and deliver them to customers.

WHAT ARE THE BENEFITS OF INTERACTIVE PRODUCT AND SERVICE INNOVATION?

 Looking at the stages of design together can improve the quality of both service and product design and process design. It also helps a design 'break even' on its investment earlier by reducing time to market. Three factors help interactive product and service innovation:

- Employ simultaneous development where design decisions are taken as early as they can be, without necessarily waiting for a whole design phase to be completed.
- Ensure early conflict resolution, which allows contentious decisions to be resolved early in the design process, thereby not allowing them to cause far more delay and confusion if they emerge later in the process.
- Use a project-based organizational structure, which can ensure that a focused and coherent team of designers is dedicated to a single design or group of design projects.

Problems and applications

All chapters have problems and application questions that will help you practice analyzing operations. They can be answered by reading the chapter. Model answers for the first question can be found on the companion website for this text.

1 ➔ One product where customers value a very wide range of product types is that of domestic paint. Most people like to express their creativity in the choice of paints and other home-decorating products that they use in their homes. Clearly, offering a wide range of paint must have serious cost implications for the companies that manufacture, distribute and sell the product. Visit a store that sells paint and get an idea of the range of products available on the market. How do you think paint manufacturers and retailers could innovate so as to increase variety but minimize costs?

2 ➔ "We have to get this new product and fast", said the operations director. "Our competitors are close behind us and I believe their products will be almost as good as ours when they launch them." She was talking about a new product that the company hoped would establish them as the leader in their market. The company had put together a special development team, together with their own development laboratory. They had spent £10,000 on equipping the laboratory, and the cost of the development engineers would be £20,000 per quarter. It was expected that the new product would be fully developed and ready for launch within six quarters. It would be done through a specialist agency that charged £10,000 per quarter and that would need to be in place two quarters prior to the launch. If the company met their launch date it was expected that they could charge a premium price that would result in profits of approximately £50,000 per quarter. Any delay in the launch would result in profits being reduced to £40,000 per quarter.

If this development project were delayed by two quarters, how far would the break even for the project be pushed back?

3 ➔ Innovation becomes particularly important at the interface between offerings and the people that use them. Consider two types of website:

a) those that are trying to sell something, such as amazon.com;
b) those that are concerned primarily with giving information – for example, reuters.com or nytimes.com.

What constitutes good innovation for these two types of website? Find examples of particularly good and particularly poor web design and explain the issues you've considered in making the distinction between them.

→ According to the Ellen MacArthur Foundation, a circular economy is 'one that is restorative and regenerative by design, and which aims to keep products, components and materials at their highest utility and value at all times, distinguishing between technical and biological cycles'. Also refer to the 'Operations in practice' example earlier in this chapter, about Newlife Paints.

What do you see as the main barriers to a more widespread adoption of the idea?

Want to know more?

Christensen, C. (1997) *The Innovator's Dilemma*, Boston: Harvard Business School Press.

→ A major influence on innovation theory.

Rose, D. (2015) *Enchanted Objects: Innovation, Design, and the Future of Technology*, New York: Scribner Book Company.

→ An interesting look at how technology is (and will be) impacting on design.

Tidd, J. and Bessant, J. (2013) *Managing Innovation: Integrating Technological, Market and Organizational Change*, 5th edition, Hoboken, NJ: John Wiley & Sons.

→ The definitive textbook on this area.

It isn't just products than must be well designed. Services, like this theme park ride, also need to go through a systematic innovation process to make sure that they will operate in practice to meet their customers' objectives.

Process design – resources

4

Introduction

This part of the text looks at how the resources and processes of operations are designed. Processes are everywhere. They are the building blocks of all operations, and their design will affect the performance of the whole organization. By 'design' we mean how the overall shape and arrangement of transforming resources impacts on the flow of transformed resources as they move through the operation. No part of the business can fully contribute to its effectiveness if its processes are poorly designed. It is not surprising, then, that process design has become such a popular topic in the management press and among consultants. In this chapter, we look at the various types of process, the different ways of arranging process resources, how the effectiveness of processes are influenced by developments in process technology and how people's jobs can be designed. The next chapter examines the activities within processes, and how they can be analyzed in order to understand better how they operate and, therefore, how their performance could be improved. Figure 4.1 shows the position of the ideas described in this chapter in the general model of operations management.

Key questions

Why is choosing the right resources important?

Do processes match volume–variety requirements?

Are process layouts appropriate?

Are process technologies appropriate?

Are job designs appropriate?

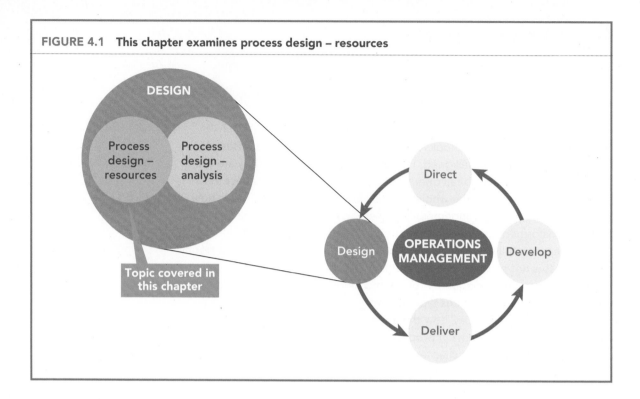

FIGURE 4.1 **This chapter examines process design – resources**

Why is choosing the right resources important?

Process design is concerned with envisioning the nature of the resources that make up the process and analyzing how the activities within the process should work. So, the first task of process design is to decide on what type of resources (people and technology) are appropriate and how they should be arranged. Processes with the wrong resources – unsuitable technology, staffed by people with inappropriately designed jobs, or resources arranged in an unsuitable manner – cannot ever realize their full potential. This is why Google (see the 'Operations in practice' box) thinks carefully about the way it designs its process resources – in its case, to promote creativity and productivity.

Process design and product/ service design are interrelated

One of the most damaging consequences of misjudging the resourcing of processes is that they will not be able to produce the services and products as they should. Often, we will treat the design of services and products, and the

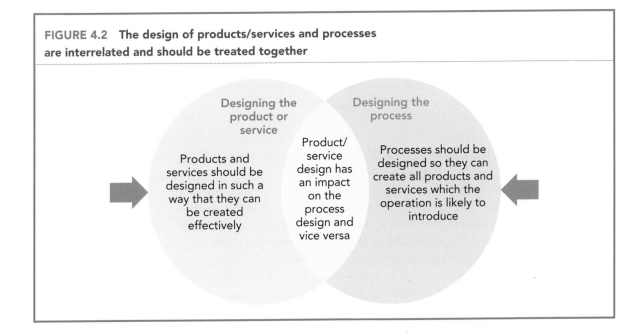

FIGURE 4.2 The design of products/services and processes are interrelated and should be treated together

Designing the product or service

Products and services should be designed in such a way that they can be created effectively

Product/ service design has an impact on the process design and vice versa

Designing the process

Processes should be designed so they can create all products and services which the operation is likely to introduce

design of the processes that make them, as though they were separate activities. Yet they are clearly interrelated. It would be foolish to commit to the detailed design of any product or service without some consideration of how it is to be produced. Small changes in the design of products and services can have profound implications for the way the operation and its processes have to produce them. Similarly, the design of a process can constrain the freedom of product and service designers to operate as they would wish (see Figure 4.2). This holds good whether the operation is producing products or services. However, the overlap is generally greater within service operations, where the customer can be an input, so, from the customer's perspective, the service cannot be separated from the process.

operations principle
The design of processes should not be done independently of the services and/or products that they are creating.

Do processes match volume–variety requirements?

Two factors are particularly important in process design: the volume and the variety of the services and products that it processes. Furthermore (as discussed in Chapter 1), volume and variety are related. Low-volume processes often have a high variety of products and services, and high-volume operations processes often have a narrow variety of products and services. We can therefore position processes on a continuum, from those producing low volume and high variety to those producing high volume and low variety. The volume–variety position of a process influences almost every aspect of its design. So, a first step in process design is to understand how volume and variety shape process characteristics, and to check whether processes have been configured in a manner that is appropriate for their volume–variety position.

The 'product–process' matrix

The most common method of illustrating the relationship between a process' volume–variety position and its design characteristics is shown in Figure 4.3. Often called the 'product–process' matrix, it can in fact be used for any type of process, whether producing products or services. Its underlying idea is that many of the more important elements of process design are strongly related to the volume–variety position of the process. So, the tasks that any process undertakes, the flow of items through the process, the layout of its resources, the technology it uses and the design of jobs, are all strongly influenced by its volume–variety position. This means that most processes should lie close to the diagonal of the matrix that represents the 'fit' between the process and its volume–variety position. This is called the 'natural' diagonal or natural line of fit.

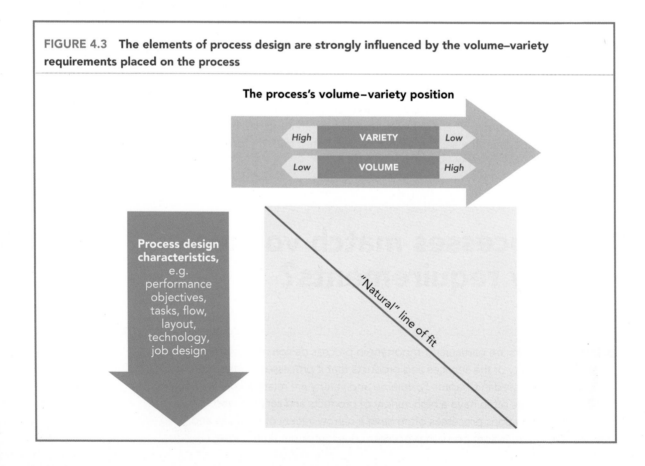

FIGURE 4.3   The elements of process design are strongly influenced by the volume–variety requirements placed on the process

The process's volume–variety position

| High | VARIETY | Low |
| Low | VOLUME | High |

Process design characteristics, e.g. performance objectives, tasks, flow, layout, technology, job design

"Natural" line of fit

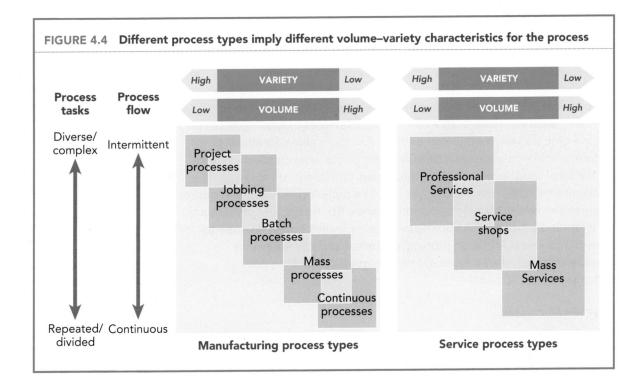

FIGURE 4.4 Different process types imply different volume–variety characteristics for the process

Process types

Processes that inhabit different points on the diagonal of the product–process matrix are sometimes referred to as 'process types'. Each process type implies differences in the set of tasks performed by the process and in the way materials, or information or customers flow through the process. Different terms are sometimes used to identify process types, depending on whether they are predominantly manufacturing or service processes, and there is some variation in how the names are used. This is especially so in service process types. It is not uncommon to find manufacturing terms used also to describe service processes. Perhaps most importantly, there is some degree of overlap between process types. The different process types are shown in Figure 4.4.

PROJECT PROCESSES

Project processes are those that deal with discrete, usually highly customized products. Often the timescale of making the product is relatively long, as is the interval between the completion of each product. The activities involved in the process may be ill-defined and uncertain, sometimes changing during the process itself. Examples include advertising agencies, shipbuilding, most construction companies, movie production companies, drilling oil wells and installing computer systems. Any process map for project processes will almost certainly be complex, partly because each unit of output is usually large, with many activities occurring at the same time, and partly because the activities often involve significant discretion to act according to professional judgement. In fact, a process map for a whole project would be extremely complex, so rarely would a project be mapped, but small parts may be.

operations principle
Process types indicate the position of processes on the volume–variety spectrum.

The major construction site shown in this picture is a project process. Each 'product' (project) is different and poses different challenges to those running the process (civil engineers).

JOBBING PROCESSES

Jobbing processes also deal with very high variety and low volumes, but whereas in project processes each project has resources devoted more or less exclusively to it, in jobbing processes each 'product' has to share the operation's resources with many others. The process will work on a series of products but, although all the products will require the same kind of attention, each will differ in its exact needs. Examples of jobbing processes include precision engineers such as specialist toolmakers, furniture restorers, 'make-to-measure' tailors and the printer who produces tickets for the local social event. Jobbing processes produce more and usually smaller items than project processes but, like project processes, the degree of repetition is low. Many jobs could be 'one-offs'. Again, any process map for a jobbing process could be relatively complex for similar reasons to project processes. Although jobbing processes sometimes involve considerable skill, they are usually more unpredictable than project processes.

This craftsperson is using general-purpose wood-crafting technology to make a product for an individual customer. The next product to be made will be different (although it may be similar), possibly for a different customer.

BATCH PROCESSES

Batch processes can look like jobbing processes, but without the degree of variety normally associated with jobbing. As the name implies, batch processes usually produce more than one 'product' at a time. So each part of the operation has periods when it is repeating itself, at least while the 'batch' is being processed. The size of the batch could be just two or three, in which case the batch process would differ little from jobbing, especially if each batch is a totally novel product. Conversely, if the batches are large, and especially if the products are familiar to the operation, batch processes can be fairly repetitive. Because of this, the batch type of process can be found over a wider range of volume and variety levels than other process types. Examples of batch processes include machine-tool manufacturing, the production of some special gourmet frozen foods, the manufacture of most of the component parts that go into mass-produced assemblies such as automobiles and the production of most clothing. Batch process maps may look straightforward, especially if different products take similar routes through the process, with relatively standard activities being performed at each stage.

In this kitchen, food is being prepared in batches. All batches go through the same sequence (preparation, cooking, storing), but each batch is a different dish.

MASS PROCESSES

Mass processes produce in high volume, usually with narrow effective variety. An automobile plant, for example, might produce several thousand variants of car if every option of engine size, colour and equipment is taken into account. Yet its effective variety is low because the different variants do not affect the basic process of production. The activities in the automobile plant, like all mass processes, are essentially repetitive and largely predictable. In addition to the automobile plant, examples of mass processes include consumer durable manufacturers, most food processes (such as a frozen-pizza manufacturer), beer-bottling plants and CD production. Process maps for this type of process will be straightforward sequences of activities.

This automobile plant is everyone's idea of a mass process. Each product is almost (but not quite) the same, and is made in large quantities.

CONTINUOUS PROCESSES

Continuous processes are one step beyond mass processes insomuch as they operate at even higher volume and often have even lower variety. Sometimes they are literally continuous, in that their products are inseparable and produced in an endless flow. Continuous processes are often associated with relatively inflexible, capital-intensive technologies with highly predictable flow. Examples of continuous processes include petrochemical refineries, electricity utilities, steel making and internet server farms. Like mass processes, process maps will show few elements of discretion, and although products may be stored during the process, the predominant characteristic of most continuous processes is of smooth flow from one part of the process to another.

This continuous water-treatment process almost never stops (it only stops for maintenance) and performs a narrow range of tasks (filters impurities). Often, we only notice the process if it goes wrong.

PROFESSIONAL SERVICES

Professional services are high-variety, low-volume processes, where customers may spend a considerable time in the service process. Such services usually provide high levels of customization, so contact staff are given considerable discretion. They tend to be people-based rather than equipment-based, with emphasis placed on the process (how the service is delivered) as much as the 'product' (what is delivered). Examples include management consultants, lawyers' practices, architects, doctors' surgeries, auditors, health-and-safety inspectors and some computer-field service operations. Where process maps are used, they are likely to be drawn predominantly at a high level. Consultants, for example, frequently use a predetermined set of broad stages, starting with understanding the real nature of the problem through to the implementation of their recommended solutions. This high-level process map guides the nature and sequence of the consultants' activities.

Here, consultants are preparing to start a consultancy assignment. They are discussing how they might approach the various stages of the assignment, from understanding the real nature of the problem, through to the implementation of their recommended solutions. They will follow a process, although it will be a very high-level one, guiding the nature and sequence of the consultants' activities.

SERVICE SHOPS

Service shops are characterized by levels of customer contact, customization, volume of customers and staff discretion that position them between the extremes of professional and mass services (see the next entry). Service is provided via a mix of front- and back-office activities. Service shops include banks, high-street shops, holiday-tour operators, car-rental companies, schools, most restaurants, hotels and travel agents. For example, an equipment-hire-and-sales organization may have a range of equipment displayed in front-office outlets, while back-office operations look after purchasing and administration. The front-office staff have some technical training and can advise customers during the process of selling the product. Essentially, the customer is buying a fairly standardized 'product', but will be influenced by the process of the sale that is customized to the individual customer's needs.

The health club shown in the picture has front-office staff who can advise on exercise programmes and other treatments. To maintain a dependable service, the staff need to follow defined processes every day.

MASS SERVICES

Mass services have many customer transactions and little customization. Such services are often predominantly equipment based and 'product' orientated, with most value added in the back office – sometimes with comparatively little judgement needed by front-office staff, who may have a closely defined job and follow set procedures. Mass services include supermarkets, national rail networks, airports and many call centres. For example, airlines move a large number of passengers on their networks. Passengers pick a journey from the range offered. The airline can advise passengers on the quickest or cheapest way to get from A to B, but they cannot 'customize' the service by putting on special flights for them.

This is an account management centre for a large retail bank. It deals with thousands of customer requests every day. Although each customer request is different, they are all of the same type – involving customers' accounts.

Moving off the natural diagonal

A process lying on the natural diagonal of the matrix shown in Figure 4.3 will normally have lower operating costs than one with the same volume–variety position that lies off the diagonal. This is because the diagonal represents the most appropriate process design for any volume–variety position. Processes that are on the right of the 'natural' diagonal would normally be associated with lower volumes and higher variety. This means that they are likely to be more flexible than seems to be warranted by their actual volume–variety position. That is, they are not taking advantage of their ability to standardize their activities. Because of this, their costs are likely to be higher than they would be with a process that was closer to the diagonal. Conversely, processes that are on the left of the diagonal have adopted a position that would normally be used for higher-volume and lower-variety processes. Processes will therefore be 'over-standardized' and probably too inflexible for their volume–variety position. This lack of flexibility can also lead to high costs because the process will not be able to change from one activity to another as readily as a more flexible process. One note of caution regarding this idea: although logically coherent, it is a conceptual model rather than something that can be 'scaled'. Although it is intuitively obvious that deviating from the diagonal increases costs, the precise amount by which costs will increase is very difficult to determine. Nevertheless, a first step in examining the design of an existing process is to check if it is on the natural diagonal of the product–process matrix. The volume–variety position of the process may have changed without any corresponding change in its design. Alternatively, design changes may have been introduced without considering their suitability for the process' volume–variety position.

operations principle
Moving off the 'natural diagonal' of the product–process matrix will incur excess costs.

LAYOUT, TECHNOLOGY AND DESIGN

If movement down the natural diagonal of the product–process matrix changes the nature of a process, then the key elements of its design will also change. At this broad level, these 'key elements' of the design are the two 'ingredients' that make up processes' resources (technology and people), and the way in which these ingredients are arranged within the process

Operations in practice

Construction of panel house

Space4 housing processes[1]

You don't usually build a house this way. It's more like the way you would expect an automobile to be made. Nevertheless, Space4's huge building in Birmingham (UK) contains what could be the future of house building. It is a production line whose 90 operators, many of whom have automobile assembly experience, are capable of producing the timber-framed panels that form the shell of the new homes at a rate of a house every hour. The automated systems within the production process control all facets of the operation, ensuring that scheduling and operations are timely and accurate. There is a direct link between the computer-aided design (CAD) systems that design the houses and the manufacturing processes that make them, reducing the time between design and manufacture. The machinery itself incorporates automatic predictive and preventative maintenance routines that minimize the chances of unexpected breakdowns. But not everything about the process relies on automation. Because of their previous automobile assembly experience, staff are used to the just-in-time (see Chapter 10), high-efficiency culture of modern mass production. After production, the completed panels are stacked and fork-lifted into trucks, where they are dispatched to building sites across the UK. Once the panels arrive at a building site, the construction workforce can assemble the exterior of a new home in a single day. Because the external structure of a house can be built in a few hours, and enclosed in a weatherproof covering, staff working on the internal fittings of the house, such as plumbers and electricians, can have a secure and dry environment in which to work, irrespective of external conditions. Furthermore, the automated production process uses a type of high-precision technology that means there are fewer mistakes in the construction process on site. This process, says Space4, speeds up the total building time from the usual 12–14 weeks to 8–10 weeks.

Also driving the adoption of mass processing were the tough new energy targets. When built, the homes also have good thermal insulation. The panels from the factory are injected with a special resin mixture that creates a foam that keeps heat in and energy bills down. Space4 also claims many other advantages for its process. It combines accurate quality conformance, flexibility, a construction routine that uses considerably less water than conventional building methods, which significantly reduces the drying-out period and surface cracking, and reduced site-generated waste, requiring fewer skips and providing a tidier, safer site. ● ● ●

relative to each other. This latter aspect is usually called 'layout'. In the remainder of the chapter, we start by discussing layout and then the design decisions that relate to process technology and the design of jobs within the process.

Are process layouts appropriate?

here is little point in having a well-sequenced process if, in reality, its activities are physically located in a way that involves excessive movement of materials, information or customers. Usually, the objective of the layout decision is to minimize movement, but, especially in information-transforming processes where distance is largely irrelevant, other criteria may dominate. For example, it may be more important to lay out processes such that similar activities or resources are grouped together. So, an international bank may group its foreign-exchange dealers together to encourage communication and discussion between them, even though the 'trades' they make are processed in an entirely different location. Some high-visibility processes may fix their layout to emphasize the behaviour of the customers who are being processed.

Layout should reflect volume and variety

The layout of a process is determined partly by its volume and variety characteristics. When volume is very low and variety is relatively high, 'flow' may not be a major issue. But, when variety is relatively small and volume is high, flow can become regularized and resources can be positioned to address the (similar) needs of the products or services, as in a classic flow line. In fact, most practical layouts are derived from only four basic layout types that correspond to different positions on the volume–variety spectrum. These are: fixed-position, functional, cell and line (sometimes called 'product') layouts. They are illustrated diagrammatically in Figure 4.5.

operations principle
Most practical layouts are derived from only four basic layout types with different volume–variety characteristics: fixed-position, functional, cell and line layouts.

FIXED-POSITION LAYOUT
Fixed-position layout is, in some ways, a contradiction in terms, since the transformed resources do not move between the transforming resources. Instead of materials, information or customers flowing through an operation, the recipient of the processing is stationary and the equipment, machinery, plant and people who do the processing move as necessary. This could be because the product or the recipient of the service is too large to be moved conveniently, or it might be too delicate to move, or perhaps it could object to being moved – for example, power-generator construction (too large to move), open-heart surgery (patients too delicate to move) or high-class restaurant (customers object to being moved).

FUNCTIONAL LAYOUT
Functional layout is so called because the functional needs and convenience of the transforming resources that constitute the processes dominate the layout

FIGURE 4.5   Different process layouts are appropriate for different volume–variety combinations

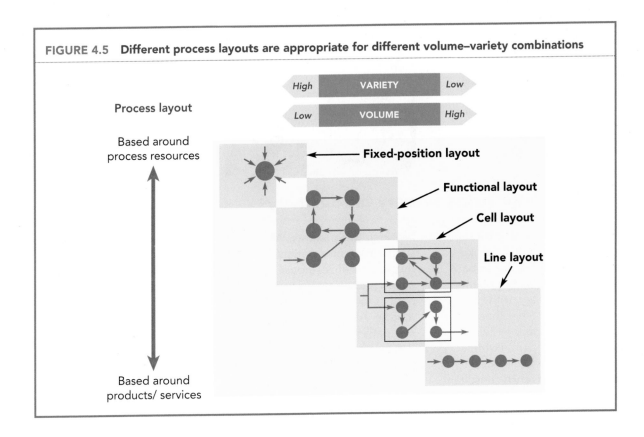

decision. (Confusingly, functional layout can also be called 'process layout'.) In functional layout, similar activities or resources (or those with similar needs) are located together. This may be because it is convenient to group them together, or that their utilization can be improved if grouped. It means that when materials, information or customers flow through the operation, they will take a route from activity to activity according to their needs. Usually this makes the flow pattern in the operation complex. Examples of process layouts include some hospital processes (e.g. radiography equipment and laboratories, required by several types of patient), high-tech machining centres (need specialist support), supermarkets (some products are convenient to restock if grouped together; some, such as frozen food, need the common technology of freezer cabinets).

CELL LAYOUT

A cell layout is one where materials, information or customers entering the operation are pre-selected (or pre-select themselves) to move to one part of the operation (or cell) in which all the transforming resources are located to meet their immediate processing needs. Internally, the cell itself may be arranged in any appropriate manner. After being processed in the cell, the transformed resources may go on to another cell. In effect, cell layout is an attempt to bring some order to the complexity of flow that characterizes functional layout. Examples of cell layouts include some computer assembly (subcontracted assembly often uses cells dedicated to each customer), the

Operations in practice

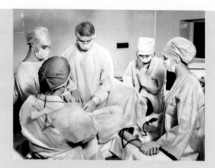

'Factory flow' helps surgery productivity[2]

Even surgery can be seen as a process, and, like any process, it can be improved. Normally patients remain stationary, with surgeons and other theatre staff performing their tasks around the patient. But this idea has been challenged by John Petri, a French consultant orthopaedic surgeon at a hospital in Norfolk in the UK. Frustrated by spending time drinking tea while patients were prepared for surgery, he redesigned the process so that now he moves continually between two theatres. While he is operating on a patient in one theatre, his anaesthetist colleagues are preparing a patient for surgery in another theatre. After finishing with the first patient, the surgeon 'scrubs up', moves to the second operating theatre and begins the surgery on the second patient. While he is doing this, the first patient is moved out of the first operating theatre and the third patient is prepared. This method of overlapping operations in different theatres allows him to work for five hours at a time, rather than the previous standard three-and-a-half-hour session. "If you were running a factory", says the surgeon, "you wouldn't allow your most important and most expensive machine to stand idle. The same is true in a hospital." Currently used on hip and knee replacements, this layout would not be suitable for all surgical procedures. But since its introduction, the surgeon's waiting list has fallen to zero and his productivity has

'lunch' products area in a supermarket (for customers who just want to purchase lunch items), the maternity unit in a hospital (customers are a well-defined group, unlikely to need the other facilities).

LINE LAYOUT
Line layout (sometimes called product layout) involves locating people and equipment entirely for the convenience of the transformed resources. Each product, piece of information or customer follows a prearranged route in which the sequence of required activities corresponds to the sequence in which the processes have been located. The transformed resources 'flow' along a 'line'. Flow is clear, predictable and therefore relatively easy to control. It is the high volume and standardized requirements of the product or service that allow product layouts. Examples of line layout include automobile assembly (almost all variants of the same model require the same sequence of processes) and self-service cafeterias (the sequence of customer requirements is common to all customers and layout helps control customer flow).

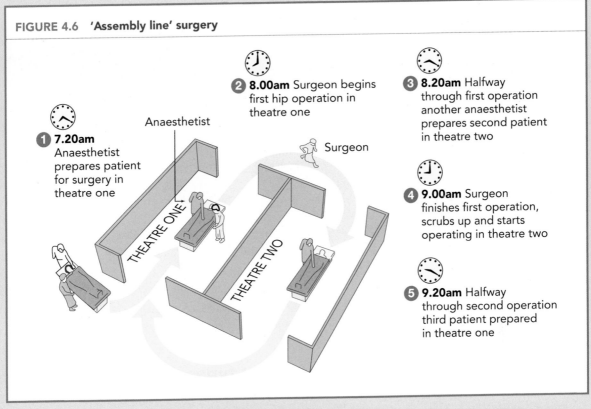

FIGURE 4.6 'Assembly line' surgery

1 7.20am Anaesthetist prepares patient for surgery in theatre one

2 8.00am Surgeon begins first hip operation in theatre one

3 8.20am Halfway through first operation another anaesthetist prepares second patient in theatre two

4 9.00am Surgeon finishes first operation, scrubs up and starts operating in theatre two

5 9.20am Halfway through second operation third patient prepared in theatre one

Anaesthetist

Surgeon

THEATRE ONE

THEATRE TWO

doubled. "For a small increase in running costs we are able to treat many more patients", said a spokesperson for the hospital management. "What is important is that clinicians. . . produce innovative ideas and we demonstrate that they are effective." ● ● ●

Layout selection

Getting the process layout right is important, if only because of the cost, difficulty and disruption of making any layout change. It is not an activity many businesses would want to repeat very often. Also, an inappropriate layout could mean that extra cost is incurred every time an item is processed.

One of the main influences on which type of layout will be appropriate is the nature of the process itself, as summarized in its 'process type'. But, process types are not the same as layout types. Process types indicate a broad approach to the organization of a process, layout is a narrower concept. Both are governed by volume and variety, but for any given process type there are usually at least two alternative layouts. Table 4.1 summarizes the alternative layouts for particular process types. Which of these is selected, or whether some hybrid layout is chosen, depends on the relative importance of the performance objectives of the process – especially cost and flexibility.

TABLE 4.1   Alternative layout types for each process type

Manufacturing process types	Potential layouts for manufacturing process types	Potential layouts for service process types	Service process Types
Project	Fixed-position layout Functional layout	Fixed-position layout Functional layout Cell layout	Professional Service
Jobbing	Functional layout Cell layout	Functional layout Cell layout	Service Shop
Batch	Functional layout Cell layout		
Mass	Cell layout Line layout	Cell layout Line layout	Mass Service
Continuous	Line layout		

Advantages and disadvantages of layout types

Fixed-position layout   has high mix and product flexibility, does not require the product or customer to be moved and gives a wide variety of tasks to staff. But, has high unit costs, scheduling of space and activities can be difficult and will mean movement of equipment and staff.

Functional layout   has high mix and product flexibility, is relatively robust in the case of disruptions and means relatively easy supervision of facilities. But, has low facilities utilization, can have very high work-in-progress or customer Queuing and flow can be difficult to control.

Cell layout   can give a good compromise between cost and flexibility for relatively high-variety operations, can give fast throughput and the associated group work can be rewarding for staff. But, can be costly to rearrange existing layout, can need more equipment and can give lower facilities utilization.

Line layout   gives low unit costs for high volume, gives opportunities for specialization and means materials or customer movement is controlled. But, can have low mix flexibility, is not very robust if there is disruption and results in repetitive tasks.

Layout and 'servicescapes'

In high-visibility processes (where the customer 'sees' much of the value-adding processing – see Chapter 1), the general look and feel of the process could be as important, if not more important, than more 'objective' criteria such as cost or distance moved. The term that is often used to describe the look and feel of the environment within an operation or process is its 'servicescape'. There are many academic studies that have shown that the servicescape of an operation plays an important role, both positive and negative, in shaping customers' views of how a high-visibility process is judged.

The general idea is that ambient conditions, space factors and signs and symbols in a service operation will create an 'environmental experience' both for employees and customers; and this environmental experience should support the service concept. The individual factors that influence this experience will then lead to certain responses (again, in both employees and customers). However, remember that a servicescape will contain not only objective, measureable and controllable stimuli, but also subjective, immeasurable and often uncontrollable stimuli, which will influence customer behaviour. The obvious example is other customers frequenting an operation. As well as controllable stimuli – such as the colour, lighting, design, space and music – the number, demographics and appearance of one's fellow customers will also shape the impression of the operation.

operations principle
Layout should include consideration of the look and feel of the operation to customers and/or staff.

Are process technologies appropriate?

Process technologies are the machines, equipment and devices that help processes 'transform' materials and information and customers. This question is a particularly important issue because few operations have been unaffected by the advances in process technology over the last two decades. And the pace of technological development is not slowing down. But, it is important to distinguish between process technology (the machines and devices that help to create products and services) and product technology (the technology that is embedded within the product or service). Some process technology, although not used for the actual creation of goods and services, nonetheless plays a key role in facilitating their creation. For example, the information technology systems that run planning and control activities can be used to help managers and operators run the processes. Sometimes, this type of technology is called 'indirect' process technology, and it is becoming increasingly important. Many businesses spend more on the computer systems that run their processes than they do on the direct process technology that creates their products and services.

Process technology should reflect volume and variety

Again, different process technologies will be appropriate for different parts of the volume–variety continuum. High-variety, low-volume processes generally require process technology that is general purpose, because it can perform the wide range of processing activities that high variety demands. High-volume, low-variety processes can use technology that is more dedicated to its narrower range of processing requirements. Within the spectrum from general purpose to dedicated process technologies, three dimensions in particular tend to vary with volume and variety. The first is the extent to which the process technology carries out activities or makes decisions for itself – that is, its degree of 'automation'. The second is the capacity of the technology to process work – that is, its 'scale' or 'scalability'. The third is the extent to which it is integrated with other technologies – that is, its degree of 'coupling' or 'connectivity'. Figure 4.7 illustrates these three dimensions of process technology.

> **operations principle**
> Process technology in high-volume, low-variety processes is relatively automated, large scale and closely coupled when compared to that in low-volume, high-variety processes.

THE DEGREE OF AUTOMATION OF THE TECHNOLOGY

To some extent, all technology needs human intervention. It may be minimal – for example, the periodic maintenance interventions in a petrochemical refinery. Conversely, the person who operates the technology may be the entire 'brains' of the process – for example, the surgeon using keyhole surgery techniques. Generally, processes that have high variety and low volume will employ process technology with lower degrees of automation than those with higher volume and lower variety. For example, investment banks trade in

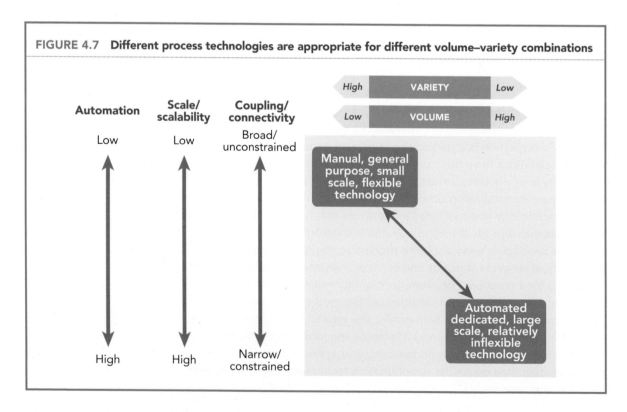

FIGURE 4.7   **Different process technologies are appropriate for different volume–variety combinations**

highly complex and sophisticated financial 'derivatives', often customized to the needs of individual clients, and each may be worth millions of dollars. The back office of the bank has to process these deals to make sure that payments are made on time, documents are exchanged and so on. Much of this processing will be done using relatively general-purpose technology, such as spreadsheets. Skilled back-office staff are making the decisions rather than the technology. Contrast this with higher-volume, low-variety products, such as straightforward equity (stock) trades. Most of these products are simple and straightforward and are processed in very high volume of several thousand per day by 'automated' technology.

THE SCALE/SCALABILITY OF THE TECHNOLOGY

There is usually some discretion as to the scale of individual units of technology. For example, the duplicating department of a large office complex may decide to invest in a single, very large, fast copier, or alternatively in several smaller, slower copiers distributed around the operation's various processes. An airline may purchase one or two wide-bodied aircraft or a larger number of smaller aircraft. The advantage of large-scale technologies is that they can usually process items cheaper than small-scale technologies, but usually need high volume and can cope only with low variety. By contrast, the virtues of smaller-scale technology are often the nimbleness and flexibility that is suited to high-variety, lower-volume processing. For example, four small machines can between them produce four different products simultaneously (albeit slowly), whereas a single large machine with four times the output can produce only one product at a time (albeit faster). Small-scale technologies are also more robust. Suppose the choice is between three small machines and one larger one. In the first case, if one machine breaks down, a third of the capacity is lost, but in the second, capacity is reduced to zero.

The equivalent to scale for some types of information processing technology is scalability. By scalability we mean the ability to shift to a different level of useful capacity quickly, and cost-effectively. Scalability is similar to absolute scale in so much as it is influenced by the same volume–variety characteristics. IT scalability relies on consistent IT platform architecture and the high process standardization that is usually associated with high-volume and low-variety operations.

THE COUPLING/CONNECTIVITY OF THE TECHNOLOGY

Coupling means the linking together of separate activities within a single piece of process technology to form an interconnected processing system. Tight coupling usually gives fast process throughput. For example, in an automated manufacturing system, products flow quickly without delays between stages, and inventory will be lower – it can't accumulate when there are no 'gaps' between activities. Tight coupling also means that flow is simple and predictable, making it easier to keep track of parts when they pass through fewer stages, or information when it is automatically distributed to all parts of an information network. However, closely coupled

Technology or people? The future of jobs[3]

Technological advances have always had an impact on the type of jobs that are in demand by businesses. Much of the highly routine work of mass manufacturing, or the standardized accounting processes that pay invoices, have been overtaken by 'the robot and the spreadsheet'. Yet the type of work that is more difficult to break down into a set of standardized elements is less prone to being displaced by technology. The obvious examples of work that is difficult to automate are the type of management tasks that involve decision making based on judgement and insight – teaching small children, diagnosing complex medical conditions and so on. However, the future may hold a less certain future for such jobs. As the convenience of data collection and analysis becomes more sophisticated, and process knowledge increases, it becomes easier to break more types of work down into routine constituents, which allows them to be automated. Carl Benedikt Frey and Michael Osborne, of the University of Oxford, maintain that the range of jobs that are likely to be automated is far higher than many assume, especially traditionally white-collar jobs such as accountancy, legal work, technical writing and (even) teaching. It is not simply that technology is getting cleverer; in addition, it can exploit the capability to access far more data. Medical samples can be analyzed cheaper and faster by image-processing software than by laboratory technicians; case precedents can be sourced by 'text-mining' programs more extensively than by para-legals; and computers can turn out new stories based on sports results or financial data. Frey and Osborne even go so far as to estimate the probability that technology will mean job losses for certain jobs in the next two decades (bravely, because such forecasting is notoriously difficult). Among jobs most at risk are telemarketers (0.99, where 1.0 = certainty), accountants and auditors (0.94), retail salespersons (0.92), technical writers (0.89) and retail estate agents (0.86). Those jobs least likely to be replaced include actors (0.37), firefighters (0.17), editors (0.06), chemical engineers (0.02), athletic trainers (0.007) and dentists (0.004). ● ● ●

technology can be both expensive (each connection may require capital costs) and vulnerable (a failure in one part of an interconnected system can affect the whole system). The fully integrated manufacturing system constrains parts to flow in a predetermined manner, making it difficult to accommodate products with very different processing requirements. So, coupling is generally more suited to relatively low variety and high volume. Higher-variety processing generally requires a more open and unconstrained level of coupling because different products and services will require a wider range of processing activities.

Are job designs appropriate?

Job design is about how people carry out their tasks within a process. It defines the way they go about their working lives. It positions the expectations of what is required of them, and it influences their perceptions of how they contribute to the organization. It also defines their activities in relation to their work colleagues and it channels the flows of communication between different parts of the operation. But, of most importance, it helps to develop the culture of the organization – its shared values, beliefs and assumptions. Inappropriately designed jobs can destroy the potential of a process to fulfill its objectives, no matter how appropriate its layout or process technology. So jobs must be designed to fit the nature of the process. However, before considering this, it is important to accept that some aspects of job design are common to all processes, irrespective of what they do or how they do it. Consider the following:

 Safety　The primary and universal objective of job design is to ensure that all staff performing any task within a process are protected against the possibility of physical or mental harm.

 Ethical issues　No individual should be asked to perform any task that is either illegal or (within limits) conflicts with strongly held ethical beliefs.

 Work/life balance　All jobs should be structured so as to promote a healthy balance between time spent at work and time away from work.

Note that all these objectives of job design are also likely to improve overall process performance. However, the imperative to follow such objectives for their own sake transcends conventional criteria.

Job design should reflect volume and variety

As with other aspects of process design, the nature and challenges of job design are governed largely by the volume–variety characteristics of a process. An architect designing major construction projects will perform a wide range of very different, often creative and complex tasks, many of which are not defined at the start of the process, and most of which have the potential to give the architect significant job satisfaction. By contrast, someone in the architect's accounts office keying in invoice details has a job that is repetitive, has little variation, is tightly defined and cannot rely on the intrinsic interest of the task itself to maintain job commitment. These two jobs will have different characteristics because they are part of processes with different volume and variety positions. Three aspects of job design in particular are affected by the volume–variety characteristics of a process: how tasks are to be allocated to each person in the process; the degree of job definition; and the methods used to maintain job commitment. Figure 4.8 illustrates these.

HOW TASKS SHOULD BE ALLOCATED – THE DIVISION OF LABOUR

The most obvious aspect of any individual's job is how big it is – that is, how many of the tasks within any process are allocated to an individual. Should a single individual perform all the process? Alternatively, should separate individuals or teams perform each task? Separating tasks into smaller parts between individuals is called the division of labour. Perhaps its epitome is the assembly line, where products move along a single path and are built up by operators continually repeating a single task. This is the predominant model of job design in most high-volume, low-variety processes. For such processes, there are some real advantages in division-of-labour principles:

  It promotes faster learning. It is obviously easier to learn how to do a relatively short and simple task than a long and complex one, so new members of staff can be quickly trained and assigned to their tasks.

operations principle

Job designs in high-volume, low-variety processes are relatively closely defined, with little decision-making discretion and needing action to help commitment when compared to those in low-volume, high-variety processes.

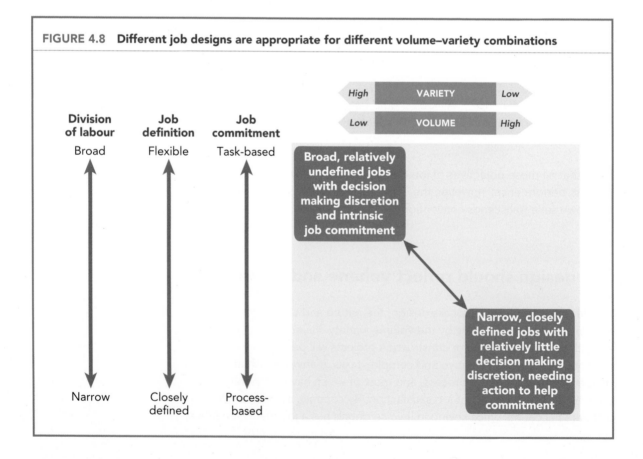

FIGURE 4.8   Different job designs are appropriate for different volume–variety combinations

| High | VARIETY | Low |
| Low | VOLUME | High |

Division of labour	Job definition	Job commitment
Broad	Flexible	Task-based
Narrow	Closely defined	Process-based

Broad, relatively undefined jobs with decision making discretion and intrinsic job commitment

Narrow, closely defined jobs with relatively little decision making discretion, needing action to help commitment

Automation becomes easier. Substituting technology for labour is considerably easier for short and simple tasks than for long and complex ones.

 Non-productive work is reduced. In large, complex tasks the proportion of time between individual value-adding elements can be very high – for example, in manufacturing, picking up tools and materials, putting them down again and generally searching and positioning.

There are also serious drawbacks to highly divided jobs:

 It is monotonous. Repeating the same task eight hours a day and five days a week is not fulfilling. This may lead to an increased likelihood of absenteeism, staff turnover and error rates.

 It can cause physical injury. The continued repetition of a very narrow range of movements can, in extreme cases, lead to physical injury. The over-use of some parts of the body (especially the arms, hands and wrists) can result in pain and a reduction in physical capability, called repetitive strain injury (RSI).

 It can mean low flexibility. Dividing a task up into many small parts often gives the job design a rigidity that is difficult to change if circumstances require it. For example, if an assembly line has been designed to make one particular product but then has to change to manufacture a quite different product, the whole line will need redesigning. This will probably involve changing every operator's set of tasks.

 It can mean poor robustness. Highly divided jobs imply items passing between several stages. If one of these stages is not working correctly, for example because some equipment is faulty, the whole operation is affected. On the other hand, if each person is performing the whole of the job, any problems will only affect that one person's output.

Even in the early days of industrialization, when standardized, repetitive jobs spread through many industries, criticisms of highly divided jobs were being voiced. In addition to the monotony of repetitive job designs, the separation of the judgemental, planning and skilled tasks (done by 'management') from the routine, standardized and low-skill tasks (done by 'operators') was causing concern. Such a separation, at the very least, deprives the majority of staff of an opportunity to contribute in a meaningful way to their jobs (and, incidentally, deprives the organization of their contribution).

To what degree should jobs be defined?

Jobs in high-variety processes are difficult to define in anything but the most general terms. Such jobs may require tacit knowledge gained over time and

Operations in practice

The stress of high customer-contact jobs[4]

Jobs dealing directly with customers can be particularly stressful. Not all customers will be reasonable, patient, courteous, or even sane. There is plenty of advice for staff that have to deal with angry customers. It usually includes such things as: acknowledge the (perceived) problem; try to put yourself in the position of the complainer; get all the facts straight; and try to rectify the problem. Not easy, but if complaints can be resolved to the satisfaction of the customer, there can be significant benefits. Nevertheless, maintaining tolerance and politeness in the face of some particularly difficult customers can be more than, even experienced, staff can

bear. That certainly was the case with Steven Slater, formerly an air steward on the US airline JetBlue. He was working on a flight to New York when he had to arbitrate when a female passenger began arguing with a male passenger about space in the overhead luggage compartment during boarding. The female passenger swore at Mr Slater and pulled down the compartment door on his head. Later, when the plane landed, she seemingly refused to follow his request to remain in her seat and got up to take her bag from the overhead locker while the plane was still taxiing. Again, the woman allegedly swore at Mr Slater. It was then that his patience ran out in a particularly

dramatic fashion. He went to the intercom and broadcast to the whole plane: "To the passenger who just called me a motherf*****: F*** you. I've been in this business for 28 years and I've had it." He then collected his hand-luggage (and two beers from the trolley), opened the cabin door, activated the inflatable chute, announced, "to those of you who have shown dignity and respect for 20 years, have a great ride" and slid out of the (fortunately stationary) plane on to the runway. As a way to give up your job, it's not recommended. He was later arrested and charged with criminal mischief and reckless endangerment. ● ● ●

through experience and often require individuals to exercise significant discretion in what they do and how they do it. Some degree of job definition is usually possible and advisable, but it may be stated in terms of the 'outcome' from the task, rather than in terms of the activities within the task. For example, the architect's job may be defined in terms of 'achieving overall coordination, taking responsibility for articulating the overall vision of the project, ensuring stakeholders are comfortable with the process, etc'. By contrast, a process with less variety and higher volume is likely to be defined more closely, with the exact nature of each activity defined and individual staff trained to follow a job step by step.

How should job commitment be encouraged?

Many factors may influence job commitment. An individual's job history and expectations, relationships with co-workers and personal circumstances can all be important. So are the volume and variety characteristics of the process by defining the possible ways in which commitment can be enhanced. In high-variety processes, especially those with a high degree of staff discretion, job commitment is likely to come from the intrinsic nature of the task itself. Exercising skill and decision making, for example, can bring its own satisfaction. Of course, commitment can be enhanced through extra responsibility, flexibility in working times and so on, but the main motivator is the job itself. By contrast, low-variety, high-volume jobs, especially those designed with a high division of labour and little discretion, can be highly alienating. Such jobs have relatively little intrinsic task satisfaction. It has to be 'designed into' the process by emphasizing the satisfaction to be gained from the performance of the process overall. A number of job design approaches have been suggested for achieving this in processes involving relatively repetitive work:

Job enlargement This involves allocating a larger number of tasks to individuals, usually by combining tasks that are broadly of the same type as those in the original job. This may not involve more demanding or fulfilling tasks, but it may provide a more complete and therefore slightly more meaningful job. If nothing else, people performing an enlarged job will not repeat themselves as often. For example, suppose that the manufacture of a product has traditionally been split up on an assembly-line basis into 10 equal and sequential jobs. If that job is then redesigned so as to form two parallel assembly lines of five people, each operator would have twice the number of tasks to perform.

Job enrichment Like job enlargement, job enrichment increases the number of tasks in a job, but also implies allocating tasks that involve more decision making, or greater autonomy, and therefore greater control over the job. These could include the maintenance of, and adjustments to, any process technology used, the planning and control of activities within the job, or the monitoring of quality levels. The effect is both to reduce repetition in the job and to increase personal development opportunities. So, in the assembly-line example, each operator could also be allocated responsibility for carrying out routine maintenance and such tasks as record-keeping and managing the supply of materials.

Job rotation This means moving individuals periodically between different sets of tasks to provide some variety in their activities. When successful, job rotation can increase skill flexibility and make a small contribution to reducing monotony. However, it is not always viewed as beneficial either by management (because it can disrupt the smooth flow of work) or by the people performing the jobs (because it can interfere with their rhythm of work).

Empowerment   This involves enhancing individuals' ability, and sometimes authority, to change how they do their jobs. Some technologically constrained processes, such as those in chemical plants, may limit the extent that staff can dilute their highly standardized task methods without consultation. Other less-defined processes to empowerment may go much further.

Team working   Closely linked to empowerment, team-based work organization (sometimes called self-managed work teams) is where staff, often with overlapping skills, collectively perform a defined task and have some discretion over how they perform the task. The team may control such things as task allocation between members, scheduling work, quality measurement and improvement, and sometimes even the hiring of staff. Groups are described as 'teams' when the virtues of working together are being emphasized and a shared set of objectives and responsibilities is assumed.

Summary answers to key questions

Each chapter has a 'Summary answers to key questions' section. Use it to check your understanding of the issues covered in the chapter.

WHY IS CHOOSING THE RIGHT RESOURCES IMPORTANT?

★ Process design is concerned with conceiving the nature of the resources that make up the process and their detailed workings. The first task of process design is to conceive the nature of the resources that make up the process and how they are arranged.

★ Without appropriate resources, it is difficult (maybe impossible) for the process ever to operate as effectively as it could do. Only after this stage should the second task (conceiving the detailed workings of the process) be attempted.

DO PROCESSES MATCH VOLUME–VARIETY REQUIREMENTS?

★ Volume and variety are particularly influential in the design of processes. They also tend to go together in an inverse relationship. High-variety processes are normally low volume, and vice versa.

★ Processes can be positioned on the spectrum between low volume and high variety and high volume and low variety. At different points on this spectrum, processes can be described as distinct process 'types'.

★ Different terms are used in manufacturing and service to identify these types. Working from low volume and high variety towards high volume and low variety, the process types are: project processes, jobbing processes, batch processes, mass processes and continuous processes. The same sequence in service types are known as: professional services, service shops and mass services.

★ Whatever terminology is used, the overall design of the process must fit its volume–variety position. This is usually summarized in the form of the 'product–process' matrix.

ARE PROCESS LAYOUTS APPROPRIATE?

★ There are different ways in which the different resources within a process (people and technology) can be arranged relative to each other. However this is done, it should reflect the process' volume–variety position.

There are pure 'types' of layout that correspond with the different volume–variety positions. These are: fixed-position layout, functional layout, cell layout and product layout.

 Many layouts are hybrids of these pure types, but the type chosen is influenced by the volume and variety characteristics of the process.

ARE PROCESS TECHNOLOGIES APPROPRIATE?

 Process technologies are the machines, equipment and devices that help processes transform materials and information and customers.

 Product technology should reflect volume and variety. In particular, the degree of automation in the technology, the scale and/or scalability of the technology and the coupling and/or connectivity of the technology should be appropriate to volume and variety.

 Generally, low volume and high variety requires relatively unautomated, general-purpose, small-scale and flexible technologies. By contrast, high-volume and low-variety processes require automated, dedicated and large-scale technologies that are sometimes relatively inflexible.

ARE JOB DESIGNS APPROPRIATE?

 Job design is about how people carry out their tasks within a process. It is particularly important because it governs people's expectations and perceptions of their contribution to the organization, as well as being a major factor in shaping the culture of the organization.

 Job designs are influenced by volume and variety – in particular, the extent of division of labour, the degree to which jobs are defined and the way in which job commitment is encouraged.

 Broadly, high-variety and low-volume processes require broad, relatively undefined jobs with decision-making discretion. Such jobs tend to have intrinsic job commitment. By contrast, high-volume and low-variety processes tend to require jobs that are relatively narrow in scope and closely defined, with relatively little decision-making discretion. In these latter cases, some deliberative action is needed in the design of the job (such as job enrichment) in order to help maintain commitment to the job.

Problems and applications

All chapters have problems and application questions that will help you practice analyzing operations. They can be answered by reading the chapter. Model answers for the first question can be found on the companion website for this text.

1 ➡ Visit a branch of a retail bank and consider the following questions: (a) what categories of service does the bank seem to offer?; (b) to what extent does the bank design separate processes for each of its types of service?; and (c) what are the different process design objectives for each category of service?

2 ➡ The International Frozen Pizza Company (IFPC) operates in three markets globally. Market 1 is its largest market, where it sells 25,000 tons of pizza per year. In this market, it trades under the name 'Aunt Bridget's Pizza' and positions itself as making pizza 'just as your Aunt Bridget used to make' (apparently she was good at it). It is also known for innovation – introducing new and seasonal pizza toppings on a regular basis. Typically, it would be selling around 20 varieties of pizza at any one time. Market 2 is smaller, selling around 20,000 tons per year under its 'Poppet's Pizza' brand. Although less innovative than market 1, it still sells around 12 varieties of pizza. Market 3 is the smallest of the three, selling 10,000 tons per year of relatively high-quality pizzas under its 'Deluxe Pizza' brand. As with Aunt Bridget's Pizza, Deluxe Pizza also sells a relatively wide product range for the size of its market. Currently, both markets 1 and 3 produce their products using relatively little automation and rely on high numbers of people, employed on a shift-system, to assemble their products. Market 2 has always been keen to adopt more automated production processes and uses a mixture of automated assembly and manual assembly. Now the management in market 2 has developed an almost fully automated pizza-assembly system (APAS). They claim that the APAS could reduce costs significantly and should be adopted by the other markets. Both markets 1 and 3 are sceptical. "It may be cheaper, but it can't cope with a high variety of products", is their response. Use the product–process matrix to explain the proposal by the management of market 2.

3 ➡ Visit a supermarket and observe people's behaviour. You may wish to try and observe which areas they move slowly past and which areas they seem to move past without paying attention to the products. (You may have to exercise some discretion when doing this; people generally don't like to be stalked around the supermarket too obviously.) Try to establish, as far as you can, some of the principles that govern its layout. What layout type is a conventional supermarket and how does it differ from a manufacturing operation using the same layout type? Some supermarkets are using customer-tracking technology that traces the flow of customers through the shop. What are the benefits of using this type of technology for supermarkets?

Want to know more?

Hammer, M. (1990) 'Re-engineering work: Don't automate, obliterate', *Harvard Business Review*, July–August.

➜ This is the paper that launched the whole idea of business processes and process management in general to a wider managerial audience. Slightly dated but worth reading.

Harrington, H.J. (2011) *Streamlined Process Improvement*, New York: McGraw Hill Professional.

➜ A comprehensive book for professionals.

Harvard Business Review (2011) *Improving Business Processes* (Harvard Pocket Mentor), Boston, MA: Harvard Business School Press.

➜ A good step-by-step guide to the practice of process design.

Hopp, W.J. and Spearman, M.L. (2011) *Factory Physics*, 3rd edition, Long Grove, IL: Waveland Press Inc.

➜ Very technical, so don't bother with it if you aren't prepared to get into the maths. However, some fascinating analysis, especially concerning Little's Law.

Jeston, J. and Nelis, J. (2014) *Business Process Management*, 3rd edition, Abingdon, UK: Routledge.

➜ Written by two consultants, it gives chapter-and-verse on the orthodoxy of business process management; a broader topic than is covered in this chapter, but useful nonetheless.

Ramaswamy, R. (1996) *Design and Management of Service Processes*, Boston, MA: Addison-Wesley Longman.

➜ A relatively technical approach to process design in a service environment.

The layout and look of all processes must fit what the operation is trying to do. So, the layout of this Google office in London reflects a casual look with plenty of opportunity for 'unscheduled' meetings between staff, all of which is intended to promote creativity.

Process design – analysis

5

Introduction

The previous chapter set the broad parameters for process design. In particular, it showed how volume and variety shape the resources of the process in terms of its appropriate layout, process technology and the design of its jobs. But this is only the beginning of process design. Within these broad resource parameters there are many, more detailed, decisions regarding the activities carried out by the process. It is these decisions that will dictate the way materials, information and customers flow through the process. Do not dismiss these detailed design decisions as merely the 'technicalities' of process design. They are important because they go a long way to determining the actual performance of the process in practice, and eventually its contribution to the performance of the whole business. Figure 5.1 shows where this topic fits within the overall model of operations management.

Key questions

Why is it important to get the details of process design correct?

What should be the objectives of process design?

How are processes currently designed?

Are process tasks and capacity configured appropriately?

Is process variability recognized?

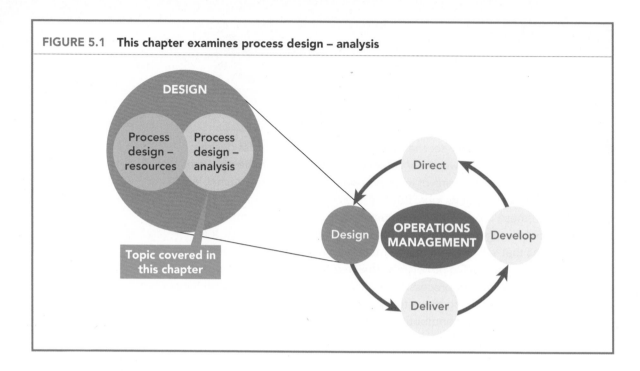

FIGURE 5.1   **This chapter examines process design – analysis**

Why is it important to get the details of process design correct?

Process design is a conceptual exercise, yet it is one that must deliver a solution that will work in practice. Process design is also an activity that can be approached at different levels of detail. One may envisage the general nature of resources and intention of a process before getting down to defining its details. This is why we devoted the previous chapter to the most common way of doing this: by looking at its volume and variety characteristics. But, it is often only through getting to grips with the detail of a design that the feasibility of a process' design can be assessed. At its simplest, this detailed design of a process involves identifying all the individual activities that are needed to meet the objectives of the process, and deciding on the sequence in which these activities are to be performed and who is going to do them. There will, of course, be some constraints to this. Some activities must be carried out before others, and certain people or equipment can only do some activities. But don't think of process design as a simple two-stage procedure, where resourcing decisions are automatically followed by its detailed analysis. There may be aspects concerned with the resourcing of the process that will need to be modified following its more detailed analysis, or details of the process modified as new or changed resources become available.

operations principle
The choice of a process' resources and the analysis of its detailed design are not totally independent decisions.

Operations in practice

Changi Airport[1]

Airports are complex operations. Really complex. Their processes handle passengers, aircraft, crew, baggage, commercial cargo, food, security and restaurants, and numerous customer services interact. The operations managers, who oversee the daily operations of an airport, must cope with aviation administration rules and regulations, a huge number of airport service contracts, usually thousands of staff with a wide variety of specialisms, airlines with sometimes competing claims to service priority, customers some of whom fly every week and others who are a family of seven with two baby strollers that flies once a decade. Also, their processes are vulnerable to disruptions from late arrivals, aircraft malfunction, weather, the industrial action of workers two continents away, conflicts, terrorism and exploding volcanoes in Iceland. Designing the processes that can operate under these conditions must be one of the most challenging operations tasks. So, to win prizes for 'Best Airport'

customer service and operating efficiency year after year has to be something of an achievement. Which is what the sixth-busiest international airport, Changi Airport in Singapore, has done. As a major air hub in Asia, Changi serves more than 100 international airlines flying to some 300 cities in about 70 countries and territories worldwide. It handles almost 60 million passengers (that's roughly 10 times the size of Singapore's population). A flight takes off or lands at Changi roughly once every 90 seconds.

Changi's new Terminal 4 can handle about 16 million passengers per year, increasing the airport's annual passenger handling capacity to 82 million. Every stage of the customers' journey through the terminal has been designed to be as smooth as possible. The aim of all the processes that make up the terminal is to provide a fast, smooth and seamless flow for passengers. Each stage in the process must have enough capacity to cope with anticipated demand. A new

overhead bridge connects T4 with Singapore's highway system and enables the movement of cars, buses and airside vehicles. Once passengers arrive at the two-storey terminal building, they pass through kiosks and automated options for self-check-in, self-bag tagging and self-bag-drops. Their bags are then transported to the aircraft via an advanced and automated baggage handling system. After security checks, passengers find themselves in 15,000 m² of shopping, dining, liquor, tobacco, perfumes, cosmetics and other retail spaces. It will implement a new walk-through retail concept featuring local, cultural and heritage-themed restaurants, as well as retail stores. This space also features a 300 m-long central galleria, with a glazed open space that visually connects the departure, check-in, arrival and transit areas across the terminal. The emphasis on the aesthetic appeal of the terminal is something that Changi has long considered important. It already boasts a butterfly garden, orchid and sunflower gardens, as well as a koi pond. ● ● ●

What should be the objectives of process design?

The detailed design of processes is important because process performance also affects the performance of the whole operation. The whole point of process design is to make sure that the performance of the process is appropriate for whatever it is trying to achieve. For example, if an operation competed primarily on its ability to respond quickly to customer requests, its processes would need to be designed to give fast throughput times. This would minimize the time between customers requesting a product or service and them receiving it. Similarly, if an operation competed on low price, cost-related objectives are likely to dominate its process design. Some kind of logic should link what the operation as a whole is attempting to achieve and the performance objectives of its individual processes. This is illustrated in Table 5.1. Here we will include 'sustainability' as an operational objective of process design, even though it is really a far broader societal issue that is part of the organization's 'triple bottom line' (see Chapter 1).

> **operations principle**
> The design of any process should be judged on its quality, speed, dependability, flexibility, cost and sustainability performance.

'Micro' objectives

Operations performance objectives translate directly to process design objectives, as shown in Table 5.1. But, because processes are managed at a very operational level, process design also needs to consider a more 'micro' and detailed set of objectives. These are largely concerned with flow through the process. When whatever is being 'processed' enters a process, it will progress through a series of activities where it is 'transformed' in some way. Between these activities it may dwell for some time in inventories, waiting to be transformed by the next activity. This means that the time that a unit spends in the process (its throughput time) will be longer than the sum of all the transforming activities that it passes through. Also, the resources that perform the processes activities may not be used all the time because not all items will necessarily require the same activities and the capacity of each resource may not match the demand placed upon it. So, neither the items moving through the process, nor the resources performing the activities may be fully utilized. Because of this, the way that items leave the process is unlikely to be exactly the same as the way they arrive at the process. It is common for more 'micro'

TABLE 5.1 The impact of strategic performance objectives on process design objectives and performance

Operations performance objective	Typical process design objectives	Some benefits of good process design
▶ Quality	▶ Provide appropriate resources, capable of achieving the specification of product or services ▶ Error-free processing	▶ Products and service produced 'on-specification' ▶ Less recycling and wasted effort within the process
▶ Speed	▶ Minimum throughput time ▶ Output rate appropriate for demand	▶ Short customer-waiting time ▶ Low in-process inventory
▶ Dependability	▶ Provide dependable process resources ▶ Reliable process output timing and volume	▶ On-time deliveries of products and services ▶ Less disruption, confusion and rescheduling within the process
▶ Flexibility	▶ Provide resources with an appropriate range of capabilities ▶ Change easily between processing states (what, how, or how much is being processed?)	▶ Ability to process a wide range of products and services ▶ Low-cost/fast product and service change • Low-cost/fast volume and timing changes • Ability to cope with unexpected events (e.g. a supply or processing failure)
▶ Cost	▶ Appropriate capacity to meet demand ▶ Eliminate process waste in terms of: • excess capacity • excess process capability • in-process delays • in-process errors • inappropriate process inputs	▶ Low processing costs ▶ Low resource costs (capital costs) ▶ Low delay/inventory costs (working capital costs)
▶ Sustainability	▶ Minimize energy usage ▶ Reduce local impact on community ▶ Produce for easy disassembly	▶ Lower negative environmental and societal impact

performance flow objectives to be used that describe process flow performance. For example:

 Throughput rate (or flow rate) is the rate at which items emerge from the process – i.e., the number of items passing through the process per unit of time.

 Cycle time, or takt time, is the reciprocal of throughput rate; it is the time between items emerging from the process. The term 'takt' time is the same, but is normally applied to 'paced' processes such as moving-belt assembly lines. It is the 'beat' or tempo of working required to meet demand.[2]

 Throughput time is the average elapsed time taken for inputs to move through the process and become outputs.

 The number of items in the process (also called the 'work in progress', or in-process inventory) are taken as an average over a period of time.

 The utilization of process resources is the proportion of available time that the resources within the process are performing useful work.

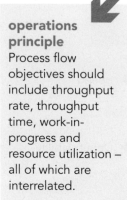

operations principle
Process flow objectives should include throughput rate, throughput time, work-in-progress and resource utilization – all of which are interrelated.

Standardization of processes

One of the most important process design objectives, especially in large organizations, concerns the extent to which process designs should be standardized. By standardization in this context we mean 'doing things in the same way' or, more formally, 'adopting a common sequence of activities, methods and use of equipment'. It is a significant issue in large organizations because, very often, different ways of carrying out similar or identical tasks emerge over time in the various parts of the organization. But, why not allow many different ways of doing the same thing? That would give a degree of autonomy and freedom to individuals and teams to exercise their discretion. The problem is that allowing numerous ways of doing things causes confusion, misunderstandings and, eventually, inefficiency. In healthcare processes, it can even cause preventable deaths. For example, the Royal College of Physicians in the UK revealed that there were more than 100 types of charts that were used for monitoring patients' vital signs in use in UK hospitals.[4] This leads to confusion, they said. Potentially, thousands of hospital deaths could be prevented if doctors and nurses used a standardized bed chart. Because hospitals can use different charts, doctors and nurses have to learn how to read new ones when they move jobs. They recommended that there should be just one chart and one process for all staff who check on patients' conditions.

Standardization is also an important objective in the design of some services and products, for similar reasons (see Chapter 3). The practical dillema for most organizations is how to draw the line between processes that are required to be standardized, and those that are allowed to be different.

operations principle
Standardizing processes can give some significant advantages, but not every process can be standardized.

Fast (but not too fast) food drive-throughs[3]

There is some dispute about who established the first drive-through (or drive-thu, if you prefer). Some claim it was the In-N-Out in California. Other claimants include the Pig Stand restaurant in Los Angeles, where Royce Hailey first promoted the drive-through service, allowing customers to simply drive by the back door of the restaurant where the chef would come out and deliver the restaurant's famous 'Barbequed Pig' sandwiches, and Red's Giant Hamburg in Springfield, Missouri. What became apparent though, as the drive-through idea began to spread (and include services other than fast food such as Banks) was that their design could have a huge impact on their efficiency and profitability. Today, drive-through processes are slicker, and far, far, faster, although most stick to a proven formula with orders generally placed by the customer using a microphone and picked up at a window. It is a system that allows drive-throughs to provide fast and dependable

service. In fact, there is strong competition between drive-throughs to design the fastest and most reliable process. For example, some Starbuck's drive-throughs have strategically placed cameras at the order boards so that servers can recognise regular customers and start making their order - even before it's placed. Other drive-throughs have experimented with simpler menu boards and see-through food bags to ensure greater accuracy. There is no point in being fast if you don't deliver what the customer ordered. These details matter. It has been estimated that sales increase one per cent for every six seconds saved at a drive-through. One experiment in making drive through process times slicker was carried out by a group of McDonalds restaurants. On California's central coast 150 miles from Los Angeles, a call centre took orders remotely from 40 McDonald's outlets around the country. The orders were then sent back to the restaurants and the food was assembled only a

few meters from where the order was placed. Although saving only a few seconds on each order, it could add up to extra sales at busy times of the day. A good drive-through process should also help customers to contribute to speeding things up. So, for example, menu items must be easy to read and understand.

This is why, what are often called, 'combo meals' (burger, fries and a cola), can save time at the ordering stage. By contrast, complex individual items or meals that require customisation can slow down the process. This can become an issue for drive-through operators when fashion moves towards customised salads and sandwiches. Yet there are signs that above a certain speed of service, other aspects of process performance become more important. As one drive-through chief operations manager points out, *"you can get really fast but ruin the overall experience, because now you're not friendly."* ● ● ●

Environmentally sensitive process design

With the issues of environmental protection becoming more important, process designers have to take account of 'green' (sustainability) issues. In many developed countries, legislation has already provided some basic standards. Interest has focused on some fundamental issues:

★ **The sources of inputs** to a product or service. (Will they damage rainforests? Will they use up scarce minerals? Will they exploit the poor, or use child labour?)

★ **Quantities and sources of energy** consumed in the process. (Do plastic beverage bottles use more energy than glass ones? Should waste heat be recovered and used in fish farming?)

★ **The amounts and type of waste material** that are created in the manufacturing processes. (Can this waste be recycled efficiently, or must it be burnt or buried in landfill sites?)

★ **The life of the product itself.** (If a product has a long, useful life, will it consume fewer resources than a short-life product?)

★ **The end-of-life of the product.** (Will the redundant product be difficult to dispose of in an environmentally friendly way?)

Designers are faced with complex trade-offs between these factors, although it is not always easy to obtain all the information that is needed to make the 'best' choices. To help make more rational decisions in the design activity, some industries are experimenting with life-cycle analysis. This technique analyses all the production inputs, the life-cycle use of the product and its final disposal, in terms of total energy used and all emitted wastes. The inputs and wastes are evaluated at *every* stage of a service or product's creation, beginning with the extraction or farming of the basic raw materials.

operations principle
The design of any process should include consideration of ethical and environmental issues.

How are processes currently designed?

Often, process design is in fact the redesign of an existing process, and a useful starting point is to fully understand how the current process operates. However, existing processes are not always sufficiently well-defined or described. Sometimes this is because they have developed over time without ever being formally recorded, or they may have been changed (perhaps improved) informally by the individuals who work in the process. But processes that are not formally defined can be interpreted in different ways, leading to confusion and inhibiting improvement. So, it is important to have some recorded visual descriptor of a process that can be agreed by all those who are involved in it. This is where process 'mapping' comes in.

operations principle
Process mapping is needed to expose the reality of process behaviour.

Process mapping

Process mapping simply involves describing processes in terms of how the activities within the process relate to each other. There are many techniques that can be used for process mapping (or process blueprinting, or process analysis, as it is sometimes called). However, all the techniques identify the different *types* of activity that take place during the process and show the flow of materials or people or information through the process.

PROCESS MAPPING SYMBOLS

Process mapping symbol**s** are used to classify different types of activity. And although there is no universal set of symbols used all over the world for any type of process, there are some that are commonly used. Most of these derive either from the early days of 'scientific' management, around a century ago or, more recently, from information system flowcharting. Figure 5.2 shows the symbols we shall use here.

These symbols can be arranged in order, and in series or in parallel, to describe any process. For example, Figure 5.3 shows one of the processes used in a theatre lighting operation. The company hires out lighting and stage effects equipment to theatrical companies and event organizers. Customers' calls are routed to the store technician. After discussing their requirements, the technician checks the equipment availability file to see if the equipment can be supplied from the company's own stock on the required dates. If the equipment cannot be supplied in-house, customers may be asked whether they want the company to try and obtain it from other possible suppliers. This offer depends on how busy and how helpful individual technicians are.

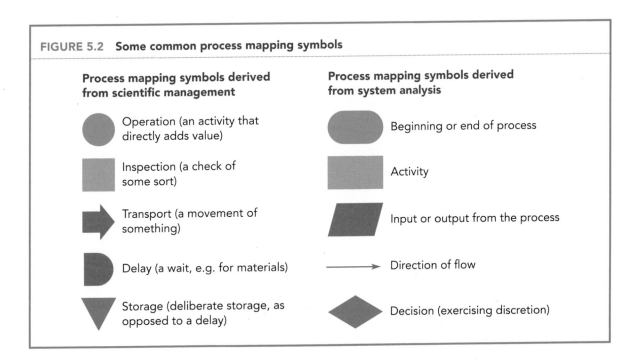

FIGURE 5.2 **Some common process mapping symbols**

Process mapping symbols derived from scientific management

- Operation (an activity that directly adds value)
- Inspection (a check of some sort)
- Transport (a movement of something)
- Delay (a wait, e.g. for materials)
- Storage (deliberate storage, as opposed to a delay)

Process mapping symbols derived from system analysis

- Beginning or end of process
- Activity
- Input or output from the process
- Direction of flow
- Decision (exercising discretion)

FIGURE 5.3   Process map for 'enquire-to-delivery' process at stage lighting operation

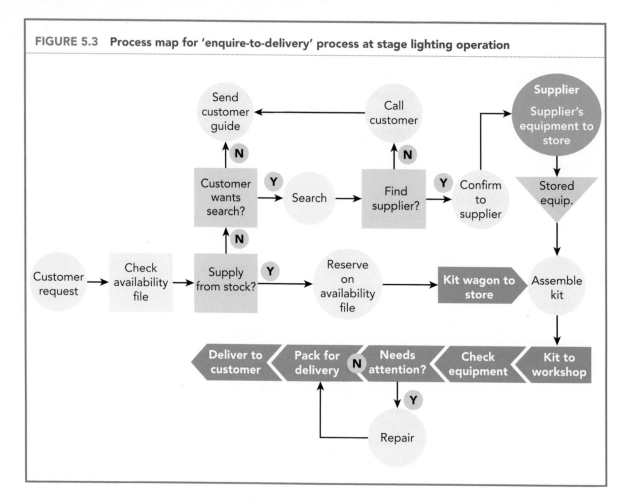

Sometimes customers decline the offer and a 'Guide to Customers' leaflet is sent to the customer. If the customer does want a search, the technician will call potential suppliers in an attempt to find available equipment. If this is not successful the customer is informed, but if suitable equipment is located it is reserved for delivery to the company's site. If equipment can be supplied from the company's own stores, it is reserved on the equipment availability file, and the day before it is required a 'kit wagon' is taken to the store where all the required equipment is assembled, taken back to the workshop, checked and if any equipment is faulty, it is repaired at this point. After that it is packed in special cases and delivered to the customer.

DIFFERENT LEVELS OF PROCESS MAPPING

For a large process, drawing process maps at this level of detail can be complex. This is why processes are often mapped at a more aggregated level, called high-level process mapping, before more detailed maps are drawn. Figure 5.4 illustrates this for the total 'supply-and-install' lighting process in the stage lighting operation. At the highest level, the process can be drawn simply as an input–transformation–output process, with materials and customers as its input resources and lighting services as outputs. No details of how inputs are transformed into outputs are included. At a slightly lower or more detailed level, what is sometimes called an outline process map (or chart) identifies the

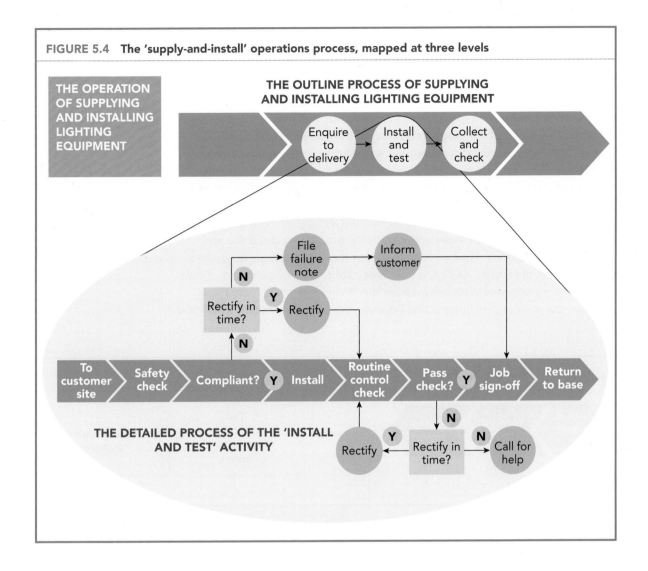

FIGURE 5.4 The 'supply-and-install' operations process, mapped at three levels

sequence of activities, but only in a general way. So, the process of 'enquire-to-delivery' that is shown in detail in Figure 5.3 is here reduced to a single activity. At the more detailed level, all the activities are shown in a 'detailed process map' (the activities within the process 'install-and-test' are shown).

Although not shown in Figure 5.4, an even more micro set of process activities could be mapped within each of the detailed process activities. Such a micro-detailed process map could specify every single motion involved in each activity. Some quick-service restaurants, for example, do exactly that. In the lighting hire company example, most activities would not be mapped in any more detail than that shown in Figure 5.4. Some activities, such as 'return to base', are probably too straightforward to be worth mapping any further. Other activities, such as 'rectify faulty equipment', may rely on the technician's skills and discretion to the extent that the activity has too much variation and is too complex to map in detail. Some activities, however, may need mapping in more detail to ensure quality or to protect the company's interests. For example, the activity of safety checking the customer's site to ensure that it is compliant with safety regulations will need specifying in some detail to ensure that the company can prove it exercised its legal responsibilities.

PROCESS VISIBILITY

It is sometimes useful to map such processes in a way that makes the degree of visibility of each part of the process obvious. This allows those parts of the process with high visibility to be designed so that they enhance the customer's perception of the process. Figure 5.5 shows yet another part of the lighting equipment company's operation: the 'collect-and-check' process. The process is mapped to show the visibility of each activity to the customer. Here, four levels of visibility are used. There is no hard and fast rule about this; many processes simply distinguish between those activities that the customer could see and those that they couldn't. The boundary between these two categories is often called the 'line of visibility'. In Figure 5.5, three categories of visibility are shown. At the very highest level of visibility, above the 'line of interaction', are those activities that involve direct interaction between the lighting company's staff and

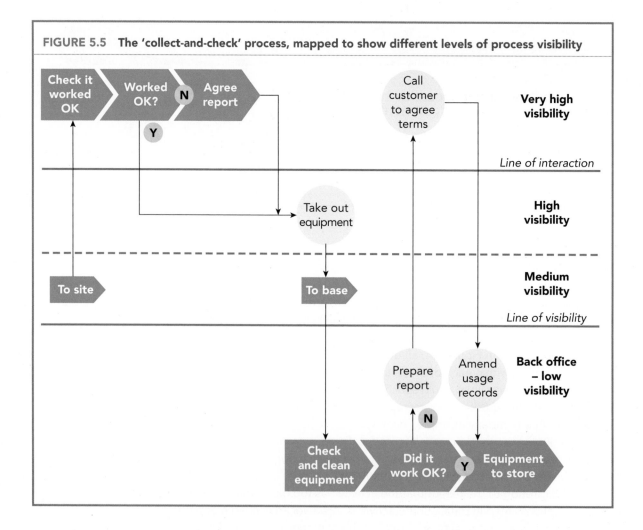

FIGURE 5.5   The 'collect-and-check' process, mapped to show different levels of process visibility

Operations in practice

Puncturing the line of visibility (by mistake)[5]

Sometimes it gets embarrassing when customers see through the line of visibility. This happened when staff at Sainsbury's, a UK supermarket, mistakenly put up in its window a poster encouraging their workers to get customers to spend more. The poster, urging staff to get people to spend an extra 50p, appeared in a store in east London. It read: 'Fifty pence challenge: Let's encourage every customer to spend an additional 50p during each shopping trip between now and the year-end.' Unfortunately, before the mistake was noticed, a customer took a picture and posted it on Twitter saying: '@sainsburys not sure this is supposed to be in your window' Quickly Sainsbury's tweeted back, saying it should have remained behind closed doors and was meant for staff only. A spokesperson for Sainsbury's said: "We often use posters to make store targets fun and achievable for our colleagues. They are intended for colleague areas in the store, but this one was mistakenly put on public display." ● ● ●

the customer. Other activities take place at the customer's site or in the presence of the customer, but involve less or no direct interaction. Yet further activities (the two transport activities in this case) have some degree of visibility because they take place away from the company's base and are visible to potential customers, but they are not visible to the immediate customer.

Are process tasks and capacity configured appropriately?

Throughput time, cycle time and work in progress

After describing a process by mapping its activities, the next stage of analysing it is to understand the nature of, and relationship between, its throughput time, cycle time and work in progress. Throughput time is the elapsed time between an item entering the process and leaving it, cycle time is the average time between items being processed and work in progress is the number of items within the process at any point in time. In addition, the 'work content' for each item will also be important for some analysis. Work content is the total amount of work required to produce a unit of output. For example, suppose that in an assemble-to-order sandwich shop, the time to assemble and sell a sandwich (the work content) is two minutes and that two people are staffing the process. Each member of staff will serve a customer every two minutes; therefore, every two minutes two customers are being served and so, on average, a customer is emerging from the process every minute (this is the cycle time of the process). When customers join the queue in the process they become work in progress (sometimes written as WIP). If the queue is ten-people long (including that customer) when the customer joins it, he or she will have to wait ten minutes to emerge from the process. Or, put more succinctly:

> **operations principle**
> Process analysis derives from an understanding of the required process cycle time.

$$\text{Throughput time} = \text{Work in progress} \times \text{Cycle time}$$

In this case:

$$10 \text{ minutes wait} = 10 \text{ people in the system} \times 1 \text{ minute per person}$$

LITTLE'S LAW

This mathematical relationship
(throughput time = work in progress × cycle time) is called Little's Law. It is simple but very useful, and it works for any stable process. Little's Law states that the average number of things in the system is the product of the average rate at which things leave the system and average time each one spends in the system. Or, put another way, the average number of objects in a queue is the product of the entry rate and the average holding time. For example, suppose it is decided that in a new sandwich-assembly and sales process, the average number of customers in the process should be limited to around ten and the maximum time a customer is in the process should be, on average, four minutes. If the time to assemble and sell a sandwich (from customer request to the customer leaving the process) in the new process has been reduced to 1.2 minutes, how many staff should be serving?

Putting this into Little's Law:

$$\text{Throughput time} = 4 \text{ minutes}$$

and

$$\text{Work in progress (WIP)} = 10$$

So, since

$$\text{Throughput time} = \text{WIP} \times \text{Cycle time}$$

$$\text{Cycle time} = \frac{\text{Throughput time}}{\text{WIP}}$$

$$\text{The Cycle time for the process} = \frac{4}{10} = 0.4 \text{ minutes}$$

Worked example

Every year it was the same. All the workstations in the building had to be renovated (tested, new software installed, etc.) and there was only one week in which to do it. The one week fell in the middle of the August vacation period, when the renovation process would cause minimum disruption to normal working. Last year the company's 500 workstations had all been renovated within one working week (40 hours). Each renovation last year took, on average, two hours, and 25 technicians had completed the process within the week. This year there would be 530 workstations to renovate but the company's IT support unit had devised a faster testing and renovation routine that would only take, on average, one and a half hours instead of two hours. How many technicians would be needed this year to complete the renovation processes within the week?

Last year:

$$\text{Work in progress (WIP)} = 500 \text{ workstations}$$
$$\text{Time available (Tt)} = 40 \text{ hours}$$
$$\text{Average time to renovate} = 2 \text{ hours}$$
$$\text{Therefore, throughput rate (Tr)} = {}^{1}/_{2} \text{ hour per technician}$$
$$= 0.5 \text{ N}$$

Where
$$N = \text{number of technicians}$$

Little's Law
$$\text{WIP} = \text{Tt} \times \text{Tr}$$
$$500 = 40 \times 0.5N$$
$$N = \frac{500}{40 \times 0.5}$$
$$= 25 \text{ technicians}$$

This year:

$$\text{Work in progress (WIP)} = 530 \text{ workstations}$$
$$\text{Time available (Tt)} = 40 \text{ hours}$$
$$\text{Average time to renovate} = 1.5 \text{ hours}$$
$$\text{Throughput rate (Tr)} = 1/1.5 \text{ per technician}$$
$$= 0.67N$$

where
$$N = \text{number of technicians}$$

Little's Law
$$\text{WIP} = \text{Tt} \times \text{Tr}$$
$$530 = 40 \times 0.67N$$
$$N = \frac{530}{40 \times 0.67}$$
$$= 19.88 \text{ (say 20) technicians}$$

Worked example

A vehicle licensing centre receives application documents, keys in details, checks the information provided on the application, classifies the application according to the type of licence required, confirms payment and then issues and mails the licence. It is currently processing an average of 5,000 licences every 8-hour day. A recent spot check found 15,000 applications that were 'in progress' or waiting to be processed. The sum of all activities that are required to process an application is 25 minutes. What is the throughput efficiency of the process?

$$\text{Work in progress} = 15000 \text{ applications}$$

$$\text{Cycle time} = \text{time producing}$$

$$\frac{\text{Time producing}}{\text{Number produced}} = \frac{8 \text{ hours}}{5000} = \frac{480 \text{ minutes}}{5000}$$

$$= 0.096 \text{ minutes}$$

From Little's Law,
throughput time = WIP × Cycle time

$$\text{Throughput time} = 15000 \times 0.096$$

$$= 1440 \text{ minutes} = 24 \text{ hours}$$

$$= 3 \text{ days of working}$$

$$\text{Throughput efficiency} = \frac{\text{Work content}}{\text{Throughput time}}$$

$$= \frac{25}{1440} = 1.74 \text{ per cent}$$

Although the process is achieving a throughput time of 3 days (which seems reasonable for this kind of process), the applications are only being worked on for 1.7 per cent of the time they are in the process. ● ● ●

That is, a customer should emerge from the process every 0.4 minutes, on average.

Given that an individual can be served in 1.2 minutes,

$$\text{the number of servers required} = \frac{1.2}{0.4} = 3$$

In other words, three servers would serve three customers in 1.2 minutes, which is one customer in 0.4 minutes.

operations principle

Little's Law states that throughput time = work in progress × cycle time.

THROUGHPUT EFFICIENCY

This idea that the throughput time of a process is different from the work content of whatever it is processing has important implications. What it means is that for significant amounts of time, no useful work is being done to the materials, information or customers that are progressing through the process. In the case of the simple example of the sandwich process described earlier, customer throughput time is restricted to 4 minutes, but the work content of the task (serving the customer) is only 1.2 minutes. So, the item being processed (the customer) is only being 'worked on' for 1.2/4 = 30 per cent of its time. This is called the 'throughput efficiency' of the process.

$$\text{Percentage throughput efficiency} = \frac{\text{Work content}}{\text{Throughput time}} \times 100$$

In this case, the throughput efficiency is very high, relative to most processes, perhaps because the 'items' being processed are customers who react badly to waiting. In most material and information-transforming processes, throughput efficiency is far lower – usually in single percentage figures.

VALUE-ADDED THROUGHPUT EFFICIENCY

The approach to calculating throughput efficiency that is described above assumes that all the 'work content' is actually needed. Changing a process can significantly reduce the time that is needed to complete the task. Therefore, work content is actually dependent upon the methods and technology used to perform the task. It may be also that individual elements of a task may not be considered 'value-added'. In the Intel expense report example, the new method eliminated some steps because they were 'not worth it' – that is, they were not seen as adding value. So, value-added throughput efficiency restricts the concept of work content to only those tasks that are literally adding value to whatever is being processed. This often eliminates activities such as movement, delays and some inspections.

For example, if in the licensing worked example, of the 25 minutes of work content only 20 minutes was actually adding value, then:

$$\text{Value-added throughput efficiency} = \frac{20}{1440} = 1.39 \text{ per cent}$$

Workflow[6]

When the transformed resource in a process is information (or documents containing information), and when information technology is used to move, store and manage the information, process design is sometimes called 'workflow' or 'workflow management'. It is defined as, 'the automation of procedures where documents, information or tasks are passed between participants according to a defined set of rules to achieve, or contribute to, an overall business goal'. Although workflow may be managed manually, it is almost always managed using an IT system. The term is also often associated with business process re-engineering (see Chapter 13). More specifically, workflow is concerned with the following:

 analysis, modelling, definition and subsequent operational implementation of business processes;

 the technology that supports the processes;

the procedural (decision) rules that move information/documents through processes;

 defining the process in terms of the sequence of work activities, the human skills needed to perform each activity and the appropriate IT resources.

Process bottlenecks

A bottleneck in a process is the activity or stage where congestion occurs because the workload placed is greater than the capacity to cope with it. In other words, it is the most overloaded part of a process. And as such it will dictate the rate at which the whole process can operate. For example, look at the simple process illustrated in Figure 5.6. It has four stages and the total amount of work to complete the work required for each item passing through the process is 10 minutes. In this simple case, each of the four stages has the same capacity. In the first case (a) the 10 minutes of work is equally allocated between the four stages, each having 2.5 minutes of work. This means that items will progress smoothly through the process without any stage holding up the flow, and the cycle time of the process is 2.5 minutes. In the second case (b) the work has not been allocated evenly. In fact, this is usually the case because usually it is difficult (in fact close to impossible) to allocate work absolutely equally. In this case, stage 4 of the process has the greatest load (3 minutes). It is the bottleneck, and will constrain the cycle time of the process to 3 minutes.

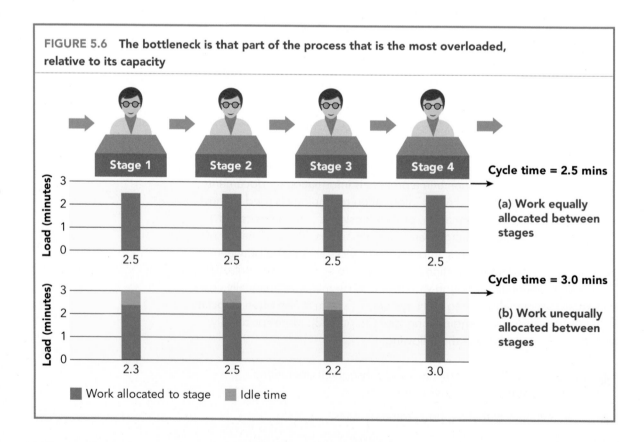

FIGURE 5.6 **The bottleneck is that part of the process that is the most overloaded, relative to its capacity**

Bottlenecks reduce the efficiency of a process because, although the bottleneck stage will be fully occupied, the other stages will be underloaded. In fact, the total amount of time invested in processing each item is four times the cycle time because, for every unit produced, all four stages have invested an amount of time equal to the cycle time. When the work is equally allocated between the stages, the total time invested in each product or service produced is $4 \times 2.5 = 10$ minutes. However, when work is unequally allocated, as illustrated, the time invested is $3.0 \times 4 = 12$ minutes. So, in total, 2 minutes of time (16.67 per cent of the total) is wasted. The activity of trying to allocate work equally between stages is called 'balancing', and the wasted time, expressed as a percentage, is called 'balancing loss'.

operations principle
Allocating work equally to each stage in a process (balancing) smooths flow and avoids bottlenecks.

Allocating work to process stages must respect the 'precedence' of the individual tasks that make up the total work content of the job that the process is performing. The most common way of showing task precedence is by using a 'precedence diagram'. This is a representation of the ordering of the elements, where individual tasks are represented by circles connected by arrows, which signify the ordering of the tasks. Figure 5.7 in the following worked example illustrates how precedence diagrams can be used.

operations principle
Process design must respect task precedence.

Arranging the stages

All the stages necessary to fulfil the requirements of the process may not be arranged in a sequential 'single line'. For example, suppose a mortgage application process requires four stages working on the task to maintain a cycle time of one application processed every 15 minutes. One possible arrangement of the four stages would be to arrange them sequentially, each stage having 15 minutes' worth of work. However (theoretically), the same output rate could also be achieved by arranging the four stages as two shorter lines, each of two stages with 30 minutes' worth of work each. Alternatively, following this logic to its ultimate conclusion, the stages could be arranged as four parallel stages, each responsible for the whole work content. Figure 5.8 shows these options.

This is a simplified example, but it represents a genuine issue. Should the process be organized as a single 'long-thin' arrangement, or as several 'short-fat' parallel arrangements, or somewhere in between? (Note that 'long' means the number of stages and 'fat' means the amount of work allocated to each stage.) In any particular situation, there are usually technical constraints that limit either how 'long and thin' or how 'short and fat' the process can be, but there is usually a range of possible options within which a choice needs to be made. The advantages of each extreme of the long thin to short fat spectrum are very different, and help to explain why different arrangements are adopted.

Worked example

Karlstad Kakes (KK) is a manufacturer of speciality cakes, which has recently obtained a contract to supply a major supermarket chain with a speciality cake in the shape of a space rocket. It has been decided that the volumes required by the supermarket warrant a special production process to perform the finishing, decorating and packing of the cake. This line would have to carry out the elements shown in Table 5.2.

Figure 5.7 shows the precedence diagram for the total job. The initial order from the supermarket is for 5,000 cakes a week, and the number of hours worked by the factory is 40 per week. From this:

$$\text{The required cycle time} = \frac{40 \text{ h} \times 60 \text{ min}}{5000}$$

$$= 0.48 \text{ min}$$

The required number of stages

$$= \frac{1.68 \text{ min (the total work content)}}{0.48 \text{ min (the required cycle time)}}$$

$$= 3.5 \text{ stages}$$

TABLE 5.2 The individual tasks that make up the total job of the finishing, decorating and packing of the cake

▶ Task (a) – De-tin and trim

▶ Task (b) – Reshape

▶ Task (c) – Apply base fondant

▶ Task (d) – Clad in top fondant

▶ Task (e) – Apply red icing

▶ Task (f) – Apply green icing

▶ Task (g) – Apply blue icing

▶ Task (h) – Fix transfers

▶ Task (i) – Transfer to base and pack

The advantages of the long-thin arrangement include:

 Controlled flow of items. which is easy to manage.

 Simple handling. especially if the items being processed are heavy, large or difficult to move.

 Lower capital requirements. If a specialist piece of equipment is needed for one task in the job, only one piece of equipment would need to be purchased; on short-fat arrangements, every stage would need one.

This means four stages.

Working from the left on the precedence diagram, tasks a and b can be allocated to stage 1. Allocating task c to stage 1 would exceed the cycle time. In fact, only task c can be allocated to stage 2, because including task d would again exceed the cycle time. Task d can be allocated to stage 3. Either task e or f can also be allocated to stage 3, but not both or the cycle time would be exceeded. In this case, task e is chosen. The remaining tasks are then allocated to stage 4. The dotted lines in Figure 5.7 show the final allocation of tasks to each of the four stages. ● ● ●

FIGURE 5.7 Precedence diagram for Karlstad Kakes, with allocation of tasks to each stage

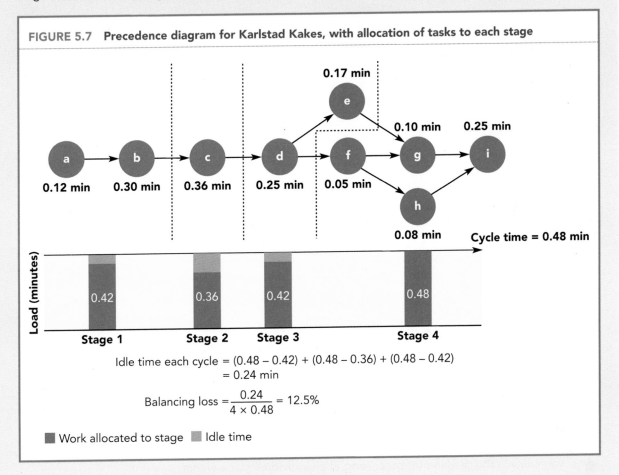

Idle time each cycle = (0.48 − 0.42) + (0.48 − 0.36) + (0.48 − 0.42)
= 0.24 min

Balancing loss = $\dfrac{0.24}{4 \times 0.48}$ = 12.5%

■ Work allocated to stage ■ Idle time

 More efficient operation. If each stage is only performing a small part of the total job, the person at the stage will have a higher proportion of direct productive work as opposed to the non-productive parts of the job, such as picking up tools and materials.

The advantages of the short-fat arrangement include:

 Higher-mix flexibility. If the process needs to work on several types of item, each stage or whole process could specialize in different types.

 Higher-volume flexibility. As volume varies, stages can simply be closed down or started up as required; long-thin arrangements would need rebalancing each time the cycle time changed.

Higher robustness.   If one stage breaks down or ceases operation in some way, the other parallel stages are unaffected; a long-thin arrangement would cease operating completely.

 Less-monotonous work.   In the mortgage example, the staff in the short-fat arrangement are repeating their tasks only every hour; in the long-thin arrangement it is every 15 minutes.

Is process variability recognized?

So far in our treatment of process design we have assumed that there is no significant variability, either in the demand to which the process is expected to respond, or in the time taken for the process to perform its various activities. Clearly, this is not the case in reality. So, it is important to look at the variability that can affect processes and to take account of it.

There are many reasons why variability occurs in processes. These can include: the late (or early) arrival of material, information or customers; a temporary malfunction or breakdown of process technology within a stage of the process; the recycling of 'mis-processed' materials, information or customers to an earlier stage in the process; or variation in the requirements of items being processed. All these sources of variation interact with each other, but result in two fundamental types of variability:

 variability in the demand for processing at an individual stage within the process, usually expressed in terms of variation in the inter-arrival times of items to be processed;

 variation in the time taken to perform the activities (i.e. process a unit) at each stage.

To understand the effect of arrival variability on process performance, it is first useful to examine what happens to process performance in a very simple process as arrival time changes under conditions of no variability. For example, the simple process shown in Figure 5.9 is comprised of one stage that performs exactly 10 minutes of work. Items arrive at the process at a constant and predictable rate. If the arrival rate is one unit every 30 minutes, then the process will be utilized for only 33.33% of the time, and the items will

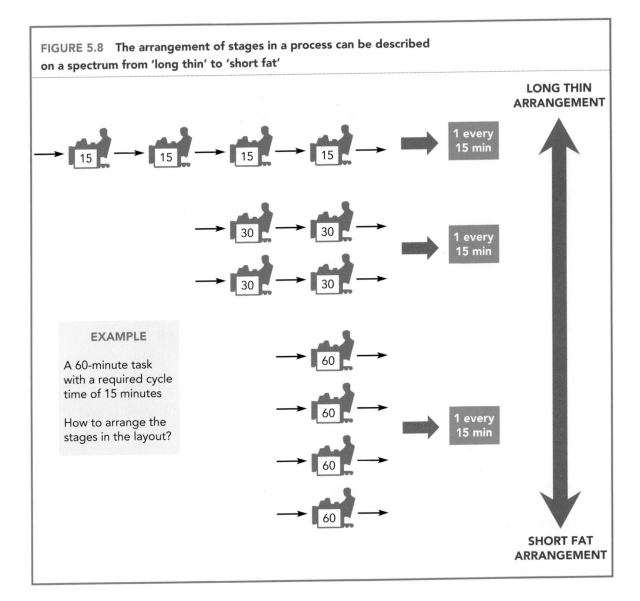

FIGURE 5.8 The arrangement of stages in a process can be described on a spectrum from 'long thin' to 'short fat'

LONG THIN ARRANGEMENT

SHORT FAT ARRANGEMENT

EXAMPLE

A 60-minute task with a required cycle time of 15 minutes

How to arrange the stages in the layout?

never have to wait to be processed. This is shown as point A on Figure 5.9. If the arrival rate increases to one arrival every 20 minutes, the utilization increases to 50%, and again the items will not have to wait to be processed. This is point B on Figure 5.9. If the arrival rate increases to one arrival every 10 minutes, the process is now fully utilized, but, because a unit arrives just as the previous one has finished being processed, no unit has to wait. This is point C on Figure 5.9. However, if the arrival rate ever exceeded one unit every 10 minutes, the waiting line in front of the process activity would build up indefinitely, as is shown as point D in Figure 5.9. So, in a perfectly constant and predictable world, the relationship between process waiting time and utilization is a rectangular function, as shown by the red line in Figure 5.9.

operations principle
Variability in a process acts to reduce its efficiency.

FIGURE 5.9   The relationship between process utilization and the number of items waiting to be processed for constant and variable arrival and process times

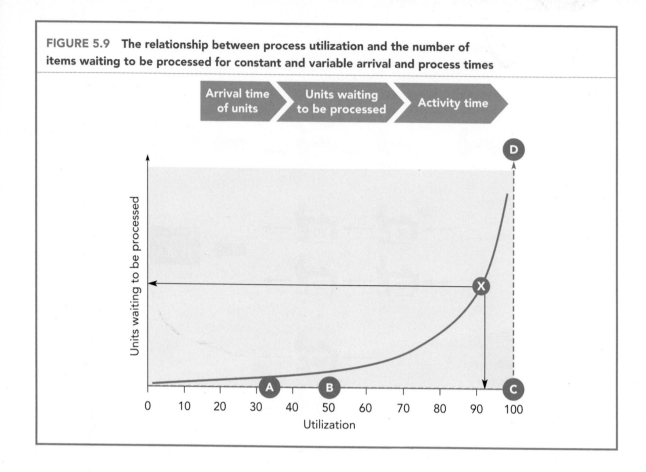

However, when arrival and process times are variable, then sometimes the process will have items waiting to be processed, while at other times the process will be idle, waiting for items to arrive. Therefore, the process will have both a 'non-zero' average queue and be underutilized in the same period. So, a more realistic point is that shown as point X in Figure 5.9. If the average arrival time were to be changed with the same variability, the blue line in Figure 5.9 would show the relationship between average waiting time and process utilization. As the process moves closer to 100% utilization, the higher the average waiting time will become. Or, to put it another way, the only way to guarantee very low waiting times for the items is to suffer low process utilization.

The greater the variability in the process, the more the waiting time-utilization deviates from the simple rectangular function of the 'no variability' conditions that were shown in Figure 5.9. A set of curves for a typical process is shown in Figure 5.10 (a). This phenomenon has important implications for the design of processes. In effect, it presents three options to process designers wishing to improve the waiting time or utilization performance of their processes, as shown in Figure 5.10 (b):

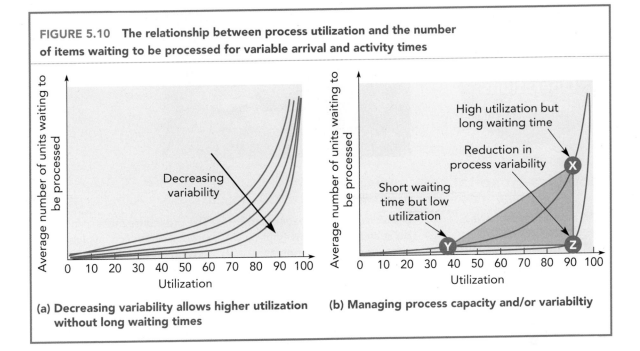

FIGURE 5.10 The relationship between process utilization and the number of items waiting to be processed for variable arrival and activity times

(a) Decreasing variability allows higher utilization without long waiting times

(b) Managing process capacity and/or variabiltiy

 accept long average waiting times and achieve high utilization (point X);

 accept low utilization and achieve short average waiting times (point Y);

 reduce the variability in arrival times, activity times, or both, and achieve higher utilization and short waiting times (point Z).

To analyze processes with both inter-arrival and activity time variability, queuing or 'waiting line' analysis can be used. But, do not dismiss the relationship shown in Figures 5.9 and 5.10 as some minor technical phenomenon. It is far more than this. It identifies an important choice in process design that could have strategic implications. Which is more important to a business – fast throughput time, or high utilization of its resources? The only way to have both of these simultaneously is to reduce variability in its processes, which may itself require strategic decisions such as limiting the degree of customization of products or services, or imposing stricter limits on how products or services can be delivered to customers, and so on. It also demonstrates an important point concerned with the day-to-day management of process – the only way to absolutely guarantee a hundred-per-cent utilization of resources, is to accept an infinite amount of work in progress and/or waiting time.

operations principle
Process variability results in simultaneous waiting and resource under-utilization.

Operations in practice

Shouldice Hospital cuts variability[7]

Shouldice Hospital is a Canadian hernia-treatment hospital. Its approach to hernia treatment started when Dr Earle Shouldice, the founder, removed the appendix from a seven-year-old girl who refused to stay quietly in bed. In spite of her activity, no harm was done. In fact, he found that encouraging post-operative activity could make recovery times shorter and more predictable. The hospital has a very standardized surgical procedure, called the 'Shouldice method', which all its surgeons follow strictly. Pre-surgery, Shouldice sends surveys to its patients asking for information that helps ensure that the patients are good candidates for the treatment Shouldice offers (this further helps reduce variability in process time).

Shouldice requires patients to be at an acceptable weight appropriate to their height. Prospective patients who are overweight must lose weight. Patients enter the hospital the day before surgery and are given a briefing about the procedures to be followed the next day. The night before the operation is also intended as an opportunity for patients to come to know each other – Shouldice encourages patients to work together to promote recovery. The hospital schedules the surgeries in such a way that variability in the arrivals of customers is virtually non-existent. This means that Shouldice can operate in a routine and regular manner. Which, in turn, means that it can keep nearly all its beds full without creating customer waits.

The procedure most commonly used at Shouldice involves sewing muscle layers together in an overlapping manner – a technique that is said to be particularly reliable. After discharge, Shouldice sends out an email newsletter to all of its patients that includes a questionnaire for Shouldice's post-operative follow-up programme, which shows that fewer than 1 per cent of patients have a recurrence after hernia repair. The questionnaire also helps the hospital to refine the knowledge that keeps its procedures reliable. So, by reducing the variability in its operations ('operations' in both senses of the word), the hospital has designed a set of processes that can both be highly utilized and reduce customer waiting time. ●●●

Summary answers to key questions

Each chapter has a 'Summary answers to key questions' section. Use it to check your understanding of the issues covered in the chapter.

WHY IS IT IMPORTANT TO GET THE DETAILS OF PROCESS DESIGN CORRECT?

★ The detailed design of processes is important because their performance, and process performance, affects the performance of the whole operation.

★ The objective of process design is to make sure that the performance of the process is appropriate for whatever it is trying to achieve.

WHAT SHOULD BE THE OBJECTIVES OF PROCESS DESIGN?

★ The purpose of process design is to meet the needs of customers and the business through achieving appropriate levels of quality, speed, dependability, flexibility and cost.

★ The design activity must also take account of environmental issues. These include examination of the source and suitability of materials, the sources and quantities of energy consumed, the amount and type of waste material, the life of the product itself and the end-of-life state of the product.

HOW ARE PROCESSES CURRENTLY DESIGNED?

★ Processes are designed initially by breaking them down into their individual activities. Often, common symbols are used to represent types of activity. The sequence of activities in a process is then indicated by the sequence of symbols representing activities. This is called 'process mapping'. Alternative process designs can be compared using process maps, and improved processes considered in terms of their operations performance objectives.

ARE PROCESS TASKS AND CAPACITY CONFIGURED APPROPRIATELY?

 Process performance in terms of throughput time, work in progress and cycle time are related by a formula known as Little's Law. Throughput time equals work in progress multiplied by cycle time.

 The stages in processes can be configured in series or in parallel. Depending on how this is done, a process can achieve a different balance between performance objectives.

IS PROCESS VARIABILITY RECOGNIZED?

 Variability has a significant effect on the performance of processes, particularly the relationship between waiting time and utilization.

Problems and applications

All chapters have Problems and application questions that will help you practice analyzing operations. They can be answered by reading the chapter. Model answers for the first question can be found on the companion website for this text.

1 ➜ One of the examples at the beginning of the chapter described 'drive-through' fast food processes. Think about (or, better still, visit) a drive-through service and try mapping what you can see of the process (plus what you can infer from what may be happening 'behind the scenes').

2 ➜ A laboratory process receives medical samples from hospitals in its area and then subjects them to a number of tests that take place in different parts of the laboratory. The average response time for the laboratory to complete all its tests and mail the results back to the hospital (measured from the time that the sample for analysis arrives) is 3 days. A recent process map has shown that, of the 60 minutes that are needed to complete all the tests, the tests themselves took 30 minutes, moving the samples between each test area took 10 minutes and double-checking the results took a further 20 minutes. What is the throughput efficiency of this process? What is the value-added throughput efficiency of the process? (State any assumptions that you are making.) If the process is rearranged so that all the tests are performed in the same area, thus eliminating the time to move between test areas, and the tests themselves are improved to half the amount of time needed for double-checking, what effect would this have on the value-added throughput efficiency?

3 ➜ "It is a real problem for us", said Angnyeta Larson. "We now have only ten working days between all the expense claims coming from the departmental coordinators and authorizing payments on the next month's payroll. This really is not long enough and we are already having problems during peak times." Angnyeta is the department head of the internal financial control department of a metropolitan authority in southern Sweden. Part of her department's responsibilities includes checking and processing expense claims from staff throughout the metropolitan authority and authorizing payment to the salaries payroll section. She has 12 staff who are trained to check expense claims and all of them are devoted full time to processing the claims in the two weeks (10 working days) prior to the deadline for informing the salaries section. The number of claims submitted over the year averages around 3,200, but this can vary between 1,000 during the quiet summer months up to 4,300 in peak months. Processing claims involve checking receipts, checking that claims meet with the strict financial allowances for different types of expenditure, checking all calculations, obtaining more data from the claimant if necessary and (eventually) sending an approval notification to salaries. The total processing time takes, on average, 20 minutes per claim. (a) How many staff does the process need, on average, for the lowest demand and for the highest demand? (b) If a more automated process involving electronic submission of claims could reduce the average processing time to 15 minutes, what effect would this have on the required staffing levels? (c) If department coordinators could be persuaded to submit their batched claims earlier (not always possible for all departments), so that the average time between submission of the claims to the finance department and the deadline for informing salaries section was increased to 15 working days, what effect would this have?

4   ➡ At the theatre, the interval during a performance of *King Lear* lasts for 20 minutes and in that time 86 people need to use the toilet cubicles. On average, a person spends 3 minutes in the cubicle. There are 10 cubicles available. (a) Does the theatre have enough toilets to deal with the demand? (b) If there are not enough cubicles, how long should the interval be to cope with demand?

5   ➡ A gourmet burger shop has a daily demand for 250 burgers and operates for 10 hours. (a) What is the required cycle time in minutes? (b) Assuming that each burger has 7.2 minutes of work required, how many servers are required? (c) If the burger shop has a three-stage process for making burgers and stage 1 takes 2.0 minutes, stage 2 takes 3.0 minutes and stage 3 takes 2.2 minutes, what is the balancing loss for the process?

Want to know more?

Chopra, S., Anupindi, R., Deshmukh S.D., Van Mieghem, J.A. and Zemel, E. (2012) *Managing Business Process Flows*, 3rd edition, Harlow, UK: Pearson.

➡ An excellent, although mathematical, approach to process design in general.

Hammer, M. (1990) 'Re-engineering work: Don't automate, obliterate', *Harvard Business Review*, July–August.

➡ This is the paper that launched the whole idea of business processes and process management in general to a wider managerial audience. Slightly dated but worth reading.

Hopp, W.J. and Spearman, M.L. (2001) *Factory Physics*, 2nd edition, New York: McGraw Hill.

➡ Very technical, so don't bother with it if you aren't prepared to get into the maths. However, some fascinating analysis, especially concerning Little's Law.

Mahal, A. (2010) *How Work Gets Done: Business Process Management, Basics and Beyond*, Buchanan, NY: Technics Publications.

➡ Certainly not a critical look at process management, but an easily digestible coverage of 'how to do it'.

Smith, H. and Fingar, P. (2003) *Business Process Management: The Third Wave*, Tampa, FL: Meghan-Kiffer Press.

➡ A popular book on process management from a BPR perspective.

Supply chain management

6

Introduction

How is it that businesses such as Apple, Toyota, Zara, and Maersk achieve notable results in highly competitive markets? Partly, it is down to their products and services, but partly also to the way they manage their supply chains. This is what supply chain management is concerned with – the way operations managers look beyond a purely internal view to also consider the performance of suppliers, and suppliers' suppliers, as well as customers, and customers' customers. In addition, operations are increasingly outsourcing many of their activities, buying more of their services and materials from outside specialists. So, the way they manage supplies to their operations becomes increasingly important, as does the integration of their distribution activities. In Chapter 2 we explored the structure and scope of operations; by contrast, this chapter is more concerned with how supply chains and networks are subsequently managed. Figure 6.1 shows the position of the ideas described in this chapter in the general model of operations management.

Key questions

What is supply chain management?

How do supply chains compete?

How should you manage supply chain relationships?

How should the supply side be managed?

How should the demand side be managed?

What are the dynamics of supply chains?

FIGURE 6.1 **This chapter examines supply chain management**

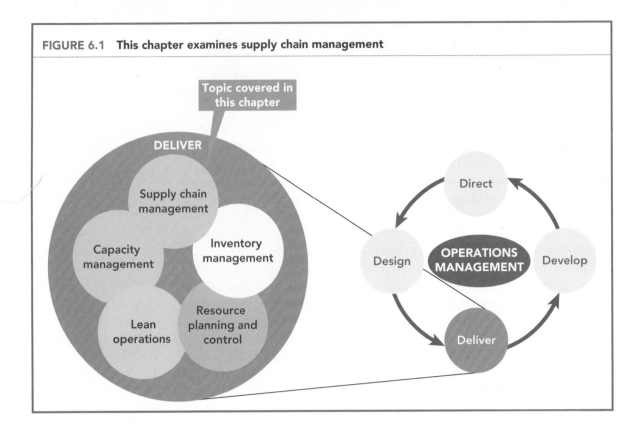

What is supply chain management?

S upply chain management (SCM) is the management of the relationships and flows between the 'string' of operations and processes that produce value in the form of products and services to the ultimate consumer. It is a holistic approach to managing across the boundaries of companies and of processes. Technically, supply *chains* are different to supply *networks*. A supply network is *all* the operations that are linked together so as to provide products and services through to end customers. In large supply networks, there can be many hundreds of supply chains of linked operations passing through a single operation (see Figures 6.2 and 6.3). Confusingly, the terms supply network management and supply chain management are often (mistakenly) used interchangeably. It is also worth noting that the 'flows' in supply chains are not restricted to the downstream flow of products and services from suppliers through to customers. Although the most obvious failure in supply chain management occurs when the downstream of products and services flow fails to meet

FIGURE 6.2 Supply chain management is concerned with managing the flow of materials and information between a string of operations, which form the strands (or 'chains') of a supply network

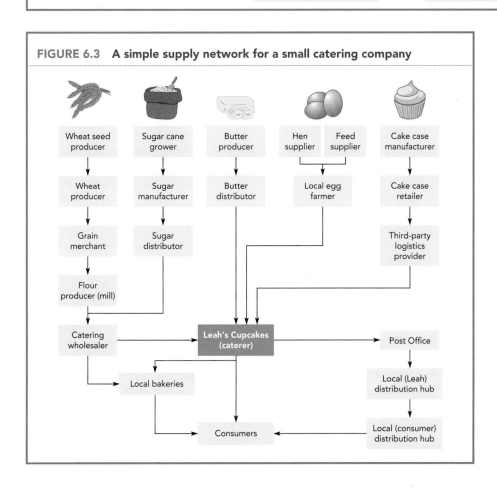

FLOW BETWEEN
PROCESSES

FLOW BETWEEN
PROCESSES

Supply network
management concerns
flow between operations

FLOW BETWEEN
PROCESSES

FLOW BETWEEN
PROCESSES

FLOW BETWEEN
PROCESSES

Supply chain management
concerns flow between a
string of operations

FLOW BETWEEN
PROCESSES

FLOW BETWEEN
PROCESSES

FIGURE 6.3 A simple supply network for a small catering company

Wheat seed producer → Wheat producer → Grain merchant → Flour producer (mill) → Catering wholesaler

Sugar cane grower → Sugar manufacturer → Sugar distributor

Butter producer → Butter distributor

Hen supplier, Feed supplier → Local egg farmer

Cake case manufacturer → Cake case retailer → Third-party logistics provider

Catering wholesaler → Leah's Cupcakes (caterer) → Post Office → Local (Leah) distribution hub → Local (consumer) distribution hub → Consumers

Catering wholesaler → Local bakeries

Leah's Cupcakes (caterer) → Local bakeries

Leah's Cupcakes (caterer) → Consumers

Local bakeries → Consumers

Operations in practice

Ocado[1]

The UK grocery market is tough. Giant retailers battle for increasingly cost-conscious customers, who also demand quality and service. So, when Mark Richardson, the head of Ocado's technology operation, was promoted to the newly created role of Operations Director it was greeted as an announcement that reinforced the importance of Ocado's high-tech operations processes. It was also seen as reflecting the urgent need for Ocado to get its state-of-the-art distribution centre operating at full efficiency. The company's on-time delivery performance, although still better than its rivals, had been slipping in the months prior to the announcement. This had been an unusual experience for Ocado, which was the only dedicated online supermarket in the UK and the largest dedicated online supermarket in the world. It had succeeded in reshaping the final 'business-to-consumer' configuration of the traditional food supply chain in its UK home market and, in the process, had become one of the most successful online grocers in the world.

In establishing itself as a major player in the online grocery market, one of Ocado's first decisions was to enter into a branding and sourcing arrangement with Waitrose, a leading high-quality UK supermarket, from where the vast majority of its products are still sourced. But, just as important, it has developed a supply process that provides both relative efficiency and high levels of service. (A typical Ocado delivery has a lower overall carbon footprint than walking to your local supermarket.) Most online grocers fulfil internet orders by gathering goods from the shelf of a local supermarket and then loading them in a truck for delivery. By contrast, from its distribution centre in Hatfield, 20 miles north of London, Ocado offers 'doorstep' delivery of around 230,000 orders per week, from a selection of over 50,000 Stock Keeping Units (SKUs), to over 588,000 active customers. The orders are centrally picked from a single, state-of-the-art, highly automated warehouse (the customer fulfilment centre or 'CFC'). This is a space the size of 10 football pitches; a 15-km system of conveyor belts handles upwards of 8,000 grocery containers an hour, which are then shipped to homes. The largely automated picking process, which was developed by its own software engineers, allows the company to pick and prepare groceries for delivery up to seven times faster than its rivals, reducing deterioration of fresh foods, in particular. Ocado's food waste at 0.3% of sales and its error rate of around 80 per million items are the lowest in the industry. Just as important as the physical distribution to the customers' doors is the ease of use of the company's website (Ocado.com) and the convenience of booking a delivery slot. Ocado offer reliable one-hour, next-day timeslots in an industry where two-hour timeslots prevail. This is made possible thanks, again, to the centralized model and world-class processes, systems and controls. Finally, Ocado makes a conscious effort to recruit people with customer-service skills and then train them as drivers, rather than vice versa. Drivers, known as 'customer service team members', are paid well above the industry norm and are empowered to process refunds and deal with customer concerns on the doorstep. ● ● ●

customer requirements, the root cause may be a failure in the upstream flow of information. Modern supply chain management is as much concerned with managing information flows (upstream and downstream) as it is with managing the flow of products and services.

Internal and external supply chains

Although we often describe supply chains as an interconnection of 'organizations', this does not necessarily mean that these 'organizations' are distinctly separate entities belonging to and managed by different owners. Earlier in the text, we pointed out how the idea of networks can be applied, not just at the supply network level of 'organization-to-organization' relationships, but also at the 'process-to-process', within-operation level and even at the 'resource-to-resource', within-process level. We also introduced the idea of internal customers and suppliers. Put these two related ideas together and one can understand how some of the issues that we will be discussing in the context of 'organization-to-organization' supply chains can also provide insight into internal 'process-to-process' supply chains.

operations principle
The supply chain concept applies to the internal relationships between processes as well as the external relationships between operations.

Tangible and intangible supply chains

Almost all the books, blogs and articles on supply chain management deal with relationships between what we call 'material transformation' operations – that is, operations concerned with the creation, movement, storage or sale of physical products. However, the idea of supply chains and supply networks applies equally to operations with largely, or exclusively, intangible inputs and outputs, such as financial services, retail shopping malls, insurance providers, healthcare operations, consultants, universities and so on. All these operations have suppliers and customers, they all purchase services, they all have to choose how they get their services to consumers. In other words, they all have to manage their supply chains.

operations principle
The supply chain concept applies to non-physical flow between operations and processes, as well as physical flow.

How do supply chains compete?

Supply chain management shares one common, and central, objective – to satisfy the end customer. All stages in the various chains that form the supply network must eventually include consideration of the final customer, no matter how far an individual operation is from the end customer. When a customer decides to make a purchase, he or she

Managing Apple's supply network

Apple is often credited with being the 'best supply chain in the world'. (In surveys, other companies voted as having excellent supply chains include McDonald's, Amazon.com, Unilever, Intel, Samsung Electronics and Coca Cola.) It is a title that is especially impressive when one considers the complexity of Apple's products and the company's strategy of frequently introducing new, and technologically advanced, products. Yet there is a connection between Apple's products and its supply chain. Innovative products that combine advanced functionality, a fast ramp-up of manufacturing capacity and customers who have a near-obsessive interest in the detail of design, will typically require innovative approaches to the development of their supply chains. In fact, because of the hyper-competitive nature of its markets and its reliance on innovative technology, Apple's supply chain organization integrates all its research and development, marketing, purchasing, outsourced manufacturing and logistics functions together. This allows it to achieve the detailed advanced planning that accelerated new-product introduction requires, sometimes by acquiring exclusive rights from its suppliers to secure strategic raw materials and components. The relationship with its suppliers is vital. Apple can use its financial muscle to guarantee sufficient supply capacity by placing large pre-orders with suppliers, which also prevents competitors from gaining access to the same manufacturing resources. Apple's supply chain is structured to give the company maximum visibility and, essentially, control over the design and nature of its products, right down to the smallest components. Apple is not alone in tightly controlling the design and manufacturing of its products and services. At about the same time, companies such as Google and Facebook were developing tighter relationships with their Asian hardware suppliers.

Although the extensive outsourcing of production has provided Apple with some significant advantages, it does not come without risk. Outsourcing can leave any company exposed to supply chain disruption caused by anything from natural disasters to alterations to international trade agreements. In addition, reputational risks over issues such as working conditions in its suppliers' factories, environmental damage from suppliers' production processes and employment practices, can damage a company's consumer image. Indeed, Apple has suffered from criticism of the work practices in its (or rather its suppliers') extended supply chain in Asia, including a large number of suicides at a giant factory in China of its major contract manufacturer Foxconn. ● ● ●

triggers action back along a whole series of supply chains in the network. All the businesses in the supply network pass on portions of that end-customer's money to each other, each retaining a margin for the value it has added. Thus, each operation in each chain should be satisfying its own customer, but also making sure that eventually the end customer is also satisfied.

Performance objectives for supply networks

The objective of any supply network is to meet the requirements of end customers by supplying appropriate products and services through its many supply chains. Doing this requires the supply network to achieve appropriate levels of the five operations performance objectives – quality, speed, dependability, flexibility and cost.

Quality   The quality of a product or service when it reaches the customer is a function of the quality performance of every operation in the chain that supplied it. The implication of this is that errors in each stage of the chain can multiply in their effect on end-customer service (if each of seven stages in a supply chain has a 1 per cent error rate, only 93.2 per cent of products or services will be of good quality on reaching the end customer – i.e. 0.99 to the power of 7). This is why only by every stage taking some responsibility for its own *and its suppliers'* performance, can a supply chain achieve high-end customer quality.

Speed   This has two meanings in a supply chain context. The first is how fast customers can be served, (the elapsed time between a customer requesting a product or service and receiving it in full). However, fast customer response can be achieved simply by over-resourcing or over-stocking within the supply chain. For example, very large stocks in a retail operation can reduce the chances of stock-out to almost zero, so reducing customer waiting time virtually to zero. Similarly, an accounting firm may be able to respond quickly to customer demand by having a very large number of accountants on standby waiting for demand that may (or may not) occur. An alternative perspective on speed is the time taken for goods and services to move through the chain – the throughput time. Products that move quickly down a supply chain from raw material suppliers through to retailers will spend little time as inventory, which has significant benefits (see Chapter 8).

Dependability   In supply chains, dependability is often measured as 'on time' and 'in full'. If the individual operations in a chain do not deliver as promised on time, there will be a tendency for customers to over-order, or order early, in order to provide some kind of insurance against late delivery. The same argument applies if there is uncertainty regarding the *quantity* of products or services delivered. As with the speed dimension, one can almost guarantee 'on-time' delivery by keeping excessive resources, such as inventory, within the chain. However, dependability of throughput time is a much more desirable aim because it reduces uncertainty within the chain.

Flexibility   In a supply chain context this is usually taken to mean the chain's ability to cope with changes and disturbances. Very often this is referred to as supply chain agility. The concept of agility includes previously discussed issues such as focusing on the end customer and ensuring fast throughput

Operations in practice

The North Face of sustainable purchasing[2]

Named for the coldest, most unforgiving side of northern hemisphere mountains, The North Face range of high-performance outdoor apparel, equipment and footwear has developed a reputation for durability, fashionable styling and, increasingly, sustainable sourcing of its materials. Owner of The North Face, VF Corporation's claim is that it 'responsibly manages the industry's most efficient and complex supply chain, which spans multiple geographies, product categories and distribution channels'.

In particular, The North Face is keen to promote sustainable purchasing in its supply chain management. Its commitment to sustainability, it says, comes from a desire to protect the natural places associated with how and where its products are used and from its concern about the effects of climate change. As a sign of its determination to pursue sustainable purchasing, The North Face has partnered with the independent bluesign® standard – a Swiss-based organization that promotes 'maximum resource productivity with a view to environmental protection, health and safety'. The idea of bluesign® is to tackle the sustainability at its roots and exclude substances and practices that are potentially hazardous to human health or the environment from all processes in the garment supply chain. So, to be considered as a supplier to The North Face, any factory must meet the rigorous, independent bluesign® standard, which ensures that suppliers address harmful chemicals at the fabric level and meet demanding requirements for consumer and worker safety, efficient resource use and environmental protection.

It is not only the monitoring of suppliers that is important in meeting sustainability targets, says The North Face – product and process innovation is also vital. 'For example', it says, 'our Venture jacket is a great illustration of innovation going hand-in-hand with environmental sustainability. We reduced the synthetic compounds in the membrane of our Venture product line by 50% by incorporating castor oil, a renewable resource. The castor bean plant, widely grown throughout the tropics, produces oil from its seeds that provides an effective substitute for half of the petroleum-derived materials in the waterproof membrane of our best-selling Venture product line.' ● ● ●

and responsiveness to customer needs. But, in addition, agile supply chains are sufficiently flexible to cope with changes, either in the nature of customer demand or in the supply capabilities of operations within the chain.

Cost In addition to the costs incurred within each operation to transform its inputs into outputs, the supply chain as a whole incurs additional costs that derive from each operation in a chain doing business with each other. These transaction costs may include such things as the costs of finding appropriate suppliers, setting up contractual agreements, monitoring supply performance, transporting products between operations, holding inventories and so on. Many of the recent developments in supply chain management, such as partnership agreements or reducing the number of suppliers, are an attempt to minimize transaction costs.

Lean versus agile supply networks

A distinction is often drawn between supply networks that are managed to emphasize efficiency – *lean supply networks* – and those that emphasize responsiveness and flexibility – *agile supply networks*. Even companies that have seemingly similar products or services may compete in different ways with different products. For example, shoe manufacturers may produce classics that change little over the years, as well as fashion shoes that last only one season. Hospitals have routine 'standardized' surgical procedures, such as cataract removal, but also have to provide emergency post-trauma surgery. Demand for the former products will be relatively stable and predictable, but demand for the latter will be far more uncertain. Also, the profit margin commanded by the innovative product will probably be higher than that of the more functional product. However, the price (and therefore the margin) of the innovative product may drop rapidly once it has become unfashionable in the market. Figure 6.4 illustrates key differences between what are typically described as 'functional' and 'innovative' products.

The supply chain policies that are seen to be appropriate for functional products and innovative products are termed efficient (or lean) and responsive (or agile) supply chain policies, respectively. Efficient supply chain policies include

---

FIGURE 6.4   'Functional' versus 'innovative' products

FUNCTIONAL ←————————————————→ INNOVATIVE

Product	 Bucket	 Bread	 Mobile phone	 Fashion handbag
Time between new product/ service introductions	10 yr+	1 yr–10 yr+	1yr–18 months	3–6 months
Profit margins	Tiny	Small	Very high	High
Volume and variety	High/very low	High/low	Moderate/ moderate	Moderate/ moderate
Demand volatility and uncertainty	Very low	Very low	Moderate	Moderate–high

keeping inventories low, especially in the downstream parts of the network, so as to maintain fast throughput and reduce the amount of working capital tied up in the inventory. What inventory there is in the network is concentrated mainly in the manufacturing operation, where it can keep utilization high and therefore manufacturing costs low. Information must flow quickly up and down the chain from retail outlets back up to the manufacturer so that schedules can be given the maximum amount of time to adjust efficiently. The chain is then managed to make sure that products flow as quickly as possible down the chain to replenish what few stocks are kept downstream.

By contrast, responsive supply chain policy stresses high service levels and responsive supply to the end customer. The inventory in the network will be deployed as closely as possible to the customer. In this way, the chain can still supply even when dramatic changes occur in customer demand. Fast throughput from the upstream parts of the chain will still be needed to replenish downstream stocks. But those downstream stocks are needed to ensure high levels of availability to end customers. Figure 6.5 illustrates how

> **operations principle**
> Supply chains with different end objectives need managing differently.

FIGURE 6.5   Matching the operations resources in the supply chain with market requirements

		Nature of demand	
		Functional products	**Innovative products**
		Predictable ⊢————————————⊣ Unpredictable	
		Few changes ⊢————————————⊣ Many changes	
		Low variety ⊢————————————⊣ High variety	
		Price stable ⊢————————————⊣ Price markdowns	
		Long lead time ⊢————————————⊣ Short lead time	
		Low margin ⊢————————————⊣ High margin	

Supply chain objectives			
Efficient Low cost / High utilization / Min. inventory / Low-cost suppliers	**Lean supply chain management**	**Mismatch**
Responsive Fast response / Low T/P time / Deployed inventory / Flexible suppliers	**Mismatch**	**Agile supply chain management**

Source: Adapted from Fisher, M.C. (1997) 'What is the right supply chain for your product?' *Harvard Business Review*, March–April, pp. 105–116.

the different supply chain policies match the different market requirements implied by functional and innovative products.

operations principle
'Functional' products and services require lean supply chain management; 'innovative' products and services require agile supply chain management.

How should you manage supply chain relationships?

The 'relationship' between operations in a supply chain is the basis on which the exchange of products, services, information and money is conducted. As such, managing supply chains is about managing relationships. Different forms of relationship will be appropriate in different circumstances. Two dimensions are particularly important – *what* the company chooses to outsource, and *who* it chooses to be its suppliers. In terms of *what* is outsourced, key questions are, 'how many activities are outsourced?' (from doing everything in-house at one extreme, to outsourcing everything at the other extreme), and 'how important are the activities outsourced?' (from outsourcing only trivial activities at one extreme, to outsourcing even core activities at the other extreme).

We discussed the first dimension in Chapter 2 when looking at the scope and structure of operations. When dealing with the second dimension of *who* is chosen to supply products and services, again two questions are important: 'how many suppliers will be used by the operation?' (from using many suppliers to perform the same set of activities at one extreme, through to only one supplier for each activity at the other extreme), and 'how close are the relationships?' (from 'arm's length' relationships at one extreme, through to close and intimate relationships at the other extreme). Figure 6.6 illustrates this way of characterizing relationships.

Contracting and relationships

There are two basic ingredients of supply interactions that are connected to the horizontal axis of Figure 6.6; they are 'contracts' and 'relationships'. Whatever the arrangement with its suppliers that a firm chooses to take, it can be described by the balance between contracts and relationships (see Figure 6.7). They complement each other, but can cause major problems with suppliers if they are not balanced. The more a supply agreement is market-based, with purchases based on relatively short-term arrangements, the more the agreement is likely to be defined in a detailed contract. By contracts we mean explicit, usually written and formal, documents that specify the legally binding obligations and roles of both parties in a relationship. The more a supply agreement is based on long-term, usually exclusive, agreements, the more a broad trust-based partnership agreement is appropriate. In any one

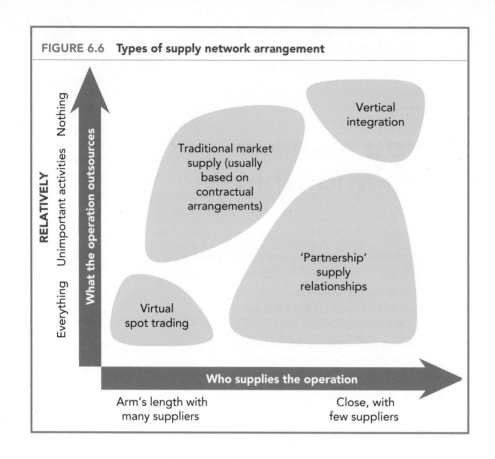

FIGURE 6.6 **Types of supply network arrangement**

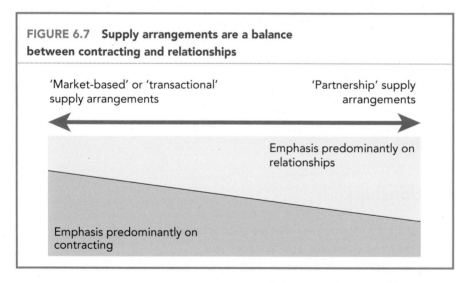

FIGURE 6.7 **Supply arrangements are a balance between contracting and relationships**

operation, a range of different approaches will be required. We will now examine contracts and relationships in more detail.

CONTRACT-BASED 'TRANSACTIONAL' RELATIONSHIPS
Contract-based, transactional relationships involve purchasing goods and services in a 'pure' market fashion, often seeking the 'best' supplier every time it is necessary to make a purchase. Each transaction effectively becomes a separate

decision and, as such, the orientation is short term. Often, price will dominate the decision-making process, with minimal information sharing between the buyer and the supplier and with no guarantee of further trading between the parties once the goods or services are delivered and payment is made. The *advantages* of contract-based 'transactional' relationships are usually seen as follows:

 They maintain competition between alternative suppliers.

 A supplier specializing in a small number of products or services, but supplying them to many customers, can gain natural economies of scale, and therefore enable lower prices than if customers performed the activities themselves on a smaller scale.

 There is inherent flexibility in outsourced supplies. If demand changes, customers can simply change the number and type of suppliers – a faster and cheaper alternative to redirecting internal activities.

 Innovations can be exploited, no matter where they originate. Specialist suppliers are more likely to come up with innovations that can be acquired faster and cheaper than developing them in-house.

There are, however, *disadvantages* of buying in a purely contractual manner:

 Suppliers owe little loyalty to customers. If supply is difficult, there is no guarantee of receiving supply.

 Choosing who to buy from takes time and effort. Gathering sufficient information and making decisions continually are activities that need to be resourced.

Short-term contractual relationships of this type may be appropriate when new companies are being considered as more regular suppliers, or when purchases are one-off or very irregular (for example, the replacement of all the windows in a company's office block would typically involve this type of competitive-tendering market relationship).

LONG-TERM 'PARTNERSHIP' RELATIONSHIPS

Partnership relationships in supply chains are sometimes seen as a compromise between vertical integration on the one hand (owning the resources that supply you) and transactional relationships on the other. Partnership (or 'collaborative') relationships involve a longer-term commitment between buyers and suppliers. These relationships emphasize cooperation, frequent interaction, information sharing and joint problem solving (see Figure 6.8). At their core, partnerships are *close* and *trusting* relationships, the degree to which is influenced by a number of factors:

 Sharing success   Both partners jointly benefit from the cooperation rather than manoeuvring to maximize their own individual contribution. This may sometimes involve formal profit-sharing arrangements.

FIGURE 6.8 The value of partnership relationships

Characteristics of partnership relationships	Dimensions of relationship value
→ High levels of trust → Collaborative problem solving → Frequent and effective communication → Higher degree of mutual understanding → Early conflict resolution → Understanding of different cultures and competencies → Emphasis on joint problem solving during failure episodes rather than assigning blame	→ Reduced transaction costs → Reduced cost of compliance monitoring → Generation of increased value through leveraging shared competencies → Fewer quality failures and unanticipated failures → Early failure identification and problem resolution

★ **Long-term expectations**   These are relatively long-term commitments, but not necessarily permanent ones.

★ **Multiple points of contact**   Communication is not restricted to formal channels, but may take place between many individuals in both organizations.

★ **Joint learning**   There is a relationship commitment to learn from each other's experiences.

★ **Few relationships**   There is a commitment on the part of both parties to limit the number of customers or suppliers with whom they do business.

★ **Joint coordination of activities**   Fewer relationships allow joint coordination of activities, such as the flow of materials or services, payment and so on.

★ **Information transparency**   Confidence is built through information exchange between the partners.

★ **Joint problem solving**   Jointly approaching problems can increase closeness over time.

★ **Trust**   This is probably the key element in partnership relationships. In this context, trust means the willingness of one party to relate to the other on the understanding that the relationship will be beneficial to both, even though that cannot be guaranteed. Trust is widely held to be the key issue in successful partnerships, but also, by far, the most difficult element to develop and maintain.

Which type of relationship?

It is very unlikely that any business will find it sensible to engage exclusively in one type of relationship over another. Most businesses will have a portfolio of, possibly, widely differing relationships. Also, there are degrees to which any particular relationship can be managed on a transactional or partnership basis. While there is no simple formula for choosing the 'ideal' form of relationship in each case, there are some important factors that can sway the decision. The most obvious issue will concern how a business intends to compete in its marketplace. If price is the main competitive factor, then the relationship could be determined by which approach offers the highest potential savings. On one hand, market-based contractual relationships could minimize the actual price paid for purchased products and services, while on the other, partnerships could minimize the transaction costs of doing business. If a business is competing primarily on product or service innovation, the type of relationship may depend on where innovation is likely to happen. If innovation depends on close collaboration between supplier and customer, partnership relationships are needed. On the other hand, if suppliers are busily competing to out-do each other in terms of their innovations, and especially if the market is turbulent and fast growing (as with many software and internet-based industries), then it may be preferable to retain the freedom to change suppliers quickly using market mechanisms.

> **operations principle**
> All supply chain relationships can be described by the balance between their 'contractual' and 'partnership' elements.

How should the supply side be managed?

The ability of any process or operation to produce outputs is dependent on the inputs it receives. So, good supply management is a necessary (but not sufficient) condition for effective operations management in general. Once a decision has been made to buy products or services (as opposed to make or do in-house), managers must decide on sourcing strategies for different products and services, select appropriate suppliers, manage ongoing supply and improve suppliers' capabilities over time. These activities are usually the responsibility of the purchasing or procurement function within the business. The purchasing department should provide a vital link between the operation itself and its suppliers. It should understand the requirements of all the processes within its own operation as well as the capabilities of the suppliers who could potentially provide products and services for the operation.

Sourcing strategy

Sourcing strategy concerns deciding how to configure the supply network. Here, we examine four key sourcing approaches – multiple sourcing, single sourcing, delegated sourcing and parallel sourcing.

Multiple sourcing

This involves obtaining a product or service component from more than one supplier. It is commonly seen in competitive markets, where switching costs are low and performance objectives are primarily focused on price and dependability. Multiple sourcing can help maintain competition in the supply market, reduce supply risk and increase flexibility in the face of supplier failure or changes in customer demand. In addition, some firms like to multi-source to prevent supplier dependence, thus allowing for changes in purchase volumes without the risk of supplier bankruptcy. However, the disadvantage of multiple sourcing is that it becomes hard to encourage supplier commitment and, as such, limits the opportunity to develop a partnership approach to supply management.

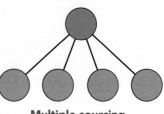

Multiple sourcing

Single sourcing

This involves buying all of one product or service component from a single supplier. Often these components represent a high proportion of total spend or are of strategic importance. In other cases, however, firms simply prefer the simplicity (and reduced transaction costs) of single sourcing. Many single-source arrangements have a longer-term focus than multiple-sourcing arrangements, and focus on a wider range of performance objectives. However, single-source arrangements can carry an increased risk of lock-in and a reduction in the firm's bargaining power.

Single sourcing

Delegated sourcing

This involves a tiered approach to managing supplier relationships. This means that one supplier is responsible for delivering an entire sub-assembly as opposed to a single part, or a package of services as opposed to an individual service. This has the advantage of reducing the number of tier-one suppliers significantly, while simultaneously allowing a focus on strategic partners. However, delegated sourcing can alter the dynamics of the supply market and risk creating 'mega-suppliers' with significant power in the network.

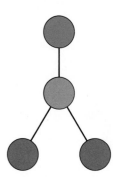

Delegated sourcing

Parallel sourcing

This has the aim of providing the advantages of both multiple sourcing and single sourcing simultaneously. It involves having single-source relationships for components or services for different product models or service packages. If a supplier is deemed unsatisfactory, it is possible to switch to the alternative supplier who currently provides the *same* component but for a *different* model. The advantage of this sourcing approach is that it maintains competition and allows for switching. However, managing parallel sourcing arrangements is relatively complex.

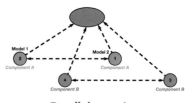

Parallel sourcing

MAKING THE SOURCING STRATEGY DECISION

Given that each sourcing strategy has its advantages and disadvantages, a key challenge is to decide which is most suitable. Here, we can explore two key questions: 'what is the risk in the supply market?' and 'what is the criticality of the product or service to the business?'. Considering risk, we can consider the number of alternative suppliers, how easy it is to switch from one

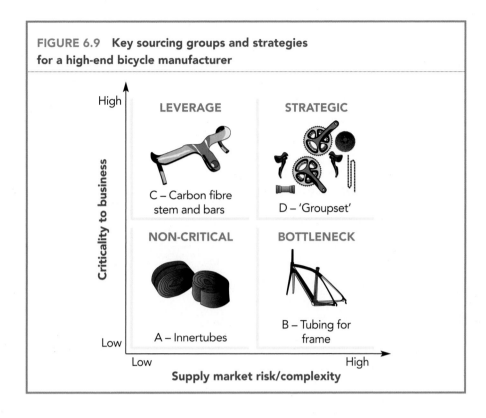

FIGURE 6.9   Key sourcing groups and strategies for a high-end bicycle manufacturer

supplier to another, exit barriers and the cost of bringing operations back in-house. For criticality, managers may consider a product or service component's importance in terms of volume purchased, percentage of total purchase cost, or the impact on business growth. By looking at these two dimensions, it is possible to position product or service components broadly in one of four key quadrants[3] – leverage, strategic, non-critical or bottleneck – and select appropriate sourcing strategies. Figure 6.9 shows this process for a high-end bicycle manufacturer.

 Non-critical   The innertubes (A) account for a relatively low proportion of the total cost of the product and, with the large number of alternative suppliers, the supply risk is low. For the non-critical purchase category, multiple-sourcing strategies tend to be most common.

 Bottleneck   The tubing (B) on the bike frame is a particular grade of carbon and is specially moulded for different types of model. While this component accounts for a relativley low proportion of the total cost of the product, the limited supply alternatives and high switching costs increase risk. For products and services in the bottleneck category, single sourcing is common because of a lack of choice in the supply market.

 Leverage   The carbon-fibre stem and bars (C) account for a high proportion of the cost of this bicycle but are relatively easy to source as there are a relatively large number of available suppliers. For leverage products and services, bundling of requirements allows a shift towards delegated sourcing in many cases.

 Strategic   The 'groupset' (D) refers to the gearing systems on the bicycle. These are complex to source and account for a high proportion of total spending. In addition, there are few suppliers capable of manufacturing these components to sufficient quality for high-end bicycles, and so the cost of switching is high. For strategic products and services, single-sourcing approaches remain popular. However, given the associated risks of single sourcing, many firms have moved to delegated or parallel approaches for this group of purchases.

Global sourcing

One of the major supply chain developments of recent years has been the expansion in the proportion of products and services that businesses are willing to source from outside their home country. Known as global sourcing, it is the process of identifying, evaluating, negotiating and configuring supply across multiple geographies. Traditionally, even companies who exported their goods and services all over the world (that is, they were international on their demand side) still sourced the majority of their supplies locally. This has changed – companies are now increasingly willing to look globally for their supplies, and for very good reasons. There can be significant savings by sourcing from low-cost-country suppliers. In addition, transportation infrastructures are considerably more sophisticated and cheaper than they once were. Super-efficient port operations in Shanghai, Singapore and Rotterdam, for example, integrated road–rail systems, jointly developed autoroute systems and cheaper air freight have all reduced some of the cost barriers to international trade.

There are, of course, problems with global sourcing. The risks of increased complexity and increased distance need managing carefully. Suppliers who are a significant distance away need to transport their products across long distances. The risks of delays and hold-ups can be far greater than when sourcing locally (see the 'Operations in practice' example on the problems that the Japanese tsunami caused). In addition, negotiating with suppliers whose native language is different from one's own makes communication more difficult and can lead to misunderstandings over contract terms. Therefore, global sourcing decisions require businesses to balance cost, performance, service and risk factors, not all of which are obvious.

Supplier selection

In conjunction with deciding on sourcing strategies for different products and services, organizations much select appropriate suppliers. Given the trends of

Operations in practice

The tsunami effect[4]

The volcanic ash from Iceland that disrupted air transport across Europe provided a preview of how natural disasters could throw global supply chains into disarray – especially those that had adopted the lean, low-inventory, just-in-time philosophy. That was in 2010. Yet the following year an even more severe disaster caused chaos in all supply chains with a Japanese connection; and that is a lot of supply chains. It was a quadruple disaster: an earthquake off Japan's eastern coast, one of the largest ever recorded, caused a tsunami that killed thousands of people and caused a meltdown at a nearby nuclear power plant, which necessitated huge evacuations and nationwide power shortages. The effect on global supply networks was immediate and drastic. Sony Corporation shut down some of its operations in Japan because of the ongoing power shortages and announced that it was giving its staff time off during the summer (when air conditioning needs are high) to save energy. Japanese automobile companies' production was among the worst affected. Toyota suspended production at most of its Japanese plants and reduced and then suspended output from its North American and European operations. Nissan said it would be suspending its UK production for three days at the end of the month due to a shortfall of parts from Japan. Honda announced that it was halving production at its factory in Swindon in the south of the UK. However, the disruption was not as severe as it might have been. Honda said that the vast majority of the parts used in Swindon are made in Europe, and added that its flexible working policy would allow it to make up for the lost production later in the year.

In the longer term, the disruption caused a debate among practitioners about how supply chains could be made more robust. Hans-Paul Bürkner, chief of the Boston Consulting Group, said, "It is very important now to think the extreme. You have to have some buffers." Some commentators even drew parallels with financial meltdowns, claiming that just as some financial institutions proved 'too big to fail', so some Japanese suppliers may be too crucial to do without. For example, at the time of the disruption, two companies, Mitsubishi Gas Chemical and Hitachi Chemical, controlled about 90 per cent of the market for a specialty resin used to make the microchips that go into smartphones and other devices. Both firms' plants were damaged and the effect was felt around the world. So maybe suppliers who have near-monopolies on vital components should spread their production facilities geographically. Similarly, businesses that rely on single suppliers may be more willing to split their orders between two or more suppliers. ● ● ●

outsourcing, supply-base rationalization, supplier involvement in new product and service development and longer-term supplier relationships, the selection process is critical to the success of organizations. Figure 6.10 outlines the four key steps in supplier selection.

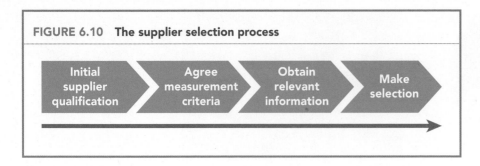

FIGURE 6.10   **The supplier selection process**

★ **Initial qualification**   This is aimed at reducing possible suppliers to a manageable set for subsequent assessment. Pre-qualification criteria often include financial viability, accreditation (such as ISO9000), location (e.g. only considering suppliers located within a certain distance of a manufacturer) and scale.

★ **Agree measurement criteria**   Determining the relative importance of key performance objectives (quality, speed, dependability, flexibility, cost and others) is critical in the selection of suppliers. For key performance objectives, measurable criteria are then needed. For example, for cost a firm might consider unit price, pricing terms (e.g. volume discounts), exchange rate effects and so on.

★ **Obtain relevant information**   As firms narrow down to a smaller group of potential suppliers, further information can be gathered to inform the selection decision. This may include additional levels of detail in delivery options and cost structure, site visits and tests (e.g. test orders in small quantities) to assess competence prior to potential ramp-up of supply.

★ **Make selection**   Having arrived at a group of viable alternatives, selection may be supported using various multi-criteria decision-making models, including the weighted score method (see worked example below) and the analytical hierarchy process (AHP). These models aim to provide quantifiable information for each key selection criteria and a weighting of their relative importance to allow for an objective assessment of different suppliers. Total cost of ownership (TCO) is an alternative approach that seeks to provide detailed information on all possible costs (rather than simply product or service price) associated with procurement, to reach more 'rational' decisions during supplier selection.

Managing on-going supply

Managing supply relationships is not just a matter of choosing the right suppliers and then leaving them to get on with day-to-day supply. It is also about ensuring that suppliers are given the right information and encouragement to maintain smooth supply and that internal inconsistency does not negatively affect their ability to supply. A basic requirement is that some mechanism should be set up that ensures the two-way flow of

Worked example

A hotel chain has decided to change its current supplier of cleaning supplies because it has become unreliable in its delivery performance. The two alternative suppliers that the hotel is considering have been evaluated, on a 1–10 scale, against the criteria shown in Table 6.1, which also shows the relative importance of each criterion on a 1–10 scale. Based on this evaluation, Supplier B has the superior overall score.

TABLE 6.1 Weighted supplier selection criteria for the hotel chain

Factor	Weight	Supplier A score	Supplier B score
Cost performance	10	8 (8 × 10 = 80)	5 (5 × 10 = 50)
Quality record	10	7 (7 × 10 = 70)	9 (9 × 10 = 90)
Delivery speed promised	7	5 (5 × 7 = 35)	5 (5 × 7 = 35)
Delivery speed achieved	7	4 (4 × 7 = 28)	8 (8 × 7 = 56)
Dependability record	8	6 (6 × 8 = 48)	8 (8 × 8 = 64)
Range provided	5	8 (8 × 5 = 40)	5 (5 × 5 = 25)
Innovation capability	4	6 (6 × 4 = 24)	9 (9 × 4 = 36)
Total weighted score		325	356

information between customer and supplier. Customers may see suppliers as having the responsibility for ensuring appropriate supply 'under any circumstances'. Suppliers themselves may be reluctant to inform customers of any potential problems with supply because they see it as risking the relationship.

Some organizations bring a degree of formality to supplier relationships by encouraging (or requiring) all suppliers to sign service-level agreements (SLAs). SLAs are formal definitions of the dimensions of service and the relationship between operations; for example, between a supplier and its customer, or between in internal supplier of service and its internal customer. SLAs are also an important tool in quality management (described more fully in Chapter 12).

Improving supplier capabilities

In any relationship other than pure market-based transactional relationships, it is in a customer's long-term interests to take some responsibility for developing supplier capabilities. Helping a supplier to improve not only enhances the service (and hopefully price) from the supplier; it may also lead to greater supplier loyalty and long-term commitment. This is why some particularly successful businesses invest in supplier development teams, whose responsibility is to help suppliers to improve their own operations processes. Of course, committing the resources to help suppliers is only worthwhile if it improves the effectiveness of the supply chain as a whole. Nevertheless, the potential for such enlightened self-interest can be significant.

How should the demand side be managed?

The management of demand-side relationships will depend partly on the nature of demand – in particular, how uncertain it is. Knowing the exact demands that customers are going to require allows a supplier to plan its own internal processes in a systematic manner. This type of demand is called 'dependent' demand (see Chapter 9 for more details). It is relatively predictable because it is dependent upon some factor that is itself predictable. For example, supplying tyres to the bicycle manufacturer described earlier involves examining the manufacturing schedules in its manufacturing plant and deriving the demand for tyres from these. Because of this, the tyres can be ordered from the tyre manufacturer to a delivery schedule that is closely in line with the demand for tyres from the plant.

However, not all operations have such predictable demand (again, noted in Chapter 9) and are instead subject to independent demand. There is a random element in demand, which is virtually independent of any obvious factors. They, like their suppliers, are required to supply demand without having any firm forward visibility of customer orders. (In Chapter 9 we use the example of a drive-in tyre replacement service. It cannot predict either the volume or the specific needs of customers. It must make decisions on how many and what type of tyres to stock, based on demand forecasts and in the light of the risks it is prepared to take of running out of stock.) Managing internal process networks when external demand is independent involves making 'best guesses' concerning future demand, attempting to put the resources in place to satisfy this demand and attempting to respond quickly if actual demand does not match the forecast.

Logistics services

Logistics means moving products to customers. Sometimes the term 'physical distribution management', or simply 'distribution', is used as being analogous to logistics. An important decision is how much of the logistical process of organizing the movement of goods to trust to outside service providers. The extent and integration of this type of service provision is often referred to as first-, second-, third- or fourth-party logistics (or 1PL, 2PL, 3PL, 4PL, for short). However, the distinction between the PL classifications can sometimes be blurred, with different firms using slightly different definitions.

First-party logistics (1PL) is when, rather than outsourcing the activity, the owner of whatever is being transported organizes and performs product movements themselves. For example, a manufacturing firm will deliver directly, or a retailer such as a supermarket will collect products from a supplier. The logistics activity is an entirely internal process.

Second-party logistics (2PL) is when a firm decides to outsource or sub-contract logistics services over a specific segment of a supply chain. It could involve a road, rail, air or maritime shipping company being hired to transport and, if necessary, store products from a specific collection point to a specific destination.

Third-party logistics (3PL) is when a firm contracts a logistics company to work with other transport companies to manage its logistics operations. It is a broader concept than 2PL and can involve transportation, warehousing, inventory management and even packaging or repackaging products. Generally, 3PL involves services that are scaled and customized to a customer's specific needs.

This is a Maersk Triple-E class vessel designed for efficiency, economy of scale and to be environmentally efficient by reducing CO2 emissions. Ships such as this play an important role in international supply chains

Fourth-party logistics (4PL) is a yet broader idea than 3PL. Accenture, the consulting group, originally used the term '4PL'. Its definition of 4PL is: 'A 4PL is an integrator that assembles the resources, capabilities and technology of its own organization and other organizations to design, build and run comprehensive supply chain solutions.' 4PL service suppliers pool transport capabilities, processes, technology support and coordination activities to provide customized supply chain services for part or all of a client's supply chain. 4PL firms can manage all aspects of a client's supply chain. They may act as a single interface between the client and multiple logistics service providers, and are often separate organizational entities founded on a long-term basis or as a joint venture between a client and one or more partners.

Fifth-party logistics (5PL) is what some firms are selling themselves as providing, mainly by defining themselves as broadening the scope further to e-business and in consolidating the needs of multiple 3PLs and 4PLs to generate greater economies of scale.

Customer relationship management (CRM)

There is a story (which may or may not be true) that is often quoted to demonstrate the importance of using information technology to analyze customer information. It goes like this. Wal-Mart, the huge US-based supermarket chain, did an analysis of customers' buying habits and found a statistically significant correlation between purchases of beer and purchases of diapers (nappies), especially on Friday evenings. The reason? Fathers were going to the supermarket to buy nappies for their babies, and because fatherhood restricted their ability to go out for a drink as often, they would also buy beer. Supposedly this led the supermarket to start locating nappies next to the beer in their stores, resulting in increased sales of both!

Whether it is true or not, it does illustrate the potential of analyzing data to understand customers. This is the basis of customer relationship management (CRM). It is a method of learning more about customers' needs and behaviours in order to develop stronger relationships with them. Although CRM usually depends on information technology, it is misleading to see it as a 'technology'. Rather, it is a process that helps to understand customers' needs and develop ways of meeting those needs while maximizing profitability. CRM brings together all the disparate information about customers in order to gain insight into their behaviour and their value to the business. It helps to sell products and services more effectively and increase revenues by:

 providing services and products that are exactly what your customers want;

 retaining existing customers and discovering new ones;

 offering better customer service;

 cross-selling products more effectively.

CRM tries to help organizations understand who their customers are and what their value is over a lifetime. It does this by building a number of steps into its customer interface processes. First, the business must determine the needs of its customers and how best to meet those needs. For example, a bank may keep track of its customers' ages and lifestyles so that it can offer appropriate products such as mortgages or pensions to them when they fit their needs. Second, the business must examine all the different ways and parts of the organization where customer-related information is collected, stored and used. Businesses may interact with customers in different ways and through different people. For example, sales people, call centres, technical staff, operations and distribution managers may all, at different times, have contact with customers. CRM systems should integrate this data. Third, all customer-related data must be analyzed to obtain a holistic view of each customer and identify where service can be improved.

Despite its name, some critics of CRM argue that the greatest shortcoming is that it is insufficiently concerned with directly helping customers. CRM systems are sold to executives as a way to increase efficiency, force standardized processes and gain better insight into the state of the business. But they rarely address the need to help organizations resolve customer problems, answer customer questions faster, or help them solve their own problems. This may explain the trend towards a shift in focus from automating internal front-office functions to streamlining processes such as online customer support.

Customer development

As noted a number of times in this text, it is imperative to understand customer expectations and perceptions of performance, and feed these into your own improvement plans. What is less common, but can be equally valuable, is to

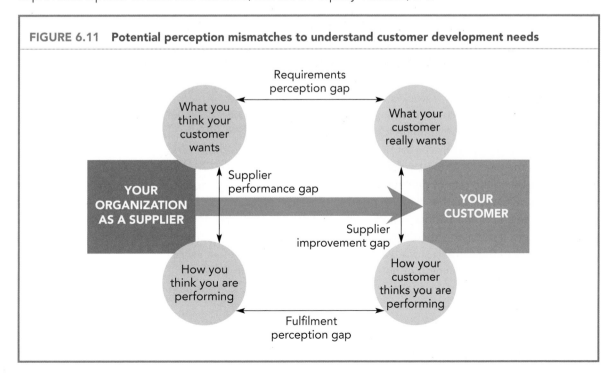

FIGURE 6.11   Potential perception mismatches to understand customer development needs

examine whether customer requirements and perceptions of performance are either accurate or reasonable (see Figure 6.11). For example, customers may be placing demands on suppliers without fully considering their consequences. It may be that slight modifications in what is demanded would not inconvenience customers and yet would provide significant benefits to suppliers that could then be passed on to customers. Similarly, customers may be incompetent at measuring supplier performance, in which case the benefits of excellent supplier service will not be recognized. So, just as customers have a responsibility to help develop their own supplier's performance, in their own as well as their supplier's interests, so suppliers have a responsibility to develop their customer's understanding of how supply should be managed.

operations principle
Unsatisfactory customer relationships can be caused by requirement and fulfilment perception gaps.

What are the dynamics of supply chains?

There are dynamics that exist between firms in supply chains that cause errors, inaccuracies and volatility. These increase for operations further upstream in the supply chain. This effect is known as the 'bullwhip effect',[5] so called because a small disturbance at one end of the chain causes increasingly large disturbances as it works its way towards the other end. Its main cause is a perfectly understandable and rational desire by the different links in the supply chain to manage their levels of activity and inventory sensibly. To demonstrate this, examine the production rate and stock levels for the supply chain shown in Table 6.2. This is a four-stage supply chain, where an original equipment manufacturer (OEM) is served by three tiers of suppliers. The demand from the OEM's market has been running at a rate of 100 items per period, but in period 2, demand reduces to 95 items per period. All stages in the supply chain work on the principle that they will keep in stock one period's demand. This is a simplification, but not a gross one. Many operations gear their inventory levels to their demand rate. The column headed 'stock' for each level of supply shows the starting stock at the beginning of the period and the finishing stock at the end of the period. At the beginning of period 2, the OEM has 100 units in stock (that being the rate of demand up to period 2). Demand in period 2 is 95 and so the OEM knows that it would need to produce sufficient items to finish up at the end of the period with 95 in stock (this being the new demand rate). To do this, it need only manufacture 90 items; these, together with five items taken out of the starting stock, will supply demand and leave a finished stock of 95 items. The beginning of period 3 finds the OEM with 95 items in stock. Demand is also 95 items and therefore its production rate to maintain a stock level of 95 will be 95 items per period. The original equipment manufacturer now operates at a steady rate of producing 95 items per period.

TABLE 6.2 Fluctuations of production levels along a supply chain in response to a small change in end-customer demand (starting stock (a) + production (b) = finishing stock (c) + demand — that is, production in previous tier down (d): see explanation in text). Note all stages in the supply chain keep one period's inventory: c = d

Period	Third-tier supplier		Second-tier supplier		First-tier supplier		Original equipment mfr		Demand
	Prodn.	Stock	Prodn.	Stock	Prodn.	Stock	Prodn.	Stock	
1	100	100 / 100	100	100 / 100	100	100 / 100	100	100 / 100	100
2	20	100 / 60	60	100 / 80	80	100 / 90	90	100 / 95	95
3	180	60 / 120	120	80 / 100	100	90 / 95	95	95 / 95	95
4	60	120 / 90	90	100 / 95	95	95 / 95	95	95 / 95	95
5	100	90 / 95	95	95 / 95	95	95 / 95	95	95 / 95	95
6	95	95 / 95	95	95 / 95	95	95 / 95	95	95 / 95	95

3 → Orders/Items → 2 → Orders/Items → 1 → Orders/Items → OEM → Orders/Items → Market

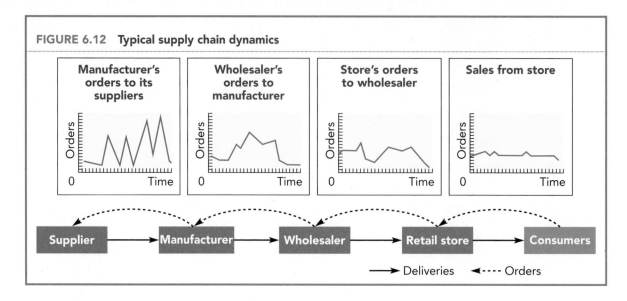

FIGURE 6.12   Typical supply chain dynamics

Note, however, that a change in demand of only five items has produced a fluctuation of 10 items in the OEM's production rate.

Carrying this same logic through to the first-tier supplier, at the beginning of period 2 the second-tier supplier has 100 items in stock. The demand that it has to supply in period 2 is derived from the production rate of the OEM. This has dropped down to 90 in period 2. The first-tier supplier therefore has to produce sufficient to supply the demand of 90 items (or the equivalent) and leave one month's demand (now 90 items) as its finish stock. A production rate of 80 items per month will achieve this. It will therefore start period 3 with an opening stock of 90 items, but the demand from the OEM has now risen to 95 items. It therefore has to produce sufficient to fulfil this demand of 95 items and leave 95 items in stock. To do this, it must produce 100 items in period 3. After period 3 the first-tier supplier then resumes a steady state, producing 95 items per month. Note again, however, that the fluctuation has been even greater than that in the OEM's production rate, decreasing to 80 items a period, increasing to 100 items a period and then achieving a steady rate of 95 items a period. Extending the logic back to the third-tier supplier, it is clear that the further back up the supply chain an operation is placed, the more drastic are the fluctuations.

operations principle
Demand fluctuations become progressively amplified as their effects work back up the supply chain.

This relatively simple demonstration ignores any time lag in material and information flow between stages. In practice, there will be such a lag, and this will make the fluctuations even more marked. Figure 6.12 shows the net result of all these effects in a typical supply chain. Note the increasing volatility further back in the chain.

Controlling supply chain dynamics

The first step in improving supply chain performance involves attempting to reduce the bullwhip effect. This usually means coordinating the activities of the operations in the chain in several ways.[6]

E-ENABLING SUPPLY NETWORKS

One of the reasons for the fluctuations in output described in the example earlier was that each operation in the chain reacted to the orders placed by its immediate customer. None of the operations had an overview of what was happening throughout the chain. If information had been available and shared throughout the chain, it is unlikely that such wild fluctuations would have occurred. It is sensible, therefore, to try to transmit information throughout the chain so that all the operations can monitor true demand, free of these distortions. An obvious improvement is to make information on end-customer demand available to upstream operations. Electronic point-of-sale (EPOS) systems used by many retailers attempt to do this. Sales data from checkouts or cash registers is consolidated and transmitted to the warehouses, transportation companies and supplier manufacturing operations that form its supply chain.

> **operations principle**
>
> The bullwhip effect can be reduced by information sharing, aligning planning and control decisions, improving flow efficiency and better forecasting.

CHANNEL ALIGNMENT IN SUPPLY NETWORKS

Channel alignment means the adjustment of scheduling, material movements, stock levels, pricing and other sales strategies in order to bring all the operations in the chain into line with each other. This goes beyond the provision of information. It means that the systems and methods of planning and control decision making are harmonized through the chain. For example, even when using the same information, differences in forecasting methods or purchasing practices can lead to fluctuations in orders between operations in the chain. One way of avoiding this is to allow an upstream supplier to manage the inventories of its downstream customer. This is known as vendor-managed inventory (VMI). So, for example, a packaging supplier could take responsibility for the stocks of packaging materials held by a food-manufacturing customer. In turn, the food manufacturer takes responsibility for the stocks of its products that are held by its customer – in the supermarket's warehouses.

OPERATIONAL EFFICIENCY IN SUPPLY NETWORKS

'Operational efficiency' in this context means the efforts that each operation in the chain makes to reduce its own complexity, the cost of doing business with other operations in the chain and its throughput time. The cumulative effect of this is to simplify throughput in the whole chain. For example, imagine a chain of operations whose performance level is relatively poor: quality defects are frequent, the lead time to order products and services is long, delivery is unreliable and so on. The behaviour of the chain would be a continual sequence of errors and effort wasted in re-planning to compensate for the errors. Poor quality would mean extra and unplanned orders being placed, and unreliable delivery and slow delivery lead times would mean high safety stocks. Just as important, most operations managers' time would be spent coping with the inefficiency. By contrast, a chain whose operations had high levels of operations performance would be more predictable and have faster throughput, both of which would help to minimize supply chain fluctuations. Improved forecast accuracy also helps to reduce the bullwhip effect by reducing the inventory-holding requirements needed to achieve customer-service targets.

Summary answers to key questions

Each chapter has a 'Summary answers to key questions' section. Use it to check your understanding of the issues covered in the chapter.

WHAT IS SUPPLY CHAIN MANAGEMENT?

★ Supply chain management is the management of relationships and flows between operations and processes. Technically, it is different from supply network management, which looks at all the operations or processes in a network, but the two terms are often used interchangeably.

★ Many of the principles of managing external supply chains (flow between operations) are also applicable to internal supply chains (flow between processes and departments).

HOW DO SUPPLY CHAINS COMPETE?

★ The central objective of supply chain management is to satisfy the needs of the end customer.

★ Each operation in the chain (and each chain in the supply network) should contribute to whatever mix of quality, speed, dependability, flexibility and cost that the end customer requires.

★ An important distinction is between lean and agile supply chain performance. Broadly, lean (or efficient) supply chains are appropriate for stable 'functional' products and services, while agile (or responsive) supply chains are more appropriate for less predictable innovative products and services.

HOW SHOULD YOU MANAGE SUPPLY CHAIN RELATIONSHIPS?

★ Supply chain relationships can be described on a spectrum from market-based, contractual, 'arm's length' relationships, through to close and long-term partnership relationships.

★ The types of relationships adopted may be dictated by the structure of the market itself.

HOW SHOULD THE SUPPLY SIDE BE MANAGED?

★ Managing supply-side relationships involves determining sourcing strategy, selecting appropriate suppliers, managing ongoing supply and improving supplier capabilities.

★ Sourcing strategies include multiple sourcing, single sourcing, delegated sourcing and parallel sourcing. Their selection is influenced by the complexity and risk of the supply market and the criticality to the business.

★ Organizations increasingly look globally when making sourcing decisions. While there are significant advantages in accessing a wider supply market, global sourcing often exposes operations to greater risks.

★ Supplier selection involves trading off different supplier attributes, often using scoring assessment methods.

★ Managing ongoing supply involves clarifying supply expectations, often using service level agreements.

★ Supplier development can benefit both suppliers and customers, especially in partnership relationships.

HOW SHOULD THE DEMAND SIDE BE MANAGED?

★ This will depend partly on whether demand is dependent or independent. Approaches such as materials requirements planning (MRP) are used in the former case, while approaches such as inventory management are used in the latter case.

★ Logistics is used to move products to customer. Often, this activity is outsourced to third- and fourth-party logistics (3PL and 4PL) providers.

★ CRM and customer development are increasingly used to improve understanding of customer behaviour, and to engage customers more proactively to influence both expectations and demands placed on the supply network.

WHAT ARE THE DYNAMICS OF SUPPLY CHAINS?

★ Supply chains have a dynamic of their own that is often called the bullwhip effect. It means that relatively small changes at the demand end of the chain increasingly amplify into large disturbances as they move upstream.

★ Three key methods can be used to reduce this effect. E-enabled supply networks can prevent over-reaction to immediate stimuli and give a better view of the whole chain. Channel alignment through standardized planning and control methods allows for easier coordination of the whole chain. Improving the operational efficiency of each part of the chain prevents local errors multiplying to affect the whole chain. In particular, improved forecasts reduce the inventory-holding requirements for supply chains while maintaining customer-service levels.

Problems and applications

All chapters have Problems and application questions that will help you practice analyzing operations. They can be answered by reading the chapter. Model answers for the first question can be found on the companion website for this text.

1 ➔ The COO of Super Cycles was considering her sourcing strategy. "I have two key questions, for each of our outsourced parts: 'what is the risk in the supply market?', and 'what is the criticality of the product or service to our business?'. As far as risk is concerned, we can consider the number of alternative suppliers, how easy it is to switch from one supplier to another, possible exit barriers and the cost of bringing operations back in-house. As far as criticality is concerned, we can consider each component's importance in terms of volume purchased, percentage of total purchase cost and the impact on business growth." Four key outsourced components are shown in Table 6.3. What approach to sourcing these components would you recommend?

TABLE 6.3   Four outsourced components for Super Cycles

Component	Cost (as a proportion of total material cost)	Suppliers	Ease of changing supplier
The innertubes	3%	Many alternative suppliers	Very easy; could do it in days
Frame tubing	15%	Only one supplier capable at the moment; could take a long time to develop a new supplier	Difficult in the short term, possible in the longer term
Carbon-fibre stem and bars	32%	Relatively large number of available suppliers	Relatively easy; would probably take a few weeks for new contract
'Groupset' gearing system	35%	Few suppliers who are capable of manufacturing these components to sufficient quality	Complex to source; could switch supplier in longer term but would pose quality risk

2

➜ A chain of women's apparel retailers had all their products made by Arropa Limited, a small but high-quality garment manufacturer. They worked on the basis of two seasons: Spring/Summer and Autumn/Winter. "Sometimes we are left with surplus items because our designers have just got it wrong", said the retailer's chief designer. "It is important that we are able to flex our order quantities from Arropa during the season. Although they are a great supplier in many ways, they can't change their production plans at short notice." Arropa Limited was aware of this: "I know that they are happy with our ability to make even the most complex designs to high level of quality. I also know that they would like us to be more flexible in changing our volumes and delivery schedules. I admit that we could be more flexible within the season. Partly, we can't do this because we have to buy in cloth at the beginning of the season based on the forecast volumes from our customers. Even if we could change our production schedules, we could not get extra deliveries of cloth. We only deal with high-quality and innovative cloth manufacturers who are very large compared to us, so we do not represent much business for them." A typical cloth supplier said: "We compete primarily on quality and innovation. Designing cloth is as much of a fashion business as designing the clothes into which it is made. Our cloth goes to tens of thousands of customers around the world. These vary considerably in their requirements, but presumably all of them value our quality and innovation."

3

➜ The example of the bullwhip effect shown in Table 6.2 shows how a simple 5 per cent reduction in demand at the end of the supply chain causes fluctuations that increase in severity the further back an operation is placed in the chain.

a) Using the same logic and the same rules (i.e. all operations keep one period's inventory), what would the effect on the chain be if demand fluctuated period by period between 100 and 95? That is, period 1 has a demand of 100, period 2 has a demand of 95, period 3 a demand of 100, period 4 a demand of 95 and so on?

b) What happens if all operations in the supply chain decided to keep only half of the period's demand as inventory?

c) Find examples of how supply chains try to reduce this bullwhip effect.

4

➜ If you were the owner of a small local retail shop, what criteria would you use to select suppliers for the goods that you wish to stock in your shop? Visit three shops that are local to you and ask the owners how they select their suppliers. In what way were their answers different from what you thought they might be?

Want to know more?

Akkermans, H. and Voss, C. (2013) 'The service bullwhip effect', *International Journal of Operations & Production Management,* **33**(6), pp. 765–88.

➡ An academic paper that deals with the important issue of service supply.

Sunil Chopra, S. and Meindl, P. (2015) *Supply Chain Management,* 5th edition, Harlow, UK: Pearson.

➡ One of the best of the specialist texts.

Christopher, M. (2011) *Logistics and Supply Chain Management: Creating Value-Adding Networks,* Upper Saddle River, NJ: Financial Times Prentice Hall.

➡ Updated version of a classic that gives a comprehensive treatment of supply chain management from a distribution perspective by one of the gurus of supply chain management.

Johnsen, T., Howard, M. and Miemczyk, J. (2014) *Purchasing and Supply Chain Management: A Sustainability Perspective,* London: Routledge.

➡ Focuses on the important topic of the longer-term implications of global sourcing and sustainability.

Zara, the fashion retailer, has designed its supply chain with a relatively high degree of vertical integration between its design, manufacturing, supply and retailing operations. It also promotes detailed feedback from its stores to its designers and continuously updates its designs. This allows Zara to match both its designs and its volumes to customer demand.

Capacity management

7

Introduction

Capacity management is the activity of understanding the nature of an operation's supply and demand, and of coping with any differences between them. It involves balancing the supply from an operation (which is a function of its capacity) with the demand placed on it by its customers. It aims to meet the needs of customers while maintaining the efficiency of the operation's resources. And to do this, operations managers must be able to understand and reconcile two competing requirements. One is the importance of maintaining customer satisfaction by delivering products and services to customers reasonably quickly. The other is the need for operations (and their extended supply networks) to maintain efficiency by minimizing the costs of excess capacity. In this chapter, we look at these competing tensions at an aggregated level, in both the long and medium terms. At this level, managers do not discriminate between the different products and services that might be produced; instead, they aim to ensure that the overall ability to supply is in line with the overall demand placed on the operation. Figure 7.1 shows where this topic fits in the overall structure of operations management.

Key questions

What is capacity management?

What are the main long-term capacity decisions?

What are the main medium-term capacity decisions?

What are the ways of coping with mismatches between medium-term demand and capacity?

How can operations understand the consequences of their medium-term capacity decisions?

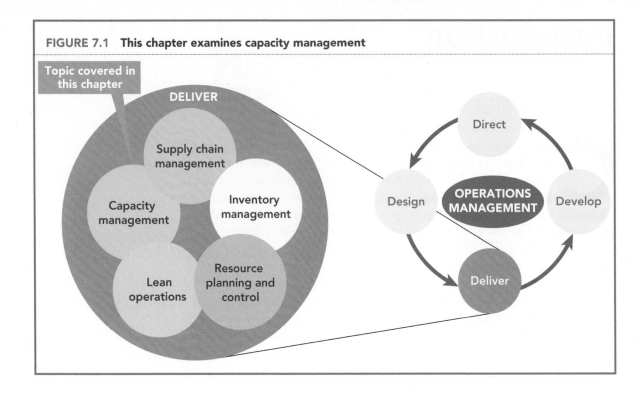

FIGURE 7.1   **This chapter examines capacity management**

What is capacity management?

The capacity of an operation is the *maximum level of value-added activity over a period of time* that the process can achieve under normal operating conditions. In other words, 'capacity' reflects not only the scale of capacity but, more importantly, its *processing capabilities*. If a pharmaceutical manufacturer has invested in a new 1000-litre capacity reactor, or a property company purchased a 500-vehicle-capacity car park, it gives you a good sense of the *scale* but it is not a particularly useful measure of capacity. The pharmaceutical company will be concerned with the level of output that can be achieved. If a batch can be produced every hour, the planned processing capacity could be as high as 24,000 litres per day. But if a batch takes four hours, and two hours are used for cleaning between batches, the vessel may only produce 4,000 litres per day. Similarly, the car park may be fully occupied only by office workers during the working day, 'processing' only 500 cars per day. Alternatively, it may be used for shoppers staying on average only one hour, and theatre-goers occupying spaces for three hours in the evening. Its processing capability could then be up to 5,000 cars per day.

operations principle
Capacity is the maximum level of value-added activity over a period of time that the process or operation can achieve under normal operating conditions.

Long-, medium- and short-term capacity management

The nature of capacity management depends on the timescale over which it is being managed. In the long term (usually meaning a period of years ahead), decisions are concerned with introducing (or removing) major increments of physical capacity. For example, 'how many distribution centres should a retailer build?' or 'how large a studio should a programme maker plan for?' Medium-term capacity management usually involves looking at the balance between demand and capacity 2–18 months ahead. However, demand forecasts are rarely totally accurate, and most operations also need to respond to changes in demand that occur on an even shorter timescale, possibly minute by minute. For example, hotels and restaurants know from experience that they can have unexpected and apparently random changes in demand from night to night. So, their operations managers also have to manage capacity in the short term, usually by temporarily flexing output. In this chapter, we briefly examine long-term capacity management before looking in detail at medium-term capacity. (Short-term capacity issues are examined in Chapter 9.)

What are the main long-term capacity decisions?

There are two sets of decisions that determine the scale of an operation's physical capacity at any point in time. The first is how big each operation should be. This is governed, at least partly, by the 'natural' economies of scale of the operation. The second is, if the long-term capacity of the operation needs to change to reflect changes in demand, what should be the timing of any change.

Economies of scale and the 'optimum' capacity level

Most organizations need to decide on the size (in terms of capacity) of each of their facilities. A chain of truck-service centres, for example, might operate centres that have various capacities. The effective cost of running each centre will depend on the average service-bay occupancy. Low occupancy because of few customers will result in a high cost per customer served, because the fixed costs of the operation are being shared between few customers. As demand, and therefore service-bay occupancy, increases, the cost per customer will reduce. However, operating at very high levels of capacity utilization (occupancy levels close to capacity) can mean longer customer waiting times and reduced customer service. There may also be less obvious cost penalties of operating centres at levels close to their capacity. For example, long periods of overtime may reduce productivity levels as well as costing more in extra payments to staff; utilizing bays at very high utilization reduces maintenance and cleaning time, which may increase breakdowns, reduce effective lifespan and so on. This usually means that average costs start to increase after a point that will often be lower than the theoretical capacity of the operation.

The blue curves in Figure 7.2 show this effect for the service centres of 5-, 10-, and 15-bay capacities. As the nominal capacity of the centres increases, the lowest cost-point at first reduces because the fixed costs of any operation do not increase proportionately as its capacity increases. A 10-bay centre has less than twice the fixed costs of a 5-bay centre, and costs less to build than twice the cost of a 5-bay centre. These two factors, taken together, are often referred to as economies of scale – a universal concept that applies (up to a point) to all types of operation. However, above a certain size, the lowest cost-point on curves such as those shown in Figure 7.2 may increase. This is because of 'diseconomies of scale', two of which are particularly important. First, complexity costs increase as size increases. The communications and coordination effort necessary to manage an operation tends to increase faster than capacity. Second, a larger centre is more likely to be partially underutilized because demand within a fixed location will be limited. The equivalent in operations that process physical items is transportation costs. For example, if a manufacturer supplies the whole of its European market from one major plant in Denmark, all supplies may have to be brought in from several countries to the single plant and all products then shipped from there throughout Europe.

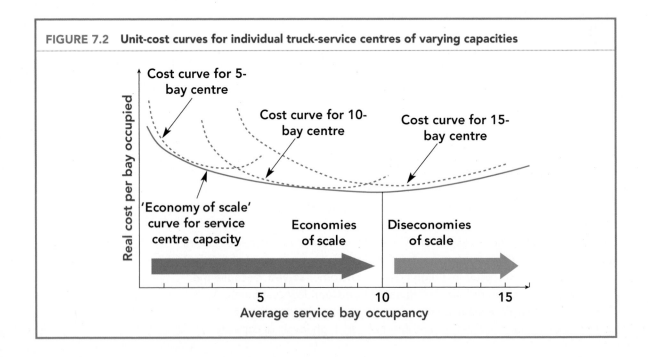

FIGURE 7.2   Unit-cost curves for individual truck-service centres of varying capacities

Operations in practice

Economies of scale in heart surgery and shipping[1]

Don't think that the idea of economies of scale only applies to manufacturing operations. It's a universal concept. Here are just two examples.

In the 1,000-bed Narayana Hrudayalaya Hospital, in Bangalore, India, Dr Devi Shetty (who has been called the 'Henry Ford' of heart surgery) has created what, according to *Forbes* magazine, is the world's largest heart factory. It is a radical new approach, Shetty says, and proves that economies of scale can transform the cost of cardiology. He calls his approach the 'Wal-Martization' of surgery – referring to the high-volume approach of the world's largest supermarket chain, Wal-Mart. The hospital has 42 surgeons who perform 6,000 heart operations each year, including 3,000 on children. This makes the hospital the busiest facility of its type in

the world. And it's needed: it is estimated that India requires 2.5 million heart operations every year, yet only 90,000 are performed. "It's a numbers game", said Dr Shetty, who has performed 15,000 heart operations. "Surgeons are technicians. The more practice they get, the more specialised they become and the better the results." The result is that costs are slashed and the hospital can be profitable, even though many patients are poor. The hospital's charges for open-heart surgery are, on average, a tenth of the cost of the cheapest procedures in the United States. But, even then, treatment is too expensive for many, so wealthier patients are charged more to subsidise the poorest.

The *Eleonora Maersk* is one of seven ships in her class that are owned by Maersk Lines, the world's biggest container-shipping company. They are

among the biggest ships ever built: almost 400 m long (the length of four football pitches). The *Eleonora Maersk* is also powerful; it has the largest internal-combustion engine ever built – as powerful as 1,000 family cars – which enables it to move all its cargo from China to Europe in just over three weeks. Yet the ship is so automated that it requires only 13 people to crew it. On board, the ship can carry 15,000 20-foot containers, each one of which can hold 70,000 T-shirts. It is these economies of scale that allow a T-shirt made in China to be sent to the Netherlands for just 2.5 cents. And the economies of scale involved in building and running these ships means that things will get bigger still. Hoping to drive costs down further, the ship's owners have ordered 20 even-larger ships with a capacity of 18,000 20-foot containers, costing $200 m each. ● ● ●

The timing of capacity change

Any operation that changes its capacity needs to decide when to make the change. For example, Figure 7.3 shows the forecast demand for a manufacturer's new product. In deciding *when* new capacity is to be

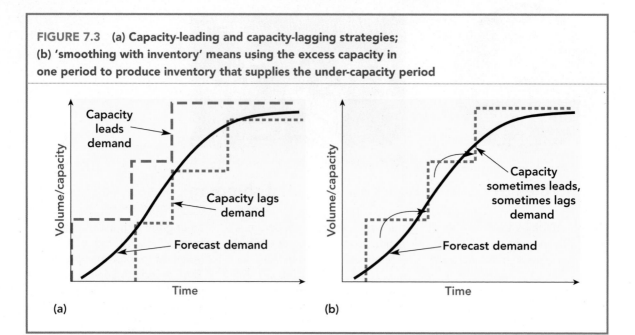

FIGURE 7.3 (a) Capacity-leading and capacity-lagging strategies; (b) 'smoothing with inventory' means using the excess capacity in one period to produce inventory that supplies the under-capacity period

introduced, the company can mix the three strategies that are illustrated in the figure. These are:

 capacity leading – timing the introduction of capacity in such a way that there is always sufficient capacity to meet forecast demand;

 capacity lagging – timing the introduction of capacity so that demand is always equal to or greater than capacity;

 capacity 'smoothing with inventory' – capacity is introduced to sometimes lead and sometimes lag demand, but inventory built up during the 'lead' times is used to help meet demand during the 'lag' times.

Each strategy has its own advantages and disadvantages. These are shown in Table 7.1. The actual approach taken by any company will depend on how it views these advantages and disadvantages. For example, if the company's access to funds for capital expenditure is limited, it is likely to find the delayed capital-expenditure requirement of the capacity-lagging strategy relatively attractive. Of course, the third strategy, 'smoothing with inventory', is only appropriate for operations that produce products that can be stored. Customer-processing operations, such as hotels, cannot satisfy demand in one year by using rooms that were vacant the previous year.

operations principle
Capacity-leading strategies increase opportunities to meet demand. Capacity-lagging strategies increase capacity utilization Using inventories to overcome demand–capacity imbalance tends to increase working capital requirements.

TABLE 7.1 The arguments for and against pure-leading, pure-lagging and smoothing-with-inventory strategies of capacity timing

Advantages	Disadvantages
Capacity-leading strategies	
▶ Always sufficient capacity to meet demand, therefore revenue is maximized and customers satisfied	▶ Utilization of the plants is always relatively low, therefore costs will be high
▶ Most of the time there is a 'capacity cushion' that can absorb extra demand if forecasts are pessimistic	▶ Risks of even greater (or even permanent) over-capacity if demand does not reach forecast levels
▶ Any critical start-up problems with new operations are less likely to affect supply	▶ Capital spending on capacity will be early
Capacity-lagging strategies	
▶ Always sufficient demand to keep the operation working at full capacity, therefore unit costs are minimized	▶ Insufficient capacity to meet demand fully, therefore reduced revenue and dissatisfied customers
▶ Over-capacity problems are minimized if forecasts prove optimistic	▶ No ability to exploit short-term increases in demand
▶ Capital spending on the operation is delayed	▶ Under-supply position even worse if there are start-up problems with the new operations
Smoothing-with-inventory strategies	
▶ All demand is satisfied, therefore customers are satisfied and revenue is maximized	▶ The cost of inventories in terms of working capital requirements can be high. This is especially serious at a time when the company requires funds for its capital expansion
▶ Utilization of capacity is high and therefore costs are low	▶ Risks of product deterioration and obsolescence
▶ Very short-term surges in demand can be met from inventories	

What are the main medium-term capacity decisions?

Capacity management in the medium term is concerned with setting capacity levels in *aggregated* terms (what we call medium-term capacity management is sometimes called 'aggregate planning'). 'Aggregated' means that information concerning different products and services is bundled together in order to get a broad view of demand and capacity. This may mean some degree of approximation. For example, a hotel might think of demand and capacity in terms of 'room nights per month'. This ignores the number of guests in each room and their individual requirements, but it is a good first approximation. A woollen knitwear factory might measure demand and capacity in the number of units (garments) it is capable of making per month, ignoring size, colour or style variations. The ultimate aggregation measure is money. For example, retailers may measure demand using revenue per month, ignoring variation in the number of items sold, their gross margin, or the number of items per customer, etc.

operations principle
In the medium term, capacity is usually expressed in aggregated terms.

The objectives of capacity management

Medium-term capacity management affects several aspects of performance:

 Costs will be affected by the balance between capacity and demand. Capacity levels in excess of demand could mean under-utilization of capacity and therefore high unit costs.

 Revenues will also be affected by the balance between capacity and demand, but in the opposite way. Capacity levels equal to or higher than demand at any point in time will ensure that all demand is satisfied and no revenue lost.

 Working capital will be affected if an operation decides to build up a finished goods inventory prior to demand. This might allow demand to be satisfied, but the organization will have to fund the inventory until it can be sold.

 Quality of goods or services might be affected by a capacity plan that involves large fluctuations in capacity levels – by hiring temporary staff, for example. The new staff and the disruption to the routine working of the operation could increase the probability of errors being made.

 Speed of response to customer demand could be enhanced, either by the build-up of inventories or by the deliberate provision of surplus capacity to avoid queuing.

 Dependability of supply will also be affected by how close demand levels are to capacity. The closer demand gets to the operation's capacity ceiling, the less able it is to cope with any unexpected disruptions and the less dependable its deliveries could be.

 Flexibility, especially volume flexibility, will be enhanced by surplus capacity. If demand and capacity are in balance, the operation will not be able to respond to any unexpected increase in demand.

Understanding medium-term demand

The first task of medium-term capacity management is to understand the nature of demand. Although demand forecasting is often the responsibility of the sales and/or marketing functions, it is a very important input into the capacity management decisions, and so is of interest to operations managers.

It is therefore important to understand the basis and rationale for these demand forecasts. As far as capacity management is concerned, there are three requirements from a demand forecast:

It is expressed in terms that are useful for capacity management   Forecasts expressed only in money terms give little indication of the demands that will be placed on an operation. They need to be translated into the effects of demand on the operation.

It is as accurate as possible   In capacity management, the accuracy of a forecast is particularly important because, whereas demand can change instantaneously, there is usually a lag between deciding to change capacity and the change taking effect.

It gives an indication of relative uncertainty   Capacity decisions are based partly on the degree of confidence in a forecast. So, an estimate of how much actual demand could differ from the average can be particularly important. Then, if demand is particularly uncertain, it may be necessary to plan for reserve capacity.

UNDERSTANDING SEASONALITY

Most markets are influenced by some kind of seasonality. Sometimes the causes of seasonality are climatic (holidays), sometimes festive (gift purchases), sometimes financial (tax processing), or social, or political; in fact, there are many factors that affect the volume of activity in everything from construction materials to clothing, from healthcare to hotels. Typically, the term 'seasonality' is used to describe changes to demand over a period of a year. Yet, similar variations in demand can also occur for some products and services over a shorter cycle. The daily and weekly demand patterns of a supermarket will fluctuate with the day of the week and even the time of day. The extent to which an operation will have to cope with very short-term demand fluctuations is partly determined by how long its customers are prepared to wait for their products or services. Operations such as emergency services, whose customers cannot wait, will have to plan for very short-term demand fluctuations.

Understanding medium-term capacity

Measuring capacity may sound simple, but can be relatively hard to define unambiguously unless the operation is standardized and repetitive. So, a government office may have the capacity to print and post 500,000 tax forms per week. A fast ride at a theme park might be designed to process 1,200 people per hour. In each case, an *output capacity measure* is the most appropriate measure because the output from the operation does not vary in its nature. But, for many operations capacity is not so obvious. When a much wider range of outputs places varying demands on the process, *input capacity measures* are frequently used to define capacity. Almost every type of operation could use a mixture of both input and output measures, but, in practice, most choose to use one or the other (see Table 7.2).

operations principle
Any measure of capacity should reflect the ability of an operation or process to supply demand.

TABLE 7.2   **Input and output capacity measures for different operations**

Operation	Input measure of capacity	Output measure of capacity
▶ Air-conditioner plant	▶ Machine hours available	▶ **Number of units per week**
▶ Hospital	▶ **Beds available**	▶ Number of patients treated per week
▶ Theatre	▶ **Number of seats**	▶ Number of customers entertained per week
▶ University	▶ **Number of students**	▶ Students graduating per year
▶ Retail store	▶ **Salesfloor area**	▶ Number of items sold per day
▶ Airline	▶ **Number of seats available on the sector**	▶ Number of passengers per week
▶ Electricity company	▶ Generator size	▶ **Megawatts of electricity generated**
▶ Brewery	▶ Volume of fermentation tanks	▶ **Litres per week**

(Note: The most commonly used measure is shown in bold.)

CAPACITY DEPENDS ON ACTIVITY MIX

How much an operation can do depends on what it is being required to do. One part of a hospital may treat patients requiring only short stays in hospital. Another could treat patients requiring long periods of observation or recuperation. Output depends on the mix of activities in which the hospital is engaged and, because most hospitals perform many different types of activities, output is difficult (though not impossible) to predict.

> **operations principle**
> Capacity is a function of service/product mix, duration and specification.

CAPACITY DEPENDS ON THE DURATION OVER WHICH OUTPUT IS REQUIRED

Capacity is the output that an operation can deliver *in a defined unit of time*. But the level of activity that may be achievable over short periods of time is not the same as the capacity that is sustainable on a regular basis. For example, a tax-return processing office, during its peak periods, may be capable of processing 120,000 applications a week. It does this by extending the working hours of its staff, discouraging its staff from taking vacations and maybe just by working intensively. Nevertheless, staff do need vacations, nor can they work long hours continually.

CAPACITY DEPENDS ON THE SPECIFICATION OF OUTPUT

Some operations can increase their output by changing the specification of their product or service (although this is more likely to apply to a service). For example, a postal service may effectively reduce its delivery dependability at peak times. So, during the busy Christmas period, the number of letters delivered within one day may drop from 95 per cent to 85 per cent.

CAPACITY 'LEAKAGE'

The theoretical capacity of a process (the capacity that it was designed to have) is not always achieved in practice. Some reasons for this are predictable: effective capacity will be lost as people switch between tasks; maintenance will need to be performed on machines; training will be required for employees; and scheduling clashes could lose time. Other reasons for

Operations in practice

Panettone – how Italy's bakers cope with seasonal demand[2]

Panettone is a light and fluffy, dome-shaped confection, dotted with sultanas and candied citrus peel. It is *the* Italian Christmas cake, and about 40 million of them are consumed throughout Italy over the holiday period. Now, they are becoming popular around the world. This boost to production is good news for the big Italian manufacturers, but although volumes are higher, the product is still seasonal, which poses a problem for even the experienced Milanese confectioners. Smaller, 'artisan' producers simply squeeze a few batches of panettone into their normal baking schedules as Christmas approaches. But for the large industrial producers who need to make millions for the Christmas season, it is not possible. And no panettone manufacturer is larger than the Bauli group. It is one of the foremost manufacturers of confectionery in Europe. The company's output of panettone accounts for 38 per cent of Italian sales, and although Bauli has diversified into year-round products such as croissants and biscuits, it is a leader in the production of products for festive occasions. So how does Bauli cope with such seasonality? Partly it is by hiring large numbers of temporary seasonal workers to staff its dedicated production lines. At peak times there can be 1,200 seasonal workers in the factory, more than its permanent staff of around 800. It also starts to build up inventories before demand begins to increase for the Christmas peak. Production of panettone lasts about four months, starting in September. "Attention to ingredients and the use of new technologies in production give a shelf-life of five months without preservatives", says Michele Bauli, deputy chairman, who comes from the firm's founding family. Temporary workers are also hired to bake other seasonal cakes, such as the *colomba* – a dove-shaped Easter treat – which keeps them occupied for a month and a half in the spring. ● ● ●

reduced capacity are less predictable – for example, labour shortages, quality problems, delays in the delivery of bought-in products and services and machine, or system, breakdown can all reduce capacity. This reduction in capacity is sometimes called 'capacity leakage'. One popular method of assessing this leakage is the overall equipment effectiveness (OEE) measure, which is calculated as follows:

$$OEE = a \times p \times q$$

where *a* is the availability of a process, *p* is the performance or speed of a process and *q* is the quality of product or services that the process creates. OEE (see Figure 7.4) brings together the capacity leakage caused by reduced availability (from things such as set-up and changeover losses, breakdown failures, or when employees are being absent), reduced speed (such as when equipment is idling or being run below its optimum

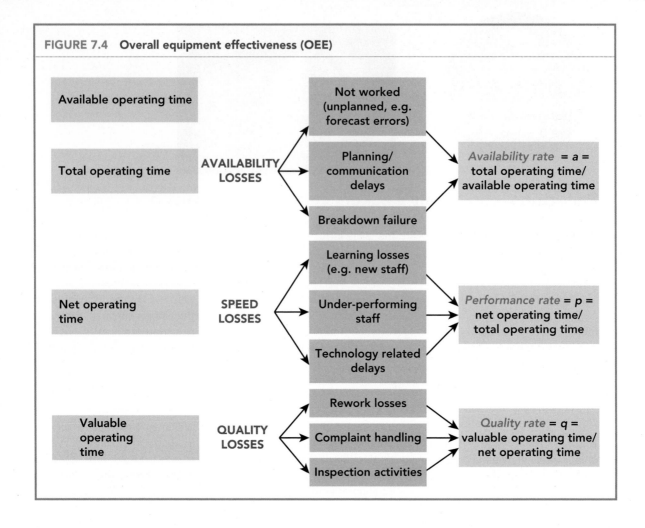

FIGURE 7.4 Overall equipment effectiveness (OEE)

work rate, or when individuals are not working at an optimum rate) and quality losses (caused by processing errors). For processes to operate effectively, they need to achieve high levels of performance against all three dimensions – availability, speed (performance) and quality. All these losses in the calculation mean that OEE represents the valuable operating time as a percentage of the capacity something was designed to have.

Both demand and capacity can vary

While many operations are most concerned with dealing with changes in demand, some operations also have to cope with variation in *capacity* (if it is defined as 'the ability to supply'). For example, Figure 7.5 shows the demand and capacity variation of two businesses. The first is a domestic appliance repair service whose capacity is relatively stable, but varies because its service people take vacations at particular times of the year. Demand, by contrast, fluctuates more significantly. The second business is a producer of frozen spinach. Here demand is relatively constant but (supply) capacity varies significantly: high during the growing season, falling almost to zero for part of the year.

operations principle
Capacity management decisions should reflect both predictable and unpredictable variations in capacity and demand.

Worked example

In a typical 7-day period, the planning department programmes a particular machine to work for 150 hours – its loading time. Changeovers and set-ups take an average of 10 hours, and breakdown failures average 5 hours every 7 days. The time when the machine cannot work because it is waiting for material to be delivered from other parts of the process is 5 hours on average, and during the period when the machine is running it averages 90 per cent of its rated speed. Three per cent of the parts processed by the machine are subsequently found to be defective in some way.

$$\text{Maximum time available} = 7 \times 24 \text{ hours} = 168 \text{ hours}$$

$$\text{Loading time} = 150 \text{ hours}$$

$$\begin{aligned}\text{Availability losses} &= 10 \text{ hours (set-ups)} \\ &+ 5 \text{ hours (breakdowns)} \\ &= 15 \text{ hours}\end{aligned}$$

$$\begin{aligned}\text{Total operating time} &= \text{loading time} \\ &- \text{availability} \\ &= 150 \text{ hours} - 15 \text{ hours} \\ &= 135 \text{ hours}\end{aligned}$$

$$\begin{aligned}\text{Speed losses} &= 5 \text{ hours (idling)} \\ &+ ((135 - 5) \times 0.1) \\ &(10\% \text{ of remaining time}) \\ &= 18 \text{ hours}\end{aligned}$$

$$\begin{aligned}\text{Net operating time} &= \text{total operating time} \\ &- \text{speed losses} \\ &= 135 - 18 \\ &= 117 \text{ hours}\end{aligned}$$

$$\begin{aligned}\text{Quality losses} &= 117 \text{ (net operating time)} \\ &\times 0.03 \text{ (error rate)} \\ &= 3.51 \text{ hours}\end{aligned}$$

$$\begin{aligned}\text{Valuable operating time} &= \text{net operating time} \\ &- \text{quality losses} \\ &= 117 - 3.51 \\ &= 113.49 \text{ hours}\end{aligned}$$

$$\text{Availability rate} = a = \frac{\text{total operating time}}{\text{loading time}}$$
$$= \frac{135}{150} = 90\%$$

$$\text{and, performance rate} = p = \frac{\text{net operating time}}{\text{total operating time}}$$
$$= \frac{117}{135} = 86.67$$

$$\text{and quality rate} = q = \frac{\text{valuable operating time}}{\text{net operating time}}$$
$$= \frac{113.49}{117} = 97\%$$

$$\text{OEE } (a \times p \times q) = 75.6\%$$

Predictable and unpredictable variation

The balance between predictable and unpredictable variation affects the nature of capacity management. When demand is stable and predictable, capacity management is straightforward. If demand is changeable, but this

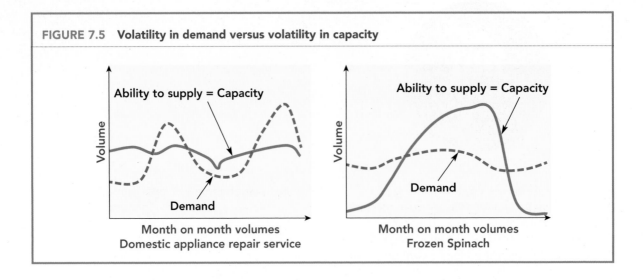

FIGURE 7.5   **Volatility in demand versus volatility in capacity**

change is predictable, capacity adjustments may be needed, but can be planned in advance. With unpredictable variation in demand, if an operation is to react to it at all, it must do so quickly; otherwise the change in capacity will have little effect on the operation's ability to satisfy demand. Figure 7.6 illustrates how the objectives and tasks of capacity management vary depending on the balance between predictable and unpredictable variation.

FIGURE 7.6   **The nature of capacity management depends on the mixture of predictable and unpredictable demand and capacity variation**

		UNPREDICTABLE VARIATION	
		Low	**High**
PREDICTABLE VARIATION	**High**	*Objective* – Adjust planned capacity as efficiently as possible *Capacity management tasks* ➜ Evaluate optimum mix of methods for capacity fluctuation ➜ Work on how to reduce cost of putting plan into effect	*Objective* – Adjust planned capacity as efficiently as possible and enhance capability for further fast adjustments *Capacity management tasks* ➜ Combination of those for predictable and unpredictable variation
	Low	*Objective* – Make sure the base capacity is appropriate *Capacity management tasks* ➜ Seek ways of providing steady capacity effectively	*Objective* – Adjust capacity as fast as possible *Capacity management tasks* ➜ Identify sources of extra capacity and/or uses for surplus capacity ➜ Work on how to adjust capacity and/or uses of capacity quickly

What are the ways of coping with mismatches between medium-term demand and capacity?

There are three 'pure' options available for coping with mismatches between supply and demand, as illustrated in Figure 7.7, although a combination of all of these are often used:

 Level capacity plan ignores demand fluctuations and keeps nominal capacity levels constant.

 Chase demand plan adjusts capacity to reflect the fluctuations in demand.

 Demand management attempts to change demand to align with capacity.

Level capacity plan

In a level capacity plan, the capacity is fixed throughout the planning period, regardless of the fluctuations in forecast demand. This means that the same number of staff operate the same processes and should therefore be capable of producing the same aggregate output in each period. Where non-perishable materials are processed, but not immediately sold, they can be transferred to finished goods inventory in anticipation of sales at a later time.

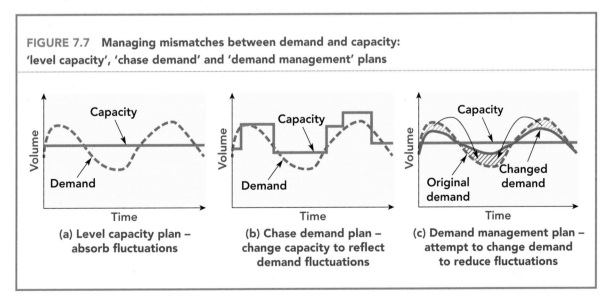

FIGURE 7.7 **Managing mismatches between demand and capacity: 'level capacity', 'chase demand' and 'demand management' plans**

(a) Level capacity plan – absorb fluctuations

(b) Chase demand plan – change capacity to reflect demand fluctuations

(c) Demand management plan – attempt to change demand to reduce fluctuations

Level capacity plans of this type can achieve the objectives of stable employment patterns, high process utilization and usually also high productivity with low unit costs. Unfortunately, they can also create considerable inventory, which has to be financed and stored. Perhaps the biggest problem, however, is that decisions have to be taken as to what to produce for inventory rather than for immediate sale. Will green woollen sweaters knitted in July still be fashionable in October? Most firms operating this plan, therefore, give priority to only creating inventory where future sales are relatively certain and unlikely to be affected by changes in fashion or design. Clearly, such plans are not suitable for 'perishable' products, such as foods and some pharmaceuticals, for products where fashion changes rapidly and unpredictably, or for customized products.

A level capacity plan could also be used by a hotel or supermarket, although this would not be the usual approach of such organizations because it usually results in a waste of staff resources, reflected in low productivity. Because service cannot be stored as inventory, a level capacity plan could involve running the operation at a uniformly high level of capacity availability, thus underutilizing both staff and facilities and making it prohibitively expensive in many service operations. However, such plans may be appropriate where the opportunity costs of individual lost sales are very high – for example, in the high-margin retailing of jewellery and in (real) estate agents. It is also possible to set the capacity somewhat below the forecast peak-demand level in order to reduce the degree of underutilization. However, in the periods where demand is expected to exceed planned capacity, customer service may deteriorate.

operations principle
Level capacity plans usually involve either inventory or underutilization costs.

Chase demand plan

The opposite of a level capacity plan is one that attempts to match capacity closely to the varying levels of forecast demand. This is much more difficult to achieve than a level capacity plan, as different numbers of staff, different working hours and even different amounts of equipment may be necessary in each period. For this reason, pure chase demand plans are unlikely to appeal to operations that manufacture standard, non-perishable products. Also, where manufacturing operations are particularly capital-intensive, the chase demand policy would require a level of physical capacity, all of which would only be used occasionally. It is for this reason that such a plan is less likely to be appropriate for an aluminium producer than for a woollen garment manufacturer, for example. A pure chase demand plan is more usually adopted by operations that are not able to store their output, such as services or manufacturers of perishable products. It avoids the wasteful provision of excess staff that occurs with a level capacity plan, and yet, with good planning, should satisfy customer demand. Where output can be stored, the chase demand policy might be adopted in order to minimize or eliminate finished goods inventory, especially if the nature of future demand (in terms of volume or mix) is relatively unpredictable. There are a number of different methods for adjusting capacity, although they all have some costs associated with them. Some of these methods are shown in Table 7.3.

TABLE 7.3 Methods of executing a chase demand plan

Method of adjusting capacity	Advantages	Disadvantages
Overtime – staff working longer than their normal working times	Quickest and most convenient	Extra payment normally necessary and agreement of staff to work; can reduce productivity over long periods
Annualized hours – staff contracted to work a set number of hours per year, rather than a set number of hours per week.	Without many of the costs associated with overtime, the number of staff time available to an organization can be varied throughout the year to reflect demand	When very large and unexpected fluctuations in demand are possible, all the negotiated annual working time flexibility can be used up before the end of the year
Staff scheduling – arranging working times (start and finish times) to vary the aggregate number of staff available for working at any time	Staffing levels can be adjusted to meet demand without changing job responsibilities or hiring in new staff	Providing start and finish (shift) times that satisfy staffs' need for reasonable working times and shift patterns, as well as providing appropriate capacity, can be difficult
Varying the size of the workforce – hiring extra staff during periods of high demand and laying them off as demand falls ('hire and fire')	Reduces basic labour costs quickly.	Hiring costs and possible low productivity while new staff go through the learning curve; lay-offs may result in severance payments and possible loss of morale in the operation, and loss of goodwill in the local labour market
Using part-time staff – recruit staff who work for less than the normal working day (at the busiest periods)	Good method of adjusting capacity to meet predictable short-term demand fluctuations	Expensive if the fixed costs of employment for each employee (irrespective of how long he or she works) are high
Skills flexibility – designing flexibility in job design and job demarcation so that staff can transfer across from less busy parts of the operation	Fast method of reacting to short-term demand fluctuations	Investment in skills training needed and may cause some internal disruption

Method of adjusting capacity	Advantages	Disadvantages
▶ Sub-contracting/ outsourcing – buying, renting or sharing capacity or output from other operations	▶ No disruption to the operation	▶ Can be very expensive because of sub-contractor's margin and sub-contractor may not be as motivated to give same service, or quality; also a risk of leakage of knowledge
▶ Changing output rate – expecting staff (and equipment) to work faster than normal	▶ No need to provide extra resources	▶ Can only be used as a temporary measure, and even then can cause staff dissatisfaction, a reduction in the quality of work, or both

Not all the methods in Table 7.3 are uncontroversial. The idea of fluctuating the workforce, or their paid hours (so-called zero-hours contracts), to match demand is regarded as unethical by some. It is any business' responsibility, they argue, to engage in a set of activities that are capable of sustaining employment at a steady level. Disrupting people's working, merely for seasonal fluctuations, which can be predicted in advance, is totally unacceptable. Even hiring people on a short-term contract, in practice, leads to them being offered poorer conditions of service and leads to a state of permanent anxiety as to whether they will keep their jobs.

> **operations principle**
> There are many ways to implement chase demand plans, but all carry costs.

Demand management plan

The third pure capacity management approach is demand management. Here, the objective is to change the pattern of demand to bring it closer to available capacity, by either stimulating off-peak demand or by constraining peak demand. There are a number of methods for achieving this:

 Constraining customer access   customers may only be allowed access to the operation's products or services at particular times – for example, reservation and appointment systems in hospitals.

 Price differentials   adjusting price to reflect demand. That is, increasing prices during periods of high demand and reducing prices during periods of low demand. For example, taxi-hiring services using apps often adopt 'surge-pricing', where prices are set as a function of demand at the point where the service is requested.

 Scheduling promotions   varying the degree of market stimulation through promotion and advertising in order to encourage demand

Operations in practice

Annualized hours at Lowaters[3]

Lowaters Nursery is a garden-plant and horticulture specialist in the South of England, employing around 25 people. Like any business that depends on seasonal weather conditions, it faces fluctuating demand for its services and products. It also prides itself on offering . . . 'the best service in partnership with our customers, by communicating in a friendly professional manner and listening to our customers to provide the result required' (Lowaters' mission statement). But to maintain its quality of service throughout the seasonal ups and down in workload means keeping your core team happy and employed throughout the year. This is why Lowaters introduced its annualized hours scheme, a method of fluctuating capacity as demand varies throughout the year without many of the costs associated with overtime or hiring temporary staff. It involves staff contracting to work a set number of hours per year rather than a set number of hours per week. The main advantage of this is that the amount of staff time available to an organization can be varied throughout the year to reflect the real state of demand. Maria Fox, one of the management team at Lowaters, says that annualized hours "simplifies administration and gives us the flexibility we need to run the business while delivering some real advantages to the employees. They are all effectively on salary with fixed monthly payments. We can flex the hours worked over the year – when we are busy we work longer and when things are quiet, in the winter, they can take time off. Everyone other than the directors is contracted to work 39 hours, on average, over 52 weeks of the year. ● ● ●

during normally low periods. For example, turkey growers in the UK and the USA make vigorous attempts to promote their products at times other than Christmas and Thanksgiving.

 Service differentials   allowing service levels to reflect demand (implicitly or explicitly) by allowing service to deteriorate in periods of high demand and increase in periods of low demand. If this strategy is used explicitly, customers are being educated to expect varying levels of service and hopefully move to periods of lower demand for their purchases.

A more radical approach attempts to create alternative products or services to fill capacity in quiet periods. It can be an effective demand management method but, ideally, new products or services should meet three criteria: (a) they can be produced via the same processes; (b) they have different demand patterns to existing offerings; and (c) they are sold through similar marketing channels. For example, most universities fill their accommodation and lecture theatres with conferences and company meetings during vacations, and ski resorts may provide mountain activity holidays in the summer.

Yield management

In operations that have relatively fixed capacities, such as airlines and hotels, it is important to use the capacity of the operation for generating revenue to its full potential. One approach used by such operations is called yield management.[4] This is really a collection of methods, some of which we have already discussed, which can be used to ensure that an operation maximizes its potential to generate profit. Yield management is especially useful where capacity is relatively fixed, the market can be fairly clearly segmented. the service cannot be stored in any way, the service is sold in advance and the marginal cost of making a sale is relatively low.

Airlines, for example, fit all these criteria. They adopt a collection of methods to try to maximize the yield (i.e. profit) from their capacity. Over-booking capacity may be used to compensate for passengers who do not show up for the flight. However, if more passengers show up than they expect, the airline will have a number of upset passengers. By studying past data on flight demand, airlines try to balance the risks of over-booking and under-booking. Operations may also use price discounting at quiet times, when demand is unlikely to fill capacity. For example, hotels will typically offer cheaper room rates outside of holiday periods to try and increase naturally lower demand. In addition, many larger chains will sell heavily discounted rooms to third parties who, in turn, take on the risk (and reward) of finding customers for these rooms.

How can operations understand the consequences of their medium-term capacity decisions?

Before an operation adopts one or more of the three 'pure' capacity plans (level capacity, chase demand or demand management), it should examine the likely consequences. Three methods are particularly useful in helping to assess the consequences of adopting particular capacity plans:

considering capacity decisions using cumulative representations;

 considering capacity decisions using queuing principles;

 considering capacity decisions over time.

Considering capacity decisions using cumulative representations

Figure 7.8 shows the forecast aggregated demand for a chocolate factory that makes confectionery products. Demand for its products is such that it must supply a demand that peaks in September. One method of assessing whether a particular level of capacity can satisfy the demand would be to calculate the degree of over-capacity below the graph, which represents the capacity levels (areas A and C), and the degree of under-capacity above the graph (area B). If over-capacity is greater than under-capacity, then that capacity *could* be regarded as adequate to satisfy demand, the assumption being that inventory has been accumulated in the periods of over-capacity. However, there are two problems with this assumption. The first is that each month shown in Figure 7.8 may not have the same amount of productive time. Some months may contain vacation periods that reduce the availability of capacity. The second problem is that a capacity level that seems adequate may only be able to supply products *after* the demand for them has occurred. For example, if the period of under-capacity occurred at the beginning of the year, no inventory could have accumulated to meet demand. A far superior way of assessing capacity plans is first to plot demand on a *cumulative* basis. This is shown as the thicker line in Figure 7.8.

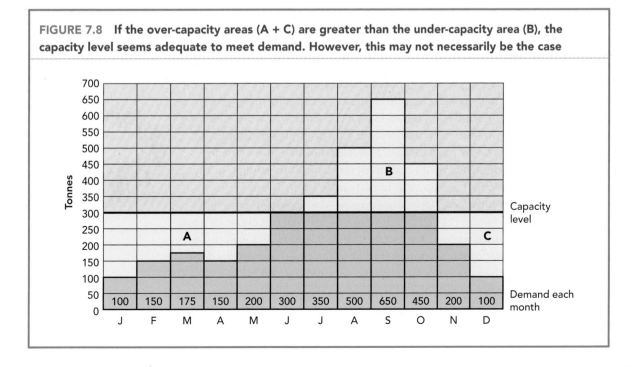

FIGURE 7.8   If the over-capacity areas (A + C) are greater than the under-capacity area (B), the capacity level seems adequate to meet demand. However, this may not necessarily be the case

The cumulative representation of demand immediately reveals that although total demand peaks in September, because of the restricted number of available productive days, the peak demand per productive day (which is more relevant to operations managers) occurs a month earlier in August. Also, it shows that the fluctuation in demand is even greater than it seemed. The ratio of monthly peak demand to monthly lowest demand is 6.5:1, but the ratio of peak to lowest demand per productive day is 10:1. Figure 7.9 also shows a level capacity plan, which produces at a rate of 14.03 tonnes per productive day. Although this meets cumulative demand by the end of the year, the plan is inadequate. Up to around day 168, the line representing cumulative production is above that representing cumulative demand, so, during this period, the factory has produced more products than has been demanded from it. So, by day 80, 1,222 tonnes have been produced but only 575 tonnes have been demanded. The surplus of 547 tonnes is the inventory at that point. When the cumulative demand line lies above the cumulative production line, the reverse is true. The vertical distance between the two lines now indicates the shortage, or lack of supply. So, by day 198, 3,025 tonnes have been demanded but only 2,778 tonnes produced. The shortage is therefore 247 tonnes. For any capacity plan to meet demand as it occurs, its cumulative production line must always lie above the cumulative demand line. This makes it a straightforward task to judge the adequacy of a plan, simply by looking at its cumulative representation. An impression of the inventory implications can also be gained from a cumulative representation by judging the area between the cumulative production and demand curves. This represents the amount of inventory carried over the period.

> **operations principle**
> For any capacity plan to meet demand as it occurs, its cumulative production line must always lie above its cumulative demand line.

Considering capacity decisions using queuing principles

Cumulative representations of capacity plans are useful where the operation has the ability to store its finished goods as inventory. However, for operations where it is not possible to produce products and services *before* demand for them has occurred, such as most service operations, capacity management is best considered using queuing ('waiting line', in US English) theory. Queuing theory accepts that while sometimes demand may be satisfied instantly, at other times customers may have to wait. This is particularly true when the arrival of individual demands on an operation are difficult to predict, or the time to produce a product or service is uncertain, or both. These circumstances make providing adequate capacity at all points in time particularly difficult. Figure 7.11 shows the general form of this capacity issue. Customers arrive according to some probability distribution and wait to be processed (unless part of the operation is idle); when they have reached the front of the queue, they are processed by one of the *n* parallel 'servers' (their processing time also being described by a probability distribution), after which they leave the operation.

FIGURE 7.9   A level capacity plan that produces shortages,
in spite of meeting demand at the end of the year

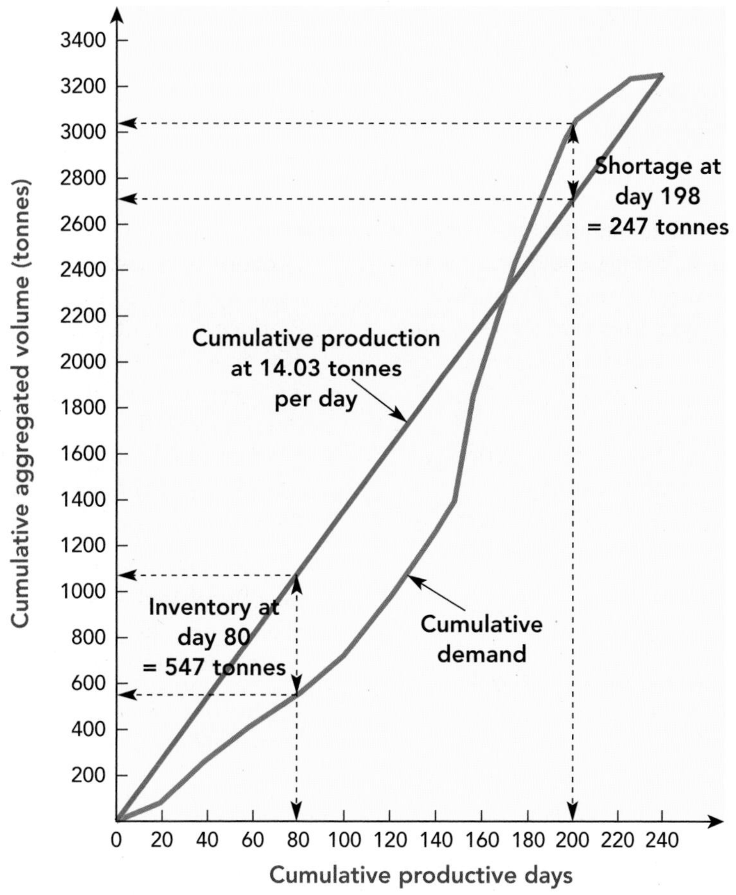

	J	F	M	A	M	J	J	A	S	O	N	D
Demand (tonnes/month)	100	150	175	150	200	300	350	500	650	450	200	100
Productive days	20	18	21	21	22	22	21	10	21	22	21	18
Demand (tonnes/day)	5	8.33	8.33	7.14	9.52	13.64	16.67	50	30.95	20.46	9.52	5.56
Cumulative days	20	38	59	80	102	124	145	155	176	198	219	237
Cumulative demand	100	250	425	575	775	1,075	1,425	1,925	2,575	3,025	3,225	3,325
Cumulative production (tonnes)	281	533	828	1,122	1,431	1,740	2,023	2,175	2,469	2,778	3,073	3,325
Ending inventory (tonnes)	181	283	403	547	656	715	609	250	(106)	(247)	(150)	0

The source of customers   'Customers' are not always human; they could
be trucks arriving at a weighbridge, orders arriving to be processed or
machines waiting to be serviced.

The arrival rate   This is the rate at which customers needing to be served
arrive at the server or servers. Rarely do customers arrive at a steady and
predictable rate. Usually there is variability in their arrival rate. Because of this,
it is necessary to describe arrival rates in terms of probability distributions.

Worked example

S uppose the chocolate manufacturer wants to reduce the inventory that would occur with a level capacity plan? It decides to explore two alternative plans, both involving some degree of demand chasing.

Plan 1

- Organize and staff the factory for a 'normal' capacity level of 8.7 tonnes per day.
- Produce at 8.7 tonnes per day for the first 124 days of the year, then increase capacity to 29 tonnes per day by heavy use of overtime, hiring temporary staff and some sub-contracting.
- Produce at 29 tonnes per day until day 194, then reduce capacity back to 8.7 tonnes per day for the rest of the year.

The costs of changing capacity by such a large amount (the ratio of peak to normal capacity is 3.33:1) are calculated by the company as being:

Cost of changing from 8.7 tonnes/day to 29 tonnes/day = £110,000

Cost of changing from 29 tonnes/day to 8.7 tonnes/day = £60,000

Plan 2

- Organize and staff the factory for a 'normal' capacity level of 12.4 tonnes per day.
- Produce at 12.4 tonnes per day for the first 150 days of the year, then increase capacity to 29 tonnes per day by overtime and hiring some temporary staff.
- Produce at 29 tonnes/day until day 190, then reduce capacity back to 12.4 tonnes per day for the rest of the year.

The costs of changing capacity in this plan are smaller because the degree of change is smaller (a peak-to-normal capacity ratio of 2.34:1), and they are calculated by the company as being:

Cost of changing from 12.4 tonnes/day to 29 tonnes/day = £35,000

Cost of changing from 29 tonnes/day to 12.4 tonnes/day = £15,000

Figure 7.10 illustrates both plans on a cumulative basis. Plan 1, which envisaged two drastic changes in capacity, has high capacity-change costs but, because its production levels are close to demand levels, it has low inventory-carrying costs. Plan 2 sacrifices some of the inventory cost advantage of Plan 1 but saves more in terms of capacity-change costs. ●●●

The queue   Customers waiting to be served form the queue itself. If there is relatively little limit on how many customers can queue at any time, we can assume that, for all practical purposes, an infinite queue is possible. Sometimes, however, there is a limit to how many customers can be in the queue at any one time.

Rejecting   If the number of customers in a queue is already at the maximum number allowed, then the customer could be rejected by the system. For example, during periods of heavy demand, some contact centres will not queue customers until the demand has declined.

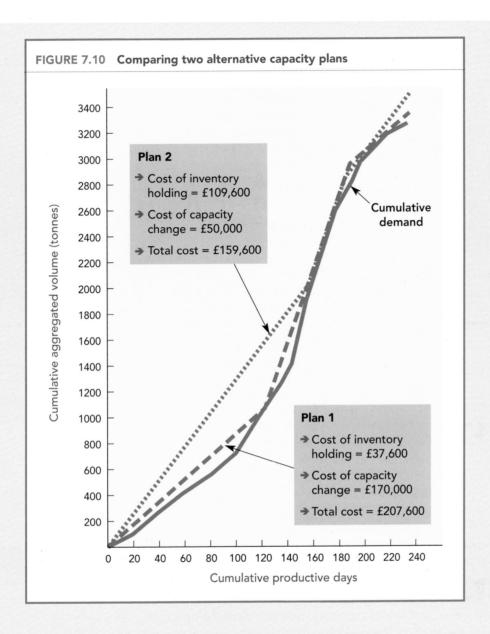

FIGURE 7.10   **Comparing two alternative capacity plans**

Plan 2
→ Cost of inventory holding = £109,600
→ Cost of capacity change = £50,000
→ Total cost = £159,600

Cumulative demand

Plan 1
→ Cost of inventory holding = £37,600
→ Cost of capacity change = £170,000
→ Total cost = £207,600

Cumulative aggregated volume (tonnes)

Cumulative productive days

Balking   When customers are humans with free will, they may refuse to join the queue and wait for service if it is judged to be too long.

Reneging   This is similar to balking, but here the customer has queued for a certain length of time and then leaves the queue.

Queue discipline   This is the set of rules that determines the order in which customers waiting in the queue are served. Most simple queues, such as those in a shop, use a *first-come-first-served* queue discipline.

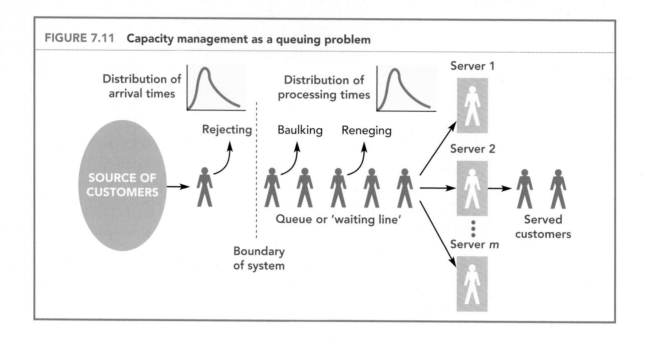

FIGURE 7.11 **Capacity management as a queuing problem**

Servers A server is the facility that processes the customers in the queue. In any queuing system there may be any number of servers configured in different ways. In Figure 7.11, servers are configured in parallel, but some may have servers in a series arrangement. For example, on entering a self-service restaurant you may join separate queues to collect a tray, order and collect a meal, order and collect a drink and finally pay for the meal. Of course, many queue systems are complex arrangements of both series and parallel connections.

BALANCING CAPACITY AND DEMAND

The dilemma in managing the capacity of a queuing system is how many servers to have available at any point in time in order to avoid unacceptably long queuing times or unacceptably low utilization of the servers. Because of the probabilistic arrival and processing times, only rarely will the arrival of customers match the ability of the operation to cope with them. Sometimes, if several customers arrive in quick succession, queues will build up in front of the operation. At other times, when customers arrive less frequently, some of the servers in the system will be idle. So even when the average capacity (processing capability) of the operation matches the average demand (arrival rate) on the system, both queues and idle time will occur. This is why the capacity planning and control problem for this type of operation is a trade-off between customer waiting time and system utilization. What is certainly important is being able to predict both of these factors for a given queuing system. Making capacity decisions about how to manage this trade-off can be done either by using simulation or mathematical models. Both these approaches are beyond the scope of this book, but some of the references in the 'Want to know more?' section at the end of this chapter explain them.

CUSTOMER PERCEPTIONS OF QUEUING

Few of us like waiting. Yet queuing is something we all have to do. So, if you have ever wondered if you are alone in particularly hating queuing, you are not – it's official. According to research involving 45,000 iPhone users who provided regular updates on their level of happiness via an app, it is one of the activities that most upsets us.[5] In fact, of all the things that make us feel unhappy, queuing is beaten only by being in bed sick. Yet, an important aspect of how they judge the service they receive from a queuing system is how they perceive the time spent queuing. It is well known that if you are told that you'll be waiting in a queue for twenty minutes and you are actually serviced in ten minutes, your perception of the queuing experience will be more positive than if you were told that you would be waiting ten minutes but the queue actually took twenty minutes. Because of this, the management of queuing systems usually involves attempting to manage customers' perceptions and expectations in some way. Below are a set of 'principles' that can help in evaluating and improving queues (that is, in cases where the queue itself can't be removed through process improvement).

operations principle
Customer reactions to having to queue will be influenced by more factors than simply waiting time.

1 Unoccupied time feels longer than occupied time.

2 Pre-process waits feel longer than in-process waits.

3 Anxiety makes the wait seem longer.

4 Uncertain waits feel longer than known, finite waits.

5 Unexplained waits feel longer than explained waits.

6 Unfair waits feel longer than equitable waits.

7 The more valuable the service, the longer a customer will 'happily' wait.

8 Solo waiting feels longer than group waiting.

9 Uncomfortable waits feel longer than comfortable waits.

10 New or infrequent users feel they wait longer than frequent users.

Considering capacity decisions over time

In practice, capacity management is a dynamic process that involves controlling and reacting to *actual* demand and *actual* capacity as it occurs. At the beginning of each period, operations management considers its forecasts of demand, its current capacity and, if appropriate, how much inventory has accumulated. Based on this, it plans the following period's capacity. During the next period, demand might or might not be as forecast

FIGURE 7.12 Capacity management strategies are partly dependent on the long- and short-term outlook for volume

SHORT-TERM OUTLOOK FOR VOLUME

	Decreasing below current capacity	Level with current capacity	Increasing above current capacity
Decreasing below current capacity	Reduce capacity (semi) permanently. For example, reduce staffing levels, reduce supply agreements.	Plan to reduce capacity (semi) permanently. For example, freeze recruitment, modify supply agreements.	Increase capacity temporarily. For example, increase working hours, and/or hire temporary staff, modify supply agreements.
Level with current capacity	Reduce capacity temporarily. For example, reduce staff working hours, modify supply agreements.	Maintain capacity at current level.	Increase capacity temporarily. For example, increase working hours, and/or hire temporary staff, modify supply agreements.
Increasing above current capacity	Reduce capacity temporarily. For example, reduce staff working hours, but plan to recruit, modify supply agreements.	Plan to increase capacity above current level, plan to increase supply agreements.	Increase capacity (semi) permanently. For example, hire staff, increase supply agreements.

LONG-TERM OUTLOOK FOR VOLUME

and the actual capacity of the operation might or might not turn out as planned. But capacity cannot usually be changed as quickly as demand changes. Which is why the difference between the long- and short-term outlook for the volume of demand is an important factor in deciding how (if at all) capacity should be adjusted. If the long-term outlook for volume is higher than current capacity can cope with, then it is unlikely that even low short-term demand volumes would cause an operation to make large, or difficult-to-reverse, cuts in capacity. Conversely, if the long-term outlook for demand is lower than current capacity, then it is unlikely that even high short-term demand volume would cause an operation to take 'difficult-to-reverse' extra capacity. Figure 7.12 illustrates some appropriate capacity management strategies, depending on the comparison of long- and short-term outlooks.

operations principle
The difference between likely short- and long-term forecasts for demand volume is an important factor in determining how capacity should be adjusted.

Summary answers to key questions

Each chapter has a 'Summary answers to key questions' section. Use it to check your understanding of the issues covered in the chapter.

WHAT IS CAPACITY MANAGEMENT?

★ The capacity of an operation is the *maximum level of value-added activity over a period of time* that the process can achieve under normal operating conditions.

★ Capacity management is the activity of understanding the nature of demand for products and services, and effectively planning and controlling capacity in the short term, medium term and long term.

WHAT ARE THE MAIN LONG-TERM CAPACITY DECISIONS?

★ Long-term capacity management focuses on planning capacity, usually over the 1–5-year period.

★ The two main long-term capacity decisions are how large an increment of capacity to plan for (influenced by the operation's economies of scale), and when to introduce or delete major increments of capacity.

WHAT ARE THE MAIN MEDIUM-TERM CAPACITY DECISIONS?

★ Medium-term capacity management focuses on adjusting aggregated capacity, usually over the 1–12-month period.

★ Demand forecasts should be expressed in terms that are useful, be as accurate as possible and give an indication of uncertainty.

★ Most demand is 'seasonal' in some way, but it is important to distinguish between predictable and unpredictable demand.

★ Capacity can be measured by the availability of its input resources or by the output that is created.

★ Effective capacity is influenced by activity mix, the time period over which activity is to be sustained and 'capacity leakage', which can be measured by overall operations effectiveness (OEE).

WHAT ARE THE WAYS OF COPING WITH MISMATCHES BETWEEN MEDIUM-TERM DEMAND AND CAPACITY?

 Demand–capacity mismatches usually call for some degree of capacity adjustment over time. There are three pure methods of achieving this, although in practice a mixture of all three may be used.

 'Level capacity' plans involve no change in capacity and require that the operation absorb demand–capacity mismatches, usually through under- or overutilization of its resources, or the use of inventory.

 'Chase demand' plans involve the changing of capacity through such methods as overtime, varying the size of the workforce and subcontracting, etc.

 'Demand management' plans involve an attempt to change demand through pricing or promotion methods, or changing product or service mix to reduce fluctuations in activity levels. When outputs cannot be stored, 'yield management' is a common method of coping with mismatches.

HOW CAN OPERATIONS UNDERSTAND THE CONSEQUENCES OF THEIR MEDIUM-TERM CAPACITY DECISIONS?

 Representing demand and output in the form of cumulative representations allows the feasibility of alternative capacity plans to be assessed.

 In many operations, especially service operations, a queuing approach can be used to explore the consequences of capacity strategies.

 Using long-term and short-term outlook for demand volume allows further evaluation of alternative capacity management decisions.

Problems and applications

All chapters have problems and application questions that will help you practice analyzing operations. They can be answered by reading the chapter. Model answers for the first question can be found on the companion website for this text.

→ A pizza company has a demand forecast for the next 12 months that is shown in Table 7.4. The current workforce of 100 staff can produce 1,500 cases of pizzas per month.

a) Prepare a production plan that keeps the output level. How much warehouse space would the company need for this plan?

b) Prepare a demand chase plan. What implications would this have for staffing levels, assuming that the maximum amount of overtime would result in production levels of only 10 per cent greater than normal working hours?

TABLE 7.4 **Pizza demand forecast**

Month	Demand (cases per month)
January	600
February	800
March	1000
April	1500
May	2000
June	1700
July	1200
August	1100
September	900
October	2500
November	3200
December	900

2

→ In a typical 7-day period, the planning department of the pizza company programmes its 'Pizzamatic' machine for 148 hours. It knows that changeovers and set-ups take 8 hours and breakdowns average 4 hours each week. Waiting for ingredients to be delivered usually accounts for 6 hours, during which the machine cannot work. When the machine is running, it averages 87 per cent of its design speed. And inspection has revealed that 2 per cent of the pizzas processed by the machine are not up to the company's quality standard. Calculate the OEE of the 'Pizzamatic' machine.

3

→ Seasonal demand is particularly important to the greetings card industry. Mother's Day, Father's Day, Halloween, Valentine's Day and other occasions have all been promoted as times to buy appropriately designed cards. Now, some card manufacturers have moved on to 'non-occasion' cards, which can be sent at any time. The cards include those intended to be sent from a parent to a child with messages such as 'Would a hug help?', 'Sorry I made you feel bad' and 'You're perfectly wonderful – it's your room that's a mess'. Other cards deal with more serious adult themes such as friendship ('You're more than a friend, you're just like family') or even alcoholism ('This is hard to say, but I think you're a much neater person when you're not drinking'). Some card companies have founded 'loyalty marketing groups' that 'help companies communicate with their customers at an emotional level'. They promote the use of greetings cards for corporate use, to show that customers and employees are valued.

a) What seem to be the advantages and disadvantages of these strategies adopted by the card companies?

b) What else could the card companies do to cope with demand fluctuations?

4

→ When footage shot by a fellow passenger showed a bloodied and unconscious man being pulled off of a United Airlines flight, the clip caused a sensation on social media. The incident began when United over-booked the flight (a problem made worse because at the last minute it decided to fly four members of staff to a connection point so they could staff another flight). The airline decided that it needed to bump four passengers to make way for the staff. They offered $400 and overnight hotel accommodation for passengers to take a later flight. No one accepted and the offer was increased to $800. Still no one accepted, so a manager announced that passengers would be selected to leave the flight, with frequent fliers and business-class passengers being given priority to stay. The first two people selected agreed to leave the plane. The third person selected also agreed. However, when the fourth man was approached, he refused, saying that he was a doctor and had to see patients in the morning. Eyewitnesses said the man was 'very upset' and tried to call his lawyer. So, instead of selecting another passenger, or increasing its offer (it could have offered a maximum of $1,350), security staff were called. The encounter with the security staff concluded with the man being wrenched from his seat onto the floor, after which he was hauled down the aisle, blood covering his face.

a) How should the airline have handled the situation?

b) After the incident attracted so much negative publicity, United announced a new upper limit of $10,000 in compensation for passengers who agree to give up a seat on a flight where United needs to free-up space, and that it would create a 'customer solutions team to provide agents with creative solutions' for getting inconvenienced customers to their destination. Do you think that these were sensible moves?

c) Within a few days another 'scandal' hit the airline. A 'potentially prize-winning' rabbit (called Simon) reportedly died while in transit from London Heathrow to O'Hare airport in Chicago. Why is this incident so important to United Airlines?

Want to know more?

Brandon-Jones, A. and Slack, N. (2008) *Quantitative analysis in Operations Management,* Harlow, UK: Pearson.

➜ Useful for operations management generally. Includes queuing theory formulae.

Gunther, N.J. (2007) *Guerrilla Capacity Planning,* New York: Springer.

➜ This book provides a tactical approach for planning capacity in both product-based and service-based contexts. Particularly interesting for those new to the ideas of capacity planning, as it covers basic and more advanced demand forecasting techniques, as well as 'classic' capacity responses.

Hansen, R.C. (2005). *Overall Equipment Effectiveness (OEE),* New York: Industrial Press.

➜ If you want to know more about OEE, its origins and applications, this is the place to start.

Van Mieghem, J. (2003). 'Capacity management, investment, and hedging: Review and recent developments', *Manufacturing and Service Operations Management,* **5**(4).

➜ An academic article reviewing the literature on strategic capacity management. It does a nice job of covering the different approaches to capacity management under conditions of stability versus volatility (demand change) and of certainty versus uncertainty (i.e., the predictability of change).

When the headlines read, 'Soaring temperatures deliver biggest rise in canned drink sales', it means that every operation in the drinks supply chain has had to increase their capacity in order to cope with the increased demand. For some products, temperature can have a huge effect on demand. In some parts of Europe, a 1° C rise in summer temperatures can lead to an increase in demand of around 12%. Which is why weather forecasting is an essential part of capacity planning for weather-dependent goods.

Inventory management

8

Introduction

Operations managers often have an ambivalent attitude towards inventories – of materials, people (queues), or information. On the one hand they can be costly (tying up working capital and valuable space in the operation), risky because items or information held in stock can deteriorate or become obsolete and annoying for customers who become an inventory when they're in a queue! On the other hand, inventories provide some security in uncertain environments that one can deliver items in stock should customers demand them. This is the dilemma of inventory management: in spite of the cost and the other disadvantages associated with holding stocks, an inventory does facilitate the smoothing of supply and demand. This chapter examines the role of inventory, and the decisions concerning how much to order, when to order and how best to control inventory. Figure 8.1 shows the position of the ideas described in the chapter within the general model of operations management.

Key questions

What is inventory?

Why do you need inventory?

How much should you order? (The volume decision)

When should you order? (The timing decision)

How can you control inventory?

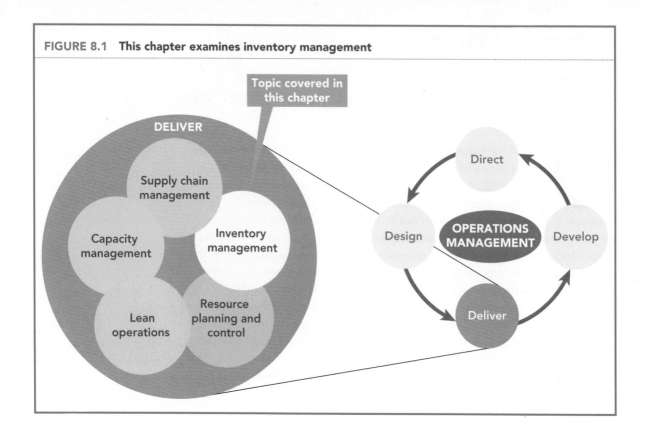

FIGURE 8.1   **This chapter examines inventory management**

What is inventory?

nventory is the accumulations of transformed resources – materials, customers or information – as they flow through processes, operations, or supply networks. Physical inventory (sometimes called 'stock') is the accumulation of physical materials such as components, parts, finished goods or physical (paper) information records. Queues are accumulations of customers, be they physical (people in an airport departure lounge) or virtual (waiting for service on the phone). Databases are stores for accumulations of digital information, such as medical records or insurance details.

Inventory management – the process of managing these accumulations – is an important task. Material inventories in a factory can represent a substantial proportion of cash tied up in working capital. Minimizing them can release large quantities of cash. However, reducing them too far can lead to customers' orders not being fulfilled. Customers held up in queues for too long can get irritated, angry and possibly leave, thus reducing revenue. Databases are critical for storing digital information, and while storage may be inexpensive, maintaining databases may not be.

Operations in practice

An inventory of energy[1]

Inventory is especially useful where there are regular mismatches between supply and demand. One of the best examples of this is the energy sector. Demand can fluctuate wildly, especially in countries that use large amounts of energy for cooling or heating. Supply, especially of the most convenient or cleaner forms of energy, is not always available at the right time. For example, wind does not blow all the time. Worse than that, it tends to be at its strongest at night when demand is low. In most countries, regulators require energy firms to preserve a safety margin over total estimated demand, in order to safeguard a reliable supply.

So, inventories are essential to smooth out differences between supply and demand. However, energy is far from easy to store. On a small scale, batteries can deliver power for short periods, but they cannot store (or discharge) energy at the high rates (hundreds of megawatts) or the huge quantities (thousands of megawatt hours) to supply a distribution grid. The most practical method of energy storage, and the most widely used, is pumped-storage hydropower (PSH). This method harnesses water and gravity to 'store' off-peak power and release it during periods of high demand by using off-peak electricity to pump water from one reservoir up to another higher one. The water is then released back down to the lower reservoir, when power is needed, through a turbine that produces electricity. The drawback to traditional PSH is that it requires the two reservoirs at different heights. More recent ideas for energy storage include: using wind turbines to pump water from a deep central reservoir out to sea, which is allowed to flow back into the reservoir through turbines that produce electricity; pumping water to raise a piston that sinks back down through a generator; using compressed air to store the energy; using argon gas to transfer heat between two vast tanks filled with gravel; and even storing energy in molten salt! For whichever method proves the most effective at creating energy inventories there will be rewards, both in terms of the potential market and in enabling the better use of sustainable energy. ● ● ●

All processes, operations and supply networks have inventories

Most things that flow do so in an uneven way. Rivers flow faster down steep sections or where they are squeezed into a ravine. Over relatively level ground they flow slowly, and form pools or even large lakes where there are natural or man-made barriers blocking their path. It's the same in operations. For example, passengers in an airport flow freely from public transport or their vehicles but then have to queue at several points, including check-in and security screening. They then have to wait (a queue, even if they are sitting) in the departure lounge as they are joined (batched) with other passengers to form a group of several hundred people who are ready to board the aircraft. They are then squeezed down the air bridge as they file in one at a time to board the plane. Similarly, a government tax department collects information about us and our finances from various sources, including our employers, our tax forms, information from banks or other investment companies, and stores this in databases until it is checked, sometimes by people, sometimes automatically, to create our tax codes and/or tax bills. In fact, because most operations involve flows of materials, customers and/or information, at some points they are likely to form inventories waiting to be processed (see Table 8.1).

Inventories are often the result of uneven flows. If there is a difference between the timing or the rate of supply and demand at any point in a process or network, then accumulations will occur. A common analogy is the water tank shown in Figure 8.2. If, over time, the rate of supply of water differs from the rate at which it is demanded, a tank of water (inventory) will be needed to maintain supply. When the rate of supply exceeds the rate of demand, inventory increases; when the rate of demand exceeds the rate of supply, inventory decreases. So, if an operation or process can match supply and demand rates, it will also succeed in reducing its inventory levels.

There is a complication when using this 'water flow' analogy to represent flows and accumulations (inventories) of information. Inventories of information can

TABLE 8.1   Examples of inventory held in processes, operations or supply networks

| Process, operation or supply network | Inventories | | |
	Physical inventories	Queues of customers	Information in databases
▶ Hotel	▶ Food items, drinks, toiletry items	▶ At check-in and check-out	▶ Customer details, loyalty card holders, catering suppliers
▶ Hospital	▶ Dressings, disposable instruments, blood	▶ Patients on a waiting list, patients in bed waiting for surgery	▶ Patient medical records
▶ Credit card application process	▶ Blank cards, forms, letters	▶ Customers waiting on the phone	▶ Customers' credit and personal information
▶ Computer manufacturer	▶ Components for assembly, packaging materials, finished computers ready for sale	▶ Customers waiting for delivery of their computer	▶ Customers' details, supplier information

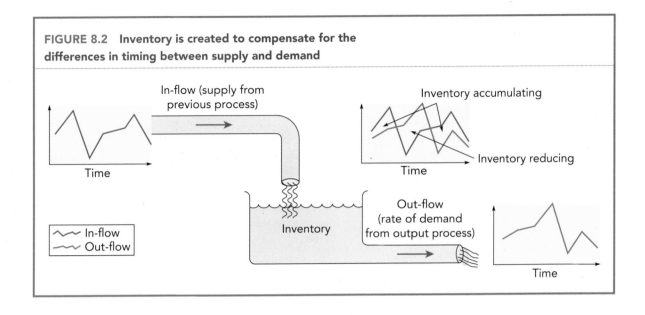

FIGURE 8.2 **Inventory is created to compensate for the differences in timing between supply and demand**

either be stored because of uneven flow, in the same way as materials and people, or stored because the operation needs to use the information to process something in the future. For example, an internet retail operation will process each order it receives, and inventories of information may accumulate because of uneven flows as we have described. But, in addition, during order processing, customer details could be permanently stored in a database. This information will then be used, not only for future orders from the same customer but also for other processes, such as targeting promotional activities. In this case, the inventory of information has turned from a transformed resource into a transforming resource, because it is being used to transform other information rather than being transformed itself. So, whereas managing physical material concerns ordering and holding the right amounts of goods or materials to deal with the variations in flow, and managing queues is about the level of resources to deal with demand, a database is the accumulation of information but it may not cause an interruption to the flow. Managing databases is about the organization of the data, its storage, security and retrieval (access and search).

Why do you need inventory?

There are plenty of reasons to avoid accumulating inventory, where possible. Table 8.2 identifies some of these – particularly those concerned with cost, space, quality and operational/organizational issues.

TABLE 8.2   **Some reasons to avoid inventories**

	Inventories		
	Physical inventories	**Queues of customers**	**Digital information in databases**
▶ Cost	▶ Ties up working capital and there could be high administrative and insurance costs	▶ Primarily a time-cost to the customer, i.e. wastes customers' time	▶ Cost of set-up, access, update and maintenance
▶ Space	▶ Requires storage space	▶ Requires areas for waiting, or phone lines for held calls	▶ Requires memory capacity; may require secure and/or special environment
▶ Quality	▶ May deteriorate over time, become damaged or obsolete	▶ May upset customers if they have to wait too long, may lose customers	▶ Data may be corrupted or lost or become obsolete
▶ Operational/ organizational	▶ May hide problems (see the chapter on 'lean' – Chapter 10)	▶ May put undue pressure on the staff and so quality is compromised for throughput	▶ Databases need constant management; access control, updating and security

So why have inventory?

On the face of it, it may seem sensible to have a smooth and even flow of materials, customers and information through operational processes and networks, and thus not have any accumulations. However, inventories provide many advantages for both operations and their customers. If a customer has to go to a competitor because a part is out of stock, or because they have had to wait too long, or because the company insists on collecting all their personal details each time they call, the value of inventories seems undisputable. The task of operations management is to allow an inventory to accumulate only when its benefits outweigh its disadvantages. The following are some of the benefits of inventory.

PHYSICAL INVENTORY IS AN INSURANCE AGAINST UNCERTAINTY

Inventory can act as a buffer against unexpected fluctuations in supply and demand. For example, a retail operation can never forecast demand perfectly over the lead-time. It will order goods from its suppliers such that there is always a minimum level of inventory to cover against the possibility that demand will be greater than expected during the time taken to deliver the goods. This is buffer, or safety, inventory. It can also compensate for the uncertainties in the process of the supply of goods into the store. The same applies with the output inventories, which is why hospitals always have a supply of blood, sutures and bandages for immediate response to accident-and-emergency patients. Similarly, auto-servicing services, factories and airlines may hold selected critical spare parts inventories so that maintenance staff can repair the most common faults without delay. Again, inventory is being used as an 'insurance' against unpredictable events.

PHYSICAL INVENTORY CAN COUNTERACT A LACK OF FLEXIBILITY

Where a wide range of customer options is offered, unless the operation is perfectly flexible, stock will be needed to ensure supply when it is engaged on other activities. This is sometimes called 'cycle inventory'. For example, Figure 8.3 shows the inventory profile of a baker who makes three types of bread. Because of the nature of the mixing and baking process, only one kind of bread can be produced at any time. The baker will have to produce each type of bread in batches large enough to satisfy the demand for each kind of bread between the times when each batch is ready for sale. So, even when demand is steady and predictable, there will always be some inventory to compensate for the intermittent supply of each type of bread.

PHYSICAL INVENTORY ALLOWS OPERATIONS TO TAKE ADVANTAGE OF SHORT-TERM OPPORTUNITIES

Sometimes opportunities arise that necessitate accumulating inventory, even when there is no immediate demand for it. For example, a supplier may be offering a particularly good deal on selected items for a limited time period, perhaps because they want to reduce their own finished goods inventories.

PHYSICAL INVENTORY CAN BE USED TO ANTICIPATE FUTURE DEMANDS

Rather than trying to make a product (consider fireworks as an example) only when it is needed, it may be produced throughout the year ahead of demand and put into inventory until it is needed. This type of inventory is called 'anticipation inventory' and is most commonly used when demand fluctuations are large but relatively predictable.

PHYSICAL INVENTORY CAN REDUCE OVERALL COSTS

Holding relatively large inventories may bring savings that are greater than the cost of holding the inventory. This may be when bulk-buying gets a lower unit

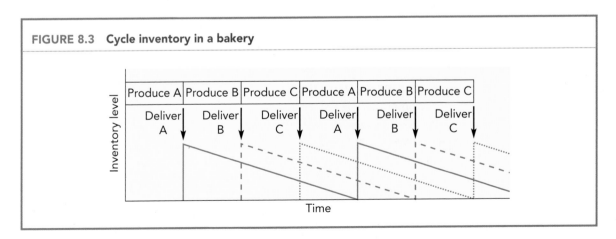

FIGURE 8.3   Cycle inventory in a bakery

cost, or when large-order quantities reduce both the number of orders placed and associated administration and material handling costs. This is the basis of the 'economic order quantity' (EOQ) approach, which will be treated later in this chapter.

PHYSICAL INVENTORY CAN INCREASE IN VALUE

Sometimes the items held as inventory can increase in value and so become an investment. For example, dealers in fine wines are less reluctant to hold inventory than dealers in wine that does not get better with age. (However, it can be argued that keeping fine wines until they are at their peak is really part of the overall process, rather than inventory as such.)

PHYSICAL INVENTORY FILLS THE PROCESSING 'PIPELINE'

When a retail store places an order, its supplier will 'allocate' the stock to the retail store in its own warehouse, pack it, load it onto its truck, transport it to its destination and unload it into the retailer's inventory. From the time that stock is allocated (and therefore it is unavailable to any other customer) to the time it becomes available for the retail store, it is called 'pipeline inventory'. In geographically dispersed supply networks, pipeline inventory is often substantial.

QUEUES OF CUSTOMERS HELP BALANCE CAPACITY AND DEMAND

This is especially useful if the main service resource is expensive – for example, doctors, consultants, lawyers or expensive equipment such as CAT scans. By waiting a short time after customers' arrival, and creating a queue, the service always has customers to process. This is also helpful where arrival times are less predictable – for example, where an appointment system is not used or is not possible.

QUEUES OF CUSTOMERS ENABLE PRIORITIZATION

In cases where resources are fixed and customers are entering the system with different levels of priority, the formation of a queue allows the organization to serve urgent customers while keeping other less urgent ones waiting. For example, in banking, high-value customers typically take priority in call-centre processing systems.

QUEUING GIVES CUSTOMERS TIME TO CHOOSE

Time spent in a queue gives customers time to decide what products/services they require. For example, customers waiting in a fast-food restaurant have time to look at the menu, so that when they get to the counter they are ready to make their order without holding up the server.

QUEUES ENABLE EFFICIENT USE OF RESOURCES

By allowing queues to form, customers can be batched together to make efficient use of operational resources. For example, a queue for an elevator makes better use of its capacity, while calling customers to the gate as a group allows more efficient boarding of an aircraft.

DATABASES PROVIDE EFFICIENT MULTI-LEVEL ACCESS

Databases are relatively cheap ways of storing information and providing many people with access. For example, the doctor's receptionist will be able to call up your records to check name and address and make an appointment, while the doctor will then be able to call up the appointment and the patient's records. There is no need to capture data at every transaction with a customer or supplier, though checks may be required.

DATABASES OF INFORMATION SPEED UP THE PROCESS

Amazon, for example, stores (with the customer's agreement) a customer's delivery address and credit card information so that purchases can be made with a single click, making it fast and easy for the customer.

Reducing physical inventory

For the remainder of this chapter we focus principally on physical inventory because this is what most operations managers assume is meant by the term 'inventory', and because customers and information are dealt with in more detail elsewhere in the text. Usually, the objective of those who manage physical inventories is to reduce the overall level (and/or cost) of inventory while maintaining an acceptable level of customer service. Table 8.3 identifies some of the ways in which physical inventory may be reduced.

TABLE 8.3 Some ways in which physical inventory may be reduced

Reason for holding inventory	Example	How inventory could be reduced
As an insurance against uncertainty	Safety stocks for when demand or supply is not perfectly predictable	Improve demand forecasting Tighten supply, e.g. through service-level penalties
To counteract a lack of flexibility	Cycle stock to maintain supply when other products are being made	Increase flexibility of processes, e.g. by reducing changeover times (see Chapter 10) Using parallel processes to produce output simultaneously (see Chapter 5)
To take advantage of relatively short-term opportunities	Suppliers offer 'time-limited' special low-cost offers	Persuade suppliers to adopt 'everyday low prices' (see Chapter 6)
To anticipate future demands	Build up stocks in low-demand periods for use in high-demand periods	Increase volume flexibility by moving towards a 'chase demand' plan (see Chapter 7)
To reduce overall costs	Purchase a batch of products in order to save delivery and administration costs	Reduce administration costs through purchasing-process efficiency gains Investigate alternative delivery channel that reduces transport costs
To fill the processing 'pipeline'	Items being delivered to customer	Reduce process time between customer request and dispatch of items Reduce throughput time in the downstream supply chain (see Chapter 7)

Operations in practice

Treasury Wine's hangover[2]

Treasury Wine Estates is a largely successful group that was founded in 1843 and today operates on three continents with more than 50 brands, including some of Australasia's premium wine brands such as Penfolds, Beringer, Lindemans and Wynns. Recently, it decided to destroy over £20 million worth of its wine because it had become 'too old', was 'deteriorating' and was in danger of 'damaging its brands'. Faced with demand that was less than they had predicted, they decided to destroy their old and aged commercial stock, to make sure that only the freshest and highest-quality wines were made available. Part of the problem is that Australia's commercial wine is intended to be consumed at a younger age than some other types of wine, so keeping the wine as inventory reduces its attractiveness. The total write-down caused by the poor forecasting was around $160 million (£96.2 million), caused by the extra cost of discounts and rebates to key distributors to help pep up the sale of remaining vintage wines. ● ● ●

Day-to-day inventory decisions

Wherever inventory accumulates, operations managers need to manage the day-to-day tasks. Orders will be received from internal or external customers; these will be dispatched and demand will gradually deplete the inventory. Orders will need to be placed for replenishment of the stocks; deliveries will arrive and require storing. In managing the system, operations managers are involved in three major types of decision:

 How much to order   Every time a replenishment order is placed, how big should it be (sometimes called the 'volume decision')?

 When to order   At what point in time, or at what level of stock, should the replenishment order be placed (sometimes called the 'timing decision')?

 How to control the system   What procedures and routines should be installed to help make these decisions?

How much should you order? (The volume decision)

To illustrate the volume decision, consider the example of the food we keep in our home. In managing this inventory, we implicitly make decisions on how much to purchase at one time. In making this decision we are balancing two sets of costs: the costs associated with going out to purchase the food items and the costs associated with holding the stocks. The option of holding very little or no inventory of food and purchasing each item only when it is needed has the advantage that it requires little money, since purchases are made only when needed. However, it would involve purchasing provisions several times a day, which is inconvenient. At the very opposite extreme, making one journey to the local superstore every few months and purchasing all the provisions we would need until our next visit reduces the time and costs incurred in making the purchase but requires a very large amount of money each time the trip is made – money that could otherwise be in the bank, earning interest. We might also have to invest in extra cupboard units and a very large freezer! Somewhere between these extremes there lies an ordering strategy that will minimize the total costs and effort involved in the purchase and storage of food.

INVENTORY COSTS

The same principles above apply in commercial order-quantity decisions. In making a decision on how much to purchase, operations managers must try to identify the costs that will be affected by their decision:

1   **Cost of placing the order**   Every time that an order is placed to replenish stock, a number of transactions are needed that incur costs to the company. These include preparing the order, communicating with suppliers, arranging for delivery, making payment and maintaining internal records of the transaction. Even if we are placing an 'internal order' on part of our own operation, there are still likely to be the same types of transaction concerned with internal administration.

2   **Price-discount costs**   Often suppliers offer discounts for large quantities and have cost penalties for small orders.

3   **Stock-out costs**   If we misjudge the order-quantity decision and our inventory runs out of stock, there will be lost revenue (opportunity costs) through failing to supply customers.

4   **Working capital costs**   After receiving a replenishment order, the supplier will demand payment. However, there will probably be a lag between

paying the suppliers and receiving payment from our customers. During this time we will have to fund the costs of inventory. This is called the 'working capital' of inventory, which includes the interest we pay the bank for borrowing it, or the opportunity costs of not investing money elsewhere.

5   **Storage costs**   These are the costs associated with physically storing the goods. Renting, heating and lighting the warehouse, as well as insuring the inventory, can be expensive, especially when special conditions are required such as low temperature or high security.

6   **Obsolescence costs**   When we order large quantities, this usually results in stocked items spending a long time stored in inventory. This increases the risk that the items might either become obsolete (in the case of a change in fashion, for example) or deteriorate with age (in the case of most foodstuffs, for example).

7   **Operating inefficiency costs**   According to just-in-time philosophies, high inventory levels prevent us seeing the full extent of problems within the operation. (This argument is fully explored in Chapter 10.)

INVENTORY PROFILES

An inventory profile is a visual representation of the inventory level over time. Figure 8.4 shows a simplified inventory profile for one particular stock item in a retail operation. Every time an order is placed, Q items are ordered. The replenishment order arrives in one batch instantaneously. Demand for the item is then steady and perfectly predictable at a rate of D units per month. When demand has depleted the stock of the items entirely, another order of Q items instantaneously arrives, and so on. Under these circumstances:

The average inventory $= \dfrac{Q}{2}$ (because the two shaded areas in Figure 8.4 are equal

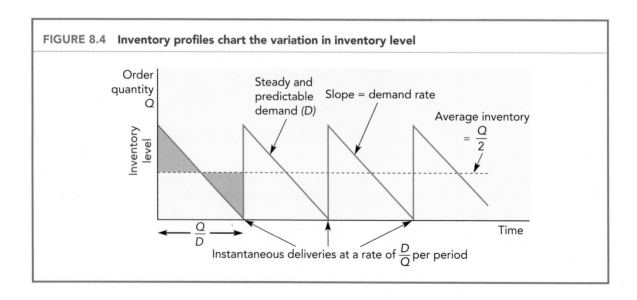

FIGURE 8.4   Inventory profiles chart the variation in inventory level

The time interval between deliveries $= \dfrac{Q}{D}$

The frequency of deliveries $=$ the reciprocal of the time interval $= \dfrac{D}{Q}$

The economic order quantity (EOQ) formula

The most common approach to deciding how much of any particular item to order when stock needs replenishing is called the economic order quantity (EOQ) approach. This approach attempts to find the best balance between the advantages and disadvantages of holding stock. For example, Figure 8.5 shows two alternative order-quantity policies for an item. Plan A, represented by the unbroken line, involves ordering in quantities of 400 at a time. Demand in this case is running at 1,000 units per year. Plan B, represented by the dotted line, uses smaller but more frequent replenishment orders. This time only 100 are ordered at a time, with orders being placed four times as often. However, the average inventory for plan B is one-quarter of that for plan A.

To find out whether either of these plans, or some other plan, minimizes the total cost of stocking the item, we need some further information – namely, the total cost of holding one unit in stock for a period of time (C_h) and the total costs of placing an order (C_o). Generally, holding costs are taken into account by including:

 working capital costs;

 storage costs;

 obsolescence risk costs.

Order costs are calculated by taking into account:

 cost of placing the order (including transportation of items from suppliers, if relevant);

 price discount costs.

FIGURE 8.5 Two alternative inventory plans with different order quantities (Q)

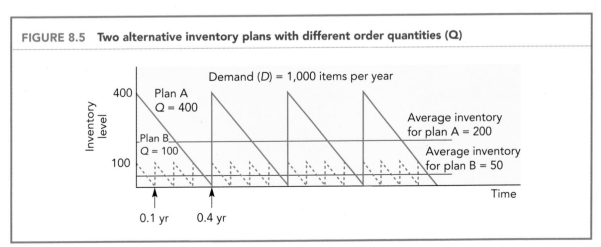

In this case, the cost of holding stocks is calculated at £1 per item per year and the cost of placing an order is calculated at £20 per order. We can now calculate total holding costs and ordering costs for any particular ordering plan as follows:

$$\text{Holding costs} = \text{holding cost per unit} \times \text{average inventory}$$

$$= C_h \times \frac{Q}{2}$$

$$\text{Ordering costs} = \text{ordering cost} \times \text{number of orders per period}$$

$$= C_o \times \frac{D}{Q}$$

$$\text{So, total cost, } C_t = \frac{C_h Q}{2} + \frac{C_o D}{Q}$$

We can now calculate the costs of adopting plans with different order quantities. These are illustrated in Table 8.4. As we would expect with low values of Q, holding costs are low but the costs of placing orders are high because orders have to be placed very frequently. As Q increases, the holding costs increase but the costs of placing orders decrease. Initially, the decrease in ordering costs is greater than the increase in holding costs and the total cost falls. After a point, however, the decrease in ordering costs slows, whereas the increase in holding costs remains constant and the total cost starts to increase. In this case, the order quantity, Q, which minimizes the sum of holding and order costs, is 200. This 'optimum' order quantity is called the economic order quantity (EOQ). This is illustrated graphically in Figure 8.6.

TABLE 8.4   Costs of adoption of plans with different order quantities

Demand (D) = 1000 units per year Order costs (C_o) = £20 per order			Holding costs (C_h) = £1 per item per year		
Order quantity (Q)	Holding costs (0.5Q × C_h)	+	Order costs ((D/Q) × C_o)	=	Total costs
50	25		20 × 20 = 400		425
100	50		10 × 20 = 200		250
150	75		6.7 × 20 = 134		209
200	**100**		**5 × 20 = 100**		**200***
250	125		4 × 20 = 80		205
300	150		3.3 × 20 = 66		216
350	175		2.9 × 20 = 58		233
400	200		2.5 × 20 = 50		250

*Minimum total cost.

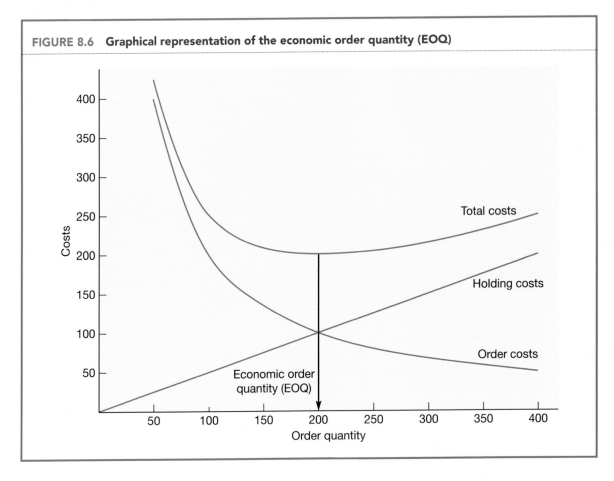

FIGURE 8.6   Graphical representation of the economic order quantity (EOQ)

A more elegant method of finding the EOQ is to derive its general expression. This can be done using simple differential calculus, as follows. From before:

$$\text{Total cost} = \text{holding cost} + \text{order cost}$$

$$C_t = \frac{C_h Q}{2} + \frac{C_o D}{Q}$$

The rate of change of total cost is given by the first differential of C_t with respect to Q:

$$\frac{dC_t}{dQ} = \frac{C_h}{2} - \frac{C_o D}{Q^2}$$

The lowest cost will occur when $\frac{dC_t}{dQ} = 0$, that is:

$$0 = \frac{C_h}{2} - \frac{C_o D}{Q_o^2}$$

where Q_o = the EOQ. Rearranging this expression gives:

$$Q_o = EOQ = \sqrt{\frac{2C_o D}{C_h}}$$

Worked example

A building-materials supplier obtains its bagged cement from a single supplier. Demand is reasonably constant throughout the year, and last year the company sold 2,000 tonnes of this product. It estimates the costs of placing an order at around £25 each time an order is placed, and calculates that the annual cost of holding inventory is 20 per cent of purchase cost. The company purchases the cement at £60 per tonne. How much should the company order at a time?

$$EOQ \text{ for cement} = \sqrt{\frac{2C_oD}{C_h}}$$

$$= \sqrt{\frac{2 \times 25 \times 2000}{0.2 \times 60}}$$

$$= \sqrt{\frac{100\,000}{12}}$$

$$= 91.287 \text{ tonnes}$$

After calculating the EOQ, the operations manager feels that placing an order for 91.287 tonnes *exactly* seems somewhat over-precise. Why not order a convenient 100 tonnes?

Total cost of ordering plan for Q = 91.287:

$$= \frac{C_hQ}{2} + \frac{C_oD}{Q}$$

$$= \frac{(0.2 \times 60) \times 91.287}{2} + \frac{25 \times 2000}{91.287}$$

$$= £1095.45$$

Total cost of ordering plan for Q = 100:

$$= \frac{(0.2 \times 60) \times 100}{2} + \frac{25 \times 2000}{100}$$

$$= £1100.00$$

The extra cost of ordering 100 tonnes at a time is £1,100.00 − £1,095.45 = £4.55. The operations manager therefore should feel confident in using the more convenient order quantity. ● ● ●

When using the *EOQ*:

$$\text{Time between orders} = \frac{EOQ}{D}$$

$$\text{Order frequency} = \frac{D}{EOQ} \text{ per period}$$

SENSITIVITY OF THE EOQ

Examination of the graphical representation of the total cost curve in Figure 8.6 shows that, although there is a single value of Q that minimizes total costs, any relatively small deviation from the EOQ will not increase total costs significantly. In other words, costs will be near optimum provided a value of Q that is reasonably close to the EOQ is chosen. Put another way, small errors in estimating either holding costs or order costs will not result in a significant deviation from the EOQ. This is a particularly convenient phenomenon because, in practice, both holding and order costs are not easy to estimate accurately.

operations principle
For any stock-replenishment activity, there is a theoretical 'optimum' order quantity that minimizes total inventory-related costs.

Gradual replacement – the economic batch quantity (EBQ) model

Although the simple inventory profile shown in Figure 8.4 made some simplifying assumptions, it is broadly applicable in most situations where each complete replacement order arrives at one point in time. In many cases, however, replenishment occurs over a time period rather than in one lot. A typical example of this is where an internal order is placed for a batch of parts to be produced on a machine. The machine will start to produce the parts and ship them in a more or less continuous stream into inventory, but at the same time demand is continuing to remove parts from the inventory. Provided the rate at which parts are being made and put into the inventory (P) is higher than the rate at which demand is depleting the inventory (D) then the size of the inventory will increase. After the batch has been completed, the machine will be reset (to produce some other part), and demand will continue to deplete the inventory level until production of the next batch begins. The resulting profile is shown in Figure 8.7. Such a profile is typical for cycle inventories supplied by batch processes, where items are produced internally and intermittently. The minimum-cost batch quantity for this profile is called the economic batch quantity (EBQ), and is also sometimes known as the economic manufacturing quantity (EMQ) or the production order quantity (POQ). It is derived as follows:

$$\text{Maximum stock level} = M$$
$$\text{Slope of inventory build-up} = P - D$$

Also, as is clear from Figure 8.7:

$$\text{Slope of inventory build-up} = M \div \frac{Q}{P}$$
$$= \frac{MP}{Q}$$

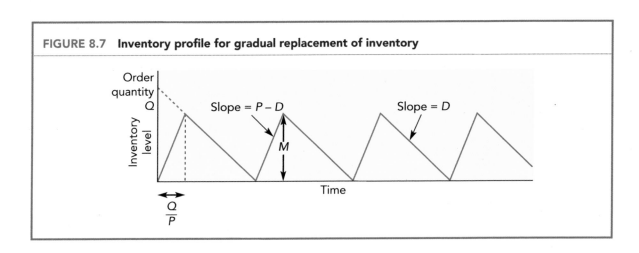

FIGURE 8.7   Inventory profile for gradual replacement of inventory

So,

$$\frac{MP}{Q} = P - D$$

$$M = \frac{Q(P - D)}{P}$$

$$\text{Average inventory level} = \frac{M}{2}$$

$$= \frac{Q(P - D)}{2P}$$

As before:

$$\text{Total cost} = \text{holding cost} + \text{order cost}$$

$$C_t = \frac{C_h Q(P - D)}{2P} + \frac{C_o D}{Q}$$

$$\frac{dC_t}{dQ} = \frac{C_h(P - D)}{2P} - \frac{C_o D}{Q^2}$$

Again, equating to zero and solving Q gives the minimum-cost order quantity EBQ:

$$EBQ = \sqrt{\frac{2C_o D}{C_h(1 - (D/P))}}$$

Criticisms of EOQ models

In order to keep EOQ-type models relatively straightforward, it is necessary to make assumptions. On the upside, the shape of the total cost curve has a relatively flat optimum point, which means that small errors will not significantly affect the total cost of a near-optimum order quantity. However, on the downside there are times when the assumptions about demand, costs and use need careful consideration.

ASSUMPTIONS ABOUT DEMAND
The assumption of steady demand (or even demand that conforms to some known probability distribution) is untrue for a wide range of the operation's inventory problems. For example, a bookseller might be very happy to adopt an EOQ-type ordering policy for some of its most regular and stable products, such as dictionaries and popular textbooks like this one! However, the demand patterns for many other books could be highly erratic, dependent on critics' reviews and word-of-mouth recommendations. In such circumstances, it is not appropriate to use EOQ models.

ASSUMPTIONS ABOUT COSTS
Other questions surround some of the assumptions made concerning the nature of stock-related costs. For example, placing an order with a supplier as part of a regular and multi-item order might be relatively inexpensive, whereas asking for a special one-off delivery of an item could prove far more costly.

Worked example

The manager of a bottle-filling plant that bottles soft drinks needs to decide how long a 'run' of each type of drink to process. Demand for each type of drink is reasonably constant at 80,000 per month (a month has 160 production hours). The bottling lines fill at a rate of 3,000 bottles per hour, but take an hour to clean and reset between different drinks. The cost (of labour and lost production capacity) of each of these changeovers has been calculated at £100 per hour. Stock-holding costs are counted at £0.1 per bottle per month.

$$D = 80{,}000 \text{ per month}$$

$$= 500 \text{ per hour}$$

$$EBQ = \sqrt{\frac{2C_oD}{C_h(1 - (D/P))}}$$

$$= \sqrt{\frac{2 \times 100 \times 80{,}000}{0.1(1 - (500/3000))}}$$

$$EBQ = 13{,}856$$

The staff who operate the lines have devised a method of reducing the changeover time from 1 hour to 30 minutes. How would that change the EBQ?

$$\text{New } C_o = £50$$

$$\text{New } EBQ = \sqrt{\frac{2 \times 50 \times 80{,}000}{0.1(1 - (500/3000))}}$$

$$= 9798$$

Similarly, many organizations underestimate the true costs of holding inventory by not recognizing prevailing interest rates, alternative uses of capital and the nature of certain products (e.g. large or hazardous items that cost more to store). In addition, the marginal costs of increasing stock-holding levels might be merely the cost of the working capital involved. On the other hand, it might necessitate the construction or lease of a whole new stock-holding facility, such as a warehouse.

ASSUMPTIONS ABOUT THE USE OF EOQ MODELS

Perhaps the most fundamental criticism of the EOQ approach again comes from the Japanese-inspired 'lean' and JIT philosophies. The EOQ tries to optimize order decisions. Implicitly, the costs involved are taken as fixed, in the sense that the task of operations managers is to find out what are the true costs rather than to change them in any way. EOQ is essentially a reactive approach. Some critics would argue that it fails to ask the right question. Rather than asking the EOQ question of 'What is the optimum order quantity?', operations managers should really be asking, 'How can I change the operation in some way, so as to reduce the overall level of inventory I need to hold?'

Operations in practice

Inventory management at Flame Electrical

Inventory management in some operations is more than just a part of their responsibility; it is their very reason for being in business. Flame Electrical was South Africa's largest independent supplier and distributor of lamps. It stocked almost 3,000 different types of lamp, which were sourced from 14 countries and distributed to customers throughout the country. "In effect, our customers are using us to manage their stocks of lighting sources for them", said Jeff Schaffer, the managing director of Flame Electrical. "They could, if they wanted to, hold their own stock but might not want to devote the time, space, money or effort to doing so. Using us they get the widest range of products to choose from, and an accurate, fast and dependable service."

Orders for the replenishment of stocks in the warehouse were triggered by a re-order point system. The re-order point for each stocked item took into account the likely demand for the product during the order lead time (forecast from the equivalent period's orders the previous year), the order lead time for the item (which varied from 24 hours to four months) and the variability of the lead time (from previous experience). Flame preferred most orders to its suppliers to be for a whole number of container loads (the shipping costs for part-container loads being more expensive). However, lower order quantities of small or expensive lamps may be used. The order quantity for each lamp was based on its demand, its value and the cost of transportation from the suppliers.

"We have to get the balance right", says Jeff Schaffer. "Excellent service is the foundation of our success. But we could not survive if we did not control stocks tightly. After all, we are carrying the cost of every lamp in our warehouse until the customer eventually pays for it. If stock levels were too high we just could not operate profitably. It is for that reason that we go as far as to pay incentives to the relevant staff based on how well they keep our working capital and stocks under control." ● ● ●

When should you order? (The timing decision)

When we assumed that orders arrived instantaneously and demand was steady and predictable, the decision on when to place a replenishment order was self-evident. An order would be placed as soon as the stock level reached zero. This would arrive instantaneously and prevent any stock-out occurring. However, if replenishment orders do not arrive instantaneously, but have a lag between the order being placed and it arriving in the inventory, we can calculate the timing of a replacement order as shown in Figure 8.8. The lead time for an order to arrive is, in this case, two weeks, so the re-order point (ROP) is the point at which stock will fall to zero minus the order lead time. Alternatively, we can define the point in terms of the level that the inventory will have reached when a replenishment order needs to be placed. In this case this occurs at a re-order level (ROL) of 200 items.

However, this assumes that both the demand and the order lead time are perfectly predictable. In most cases, of course, this is not so. Both demand and the order lead time are likely to vary to produce a profile that looks something like that in Figure 8.9. In these circumstances, it is necessary to make the replenishment order somewhat earlier than would be the case in a purely

FIGURE 8.8 The re-order level (ROL) and re-order point (ROP) are derived from the order lead time and demand rate

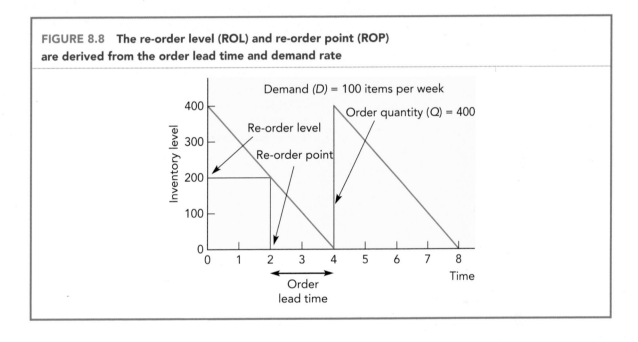

FIGURE 8.9 Safety stock (s) helps to avoid stock-outs when demand and/or order lead time are uncertain

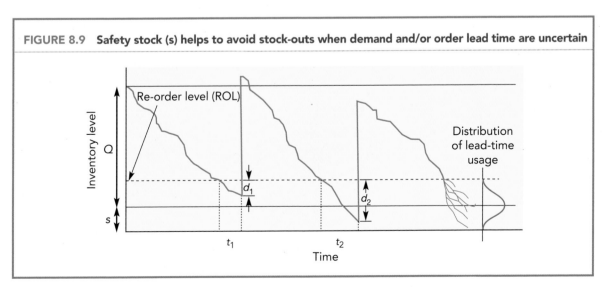

Worked example

Acompany that imports running shoes for sale in its sports shops can never be certain of how long, after placing an order, the delivery will take. Examination of previous orders reveals that out of ten orders, one took one week, two took two weeks, four took three weeks, two took four weeks and one took five weeks. The rate of demand for the shoes also varies between 110 pairs per week and 140 pairs per week. There is a 0.2 probability of the demand rate being either 110 or 140 pairs per week, and a 0.3 chance of demand being either 120 or 130 pairs per week. The company needs to decide when it should place replenishment orders if the probability of a stock-out is to be less than 10 per cent.

Both lead time and the demand rate during the lead time will contribute to the lead-time usage. So, the distributions that describe each will need to be combined. Figure 8.10 and Table 8.5 show how this can be done. Taking lead time to be either one, two, three, four or five weeks, and demand rate to be either 110, 120, 130 or 140 pairs per week, and also assuming the two variables to be independent, the distributions can be combined as shown in Table 8.5. Each element in the matrix shows a possible lead-time usage,

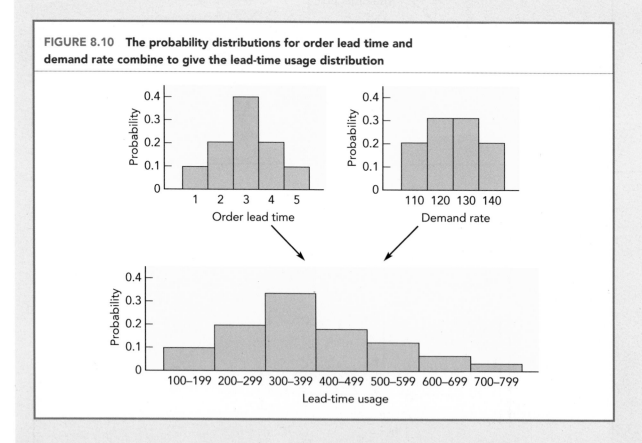

FIGURE 8.10   **The probability distributions for order lead time and demand rate combine to give the lead-time usage distribution**

with the probability of its occurrence. So, if the lead time is one week and the demand rate is 110 pairs per week, the actual lead-time usage will be 1 × 110 = 110 pairs. Since there is a 0.1 chance of the lead time being one week, and a 0.2 chance of demand rate being 110 pairs per week, the probability of both these events occurring is 0.1 × 0.2 = 0.02.

We can now classify the possible lead-time usages into histogram form. For example, summing the probabilities of all the lead-time usages that fall within the range 100–199 (all the first column)

gives a combined probability of 0.1. Repeating this for subsequent intervals results in Table 8.6.

This shows the probability of each possible range of lead-time usage occurring, but it is the cumulative probabilities that are needed to predict the likelihood of stock-out (see Table 8.7).

Setting the re-order level at 600 would mean that there is only a 0.08 (8 per cent) chance of usage being greater than available inventory during the lead time – that is, there is a less than 10 per cent chance of a stock-out occurring. ● ● ●

TABLE 8.5 Matrix of lead-time and demand-rate probabilities

			Lead-time probabilities				
			1	2	3	4	5
			0.1	0.2	0.4	0.2	0.1
Demand-rate probabilities	110	0.2	110 (0.02)	220 (0.04)	330 (0.08)	440 (0.04)	550 (0.02)
	120	0.3	120 (0.03)	240 (0.06)	360 (0.12)	480 (0.06)	600 (0.03)
	130	0.3	130 (0.03)	260 (0.06)	390 (0.12)	520 (0.06)	650 (0.03)
	140	0.2	140 (0.02)	280 (0.04)	420 (0.08)	560 (0.04)	700 (0.02)

TABLE 8.6 Combined probabilities

Lead-time usage	100–199	200–299	300–399	400–499	500–599	600–699	700–799
Probability	0.1	0.2	0.32	0.18	0.12	0.06	0.02

TABLE 8.7 Cumulative probabilities

Lead-time usage X	100	200	300	400	500	600	700	800
Probability of usage being greater than X	1.0	0.9	0.7	0.38	0.2	0.08	0.02	0

deterministic situation. This will result in, on average, some stock still being in the inventory when the replenishment order arrives. This is buffer (safety) stock. The earlier the replenishment order is placed, the higher will be the expected level of safety stock(s) when the replenishment order arrives. But because of the variability of both lead time (t) and demand rate (d), there will sometimes be a higher-than-average level of safety stock and sometimes lower. The main consideration in setting safety stock is not so much the average level of stock when a replenishment order arrives, but rather the probability that the stock will not have run out before the replenishment order arrives.

The key statistic in calculating how much safety stock to allow is the probability distribution that shows the lead-time usage. The lead-time usage distribution is a combination of the distributions that describe lead-time variation and the demand rate during the lead time. If safety stock is set below the lower limit of this distribution, then there will be shortages every single replenishment cycle. If safety stock is set above the upper limit of the distribution, there is no chance of stock-outs occurring. Usually, safety stock is set to give a predetermined likelihood that stock-outs will not occur. Figure 8.9 shows that, in this case, the first replenishment order arrived after t_1, resulting in a lead-time usage of d_1. The second replenishment order took longer, t_2, and demand rate was also higher, resulting in a lead-time usage of d_2. The third order cycle shows several possible inventory profiles for different conditions of lead-time usage and demand rate.

operations principle
For any stock-replenishment activity, the timing of replenishment should reflect the effects of uncertain lead time and uncertain demand during that lead time.

Continuous and periodic review

The approach we have described for making the replenishment timing decision is often called the 'continuous review' approach. This is because, to make the decision in this way, there must be a process to review the stock level of each item continuously and then place an order when the stock level reaches its re-order level. The virtue of this approach is that, although the timing of orders may be irregular (depending on the variation in demand rate), the order size (Q) is constant and can be set at the optimum economic order quantity. Such continual checking on inventory levels can be time-consuming, especially when there are many stock withdrawals compared with the average level of stock, but in an environment where all inventory records are computerized, this should not be a problem unless the records are inaccurate.

An alternative and far simpler approach, but one that sacrifices the use of a fixed (and therefore possibly optimum) order quantity, is called the 'periodic review' approach. Here, rather than ordering at a predetermined re-order level, the periodic approach orders at a fixed and regular time interval. So the stock level of an item could be checked, for example, at the end of every month and a replenishment order placed to bring the stock up to a predetermined level. This level is calculated to cover demand between the replenishment order being placed and the following replenishment order arriving. Figure 8.11 illustrates the parameters for the periodic review approach.

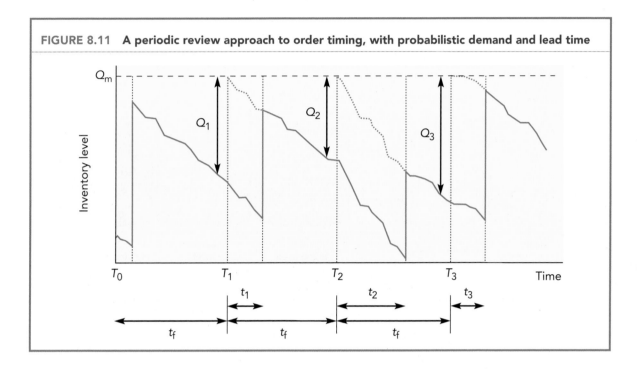

FIGURE 8.11 A periodic review approach to order timing, with probabilistic demand and lead time

At time T_1 in Figure 8.11, the inventory manager would examine the stock level and order sufficient to bring it up to some maximum, Q_m. However, that order of Q_1 items will not arrive until a further time of t_1 has passed, during which demand continues to deplete the stocks. Again, both demand and lead time are uncertain. The Q_1 items will arrive and bring the stock up to some level lower than Q_m (unless there has been no demand during t_1). Demand then continues until T_2, when again an order Q_2 is placed that is the difference between the current stock at T_2 and Q_m. This order arrives after t_2, by which time demand has depleted the stocks further. Thus, the replenishment order placed at T_1 must be able to cover the demand that occurs until T_2 and t_2. Safety stocks will need to be calculated, in a similar manner to before, based on the distribution of usage over this period.

THE TIME INTERVAL

The interval between placing orders, t_1, is usually calculated on a deterministic basis, and derived from the EOQ. So, for example, if the demand for an item is 2,000 per year, the cost of placing an order £25 and the cost of holding stock £0.5 per item per year, then:

$$EOQ = \sqrt{\frac{2C_oD}{C_h}} = \sqrt{\frac{2 \times 2000 \times 25}{0.5}} = 447$$

The optimum time interval between orders, t_f, is therefore:

$$t_f = \frac{EOQ}{D} = \frac{447}{2000} \text{ years}$$

$$= 2.68 \text{ months}$$

It may seem paradoxical to calculate the time interval assuming constant demand when demand is, in fact, uncertain. However, uncertainties in both

---

FIGURE 8.12   **The two-bin and three-bin systems of re-ordering**

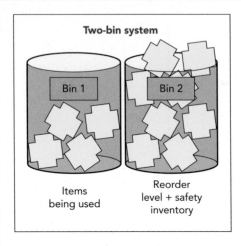

Two-bin system

Bin 1   Bin 2

Items
being used

Reorder
level + safety
inventory

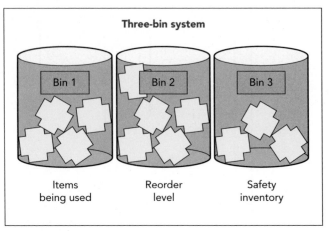

Three-bin system

Bin 1   Bin 2   Bin 3

Items
being used

Reorder
level

Safety
inventory

---

demand and lead time can be allowed for by setting Q_m to allow for the desired probability of stock-out based on usage during the period t_f + lead time.

TWO-BIN AND THREE-BIN SYSTEMS

Keeping track of inventory levels is especially important in continuous review approaches to re-ordering. A simple and obvious method of indicating when the re-order point has been reached is necessary, especially if there are a large number of items to be monitored. The two- and three-bin systems illustrated in Figure 8.12 are such methods. The simple two-bin system involves storing the re-order point quantity plus the safety inventory quantity in the second bin and using parts from the first bin. When the first bin empties, that is the signal to order the next re-order quantity. Sometimes the safety inventory is stored in a third bin (the three-bin system), so it is clear when demand is exceeding that which was expected. Different 'bins' are not always necessary to operate this type of system. For example, a common practice in retail operations is to store the second 'bin' quantity upside-down behind or under the first 'bin' quantity. Orders are then placed when the upside-down items are reached.

How can you control inventory?

The models we have described, even the ones that take a probabilistic view of demand and lead time, are still simplified compared with the complexity of real stock management. Coping with many thousands of stocked items, supplied by many hundreds of different suppliers, with possibly tens of thousands of individual customers, makes for a complex and dynamic operations task. In order to control such

Operations in practice

Amazon's 'anticipatory shipping'[3]

Forecast accuracy and time to deliver are related. Poor forecasts mean that the wrong items will be stored, which in turn means that delivery will be delayed until the right items are received. But what if a supplier could know what its customers were going to order, even before they do? That is the ambition of Amazon's online retail operation. It filed a patent to protect its system for the technology that hopes to predict what its customers will buy, even before they have clicked the 'order' button. The company, which is the world's largest online retailer, calls its new system 'anticipatory shipping', and perceives it as a way to speed up its delivery times. Amazon's patent application reveals the thinking behind the system. Its application says that: 'One substantial disadvantage to the virtual storefront model is that in many instances, customers cannot receive their merchandise immediately upon purchase, but must instead wait for a product to be shipped to them. The availability of expedited shipping methods from various common carriers may mitigate the delay in shipment, but often at substantial additional cost that may rival the price paid for the merchandise. Such delays may dissuade customers from buying items from online merchants, particularly if those items are more readily available locally.' The approach is reported as using several elements to predict what purchases a person may make. Factors to be taken into account could include age, income, previously purchased items, searched-for items, 'wish lists' and maybe even the time a user's cursor lingers over a product. Armed with this information, Amazon could ship items that are likely to be ordered to the inventory 'hub' nearest to the customer. So, when a customer really does order, the item can be delivered far faster. ● ● ●

complexity, operations managers have to do two things. First, they have to discriminate between different stocked items, so that they can apply a degree of control to each item that is appropriate to its importance. Second, they need to invest in an information-processing system that can cope with their particular set of inventory-control circumstances.

Using the ABC system to prioritize inventories

In any inventory setting, some items will be more important to the organization than others. Some, for example, might have a very high usage rate, so if they ran out many customers would be disappointed. Other items might be of particularly high value, so excessively high inventory levels would be particularly expensive. One common way of discriminating between different stock items is to rank them by the usage value (their usage rate multiplied by their individual value). Items with a particularly high usage value are deemed to warrant the most careful control, whereas those with low usage values need not be controlled quite so rigorously. Generally, a relatively small proportion of the total range of items contained in an inventory will account for a large proportion of the total usage value. This phenomenon is known as the Pareto law (after the person who described it), sometimes also referred to as the '80/20 rule'. It is called this because, typically, 80 per cent of an operation's sales are accounted for by only 20 per cent of all stocked item types. Here, the relationship can be used to classify the different types of items kept in an inventory by their usage value. ABC inventory control allows inventory managers to concentrate their efforts on controlling the more significant items of stock:

 Class A items   are those 20 per cent or so of high usage-value items that account for around 80 per cent of the total usage value.

 Class B items   are those of medium usage value, usually the next 30 per cent of items, which often account for around 10 per cent of the total usage value.

 Class C items   are those low usage value items that, although comprising around 50 per cent of the total types of items stocked, probably only account for around 10 per cent of the total usage value of the operation.

> **operations principle**
> Different inventory management decision rules are needed for different classes of inventory.

Although annual usage and value are the two criteria most commonly used to determine a stock classification system, other criteria might also contribute towards the (higher) classification of an item:

 Consequence of stock-out   High priority might be given to those items that would seriously delay or disrupt other operations, or the customers, if they were not in stock.

 Uncertainty of supply   Some items, although of low value, might warrant more attention if their supply is erratic or uncertain.

 High obsolescence or deterioration risk   Items that could lose their value through obsolescence or deterioration might need extra attention and monitoring.

Some more complex stock classification systems might include these criteria by classifying on an A, B, C basis for each. For example, a part might be classed as A/B/A, meaning it is an A category item by value, a class B item by consequence of stock-out and a class A item by obsolescence risk. While ABC classifications remain popular, some operations managers note that it is, in fact, the slow-moving items (the C-category items) that pose the greatest challenge in inventory management. These slow-moving items, although only accounting for 20 per cent of sales, often require a large part (typically between one half and two thirds) of the total investment in stock. Moreover, if errors in forecasting or ordering result in excess stock in 'A class' fast-moving items, it is relatively unimportant in the sense that excess stock can be sold quickly. However, excess stock in a slow-moving C item will be there a long time.

Measuring inventory

In our example of ABC classifications, we used the monetary value of the annual usage of each item as a measure of inventory usage. Monetary value can also be used to measure the absolute level of inventory at any point in time. This would involve taking the number of each item in stock, multiplying it by its value (usually the cost of purchasing the item) and summing the value of all the individual items stored. This is a useful measure of the investment that an operation has in its inventories, but gives no indication of how large that investment is relative to the total throughput of the operation. To do this we must compare the total number of items in stock against their rate of usage. There are two ways of doing this. The first is to calculate the amount of time the inventory would last, subject to normal demand, if it were not replenished. This is sometimes called the number of weeks' (or days', months', years', etc.) 'cover' of the stock. The second method is to calculate how often the stock is used up within a set period – usually one year. This is called the 'stock turn', or turnover of stock, and is the reciprocal of the stock-cover figure.

Inventory information systems

Most inventories of any significant size are, of course, managed by computerized systems. While each varies in some way, they tend to share certain common functions.

UPDATING STOCK RECORDS
Every time a transaction takes place (such as the sale of an item, the movement of an item from a warehouse into a truck, or the delivery of an item into a warehouse), the position, status and possible value of the stock will have changed. This information must be recorded so that operations managers can determine their current inventory status at any time.

GENERATING ORDERS
The two major decisions we have described previously – namely, how much to order and when to order, can both be made by a computerized stock-control system. The first decision, setting the value of how much to order (Q), is likely to be taken only at relatively infrequent intervals. Originally almost all computer systems automatically calculated order quantities by

Worked example

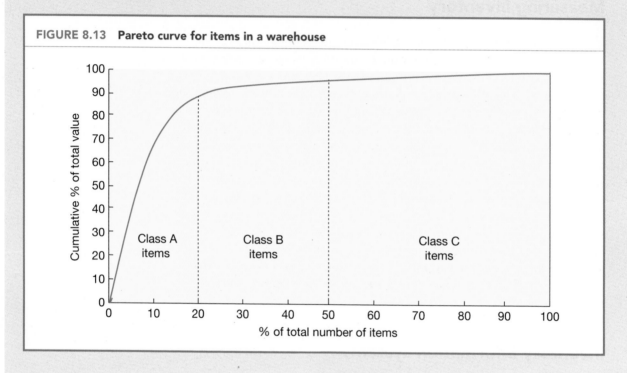

FIGURE 8.13 **Pareto curve for items in a warehouse**

Table 8.8 shows all the parts stored by an electrical wholesaler. The 20 different items stored vary in terms of both their usage per year and cost per item, as shown. However, the wholesaler has ranked the stock items by their usage value per year. The total usage value per year is £5,569,000. From this it is possible to calculate the usage value per year of each item as a percentage of the total usage value, and from that a running cumulative total of the usage value, as shown. The wholesaler can then plot the cumulative percentage of all stocked items against the cumulative percentage of their value. So, for example, the part with stock number A/703 is the highest-value part and accounts for 25.14 per cent of the total inventory value. As a part, however, it is only one-twentieth (or 5 per cent) of the total number of items stocked. This item together with

the next-highest-value item (D/012) account for only 10 per cent of the total number of items stocked, yet account for 47.37 per cent of the value of the stock, and so on.

This is shown graphically in Figure 8.13. Here, the wholesaler has classified the first four part numbers (20 per cent of the range) as Class A items, and will monitor the usage and ordering of these items very closely and frequently. A few improvements in order quantities or safety stocks for these items could bring significant savings. The six next part numbers, C/375 through to A/138 (30 per cent of the range), are to be treated as Class B items, with slightly less effort devoted to their control. All other items are classed as Class C items, whose stocking policy is reviewed only occasionally. ● ● ●

TABLE 8.8 Warehouse items ranked by usage value

Stock no.	Usage (items/year)	Cost (£/item)	Usage value (£000/year)	% of total value	Cumulative % of total value
A/703	700	20.00	1 400	25.14	25.14
D/012	450	2.75	1 238	22.23	47.37
A/135	1 000	0.90	900	16.16	63.53
C/732	95	8.50	808	14.51	78.04
C/375	520	0.54	281	5.05	83.09
A/500	73	2.30	168	3.02	86.11
D/111	520	0.22	114	2.05	88.16
D/231	170	0.65	111	1.99	90.15
E/781	250	0.34	85	1.53	91.68
A/138	250	0.30	75	1.34	93.02
D/175	400	0.14	56	1.01	94.03
E/001	80	0.63	50	0.89	94.92
C/150	230	0.21	48	0.86	95.78
F/030	400	0.12	48	0.86	96.64
D/703	500	0.09	45	0.81	97.45
D/535	50	0.88	44	0.79	98.24
C/541	70	0.57	40	0.71	98.95
A/260	50	0.64	32	0.57	99.52
B/141	50	0.32	16	0.28	99.80
D/021	20	0.50	10	0.20	100.00
Total			5 569	100.00	

Worked example

TABLE 8.9 Stock, cost and demand for three stocked items			
Item	Average number in stock	Cost per item (£)	Annual demand
Chateau A	500	3.00	2000
Chateau B	300	4.00	1500
Chateau C	200	5.00	1000

A small specialist wine importer holds stocks of three types of wine – Chateau A, Chateau B and Chateau C. Current stock levels are 500 cases of Chateau A, 300 cases of Chateau B and 200 cases of Chateau C. Table 8.9 shows the number of each held in stock, their cost per item and the demand per year for each.

$$\text{The total value of stock} = \Sigma(\text{average stock level} \times \text{cost per item})$$
$$= (500 \times 3) + (300 \times 4) + (200 \times 5)$$
$$= 3700$$

The amount of stock cover provided by each item stocked is as follows (assuming 50 sales weeks per year):

$$\text{Chateau A stock cover} = \frac{\text{stock}}{\text{demand}} = \frac{500}{2000} \times 50 = 12.5 \text{ weeks}$$
$$\text{Chateau B stock cover} = \frac{\text{stock}}{\text{demand}} = \frac{300}{1500} \times 50 = 10 \text{ weeks}$$
$$\text{Chateau C stock cover} = \frac{\text{stock}}{\text{demand}} = \frac{200}{1000} \times 50 = 10 \text{ weeks}$$

The stock turn for each item is calculated as follows:

$$\text{Chateau A stock turn} = \frac{\text{demand}}{\text{stock}} = \frac{2000}{500} = 4 \text{ times/year}$$
$$\text{Chateau B stock turn} = \frac{\text{demand}}{\text{stock}} = \frac{1500}{300} = 5 \text{ times/year}$$
$$\text{Chateau C stock turn} = \frac{\text{demand}}{\text{stock}} = \frac{1000}{200} = 5 \text{ times/year}$$

To find the average stock cover or stock turn for the total items in the inventory, the individual item measures can be weighted by their demand levels as a proportion of total demand (4500). Thus:

$$\text{Average stock cover} = \left(12.5 \times \frac{2000}{4500}\right) + \left(10 \times \frac{1500}{4500}\right) + \left(10 \times \frac{1000}{4500}\right)$$
$$= 11.11$$

$$\text{Average stock turn} = \left(4 \times \frac{2000}{4500}\right) + \left(5 \times \frac{1500}{4500}\right) + \left(5 \times \frac{1000}{4500}\right)$$
$$= 4.56$$

using the EOQ formulae covered earlier. Increasingly, more sophisticated algorithms are employed beyond the EOQ formulae, often using probabilistic data and based on examining the marginal return on investing in stock. The system will hold all the information that goes into the ordering algorithm, but might periodically check to see if demand or order lead times, or any of the other parameters, have changed significantly and then recalculate Q accordingly. The decision on when to order, on the other hand, is a far more routine affair, which computer systems make according to whatever decision rules operations managers have chosen to adopt: either continuous review or periodic review. Furthermore, the systems can automatically generate whatever documentation is required and share this with suppliers.

GENERATING INVENTORY REPORTS

Inventory control systems can generate regular reports of stock value for the different items stored, which can help management monitor its inventory control performance. Similarly, customer service performance, such as the number of stock-outs or the number of incomplete orders, can be regularly monitored.

FORECASTING

Inventory replenishment decisions should ideally be made with a clear understanding of forecast future demand. The inventory control system can compare actual demand against forecast and adjust the forecast in the light of actual levels of demand. (Control systems of this type are treated in more detail in Chapter 9.)

Common problems with inventory systems

Our description of inventory systems has been based on the assumption that operations (a) have a reasonably accurate idea of costs, such as holding cost or order cost, and (b) have accurate information that really does indicate the actual level of stock and sales. But data inaccuracy often poses one of the most significant problems for inventory managers. This is because most computer-based inventory management systems are based on what is called the 'perpetual inventory principle'. This is the simple idea that stock records are (or should be) automatically updated every time that items are recorded as having been received into an inventory, or taken out of the inventory. So,

opening stock level + receipts in − dispatches out = new stock level

Any errors in recording these transactions, and/or in handling the physical inventory, can lead to discrepancies between the recorded and actual inventory, and these errors are perpetuated until physical stock checks are made (usually quite infrequently). In practice, there are many opportunities for errors to occur, if only because inventory transactions are numerous. This means that it is surprisingly common for the majority of inventory records to be inaccurate. The underlying causes of errors include:

★ keying errors – entering the wrong product code;

★ quantity errors – a miscount of items put into or taken from stock;

★ damaged or deteriorated inventory not recorded as such, or not correctly deleted from the records when it is destroyed;

★ the wrong items being taken out of stock, but the records not being corrected when they are returned to stock;

★ delays between the transactions being made and the records being updated;

★ items stolen from inventory (common in retail environments, but also not unusual in industrial and commercial inventories).

operations principle
The maintenance of data accuracy is vital for the day-to-day effectiveness of inventory management systems.

Summary answers to key questions

Each chapter has a 'Summary answers to key questions' section. Use it to check your understanding of the issues covered in the chapter.

WHAT IS INVENTORY?

★ Inventory, or stock, is the stored accumulation of the transformed resources in an operation. Sometimes the words 'stock' and 'inventory' are also used to describe transforming resources, but the terms 'stock control' and 'inventory control' are nearly always used in connection with transformed resources.

★ Almost all operations keep some kind of inventory, most usually of materials but also of information and customers (customer inventories are normally called queues).

★ Inventory invariably takes up space (for example, in a warehouse), and has to be managed, stored in appropriate conditions, insured and physically handled when transactions occur. It therefore contributes to overhead costs.

★ If inventory is not used quickly, there is an increasing risk of damage, loss, deterioration or obsolescence.

WHY DO YOU NEED INVENTORY?

★ Inventory occurs in operations because the timing of supply and the timing of demand do not always match. Inventories are needed, therefore, to smooth the differences between supply and demand.

★ There are five main reasons for keeping physical inventory:

- to cope with random or unexpected interruptions in supply or demand (buffer inventory);
- to cope with an operation's inability to make all products simultaneously (cycle inventory);
- to allow different stages of processing to operate at different speeds and with different schedules (de-coupling inventory);
- to cope with planned fluctuations in supply or demand (anticipation inventory);
- to cope with transportation delays in the supply network (pipeline inventory).

★ Inventory is often a major part of working capital, tying up money that could be used more productively elsewhere.

HOW MUCH SHOULD YOU ORDER? (THE VOLUME DECISION)

 This depends on balancing the costs associated with holding stock against the costs associated with placing an order. The main stock-holding costs are usually related to working capital, whereas the main order costs are usually associated with the transactions necessary to generate the information to place an order.

 The best-known approach to determining the amount of inventory to order is the economic order quantity (EOQ) formula. The EOQ formula can be adapted to different types of inventory profile using different stock-behaviour assumptions.

 The EOQ approach, however, has been subject to a number of criticisms regarding the true cost of holding stock, the real cost of placing an order and the use of EOQ models as prescriptive devices.

WHEN SHOULD YOU ORDER? (THE TIMING DECISION)

 This depends partly on the uncertainty of demand. Orders are usually timed to leave a certain level of average safety stock when the order arrives. The level of safety stock is influenced by the variability of both demand and the lead time of supply. These two variables are usually combined into a lead-time usage distribution.

 Using re-order level as a trigger for placing replenishment orders necessitates the continual review of inventory levels. This can be time-consuming and expensive. An alternative approach is to make replenishment orders of varying size but at fixed time periods.

HOW CAN YOU CONTROL INVENTORY?

 The key issue here is how managers discriminate between the levels of control they apply to different stock items. The most common way of doing this is by what is known as the 'ABC classification' of stock. This uses the Pareto law principle to distinguish between the different values of, or significance placed on, types of stock.

 Inventory is usually managed through sophisticated computer-based information systems, which have a number of functions: the updating of stock records, the generation of orders, the generation of inventory status reports and demand forecasts. These systems critically depend on maintaining accurate inventory records.

Problems and applications

All chapters have problems and application questions that will help you practice analyzing operations. They can be answered by reading the chapter. Model answers for the first question can be found on the companion website for this text.

1 A supplier makes monthly shipments to 'House & Garden Stores', in average lot sizes of 200 coffee tables. The average demand for these items is 50 tables per week, and the lead time from the supplier is 3 weeks. 'House & Garden Stores' must pay for inventory from the moment the supplier ships the products. If they are willing to increase their lot size to 300 units, the supplier will offer a lead time of 1 week.

What will be the effect on cycle and pipeline inventories?

2 A local shop has a relatively stable demand for tins of sweetcorn throughout the year, with an annual total of 1,400 tins. The cost of placing an order is estimated at £15 and the annual cost of holding inventory is estimated at 25 per cent of the product's value. The company purchases tins for 20p.

How much should the shop order at a time, and what is the total cost of the plan?

3 A fruit-canning plant has a single line for three different fruit types. Demand for each type of tin is reasonably constant at 50,000 per month (a month has 160 production hours). The tinning process rate is 1,200 per hour, but it takes 2 hours to clean and re-set between different runs. The cost of these changeovers (C_o) is calculated at £250 per hour. Stock-holding is calculated at $0.1 per tin per month.

How big should the batch size be?

4 "Our suppliers often offer better prices if we are willing to buy in larger quantities. This creates a pressure on us to hold higher levels of stock. Therefore, to find the best quantity to order we must compare the advantages of lower prices for purchases and fewer orders, with the disadvantages of increased holding costs. This means that calculating total annual inventory-related costs should now not only include holding costs and ordering costs, but also the cost of purchased items themselves." (Manager, Tufton Bufton

Port Importers Inc.) One supplier to Tufton Bufton Port Importers Inc. (TBPI) has introduced quantity discounts to encourage larger order quantities. The discounts are shown below:

Order quantity	Price per bottle
0–100	€15.00
101–250	€13.50
250+	€11.00

Want to know more?

Axsäter, S. (2015) *Inventory Control*, 3rd edition, New York: Springer.

➡ A traditional, but comprehensive textbook that takes an 'operational research' quantitative approach.

Bragg, S.M. (2013) *Inventory Management*, Accounting Tools.

➡ A financial approach to the subject.

Muller, M. (2011) *Essentials of Inventory Management*, 2nd edition, New York: Amacom.

➡ Straightforward treatment.

Relph, G. and Milner, C. (2015) *Inventory Management: Advanced Methods for Managing Inventory Within Business Systems*, London: Kogan Page.

➡ An advanced book that covers most topics in the subject, including the 'k-curve', which is not included in this chapter.

In the colder parts of the world, road gritting is big news every winter when snow and ice can cause huge disruption to everyday life. This is why local government authorities cope with freezing weather by spreading grit (actually a mixture of salt and grit) on the roads. It is one of their most important inventory management decisions. Too big an inventory of grit and it may not all be used so the cost of carrying it over to next year will be borne by local taxpayers. Too small an inventory and the wrath of local voters will be incurred when the roads are difficult to negotiate. The picture shows a gritter being loaded before heading out in preparation for the forecast snow and ice.

Resource planning and control

9

Introduction

Central to an operation's ability to deliver is the way it plans and controls its resources and the activities that they perform, so that customers' demands are satisfied. All operations require plans and need to be controlled, although the degree of formality and detail may vary. This chapter introduces and provides an overview of some of the principles and methods of resource planning and control, and how planning and control systems, particularly enterprise resource planning (ERP), manages the information that ensures effective delivery. Figure 9.1 shows where this topic fits into the activities of operations management.

Key questions

What is resource planning and control?

What is the difference between planning and control?

How do supply and demand affect planning and control?

What are the activities of planning and control?

What is enterprise resource planning (ERP)?

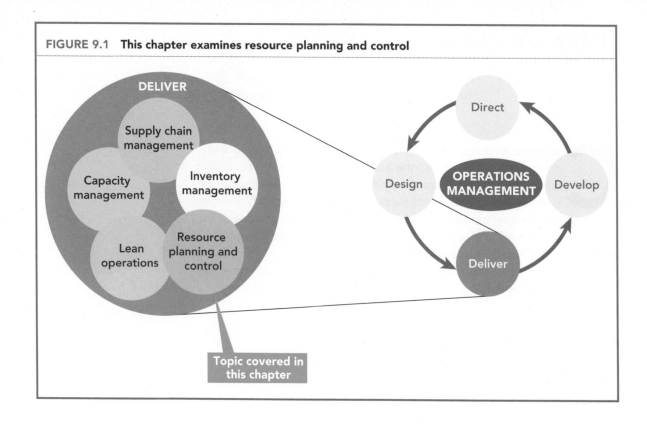

FIGURE 9.1 **This chapter examines resource planning and control**

What is resource planning and control?

Resource planning and control is concerned with the activities that attempt to reconcile the demands of the market and the ability of the operation's resources to deliver. It provides the systems, procedures and decisions that bring different aspects of supply and demand together. Consider, for example, the way in which routine surgery is organized in a hospital. When a patient is admitted, much of the planning for the surgery will already have happened. The operating theatre will have been reserved, and the doctors and nurses who staff the operating theatre will have been provided with all the information regarding the patient's condition. Appropriate preoperative and postoperative care will have been organized. All this will involve staff and facilities in different parts of the hospital – all of whom must have been given the same information, and their activities coordinated. Soon after the patient arrives, he or she will be checked to make sure that their condition is as expected. Blood, if required, will be cross-matched and reserved, and any medication will be made ready. Any

Operations in practice

Joanne manages the schedule[1]

Joanne Cheung is the senior service adviser at a premier BMW dealership. She and her team act as the interface between customers who want their cars serviced and repaired, and the 16 technicians who carry out the work in their state-of-the-art workshop. "There are three types of work that we have to organize", says Joanne. "The first is performing repairs on customers' vehicles. They usually want this doing as soon as possible. The second type of job is routine servicing. It is usually not urgent, so customers are generally willing to negotiate a time for this. The remainder of our work involves working on the pre-owned cars that our buyer has bought-in to sell-on to customers. Before any of these cars can be sold, they have to undergo extensive checks. To some extent we treat these categories of work slightly differently. We have to give good service to our internal car buyers, but there is some flexibility in planning these jobs. At the other extreme, emergency repair work for customers has to be fitted into our schedule as quickly as possible. If someone is desperate to have their car repaired at very short notice, we sometimes ask them to drop their car in as early as they can and pick it up as late as possible. This gives us the maximum amount of time to fit it into the schedule.

"There are a number of service options open to customers. We can book short jobs in for a fixed time and do it while they wait. Most commonly, we ask the customer to leave the car with us and collect it later. To help customers, we have ten loan cars that are booked out on a first-come-first-served basis. Alternatively, the vehicle can be collected from the customer's home and delivered back there when it is ready. Our four drivers who do this are able to cope with up to 12 jobs a day.

"Most days we deal with 50 to 80 jobs, taking from half-an-hour up to a whole day. To enter a job into our process, all service advisers have access to the computer-based scheduling system. On-screen it shows the total capacity we have day by day, all the jobs that are booked in, the amount of free capacity still available, the number of loan cars available and so on. We use this to see when we have the capacity to book a customer in, and then enter all the customer's details. BMW have issued 'standard times' for all the major jobs. However, you have to modify these standard times a bit to take account of circumstances. That is where the service adviser's experience comes in.

"We keep all the most commonly used parts in stock, but if a repair needs a part that is not in stock, we can usually get it from the BMW parts distributors within a day. Every evening our planning system prints out the jobs to be done the next day and the parts that are likely to be needed for each job. This allows the parts staff to pick out the parts for each job so that the technicians can collect them first thing the next morning without any delay.

"Every day we have to cope with the unexpected. A technician may find that extra work is needed, customers may want extra work doing and technicians are sometimes ill, which reduces our capacity. Occasionally parts may not be available, so we have to arrange with the customer for the vehicle to be rebooked for a later time. Every day up to four or five customers just don't turn up. Usually they have just forgotten to bring their car in so we have to rebook them for a later time. We can cope with most of these uncertainties because our technicians are flexible in terms of the skills they have and also are willing to work overtime when needed. Also, it is important to manage customers' expectations. If there is a chance that the vehicle may not be ready for them, it shouldn't come as a surprise when they try and collect it." ● ● ●

last-minute changes may require some degree of re-planning. For example, if the patient shows unexpected symptoms, observation may be necessary before the surgery can take place. Not only will this affect the patient's own treatment, but other patients' treatment may also have to be rescheduled. All these activities of scheduling, coordination and organization are concerned with the planning and control of the hospital.

operations principle
Customers' perceptions of an operation will be shaped partially by the customer interface of its planning and control system.

What is the difference between planning and control?

Notice that we have chosen to treat 'planning and control' together. This is because the division between 'planning' and 'control' is not always clear. However, there are some general features that help to distinguish between the two. Planning is a formalization of what is intended to happen at some time in the future. But a plan does not guarantee that an event will actually happen. Rather, it is a statement of intention, but things do not always happen as expected. Customers change their minds about what they want and when they want it. Suppliers may not always deliver on time, process technology may fail, or staff may be absent through illness. Control is the process of coping with these types of change. It may mean that plans need to be redrawn. It may also mean that an 'intervention' will need to be made in the operation to bring it back 'on track' – for example, finding a new supplier who can deliver quickly, getting process technology up and running again, or moving staff from another part of the operation to cover for the absentees. Control activities make the adjustments that allow the operation to achieve the objectives that the plan has set, even when the assumptions on which the plan was based do not hold true.

operations principle
Planning and control are separate but closely related activities.

Long-, medium- and short-term resource planning and control

The nature of resource planning and control activities changes over time. In the very long term, operations managers make plans concerning what they intend to do, what resources they need and what objectives they hope to achieve. The emphasis is on planning rather than control, because there is little to control, as such. They will use forecasts of likely demand described in aggregated terms. For example, a hospital will make plans for '2,000 patients' without necessarily going into the details of the individual needs of those 2,000 patients. Similarly, the hospital might plan to have 100 nurses and 20 doctors, but again without deciding on the specific attributes of the staff. Operations managers will focus mainly on volume and financial targets.

Medium-term planning and control is more detailed. It looks ahead to assess the overall demand that the operation must meet in a partially disaggregated manner. By this time, for example, the hospital must distinguish between different types of demand. The number of patients coming as accident-and-emergency cases will need to be distinguished from those requiring routine operations. Similarly, different categories of staff will have been identified and broad staffing levels in each category set.

In short-term planning and control, many of the resources will have been set and it will be difficult to make large changes. However, short-term interventions are possible if things are not going to plan. By this time, demand will be assessed on a totally disaggregated basis, with all types of surgical procedures treated as individual activities. More importantly, individual patients will have been identified by name, and specific time slots booked for their treatment. In making short-term interventions and changes to the plan, operations managers will be attempting to balance the quality, speed, dependability, flexibility and costs of their operation dynamically, on an ad hoc basis. It is unlikely that they will have the time to carry out detailed calculations of the effects of their short-term planning and control decisions on all these objectives, but a general understanding of priorities will form the background to their decision making. Figure 9.2 shows how aspects of planning and control change depending on the time horizon being considered.

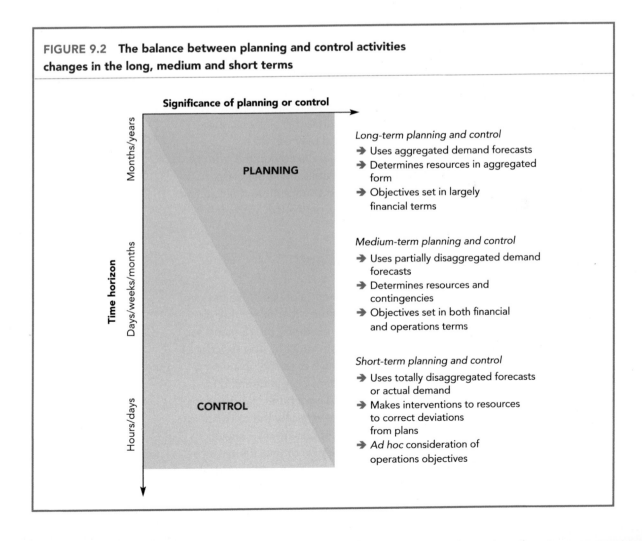

FIGURE 9.2   The balance between planning and control activities changes in the long, medium and short terms

How do supply and demand affect planning and control?

I f planning and control is the process of reconciling demand with supply, then the nature of the decisions taken to plan and control an operation will depend on both the nature of demand and the nature of supply in that operation. In this next section, we examine some differences in demand and supply that can affect the way in which operations managers plan and control their activities.

Uncertainty in supply and demand

Uncertainty is important in planning and control because it makes it more difficult. Sometimes the supply of inputs to an operation may be uncertain. Local village carnivals, for example, rarely work to plan. Events take longer than expected, some of the acts scheduled in the programme may be delayed *en route* and some traders may not even arrive. In other operations, supply is relatively predictable and the need for control is minimal. For example, cable TV services provide programmes to a schedule into subscribers' homes. It is rare to change the programme plan. Similarly, demand may be unpredictable. A fast-food outlet inside a shopping centre does not know how many people will arrive, when they will arrive and what they will order. It may be possible to predict certain patterns, but a sudden rainstorm that drives shoppers indoors could significantly increase demand in the very short term. Conversely, demand may be more predictable. In a school, for example, once classes are fixed and the term or semester has started, a teacher knows how many pupils are in the class. Both supply and demand uncertainty make planning and control more difficult, but a combination of supply *and* demand uncertainty is particularly difficult.

operations principle
Planning and control systems should be able to cope with uncertainty in demand.

Dependent and independent demand

Some operations can predict demand with relative certainty because demand for their services or products is dependent upon some other factor that is known. This is known as 'dependent demand'. For example, the demand for tyres in an automobile factory is not a totally random variable. The process of demand forecasting is relatively straightforward. It will consist of examining the manufacturing schedules in the car plant and deriving the demand for tyres from these. If 600 cars are to be manufactured on a particular day, then it is simple to calculate that 3,000 tyres will be demanded by the car plant (each car has four tyres and a spare) – demand is dependent on a known factor: the number of cars to be manufactured. Because of this, the tyres can be ordered from the tyre manufacturer to a delivery schedule that is closely related to the demand for tyres from the plant (as shown in Figure 9.3).

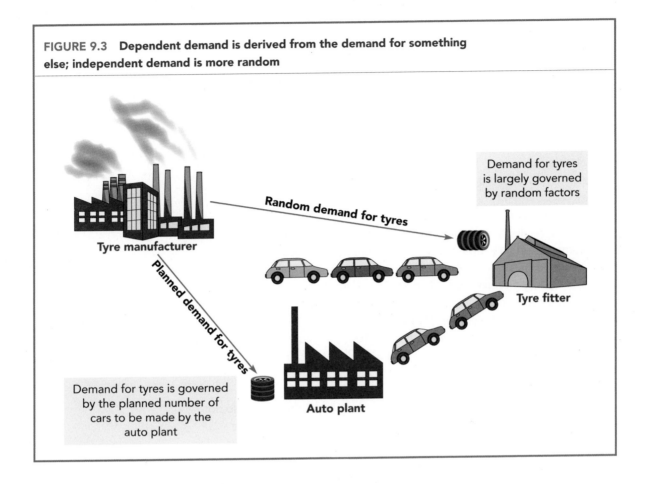

FIGURE 9.3 Dependent demand is derived from the demand for something else; independent demand is more random

By contrast, some operations are subject to independent demand. They need to supply future demand without knowing exactly what that demand will be; or, in the terminology of planning and control, they do not have firm 'forward visibility' of customer orders. For example, the Ace Tyres Company, which operates a drive-in tyre replacement service, will need to manage a stock of tyres. In that sense it is exactly the same task that faced the manager of tyre stocks in the car plant. However, demand is very different for Ace Tyres. It cannot predict either the volume or the specific needs of customers. It must make decisions on how many and what type of tyres to stock, based on demand forecasts and in the light of the risks it is prepared to run of being out of stock. This is the nature of 'independent demand' planning and control. It makes 'best guesses' concerning future demand, attempts to put the resources in place that can satisfy this demand and attempts to respond quickly if actual demand does not match the forecast. Inventory planning and control (treated in Chapter 8) is typical of independent demand planning and control.

operations principle
Planning and control systems should distinguish between dependant and independent demand.

Responding to demand

It is clear, then, that the nature of planning and control in any operation will depend on how it responds to demand, which is, in turn, related to the type of services or products it produces. For example, an advertising agency will only start the process of planning and controlling the creation of an advertising campaign when the customer (or 'client', as the agency will refer to them) confirms the contract with the agency. The creative 'design' of the advertisements will be based on a brief from the client. Only after the design is approved, are the appropriate resources (director, scriptwriters, actors, production company, etc.) contracted. The actual shooting of the advertisement and post-production (editing, putting in the special effects, etc.) then goes ahead, after which the finished advertisement is 'delivered' through television slots. This is shown in Figure 9.4 as a 'design, resource, create and deliver to order' operation.

Another operation might be sufficiently confident of the nature of demand, if not its exact details, to keep 'in stock' most of the resources it requires to satisfy its customers. Certainly it will keep its transforming resources, if not its transformed resources. However, it would still make the actual service or product only when it receives a firm customer order. For example, a website designer will have most of its resources (graphic designers, software developers, specialist development software, etc.) in place, but must still design, create and deliver the website after it understands its customer's requirements. (See the 'Operations in practice' example – Torchbox, in Chapter 1.) This is shown in Figure 9.4 as a 'design, create and deliver to order' operation.

Some operations offer relatively standard services or products, but do not create them until the customer has chosen which particular service or product to have. So, a house builder who has standard designs might choose to build each house only when a customer places a firm order. Because the design of the house is relatively standard, suppliers of materials will have been identified, even if the building operation does not keep the items in stock itself. This is shown in Figure 9.4 as a 'create and deliver to order' operation. In manufacturing, it would be called a 'make to order' operation.

Some operations have services or products that are so predictable that they can start to 'create' them before specific customer orders arrive. Possibly the best-known example of this is Dell Computers, where customers can 'specify' their computer by selecting between various components through the company's website. These components will have already been created (usually by suppliers) but are then assembled to a specific customer order. This is shown in Figure 9.4 as a 'partially create and deliver to order' operation. In manufacturing, it would be called an 'assemble to order' operation.

When an operation's services or products are standardized, there is the potential to create them entirely before demand is known. Almost all domestic products, for example, are 'created to stock', or 'make to stock' (shown in Figure 9.4), from which they are delivered to customers. Taking this evolving logic to its conclusion, some operations require their customers to collect their own services or products. This is the 'choose/collect from stock' illustration in Figure 9.4. IKEA, and most other high-street retail operations, operate like this.

operations principle
The planning and control activity will vary depending on how much work is done before demand is known.

FIGURE 9.4 The P:D ratio of an operation indicates how long the customer has to wait for the service or product, as compared with the total time needed to carry out all the activities to make the service or product available to the customer

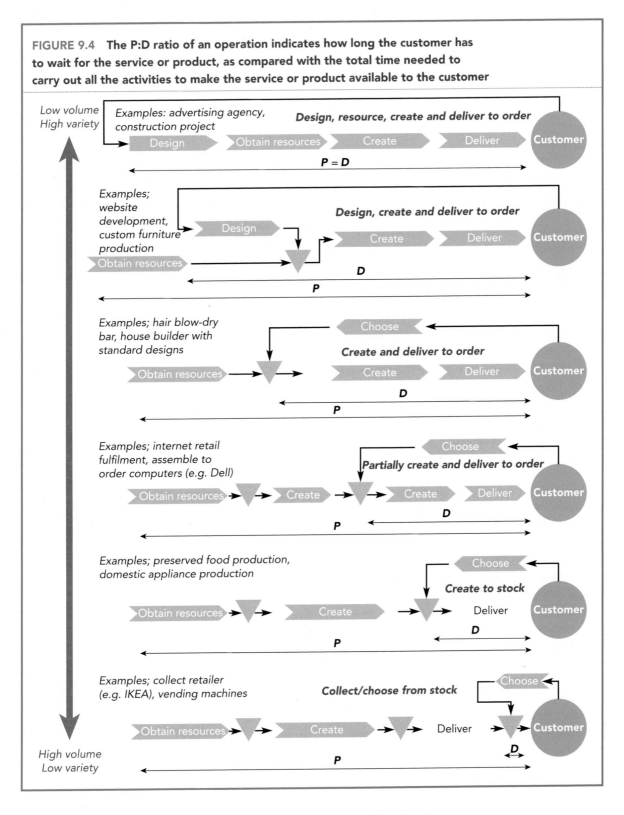

One point to note in the operations illustrated in Figure 9.4 is that there is a relationship between how operations respond to demand and their volume–variety characteristics. It is easy to see that 'design, resource, create and

deliver to order' operations are intended for low-volume and high-variety businesses. By definition, designing different services or products will result in high variety, and performing each activity for each customer would be too cumbersome for a high-volume business. Conversely, 'create for stock' or 'choose/collect from stock' clearly rely on standardized services or products.

P:D ratios[2]

Another way of characterizing the graduation between 'design, resource, create and deliver to order' and 'choose/collect from stock' planning and control is by using a P:D ratio. This contrasts the total length of time customers have to wait between asking for the service or product and receiving it, called the demand time – D, and the total throughput time from start to finish – P. Throughput time is how long the operation takes to design the service or product (if it is customized), obtain the resources, create and deliver it.

P AND D TIMES DEPEND ON THE OPERATION

P and D are illustrated for each type of operation in Figure 9.4. Generally, the ratio of P to D gets larger as operations move from 'design, resource, create and deliver to order' to 'choose/collect from stock'. In other words, as one moves down this spectrum towards the 'create to stock' and 'choose/collect from stock' end, the operation has anticipated customer demand and already created the services and products, even though it has no guarantee that the anticipated demand will really happen. This is a particularly important point for the planning and control activity. The larger the P:D ratio, the more speculative the operation's planning and control activities will be. In its extreme form, the 'choose/collect from stock' operation, such as a high-street retailer, has taken a gamble by designing, resourcing, creating and delivering (or more likely, paying someone else to do so) products to its shops before it has any certainty that any customers will want them. Contrast this with a 'design, resource, create and deliver-to-order' operation, as in the advertising agency mentioned earlier. Here, D is the same as P, and speculation regarding the volume of demand in the short term is eliminated because everything happens in response to a firm order. So, by reducing their P:D ratio, operations reduce their degree of speculative activity and also reduce their dependence on forecasting (although bad forecasting will lead to other problems).

But do not assume that when the P:D ratio approaches 1, all uncertainty is eliminated. The volume of demand (in terms of the number of customer 'orders') may be known, but not the time taken to perform each 'order'. Take the advertising agency again: during each stage of the process, from design to delivery, it is common to have to seek the customer's approval and/or feedback many times. Moreover, there will almost certainly be some recycling back through stages as modifications are made. And, in a similar way to how simultaneous development works in new service and product design, a stage can be started before the previous one has been completed. So, for example, the video-shoot director will have started prior to the artwork design being completed.

operations principle
The P:D ratio of an operation contrasts how long customers have to wait for a service or product with its total throughput time.

What are the activities of planning and control?

Planning and control requires the reconciliation of supply and demand in terms of volumes, timing and quality. In this chapter we will focus on an overview of the activities that plan and control volume and timing (most of this part of the text is concerned with these issues). There are four overlapping activities: loading, sequencing, scheduling and, lastly, monitoring and control (see Figure 9.5). Some caution is needed when using these terms. Different organizations may use them in different ways, and even textbooks in the area adopt different definitions. For example, some authorities term what we have called 'planning and control' as 'operations scheduling'. However, the terminology of planning and control is less important than understanding the basic ideas described in the remainder of this chapter.

operations principle
Planning and control activities include loading, sequencing, scheduling and monitoring and control.

Loading

Loading is the amount of work that is allocated to a work centre. For example, a machine on the shop floor of a manufacturing business is available, in theory, 168 hours a week. However, this does not necessarily mean that 168 hours of work can be loaded onto that machine. For example, it may not be available on statutory holidays and weekends, time may be lost while changing over from making one component to another, it may break down occasionally and so on. The load put onto the machine must take all these factors into account (see the explanation of OEE in Chapter 7).

operations principle
For any given level of demand, a planning and control system should be able to indicate the implications for the loading on any part of the operation.

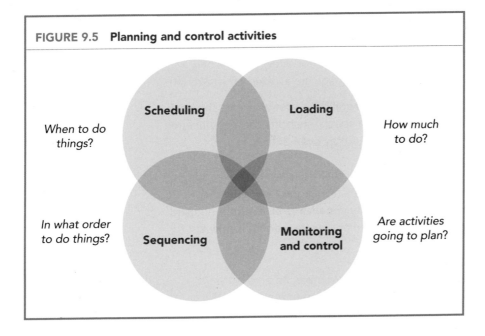

FIGURE 9.5 **Planning and control activities**

When to do things? — **Scheduling**

How much to do? — **Loading**

In what order to do things? — **Sequencing**

Are activities going to plan? — **Monitoring and control**

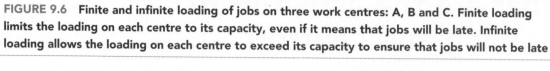

FIGURE 9.6 Finite and infinite loading of jobs on three work centres: A, B and C. Finite loading limits the loading on each centre to its capacity, even if it means that jobs will be late. Infinite loading allows the loading on each centre to exceed its capacity to ensure that jobs will not be late

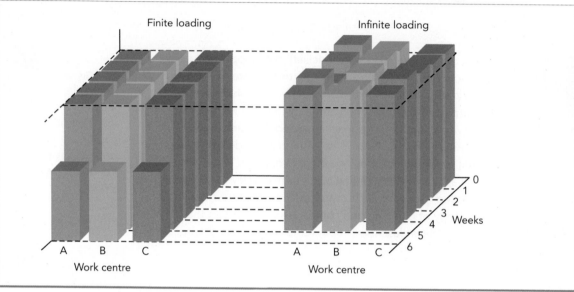

FINITE AND INFINITE LOADING

Finite loading is an approach that allocates work to a work centre (a person, a machine, or perhaps a group of people or machines) only up to a set limit. This limit is the estimate of capacity for the work centre (based on the times available for loading). Work over and above this capacity is not accepted. Figure 9.6 first shows how the load on the work centres is not allowed to exceed the capacity limit. Finite loading is particularly relevant for operations where:

 it is possible to limit the load for example, it is possible to run an appointment system for a general medical practice or a hairdresser;

 it is necessary to limit the load for example, for safety reasons only a finite number of people and weight of luggage are allowed on an aircraft;

 the cost of limiting the load is not prohibitive for example, the cost of maintaining a finite order book at a specialist sports car manufacturer does not adversely affect demand, and may even enhance it.

Infinite loading is an approach to loading work that does not limit accepting work, but instead tries to cope with it. The second diagram in Figure 9.6 illustrates this loading pattern, where capacity constraints have not been used to limit loading so the work is completed earlier. Infinite loading is relevant for operations where:

 it is not possible to limit the load for example, an accident-and-emergency department in a hospital should not turn away arrivals needing attention;

it is not necessary to limit the load for example, fast-food outlets are designed to flex capacity up and down to cope with varying arrival rates of customers; during busy periods, customers accept that they must queue for some time before being served and, unless this is extreme, the customers will not go elsewhere;

 the cost of limiting the load is prohibitive for example, if a retail bank turned away customers at the door because a set amount were inside, customers would feel less than happy with the service.

In complex planning and control activities where there are multiple stages, each with different capacities and with a varying mix arriving at the facilities (such as a machine shop in an engineering company), the constraints imposed by finite loading make loading calculations complex and not worth the considerable computational power that would be needed.

Sequencing

Whether the approach to loading is finite or infinite, when work arrives, decisions must be taken on the order in which the work will be tackled. This activity is termed 'sequencing'. The priorities given to work in an operation are often determined by some predefined set of rules, some of which are relatively complex. Some of these are summarized below.

PHYSICAL CONSTRAINTS

The physical nature of the inputs being processed may determine the priority of work. For example, in an operation using paints or dyes, lighter shades will be sequenced before darker shades. On completion of each batch, the colour is slightly darkened for the next batch. This is because darkness of colour can only be added to and not removed from the colour mix. Sometimes the mix of work arriving at a part of an operation may determine the priority given to jobs. For example, when fabric is cut to a required size and shape in garment manufacture, the surplus fabric would be wasted if not used for another product. Therefore, jobs that physically fit together may be scheduled together to reduce waste. The sequencing issue described in the 'Operations in practice' example 'Can airline passengers be sequenced?' is of this type.

CUSTOMER PRIORITY

Operations will sometimes use customer priority sequencing, which allows an important or aggrieved customer, or item, to be 'processed' prior to others, irrespective of the order of arrival of the customer or item. This approach is typically used by operations whose customer base is skewed, containing a mass of small customers and a few large, very important customers. Some banks, for example, give priority to important customers. Similarly, in hotels, complaining customers will be treated as a priority because their complaint may have an adverse effect on the perceptions of other customers. More seriously, the emergency services often have to use their judgement in

Operations in practice

Can airline passengers be sequenced?[3]

Like many before him, Dr Jason Steffen, a professional astrophysicist from the world-famous Fermilab, was frustrated by the time it took to load him and his fellow passengers onto an aircraft. He decided to devise a way to make the experience a little less tedious. So, for a while, he neglected his usual work of examining extra-solar planets, dark matter and cosmology, and experimentally tested a faster method of boarding aircraft. He found that, by changing the sequence in which passengers are loaded onto the aircraft, airlines could potentially save both time and money. Using a computer simulation and the arithmetic techniques routinely used in his day-to-day job, he was able to find what seemed to be a superior sequencing

method. In fact, the most common way of boarding passenger planes proved to be the least efficient. This is called the 'block' method, where blocks of seats are called for boarding, starting from the back. Previously, other experts in the airline industry had suggested boarding those in window seats first, followed by middle and aisle seats. This is called the 'Wilma' method. But, according to Dr Steffen's simulations, two things slow down the boarding process. The first is that passengers may be required to wait in the aisle while those ahead of them store their luggage before they can take their seat. The second is that passengers already seated in aisle or middle seats frequently have to rise and move into the aisle to let others take seats nearer the window. So Dr Steffen

suggested a variant of the Wilma method that minimized the first type of disturbance and eliminated the second. He suggested boarding in alternate rows, progressing from the rear forward, window seats first. Using this approach (now called the Steffen method), first the window seats for every other row on one side of the plane are boarded. Next, alternate rows of window seats on the opposite side are boarded. Then, the window seats in the skipped rows are filled in on each side. The procedure then repeats with the middle seats and the aisle seats (see Figure 9.7).

Later, the effectiveness of the various approaches was tested using a mock-up of a Boeing 757 aircraft and 72 luggage-carrying volunteers. Five different

prioritizing the urgency of requests for service. For example, Figure 9.8 shows a typical triage system used in hospitals to prioritize patients.

DUE DATE (DD)
Prioritizing by due date means that work is sequenced according to when it is 'due' for delivery, irrespective of the size of each job or the importance of each customer. For example, a support service, such as a printing unit, will often ask when copies are required, and then sequence the work according to that due date. Due date sequencing usually improves the delivery dependability and average delivery speed. However, it may not provide

FIGURE 9.7 The best way to sequence passengers onto an aircraft

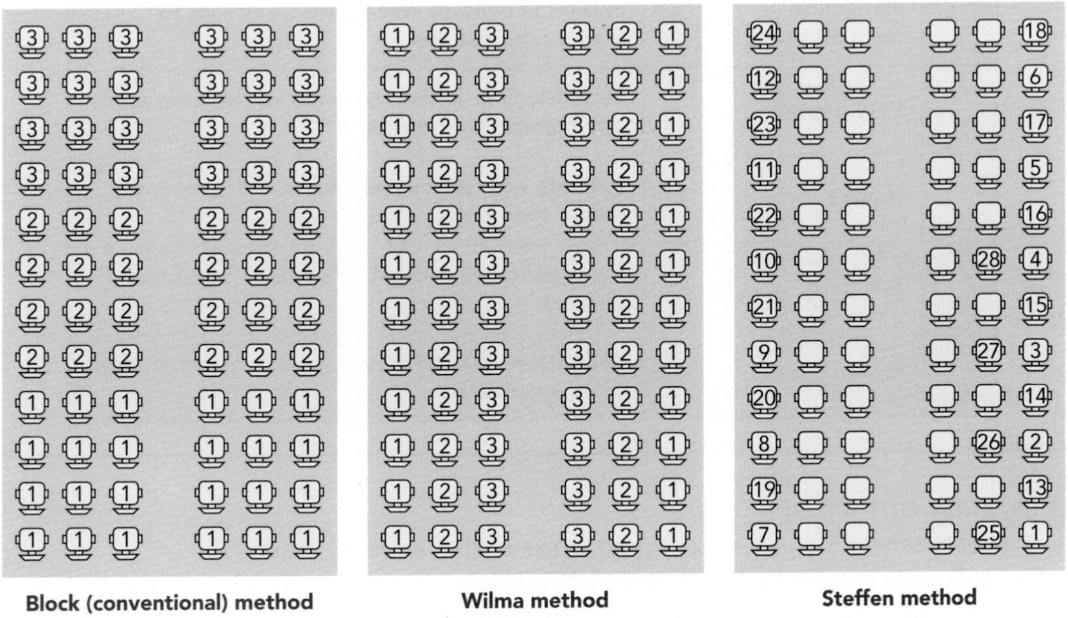

Block (conventional) method

Wilma method

Steffen method

scenarios were tested: 'block' boarding in groups of rows from back to front; one by one from back to front; the 'Wilma method'; the 'Steffen' method; and completely random boarding. In all cases, parent–child pairs were allowed to board first. It was assumed that families were likely to want to stay together. As Dr Steffen had predicted, the conventional block approach came out as the slowest, with the strict back-to-front approach not much better. Completely random boarding (unallocated seating), which is used by several low-cost airlines, fared much better – most probably because it randomly avoids space conflicts. The times for fully boarding the 72 passengers using each method were as follows: 'block' boarding – 6:54 minutes; back-to-front – 6:11 minutes; random boarding – 4:44 minutes; 'Wilma' method – 4:13 minutes; and 'Steffen' method - 3:36 minutes.

The big question is, 'would passengers really be prepared to be sequenced in this way as they queue to board the aircraft?'. Some airlines argue that directing passengers on to a plane is a little like herding cats. But if they could adopt Dr Steffen's system it would save time for customers and very significant amounts of money for the airlines. ● ● ●

optimal productivity, as a more efficient sequencing of work may reduce total costs. However, it can be flexible when new, urgent work arrives at the work centre.

LAST IN, FIRST OUT (LIFO)

Last in, first out (LIFO) is a method of sequencing usually selected for practical reasons. For example, unloading an elevator is more convenient on a LIFO basis, as there is only one entrance and exit. However, it is not an equitable approach. Patients at hospital clinics may be infuriated if they see newly arrived patients examined first.

FIGURE 9.8   A triage prioritization scale

1	Immediate resuscitation	Patient in need of immediate treatment for preservation of life
2	Very urgent	Seriously ill or injured patients whose lives are not in immediate danger
3	Urgent	Patients with serious problems, but apparently stable conditions
4	Standard	Standard cases without immediate danger or distress
5	Non-urgent	Patients whose conditions are not true accidents or emergencies

FIRST IN, FIRST OUT (FIFO)

Some operations serve customers in exactly the sequence they arrive in. This is called first in, first out sequencing (FIFO), or sometimes 'first come, first served' (FCFS). For example, UK passport offices receive mail, and sort it according to the day when it arrived. They work through the mail, opening it in sequence, and process the passport applications in order of arrival.

LONGEST OPERATION TIME (LOT)

Operations may feel obliged to sequence their longest jobs first, called longest operation time sequencing. This has the advantage of occupying work centres for long periods. By contrast, relatively small jobs progressing through an operation will take up time at each work centre because of the need to change over from one job to the next. However, although longest operation time sequencing keeps utilization high, this rule does not take into account delivery speed, reliability or flexibility. Indeed, it may work directly against these performance objectives.

SHORTEST OPERATION TIME (SOT)

Most operations at some stage become cash constrained. In these situations, the sequencing rules may be adjusted to tackle short jobs first; this is called shortest operation time sequencing. These jobs can then be invoiced and payment received to ease cash-flow problems. Larger jobs that take more time will not enable the business to invoice as quickly. This has an effect of improving delivery performance, if the unit of measurement of delivery is jobs. However, it may adversely affect total productivity and can damage service to larger customers.

JUDGING SEQUENCING RULES

All five performance objectives, or some variant of them, could be used to judge the effectiveness of sequencing rules. However, the objectives of dependability, speed and cost are particularly important. So, for example, the following performance objectives are often used:

meeting 'due date' promised to customer (dependability);

 minimizing the time the job spends in the process, also known as 'flow time' (speed);

 minimizing work-in-progress inventory (an element of cost);

 minimizing idle time of work centres (another element of cost).

Scheduling

Having determined the sequence that work is to be tackled in, some operations require a detailed timetable showing at what time or date jobs should start and when they should end – this is scheduling. Schedules are familiar statements of volume and timing in many consumer environments. For example, a bus schedule shows that more buses are put on routes at more frequent intervals during rush-hour periods. The bus schedule shows the time each bus is due to arrive at each stage of the route. Schedules of work are used in operations where some planning is required to ensure that customer demand is met. Other operations, such as rapid-response service operations where customers arrive in an unplanned way, cannot schedule the operation in a short-term sense. They can only respond at the time demand is placed upon them.

THE COMPLEXITY OF SCHEDULING

The scheduling activity is one of the most complex tasks in operations management. First, schedulers must deal with several different types of resource simultaneously. Equipment will have different capabilities and capacities; staff will have different skills. More importantly, the number of possible schedules increases rapidly as the number of activities and processes increases. For example, suppose one machine has five different jobs to process. Any of the five jobs could be processed first and, following that, any one of the remaining four jobs, and so on. This means that there are:

$$5 \times 4 \times 3 \times 2 = 120 \text{ different schedules possible}$$

In other words, for n jobs there are $n!$ (factorial n) different ways of scheduling the jobs through a single process. But when there are (say) two machines, there is no reason why the sequence on machine 1 would be the same as the sequence on machine 2. If we consider the two sequencing tasks to be independent of each other, for two machines there would be:

$$120 \times 120 = 14,400 \text{ possible schedules of the two machines and five jobs}$$

So, a general formula can be devised to calculate the number of possible schedules in any given situation, as follows:

$$\text{Number of possible schedules} = (n!)^m$$

where n is the number of jobs and m is the number of machines.

TABLE 9.1   **The effects of forward and backward scheduling**

Task	Duration	Start time (backwards)	Start time (forwards)
▶ Press	▶ 1 hour	▶ 3.00 pm	▶ 1.00 pm
▶ Dry	▶ 2 hours	▶ 1.00 pm	▶ 11.00 am
▶ Wash	▶ 3 hours	▶ 10.00 am	▶ 8.00 am

In practical terms, this means that there are often many millions of feasible schedules, even for relatively small scheduling tasks. This is why scheduling rarely attempts to provide an 'optimal' solution, but rather satisfies itself with an 'acceptable', feasible one.

FORWARD AND BACKWARD SCHEDULING

Forward scheduling involves starting work as soon as it arrives. Backward scheduling involves starting jobs at the last possible moment, to prevent them from being late. For example, assume that it takes six hours for a contract laundry to wash, dry and press a batch of overalls. If the work is collected at 8.00 am and is due to be picked up at 4.00 pm, there are more than six hours available to do it. Table 9.1 shows the different start times of each job, depending on whether they are forward or backward scheduled.

The choice of backward or forward scheduling depends largely upon the circumstances. Table 9.2 lists some advantages and disadvantages of the two approaches. In theory, both materials requirement planning (MRP – see later in the chapter) and lean (see Chapter 10) use backward scheduling, only starting work when it is required. In practice, however, users of MRP have tended to allow too long for each task to be completed, and therefore each task is not started at the latest possible time.

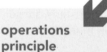

operations principle
An operation's planning and control system should allow for the effects of alternative schedules to be assessed.

GANTT CHARTS

One crude but simple method of scheduling is by use of the Gantt chart. This is a simple device that represents time as a bar, or channel, on a chart. The start and finish times for activities can be indicated on the chart and sometimes the

TABLE 9.2   **Advantages of forward and backward scheduling**

Advantages of forward scheduling	Advantages of backward scheduling
▶ High-labour utilization – workers always start work to keep busy	▶ Lower material costs – materials are not used until they have to be, therefore delaying added value until the last moment
▶ Flexible – the time slack in the system allows unexpected work to be loaded	▶ Less exposed to risk in case of schedule change by the customer
	▶ Tends to focus the operation on customer due dates

FIGURE 9.9 Gantt chart showing the schedule for jobs at each process stage

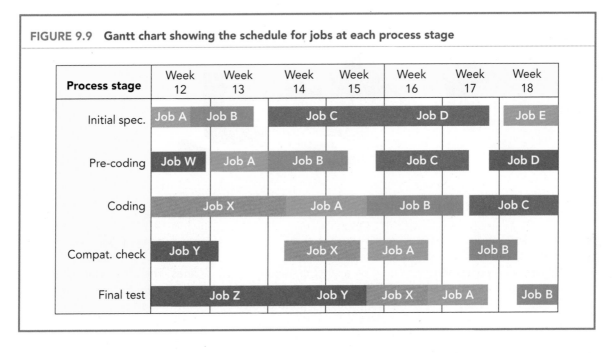

Process stage	Week 12	Week 13	Week 14	Week 15	Week 16	Week 17	Week 18
Initial spec.	Job A	Job B	Job C		Job D		Job E
Pre-coding	Job W	Job A	Job B		Job C		Job D
Coding	Job X		Job A		Job B		Job C
Compat. check	Job Y		Job X	Job A		Job B	
Final test	Job Z		Job Y	Job X	Job A		Job B

actual progress of the job is also indicated. The advantages of Gantt charts are that they provide a simple visual representation, both of what should be happening and of what actually is happening in the operation. Furthermore, they can be used to 'test out' alternative schedules. It is a relatively simple task to represent alternative schedules (even if it is a far-from-simple task to find a schedule that fits all the resources satisfactorily). Figure 9.9 illustrates a Gantt chart for a specialist software developer. It indicates the progress of several jobs as they are expected to move through five stages of the process. Gantt charts are not an optimizing tool – they merely facilitate the development of alternative schedules by communicating them effectively.

SCHEDULING WORK PATTERNS

Where the dominant resource in an operation is its staff, then the schedule of work times effectively determines the capacity of the operation itself. The main task of scheduling, therefore, is to make sure that sufficient numbers of people are working at any point in time to provide a capacity appropriate for the level of demand at that point in time. This is often called 'staff rostering'. Operations such as call centres, postal delivery, policing, holiday couriers, retail shops and hospitals will all need to schedule the working hours of their staff with demand in mind. This is a direct consequence of these operations having relatively high 'visibility' (we introduced this idea in Chapter 1). Such operations cannot store their outputs in inventories and so must respond directly to customer demand. For example, Figure 9.12 shows the scheduling of shifts for a small technical 'hot line' support service for a small software company. It gives advice to customers on their technical problems. Its service times are 4.00 hrs to 20.00 hrs on Monday, 4.00 hrs to 22.00 hrs Tuesday to Friday, 6.00 hrs to 22.00 hrs on Saturday, and 10.00 hrs to 20.00 hrs on Sunday. Demand is heaviest Tuesday to Thursday, starts to decrease on Friday, is low over the weekend and starts to increase again on Monday.

The life and times of a chicken salad sandwich[4]

Pre-packed sandwiches are a growth product around the world as consumers put convenience and speed above relaxation and cost. But if you have recently consumed a pre-packed sandwich, think about the schedule of events that has gone into its making. For example, take a chicken salad sandwich. Less than five days ago, the chicken was on the farm unaware that it would never see another weekend. The Gantt chart schedule shown in Figure 9.10 tells the story of the sandwich and (posthumously) of the chicken.

From the forecast, orders for non-perishable items are placed for goods to arrive up to a week in advance of their use. Orders for perishable items will be placed daily, a day or two before the items are required. Tomatoes, cucumbers and lettuces have a three-day shelf life so may be received up to three days before production. Stock is held on a strict first-in-first-out (FIFO) basis. If today is (say) Wednesday, vegetables are processed that have been received during the last three days. This morning the bread arrived from a local bakery and the chicken arrived fresh, cooked and in strips ready to be placed directly in the sandwich during assembly. Yesterday (Tuesday) it had been killed, cooked, prepared and sent on its journey to the factory. By midday, orders for tonight's production will have been received on the internet. From 2.00 pm until 10.00 pm the production lines are closed down for maintenance and a very thorough cleaning. During this time the production planning team is busy planning the night's production run. Production for delivery to customers furthest away from the factory will have to be scheduled first. By 10.00 pm production is ready to start. Sandwiches are made on production lines. The bread is loaded into a conveyor belt by hand and butter is spread automatically by a machine. Next the various fillings are applied at each stage according to the specified sandwich 'design' (see Figure 9.11). After the filling has been assembled, the top slice of bread is placed on the sandwich and machine-chopped into two triangles, then packed and sealed by machine. It is now early Thursday morning, and by 2.00 am the first refrigerated lorries are already departing on their journeys to various customers. Production continues through until 2.00 pm on the Thursday, after which, once again, the maintenance and cleaning teams move in. The last sandwiches are dispatched by 4.00 pm on the Thursday. There is no finished goods stock. ● ● ●

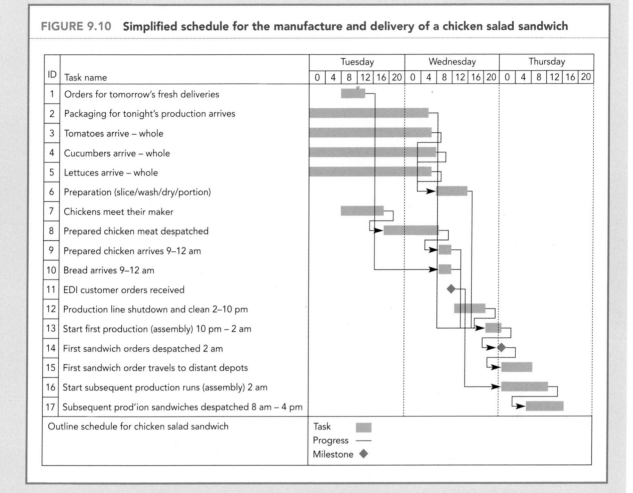

FIGURE 9.10 Simplified schedule for the manufacture and delivery of a chicken salad sandwich

ID	Task name
1	Orders for tomorrow's fresh deliveries
2	Packaging for tonight's production arrives
3	Tomatoes arrive – whole
4	Cucumbers arrive – whole
5	Lettuces arrive – whole
6	Preparation (slice/wash/dry/portion)
7	Chickens meet their maker
8	Prepared chicken meat despatched
9	Prepared chicken arrives 9–12 am
10	Bread arrives 9–12 am
11	EDI customer orders received
12	Production line shutdown and clean 2–10 pm
13	Start first production (assembly) 10 pm – 2 am
14	First sandwich orders despatched 2 am
15	First sandwich order travels to distant depots
16	Start subsequent production runs (assembly) 2 am
17	Subsequent prod'ion sandwiches despatched 8 am – 4 pm

Outline schedule for chicken salad sandwich

Task
Progress
Milestone

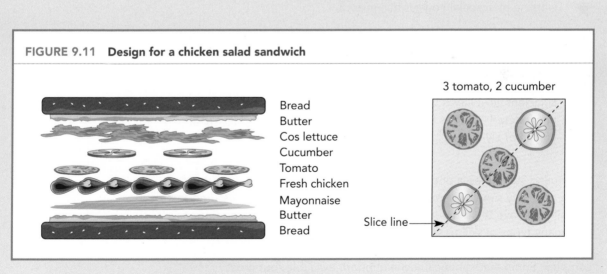

FIGURE 9.11 Design for a chicken salad sandwich

Bread
Butter
Cos lettuce
Cucumber
Tomato
Fresh chicken
Mayonnaise
Butter
Bread

3 tomato, 2 cucumber

Slice line

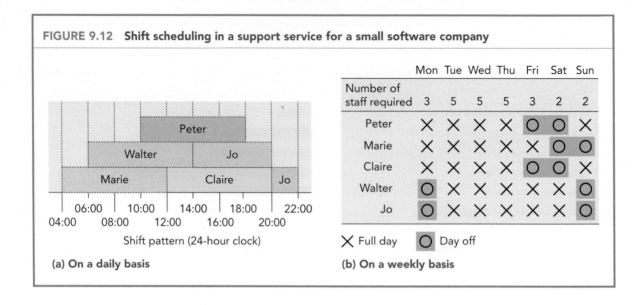

FIGURE 9.12   **Shift scheduling in a support service for a small software company**

The scheduling task for this kind of problem can be considered over different time scales, two of which are shown in Figure 9.12. During the day, working hours need to be agreed with individual staff members. During the week, days off need to be agreed. During the year, vacations, training periods and other blocks of time where staff are unavailable need to be agreed. All this has to be scheduled such that:

 capacity matches demand;

 the length of each shift is neither excessively long nor too short to be attractive to staff;

 working at unsocial hours is minimized;

 days off match agreed staff conditions (in this example, staff prefer two consecutive days off every week);

 vacation and other 'time-off' blocks are accommodated;

 sufficient flexibility is built into the schedule to cover for unexpected changes in supply (staff illness) and demand (surge in customer calls).

Scheduling staff times is one of the most complex of scheduling problems. In the relatively simple example shown in Figure 9.12, we have assumed that all staff have the same level and type of skill. In very large operations with many types of skill to schedule and with uncertain demand (for example, a large hospital), the scheduling problem becomes extremely complex. Some mathematical techniques are available, but most scheduling of this type is, in practice, solved using heuristics (rules of thumb), some of which are incorporated into commercially available software packages.

Monitoring and controlling the operation

Having created a plan for the operation through loading, sequencing and scheduling, each part of the operation has to be monitored to ensure that planned activities are indeed happening. Any deviation from the plans can then be rectified through some kind of intervention in the operation, which itself will probably involve some re-planning. Figure 9.13 illustrates a simple view of control. The output from a work centre is monitored and compared with a plan that indicates what the work centre is supposed to be doing. Deviations from this plan are taken into account through a re-planning activity and the necessary interventions made to the work centre, which will (hopefully) ensure that the new plan is carried out. Eventually, however, some further deviation from planned activity will be detected and the cycle is repeated.

operations principle
A planning and control system should be able to detect deviations from plans within a timescale that allows an appropriate response.

PUSH AND PULL CONTROL

One element of control, then, is periodic intervention into the activities of the operation. An important decision is how this intervention takes place. The key distinction is between intervention signals that push work through the processes within the operation and those that pull work only when it is required. In a push system of control, activities are scheduled by means of a central system and completed in line with central instructions. Each work centre pushes out work without considering whether the succeeding work centre can make use of it. Work centres are coordinated by means of the central operations planning and control system. In practice, however, there are many reasons why actual conditions differ from those planned. As a consequence, idle time, inventory and queues often characterize push systems. By contrast, in a pull system of control, the pace and specification of what is done are set by the 'customer' workstation, which 'pulls' work from the preceding (supplier) workstation. The customer acts as the only 'trigger' for movement. If a request is not passed back from the customer to the supplier, the supplier cannot produce anything or move any materials. A request from a

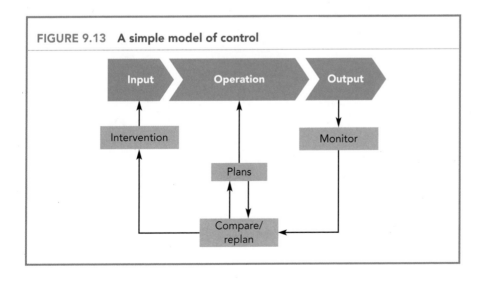

FIGURE 9.13 **A simple model of control**

customer not only triggers production at the supplying stage, but also prompts the supplying stage to request a further delivery from its own suppliers. In this way, demand is transmitted back through the stages from the original point of demand by the original customer.

The inventory consequences of push and pull

Understanding the differing principles of push and pull is important because they have different effects in terms of their propensities to accumulate inventory in the operation. Pull systems are far less likely to result in inventory build-up and are therefore favoured by lean operations (see Chapter 10). To understand why this is so, consider the 'gravity' analogy, as illustrated in Figure 9.14. Here, a push system is represented by an operation, each stage of which is on a lower level than the previous stage. When items are processed by each stage, gravity pushes them down the slope to the next stage. Any delay or variability in processing time at that stage will result in the items accumulating as inventory. In the pull system, items cannot naturally flow uphill, so they can only progress if the next stage along deliberately pulls them forward. Under these circumstances, inventory cannot accumulate as easily.

operations principle

Pull control reduces the build-up of inventory between processes or stages.

Drum, buffer, rope

The drum, buffer, rope concept comes from the theory of constraints (TOC) and a concept called optimized production technology (OPT), originally described by Eli Goldratt in his novel *The Goal*.[5] It is an idea that helps to

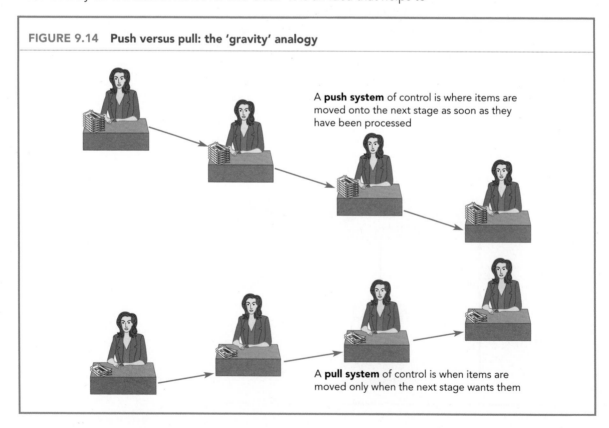

FIGURE 9.14   **Push versus pull: the 'gravity' analogy**

A **push system** of control is where items are moved onto the next stage as soon as they have been processed

A **pull system** of control is when items are moved only when the next stage wants them

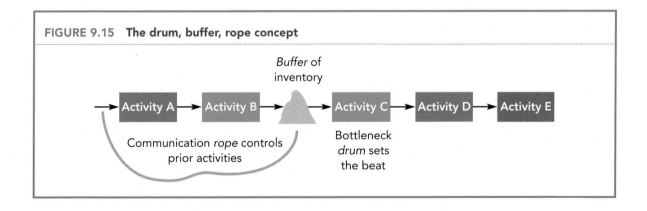

FIGURE 9.15   The drum, buffer, rope concept

decide exactly *where* in a process control should occur. Most operations do not have the same amount of work loaded onto each separate work centre (that is, they are not perfectly balanced). This means there is likely to be a part of the process that is acting as a bottleneck on the work flowing through the process. Goldratt argued that the bottleneck in the process should be the control point of the whole process. It is called the 'drum' because it sets the 'beat' for the rest of the process to follow. Because it does not have sufficient capacity, a bottleneck is (or should be) working all the time. Therefore, it is sensible to keep a 'buffer' of inventory in front of it, to make sure that it always has something to work on. Because it constrains the output of the whole process, any time lost at the bottleneck will affect the output of the whole process. So, it is not worthwhile for the parts of the process before the bottleneck to work to their full capacity. All they would do is produce work that would accumulate further along in the process, up to the point where the bottleneck is constraining the flow. Therefore, some form of communication between the bottleneck and the input to the process is needed to make sure that activities before the bottleneck do not overproduce. This is called the 'rope' (see Figure 9.15).

operations principle
The constraints of bottleneck processes and activities should be a major input to the planning and control activity.

What is enterprise resource planning (ERP)?

One of the most important issues in planning and controlling operations is managing the, sometimes vast, amounts of information generated by the activity. It is not just the operations function that is the author and recipient of this information; almost every other function of a business will be involved. So, it is important that all relevant information that is spread throughout the organization is brought together, and that, based on this information, appropriate decisions are taken. This is what enterprise resource planning does.

An easy way of thinking about enterprise resource planning (ERP) is to imagine that you have decided to hold a party in two weeks' time and expect about 40 people to attend. As well as drinks, you decide to provide sandwiches and snacks. You will probably do some simple calculations, estimating guests' preferences and how much people are likely to drink and eat. You may already have some food and drink in the house that you will use, so you will take that into account when making your shopping list. If any of the food is to be cooked from a recipe, you may have to multiply up the ingredients to cater for 40 people. Also, you may wish to take into account the fact that you will prepare some of the food the week before and freeze it, while you will leave the rest to either the day before or the day of the party. So, you will need to decide when each item is required, so that you can shop in time. In fact, planning a party requires a series of interrelated decisions about the volume (quantity) and timing of the materials needed. This is the basis of the foundation concept for ERP, called materials requirement planning (MRP). It is a process that helps companies make volume and timing calculations (similar to those for the party, but on a much larger scale, and with a greater degree of complexity). But your planning may extend beyond 'materials'. You may want to hire in a sound system from a local supplier – you will have to plan for this. The party also has financial implications. You may have to agree a temporary increase to your credit-card limit. Again, this requires some forward planning and calculations of how much it is going to cost, and how much extra credit you require. Both the equipment and financial implications may vary if you increase the number of guests. But, if you postpone the party for a month, these arrangements will change. There are also other implications of organizing the party. You will need to give any friends who are helping with the organization an idea of when they should come and for how long. This will depend on the timing of the various tasks to be done (decorating the room, making sandwiches, etc.).

So, even for this relatively simple activity, the key to successful planning is how we generate, integrate and organize all the information on which planning and control depends. Of course, in business operations it is more complex than this. Companies usually sell many different products to many hundreds of customers who are likely to vary their demand for the products. This is a bit like organizing 200 parties one week, 250 the next and 225 the following week, all for different groups of guests with different requirements who keep changing their minds about what they want to eat and drink. This is what an ERP system does; it automates and integrates core business processes such as customer demand, scheduling operations, ordering items, keeping inventory records and updating financial data. It helps companies 'forward plan' these types of decisions and understand all the implications of any changes to the plan.

operations principle
ERP systems automate and integrate core business processes.

How did ERP develop?

Enterprise resource planning is the latest, and the most significant, development of the original materials requirement planning (MRP) philosophy. The now-large companies that have grown almost exclusively on the basis of providing ERP systems include SAP and Oracle. Yet to understand ERP, it is important to understand the various stages in its development, summarized in Figure 9.16. The original MRP became popular during the 1970s, although the planning and control logic that underlies it had, by then, been known for some time. What popularized MRP was the availability of computer power to drive the basic planning and control mathematics.

Manufacturing resource planning (MRP II) expanded out of MRP during the 1980s. Again, it was a technology innovation that allowed the development. Connected networks, together with increasingly powerful desktop computers, allowed a much higher degree of processing power and communication between different parts of a business. Also, MRP II's extra sophistication allowed the forward modelling of 'what-if' scenarios. The strength of MRP and MRP II lay always in the fact that they could explore the *consequences* of any changes to what an operation was required to do. So, if demand changed, the MRP system would calculate all the 'knock-on' effects and issue instructions accordingly. This same principle also applies to ERP, but on a much wider basis. Enterprise resource planning (ERP) has been defined as, 'a complete enterprise-wide business solution. The ERP system consists of software support modules such as: marketing and sales, field service, product design and development, production and inventory control, procurement, distribution, industrial facilities management, process design and development, manufacturing, quality, human resources, finance and accounting, and information services. Integration between the modules is stressed without the duplication of information.'[6]

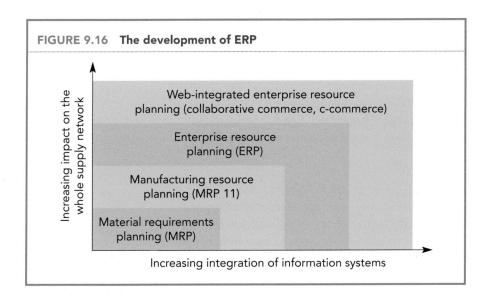

FIGURE 9.16 **The development of ERP**

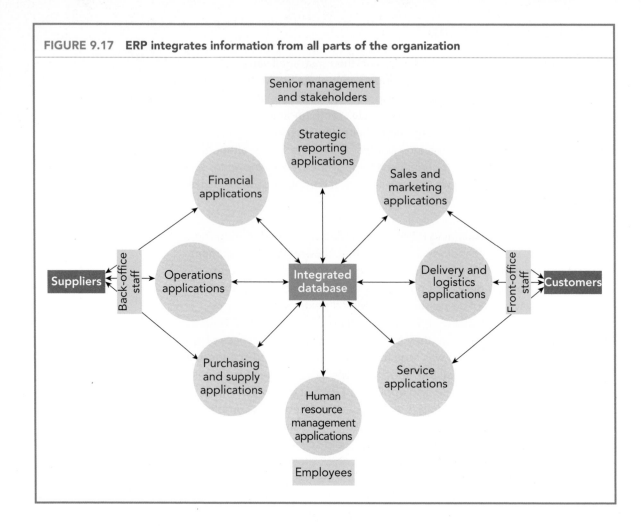

FIGURE 9.17   ERP integrates information from all parts of the organization

ERP systems allow decisions and databases from all parts of the organization to be integrated so that the consequences of decisions in one part of the organization are reflected in the planning and control systems of the rest of the organization (see Figure 9.17). ERP is the equivalent of the organization's central nervous system, sensing information about the condition of different parts of the business and relaying the information to other parts of the business that need it. The information is updated in real time by those who use it, and yet is always available to everyone connected to the ERP system.

Also, the potential of internet-based communication has provided a further boost to ERP development. Many companies have suppliers, customers and other businesses with whom they collaborate, who themselves have ERP-type systems. An obvious development is to allow these systems to communicate. However, the technical, as well as organizational and strategic, consequences of this can be formidable. Nevertheless, many authorities believe that the true value of ERP systems is only fully exploited when such web-integrated ERP becomes widely implemented.

Summary answers to key questions

Each chapter has 'Summary answers to key questions' section. Use it to check your understanding of the issues covered in the chapter.

WHAT IS RESOURCE PLANNING AND CONTROL?

 Resource planning and control is the reconciliation of the potential of the operation to supply products and services, and the demands of its customers on the operation. It is the set of day-to-day activities that run the operation on an ongoing basis.

WHAT IS THE DIFFERENCE BETWEEN PLANNING AND CONTROL?

 A plan is a formalization of what is intended to happen at some time in the future. Control is the process of coping with changes to the plan and the operation to which it relates. Although planning and control are theoretically separable, they are usually treated together.

 The balance between planning and control changes over time. Planning dominates in the long term and is usually done on an aggregated basis. In the short term, control usually operates within the resource constraints of the operation, but makes interventions into the operation to cope with short-term changes in circumstances.

HOW DO SUPPLY AND DEMAND AFFECT PLANNING AND CONTROL?

 The degree of uncertainty in demand affects the balance between planning and control. The greater the uncertainty, the more difficult it is to plan, and greater emphasis must be placed on control.

 This idea of uncertainty is linked with the concepts of dependent and independent demand. Dependent demand is relatively predictable because it is dependent on some known factor. Independent demand is less predictable because it depends on the chances of the market or customer behaviour.

 The different ways of responding to demand can be characterized by differences in the P:D ratio of the operation. The P:D ratio is the ratio of total throughput time of services or products to demand time of the customer.

WHAT ARE THE ACTIVITIES OF PLANNING AND CONTROL?

 In planning and control, four distinct activities are necessary:

- loading, which dictates the amount of work that is allocated to each part of the operation;
- sequencing, which decides the order in which work is tackled within the operation;
- scheduling, which determines the detailed timetable of activities and when activities are started and finished;
- monitoring and control, which involve detecting what is happening in the operation, re-planning if necessary and intervening in order to impose new plans.

 Pull control is a system whereby demand is triggered by requests from a work centre's (internal) customer. Push control is a centralized system, whereby control decisions are issued to work centres that are then required to perform the task and supply the next workstation.

WHAT IS ENTERPRISE RESOURCE PLANNING (ERP)?

 Enterprise resource planning (ERP) systems are information technology systems that integrate planning and control information from various parts of the business.

 ERP is a development of materials requirement planning (MRP), and is now used to integrate not only internal activities but those of customers and suppliers also.

Problems and applications

All chapters have problems and application questions that will help you practise analyzing operations. They can be answered by reading the chapter. Model answers for the first question can be found on the companion website for this text.

➜ Re-read the 'Operations in practice' at the beginning of the chapter: 'Joanne manages the schedule'.

What are the main objectives of this planning and control task, and how does Joanne try to achieve these objectives?

➜ A specialist sandwich retailer must order sandwiches at least 8 hours before they are delivered. When they arrive in the shop, they are immediately displayed in a temperature-controlled cabinet. The average time that the sandwiches spend in the cabinet is 6 hours.

What is the P:D ratio for this retail operation?

3 → Mark Key is an events coordinator for a small company. Returning from his annual holiday in France, he is given six events to plan. He gives them the codes A to F. He needs to decide upon the sequence in which to plan the events, and wants to minimize the average time the jobs are tied up in the office and, if possible, meet the deadlines allocated. The six jobs are detailed in Table 9.3.

Determine a sequence based on using (a) the FIFO rule, (b) the due date rule and (c) the shortest operation time rule.

Which of these sequences gives the most efficient solution and which gives the least lateness?

TABLE 9.3 The six jobs that Mark has to sequence

Sequence of jobs	Process time (days)	Due date
A	4	12
B	3	5
C	1	7
D	2	9
E	2	15
F	5	8

4 → It takes 3 hours for a bakery to prepare, bake and decorate (in that order) a batch of cakes for a business contract. Each batch of cakes takes 1.5 hours to prepare, 1 hour to bake and 30 minutes to decorate with the firm's logo. Usually the team is ready to begin work at 8.00 am and the orders are picked up at 4.00 pm. The two people who work in the bakery have different approaches to how they schedule the work. One schedules 'forward', which involves starting work as soon as it arrives. The other schedules 'backwards', which involves starting jobs at the last possible moment that will prevent them from being late.

a) Draw up a schedule indicating the start and finish time for each activity (prepare, bake, decorate) for both forward and backward approaches.

b) What do you think are the advantages and disadvantages of these two approaches?

Want to know more?

Chapman, S.N. (2005) *Fundamentals of Production Planning and Control*, Harlow, UK: Pearson.

➜ A detailed textbook, intended for those studying the topic in depth.

Goldratt, E.Y. and Cox, J. (1984) *The Goal*, Great Barrington, MA: North River Press.

➜ Don't read this if you like good novels, but do read this if you want an enjoyable way of understanding some of the complexities of scheduling. It particularly applies to the drum, buffer, rope concept described in this chapter.

Kehoe, D.F. and Boughton, N.J. (2001) 'New paradigms in planning and control across manufacturing supply chains: The utilization of internet technologies', *International Journal of Operations & Production Management*, **21**(5/6), pp. 582–93.

➜ Gives a good indication of how technology started to affect the planning and control activity.

Vollmann, T.E., Berry, W.L., Whybark, D.C. and Jacobs, F.R. (2004) *Manufacturing Planning and Control Systems for Supply Chain Management: The Definitive Guide for Professionals*, New York: McGraw Hill Higher Education.

➜ The latest version of the 'bible' of manufacturing planning and control.

This is a NATS air traffic controller at Heathrow airport, London. NATS is the organisation that provides air traffic navigation services to aircraft flying through UK controlled airspace. Its guiding principle is that safety is paramount. Controllers must keep the aircraft they handle safely separated using internationally agreed standards. Their main objective is to stop collisions, plan and control the flow of air traffic, and offer information to pilots. In many ways, it is a typical planning and control activity. All flights must be planned in advance to fit the capacity of an airport, yet there will always be deviations from this plan, caused by flight delays, problems on the ground, and of course, weather. Controllers must constantly adapt their plans to cope with these routine glitches, and even the occasional emergency.

10

Introduction

Lean is simultaneously a philosophy, a method of operations planning and control, and an approach to improvement. Lean aims to meet demand instantaneously, with perfect quality, no waste and at low cost. This involves supplying products and services in perfect synchronization with the demand for them. These principles were once a radical departure from traditional operations practice, but have now become orthodox in promoting the synchronization of flow through processes, operations and supply networks. And although the topic was once narrowly treated as a manufacturing phenomenon (perhaps unsurprisingly, given the pioneering role of Toyota in lean management), lean principles are now applied across all sectors, including finance, healthcare, IT, retailing, construction, agriculture and the public sector. Figure 10.1 shows the position of the ideas described in the chapter in the general model of operations management.

Key questions

What is lean?

How does lean eliminate waste?

How does lean apply throughout the supply network?

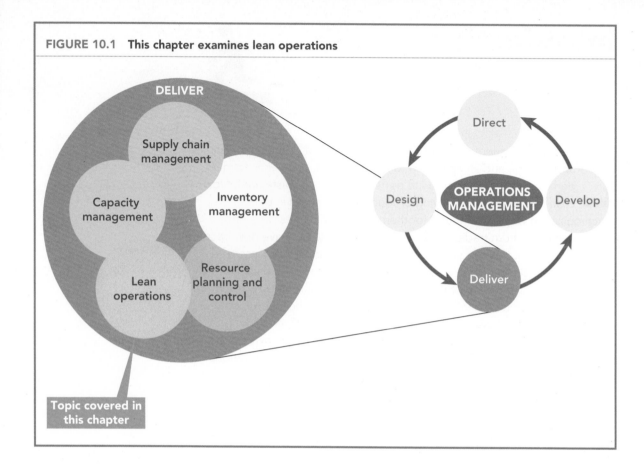

FIGURE 10.1   This chapter examines lean operations

What is lean?

The focus of lean is to achieve a flow of or materials, information or customers that delivers exactly what customers want, in exact quantities, exactly when needed, exactly where required and at the lowest possible cost. It is a concept that is almost synonymous with terms such as 'just-in-time' (JIT), the 'Toyota Production System' (TPS), 'stockless production' and 'lean synchronization'. It results in items flowing rapidly and smoothly through processes, operations and supply networks.

In this chapter, we provide examples of organizations in a wide range of sectors that apply facets of lean to their operations and supply networks. Many of the examples of lean philosophy and lean techniques in service industries are directly analogous to those found in manufacturing. For example, supermarkets usually replenish their shelves only when customers have taken sufficient products off the shelf. The movement of goods from the 'back office' store to the shelf is triggered only by the 'empty-shelf' demand signal. Construction companies increasingly make a rule of only calling for

Operations in practice

Jamie's 'lean' meals[1]

For most people working long hours, cooking is something they do not have time for. Knowing this, the celebrity chef Jamie Oliver has written a book, *Jamie's 30-Minute Meals*, with 50 menus designed to take no more than 30 minutes to prepare. To achieve this performance, Jamie has, perhaps inadvertently, applied the principles and methods of lean synchronization to cooking. Jamie's approach works significantly by ensuring dishes are prepared exactly when the next step in the process needs it, regardless of which dish it is. In other words, dishes are not cooked in sequence, one after another, but they are prepared and completed simultaneously.

If we identify all the tasks related to preparing the salad (e.g., chopping the vegetables) with the letter A, cooking the rice (e.g., blending) with letter B, cooking the chicken with letter C and finally making the dessert with the letter D, then in the traditional way of cooking, our task scheduling would look something like AAAA BBBBBBB CCCCCCC DDDD. This results in batching, waiting time and causing dishes to be ready before the dinner is supposed to be served. Conversely, Jamie Oliver's 30-minute cooking involves scheduling tasks in a sequence such as ABCDACBADCBABDC, where single tasks related to different dishes follow smoothly, as the chef chops a salad ingredient, then blends the rice, then chops some more salad ingredients while the chicken is being roasted in the oven and a part of the desert is being prepared. This way, all dishes are ready at the same time, just in time, and nothing is prepared before it has to be, avoiding any form of waste. Such a levelled approach to scheduling is called *heijunka* (mixed modelling) in lean synchronization.

In addition, Jamie's lean cooking builds on reduced set-up times. At the beginning of each recipe, the equipment needed to prepare the menu is presented under the headline 'To Start'. Other necessary preparations, such as heating the oven, are also specified. Having all equipment ready from the start saves time in the process and is, according to Jamie, a prerequisite for getting done in 30 minutes. The use of simple equipment that is suitable for many different purposes also makes the process quicker, as changeovers are minimized. The rationale is to make the most out of the time available, eliminating the 'faffing around' in cooking (non-value-added activity in OM language!) and leaving only what is strictly 'good, fast cooking', without compromising on quality. ● ● ●

material deliveries to their sites the day before materials are needed. This reduces clutter and the chances of theft. Both are examples of the application of 'pull control' principles. Other examples of lean concepts and methods apply even when most of the service elements are intangible. For example, new publishing technologies allow professors to assemble printed and e-learning course material customized to the needs of individual courses, or even individual students. Here, we see the lean principles of flexibility and small batch sizes allowing customization and rapid delivery.

Three perspectives of lean

Defining lean is not entirely straightforward! In many ways, lean can be viewed as three related but distinct things: a philosophy, a method of planning and control, with useful prescriptions of how to manage day-to-day operations, and a set of improvement tools.

LEAN IS A PHILOSOPHY OF HOW TO RUN OPERATIONS

It is a coherent set of principles that are founded on smoothing flow through processes by doing all the simple things well, on gradually doing them better, on meeting customer needs exactly and (above all) on squeezing out waste every step of the way. Three key issues define the lean philosophy: the involvement of staff in the operation, the drive for continuous improvement and the elimination of waste. Other chapters look at the first two issues, so we devote much of this chapter to the central idea of waste elimination.

LEAN IS A METHOD OF PLANNING AND CONTROLLING OPERATIONS

Many lean ideas are concerned with how items (materials, information, customers) flow through operations; and, more specifically, how operations managers can manage this flow. For this reason, lean can be viewed as a method of planning and control. Yet it is planning and control in pursuit of lean's philosophical aims. Uncoordinated flow causes unpredictability, and unpredictability causes waste because people hold inventory, capacity or time to protect themselves against it. So, lean planning and control uses several methods to achieve synchronized flow and reduce waste. Above all, it uses 'pull' control (described in Chapter 9), usually using some sort of Kanban system (described later). In addition, the other lean planning and control methods that promote smooth flow include levelled scheduling and delivery, and mixed modelling (again described later in this chapter).

LEAN IS A SET OF TOOLS THAT IMPROVE
OPERATIONS PERFORMANCE

The 'engine room' of the lean philosophy is a collection of improvement tools and techniques that are the means for cutting out waste. There are many techniques that could be termed 'lean techniques' and, again, many of them follow on naturally and logically from the overall lean philosophy. What is just as important to understand is how the introduction of lean as a philosophy helped to shift the focus of operations management generally towards viewing improvement as its main purpose. In addition, the rise of lean ideas gave birth to techniques that have now become mainstream in operations management. Some of these tools and techniques are well known outside the lean sphere, and are covered in other chapters of this book.

How lean operations consider flow

The best way to understand how lean differs from more traditional approaches to managing flow is to contrast the two simple processes in Figure 10.2. The traditional approach assumes that each stage in the process will place its

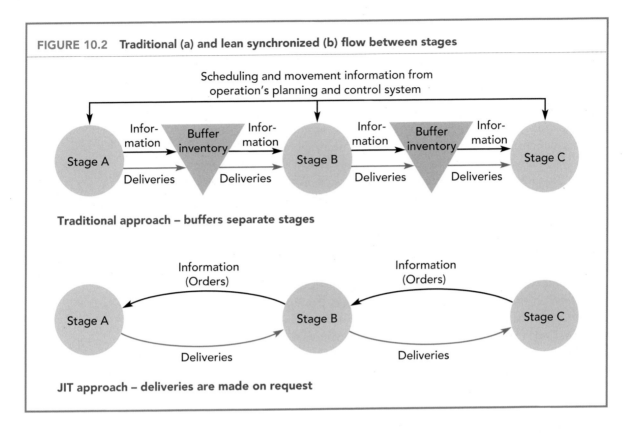

FIGURE 10.2 Traditional (a) and lean synchronized (b) flow between stages

output in an inventory that 'buffers' that stage from the next one downstream in the process. The next stage down will then (eventually) take outputs from the inventory, process them and pass them through to the next buffer inventory. These buffers are there to 'insulate' each stage from its neighbours, making each stage relatively independent so that if, for example, stage A stops operating for some reason, stage B can continue, at least for a time. The larger the buffer inventory, the greater the degree of insulation between the stages. This insulation has to be paid for in terms of inventory or queues and slow throughput times because products, customers or information will spend time waiting between stages in the process.

The main argument against this traditional approach lies in the very conditions it seeks to promote – namely, the insulation of the stages from one another. When a problem occurs at one stage, the problem will not immediately be apparent elsewhere in the system. The responsibility for solving the problem will be centred largely on the people within that stage, and the consequences of the problem will be prevented from spreading to the whole system. However, contrast this with the pure lean process illustrated in Figure 10.2. Here, products, customers or information are processed and then passed directly to the next stage in a synchronized manner, 'just-in-time' for them to be processed further. Problems at any stage have a very different effect in such a system. Now, if stage A stops processing, stage B will notice immediately and stage C very soon after. Stage A's problem is now quickly exposed to the whole process, which is immediately affected by the problem. This means that the responsibility for solving the problem is no longer confined to the staff at stage A. It is now shared by everyone, considerably improving the chances of the problem being solved, if only because it is now too important to be ignored. In other words, by preventing items accumulating between stages, the operation has increased the chances of improvement. Non-synchronized approaches seek to encourage efficiency by protecting each part of the process from disruption. The lean approach takes the opposite view. Exposure of the system (although not suddenly, as in our simplified example) to problems can both make them more evident and change the 'motivation structure' of the whole system towards problem solving. Lean sees accumulations of inventory, be they product, customer or information inventories, as a 'blanket of obscurity' that lies over the system and prevents problems being noticed.

operations principle
Buffer inventory, used to insulate stages or processes, localizes the motivation to improve.

Now think of the logic behind the explanation above. There are four interrelated ideas that 'mesh' with each other to form a logical chain. First, between each stage, it is the downstream 'customer' stage that signals the need for action. It is the customer who, in effect, 'pulls' items through the process. The starting point of the lean philosophy is a customer focus. Second, this customer 'pull' encourages items to flow through the process in a synchronized manner (rather than dwelling in inventory). Third, the smooth, synchronized flow and resulting reduction in inventory affects the motivation to improve because stages are no longer decoupled. Fourth, the increased motivation to improve exposes waste and encourages its elimination. These four related ideas are illustrated in Figure 10.3, and we will discuss them further in the rest of this chapter.

How lean operations consider inventory

The idea of obscuring effects of inventory is often illustrated diagrammatically, as in Figure 10.4. The many problems of the operation are shown as rocks in a river bed that cannot be seen because of the depth of the water. The water in

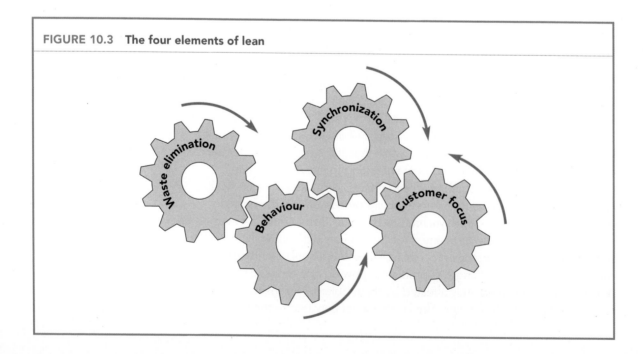

FIGURE 10.3   The four elements of lean

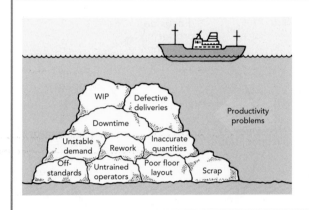
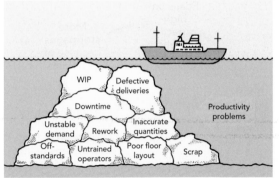

FIGURE 10.4 Reducing the level of inventory or queues (water) allows operations management (the ship) to see the problems in the operation (the rocks) and work to reduce them

this analogy represents the inventory in the operation. Yet, even though the rocks cannot be seen, they slow the progress of the river's flow and cause turbulence. Gradually reducing the depth of the water (inventory) exposes the worst of the problems, which can be resolved, after which the water is lowered further exposing more problems, and so on. The same argument will also apply for the flow between whole processes, or whole operations. For example, stages A, B and C in Figure 10.2 could be a supplier operation, a manufacturer and a customer's operation, respectively.

operations principle
Focusing on synchronous flow exposes sources of waste.

How lean operations consider capacity utilization

Lean has many benefits, but these come at the cost of capacity utilization. Return to the process shown in Figure 10.2. When stoppages occur in the traditional system, the buffers allow each stage to continue working and thus achieve high capacity utilization. However, the high utilization does not necessarily make the process as a whole produce more. Often, extra 'production' goes into buffer inventories or queues of customers. In a lean process, any stoppage will affect the whole process and lead to lower capacity utilization, at least in the short term. In organizations that place a high value on the utilization of capacity this can prove particularly difficult to accept. However, there is no point in producing output just for its own sake. In fact, producing just to keep utilization high is not only pointless, it is counter-productive, because the extra inventory produced merely serves to make improvements less likely. Figure 10.5 illustrates the two approaches to capacity utilization.

operations principle
Focusing on lean synchronization can initially reduce resource utilization.

How lean operations consider the role of people

Lean proponents frequently stress the importance of involving all staff in the lean approach. In this way it is similar to other improvement-based concepts, such as 'total quality' (which is discussed in detail in Chapter 12). However, the

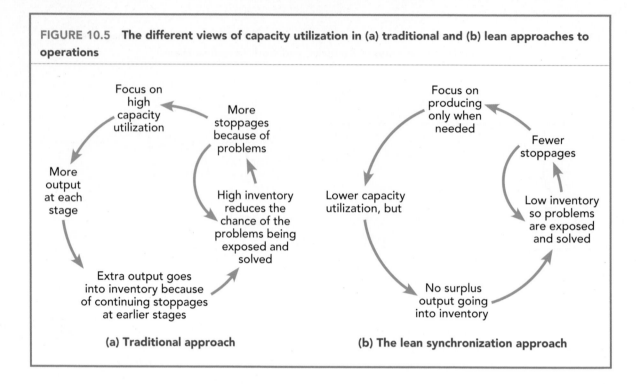

FIGURE 10.5 **The different views of capacity utilization in (a) traditional and (b) lean approaches to operations**

lean approach to people management is very much influenced by its Japanese origins, which is evident both from the terminology and the concepts themselves. So, for example, the original lean advocates called their approach the 'respect-for-humans' system. It encourages (and often requires) team-based problem solving, job enrichment (by including maintenance and set-up tasks in operators' jobs), job rotation and multi-skilling. The intention is to encourage a high degree of personal responsibility, engagement and 'ownership' of the job. Similarly, what are called 'basic working practices' are sometimes used to implement the 'involvement of everyone' principle. These include the following:

 Discipline Work standards that are critical for the safety of staff, the environment and quality must be followed by everyone all the time.

 Flexibility It should be possible to expand responsibilities to the extent of people's capabilities. This applies as equally to managers as it does to shop-floor personnel. Barriers to flexibility, such as grading structures and restrictive practices, should be removed.

 Equality Unfair and divisive personnel policies should be discarded. Many companies implement the egalitarian message through to company uniforms, consistent pay structures that do not differentiate between full-time staff and hourly-rated staff and open-plan offices.

 Autonomy Delegate responsibility to people involved in direct activities so that management's task becomes one of supporting processes. Delegation includes giving staff the responsibility for stopping processes in the event of problems, scheduling work, gathering performance-monitoring data and general problem solving.

Operations in practice

Toyota's lean DNA

Seen as the leading practitioner and the main originator of the lean approach, the Toyota Motor Company has progressively synchronized all its processes to give high quality, fast throughput and exceptional productivity. It has done this by developing a set of practices that have largely shaped what we now call 'lean' or 'just-in-time', but which Toyota calls the 'Toyota Production System' (TPS). The TPS has two themes: 'just-in-time' and '*jidoka*'. Just-in-time is defined as the rapid and coordinated movement of parts throughout the production system and supply network to meet customer demand. It is operationalized by means of *heijunka* (levelling and smoothing the flow of items), *kanban* (signalling to the preceding process that more parts are needed) and *nagare* (laying out processes to achieve smoother flow of parts throughout the production process). *Jidoka* is described as 'humanizing the interface between operator and machine'. Toyota's philosophy is that the machine is there to serve the operator's purpose. The operator should be left free to exercise his/her judgment. *Jidoka* is operationalized by means of fail-safeing (or machine *jidoka*), line-stop authority (or human *jidoka*) and visual control (at-a-glance status of production processes and visibility of process standards).

Toyota believes that both just-in-time and *jidoka* should be applied ruthlessly to the elimination of waste, where waste is defined as 'anything other than the minimum amount of equipment, items, parts and workers that are absolutely essential to production'. Fujio Cho of Toyota identified seven types of waste that must be eliminated from all operations processes. They are: waste from over production, waste from waiting time, transportation waste, inventory waste, processing waste, waste of motion and waste from product defects. Beyond this, authorities on Toyota claim that its strength lies in understanding the differences between the tools and practices used with Toyota operations and the overall philosophy of its approach. This is what some have called the apparent paradox of the Toyota Production System – 'namely, that activities, connections and production flows in a Toyota factory are rigidly scripted, yet at the same time Toyota's operations are enormously flexible and adaptable. Activities and processes are constantly being challenged and pushed to a higher level of performance, enabling the company to continually innovate and improve'. Whilst some adopters of lean principles may think they have 'done lean', Toyota simply changes the goal to constantly challenge improvement. As such, we see a key distinction between those that see lean as a specific end-point to be achieved through the application of a series of improvement tools, and those such as Toyota who treat lean as a philosophy that defines a way of conducting business. ● ● ●

Development of personnel   Over time, the aim is to create more company members who can support the rigours of being competitive.

 Quality of working life (QWL)   This may include, for example, involvement in decision making, security of employment, enjoyment and working-area facilities.

 Creativity   This is one of the indispensable elements of motivation. Creativity in this context means not just doing a job, but also improving how it is done, and building the improvement into the process.

 Total people involvement   Staff take on more responsibility to use their abilities to the benefit of the company as a whole. They are expected to participate in activities such as the selection of new recruits, dealing directly with suppliers and customers over schedules, quality issues, delivery information, spending-improvement budgets and planning and reviewing work done each day through communication meetings.

How lean operations consider improvement

Lean objectives are often expressed as ideals, such as our definition: 'to meet demand instantaneously with perfect quality and no waste'. While any operation's current performance may be far removed from such ideals, a fundamental lean belief is that it is possible to get closer to them over time. Without such beliefs to drive progress, lean proponents argue that improvement is more likely to be transitory than continuous. This is why the concept of continuous improvement is such an important part of the lean philosophy. If its aims are set in terms of ideals that individual organizations may never fully achieve, then the emphasis must be on the way in which an organization moves closer to the ideal state. The Japanese word for continuous improvement is *kaizen*, and it is a key part of the lean philosophy. (It is explained fully in Chapter 11.)

How does lean eliminate waste?

Arguably the most significant part of the lean philosophy is its focus on the elimination of all forms of waste. Waste can be defined as any activity that does not add value. For example, studies often show that as little as 5 per cent of total throughput time is actually spent directly adding value. This means that for 95 per cent of its time, an operation is adding cost to the service or product, not adding value. Such calculations can alert even relatively efficient operations to the enormous waste that is dormant within all operations. This same phenomenon applies as much to service processes as it does to manufacturing ones. Relatively simple requests, such as applying for a driving licence, may only take a few minutes to actually process, yet take days (or weeks) to be returned.

Causes of waste – *muda, mura, muri*

As so often happens in lean philosophy, Japanese terms are used to describe core ideas. The terms *muda*, *mura* and *muri* are Japanese words conveying three causes of waste that should be reduced or eliminated:

 Muda are activities in a process that are wasteful because they do not add value to the operation or the customer. The main causes of these wasteful activities are likely to be poorly communicated objectives (including not understanding the customer's requirements), or the inefficient use of resources. The implication of this is that for an activity to be effective, it must be properly recorded and communicated to whoever is performing it.

 Mura means 'lack of consistency' or 'unevenness', which results in periodic overloading of staff or equipment. So, for example, if activities are not properly documented and different people at different times perform a task differently, then, not surprisingly, the result of the activity may be different. The negative effects of this are similar to a lack of dependability.

 Muri means 'absurd' or 'unreasonable'. It is based on the idea that unnecessary or unreasonable requirements put on a process will result in poor outcomes. The implication of this is that appropriate skills, effective planning and accurate estimation of times and schedules will avoid this *muri* overloading waste. In other words, waste can be caused by failing to carry out basic operations planning tasks, such as prioritizing activities (sequencing) and understanding the necessary time (scheduling) and resources (loading) to perform activities. (All these issues are discussed in Chapter 9.)

These three causes of waste are obviously related. When a process is inconsistent (*mura*), it can lead to the overburdening of equipment and people (*muri*) which, in turn, will cause all kinds of non-value-adding activities (*muda*).

Types of waste

Muda, mura and *muri* are three *causes* of waste. Now we turn to *types* of waste, which apply in many different types of operations – both service and production – and which form the core of lean philosophy. Here we consolidate these into four broad categories.

WASTE FROM IRREGULAR FLOW

Perfect synchronization means smooth and even flow through processes, operations and supply networks. Barriers that prevent streamlined flow include the following:

 Waiting time   Machine efficiency and labour efficiency are two popular measures that are widely used to measure machine and labour waiting time, respectively. Less obvious is the time when products, customers or information wait as inventory or queues – there simply to keep operators busy.

 Transport   Moving items or customers around the operation, together with double and triple handling, does not add value. Layout changes that bring processes closer together, improvements in transport methods and workplace organization can all reduce waste.

 Process inefficiencies   The process itself may be a source of waste. Some operations may only exist because of poor component design, or poor maintenance, and so could be eliminated.

 Inventory   Regardless of type (product, customer, information), all inventories should become a target for elimination. However, it is only by tackling the causes of inventory or queues, such as irregular flow, that they can be reduced.

 Wasted motion   An operator may look busy, but sometimes no value is being added by the work. Simplification of work is a rich source of reduction in the waste of motion.

WASTE FROM INEXACT SUPPLY

Perfect synchronization also means supplying exactly what is wanted, exactly when it is needed. Any under- or over-supply and any early or late delivery will result in waste, something we have already explored in the capacity management chapter in particular. Barriers to achieving and exact matches between supply and demand include the following:

 Over-production or under-production   Supplying more than, or less than, is immediately needed by the next stage, process or operation.

 Early or late delivery   Items should only arrive exactly when they are needed. Early delivery is as wasteful as late delivery.

 Inventory   Again, all inventories should become a target for elimination. However, it is only by tackling the causes of inventory, such as inexact supply, that it can be reduced.

WASTE FROM INFLEXIBLE RESPONSE

Customer needs can vary, in terms of what they want, how much they want and when they want it. However, processes usually find it more convenient to change what they do relatively infrequently, because every change implies some kind of cost. That is why hospitals schedule specialist clinics only at particular times, and why machines often make a batch of similar products together. Yet responding to customer demands exactly and instantaneously requires a high degree of process flexibility. Symptoms of inadequate flexibility include the following:

 Large batches   Sending large batches of items through a process inevitably increases inventory as the batch moves through the whole process.

 Delays between activities   The longer the time (and the cost) of changing over from one activity to another, the more difficult it is to synchronize flow to match customer demand instantaneously.

 More variation in activity mix than in customer demand   If the mix of activities in different time periods varies more than customer demand varies, then some 'batching' of activities must be taking place.

WASTE FROM VARIABILITY

Synchronization implies exact levels of quality. If there is variability in quality levels, then customers will not consider themselves as being adequately supplied. Variability, therefore, is an important barrier to achieving synchronized supply. Symptoms of poor variability include the following:

 Poor reliability of equipment   Unreliable equipment usually indicates a lack of conformance in quality levels. It also means that there will be irregularity in supplying customers. Either way, it prevents synchronization of supply.

 Defective products or services   Waste caused by poor quality is significant in most operations. Service or product errors cause both customers and processes to waste time until they are corrected.

Looking for waste (and *kaizen* opportunities) – the '*gemba* walk'

Gemba (also sometimes called *ganba*), when roughly translated from the Japanese means 'the actual place' where something happens. It is a term often used in lean philosophy or in improvement generally, to convey the idea that, if you really want to understand something, you go to where it actually takes place. Only then can a true appreciation of the realities of improvement opportunities be gained. Lean improvement advocates often use the idea of the '*gemba* walk' to make problems visible. By this they mean that managers should regularly visit the place where the job is done to seek out waste. (The Western idea of 'management by walking around' is similar.) The concept of the *gemba* walk is also used in new service or product development to mean that designers should go to where the service happens, or where the product is used, to develop their ideas.

Eliminating waste through streamlined flow

The smooth flow of materials, information and people in the operation is a central idea of lean synchronization. Long process routes provide

operations principle
There is no substitute for seeing the way processes actually operate in practice.

opportunities for delay and inventory build-up, add no value and slow down throughput time. So, the first contribution any operation can make to streamlining flow is to reconsider the basic layout of its processes. Primarily, reconfiguring the layout of a process to aid lean synchronization involves moving it down the 'natural diagonal' of process design that was discussed in Chapter 4. Broadly speaking, this means moving from functional layouts towards cell-based layouts, or from cell-based layouts towards line layouts. Either way, it is necessary to move towards a layout that brings more systematization and control to the process flow. At a more detailed level, typical layout techniques include placing workstations close together so that inventory physically just cannot build up because there is no space for it to do so, and arranging workstations in such a way that all those who contribute to a common activity are in sight of each other and can provide mutual help. For example, at the Virginia Mason Medical Centre, Seattle, USA, a leading proponent of lean synchronization in healthcare, many of the waiting rooms have been significantly reduced in their capacity, or removed entirely. This forces a focus on the flow of the whole process because patients have literally nowhere to be stored.

EXAMINING ALL ELEMENTS OF THROUGHPUT TIME

Throughput time is often taken as a surrogate measure for waste in a process. The longer that items being processed are held in inventory, moved, checked or subject to anything else that does not add value, the longer they take to progress through the process. So, looking at exactly what happens to items within a process is an excellent method of identifying sources of waste.

Value-stream mapping (also known as 'end-to-end' system mapping) is a simple but effective approach to understanding the flow of material and information as a product or service has value added as it progresses through a process, operation or supply chain. It visually maps a product or service's 'production' path from start to finish. In doing so it records not only the direct activities of creating products and services, but also the 'indirect' information systems that support the direct process. It is called 'value-stream' mapping because it focuses on value-adding activities and distinguishes between value-adding and non-value-adding activities. It is similar to process mapping (see Chapter 5) but different in four ways:

 It uses a broader range of information than most process maps.

 It is usually at a higher level (5–10 activities) than most process maps.

 It often has a wider scope, frequently spanning the whole supply chain.

 It can be used to identify where to focus future improvement activities.

A value-stream perspective involves working on (and improving) the 'big picture', rather than just optimizing individual processes. Value-stream mapping is seen by many practitioners as a starting point to help recognize waste and identify its causes. It is a four-step technique that identifies waste and suggests ways in which activities can be streamlined. First, it involves identifying the value stream (the process, operation or supply chain) to map. Second, it involves physically mapping a process, then above it mapping the information flow that enables the process to occur. This is the so-called 'current state' map. Third, problems are diagnosed and changes suggested making a 'future state' map that represents the improved process, operation or supply chain. Fourth, the changes are implemented. Figure 10.6 shows a value-stream map for an industrial air-conditioning installation service. The service process itself is broken down into five relatively large stages, and various items of data for each stage are marked on the chart. The type of data collected here do vary, but all types of value-stream map compare the total throughput time with the amount of value-added time within the larger process. In this case, only 8 of the 258 hours of the process are value adding.

ADOPTING VISUAL MANAGEMENT

Visual management is one of the lean techniques designed to make the current and planned state of the operation or process transparent to everyone, so that anyone (whether working in the process or not) can very quickly see what is going on. It usually employs some kind of visual sign, such as a notice board, computer screen or simply lights or other signals that

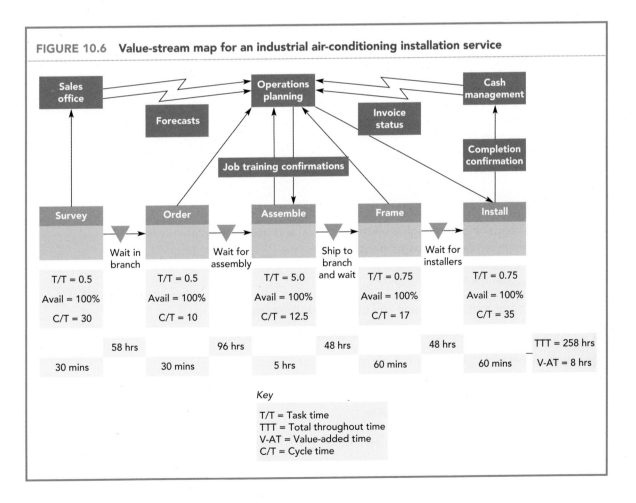

FIGURE 10.6   Value-stream map for an industrial air-conditioning installation service

Key
T/T = Task time
TTT = Total throughout time
V-AT = Value-added time
C/T = Cycle time

Operations in practice

Waste reduction in airline maintenance[2]

Aircraft maintenance is important. Planes have a distressing tendency to fall out of the sky unless they are checked, repaired and generally maintained regularly! So, the overriding objective of the operations that maintain aircraft must be the quality of maintenance activities. But it is not the only objective. Improving maintenance turnaround time can reduce the number of aircraft an airline needs to own, because they are not out of action for as long. Also, the more efficient the maintenance process, the more profitable is the activity and the more likely a major airline with established maintenance operations can create additional revenue streams by doing maintenance for other airlines. Figure 10.7 shows how one airline maintenance operation applied lean principles to achieve all these objectives. The objectives of the lean analysis were to preserve, or even improve, quality levels, while at the same time improving the cost of maintaining airframes and increasing the availability of airframes by reducing turnaround time.

The lean analysis focused on identifying waste in the maintenance process. Two findings emerged from this. First, the sequence of activities on the airframe itself was being set by the tasks identified in the technical manuals supplied by the engine, body, control system and other suppliers. No one had considered all the individual activities together to work out a sequence that would save maintenance staff time and effort. The overall sequence of activities was defined and allocated with structured work preparation of tools, materials and equipment. Figure 10.7 shows the path taken by maintenance staff before and after the lean analysis. Second, maintenance staff would often be waiting until the airframe became available. Yet some of the preparatory work and

convey what is happening. Although a seemingly trivial and usually simple device, visual management has several benefits:

 acts as a common focus for team meetings;

 demonstrates methods for safe and effective working practice;

 communicates to everyone how performance is being judged;

 assesses at a glance the current status of the operation;

 understands tasks and work priorities;

 judges your and others' performance;

 identifies the flow of work – what has been and is being done;

 identifies when something is not going to plan;

FIGURE 10.7   Aircraft maintenance procedures subject to waste-reduction analysis

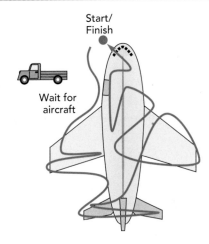
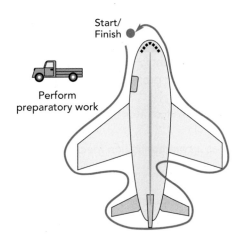

Before:
→ Maintenance staff follow the steps as detailed in the technical documentation.
→ The overall sequence of tasks is not optimized.
→ Preparation work and set-ups included as part of the task.

After:
→ The overall sequence of tasks is defined and allocated to minimize non-value-added.
→ Preparation work and set-ups may be done ahead of time to minimize aircraft contact time.
→ Increased productivity and reduced aircraft waiting time.

set-ups did not need to be done while the airframe was present. Therefore, why not get maintenance staff to do these tasks when they would otherwise be waiting before the airframe became available? The result of these changes was a substantial improvement in cost and availability. In addition, work preparation was conducted in a more rigorous and routine manner and maintenance staff were more motivated because many minor frustrations and barriers to their efficient working were removed. ● ● ●

 shows what agreed standards should be;

 provides real-time feedback on performance to everyone involved;

 reduces the reliance on formal meetings.

As an example of how visual management works, a finance office in a web-based retailer was having problems. Service levels were low, and complaints high, as the office attempted to deal with payments from customers, invoices from suppliers and requests for information from its distribution centre, all while demand was increasing. It was agreed that the office's processes were chaotic and poorly managed, with little understanding of priorities or how each member of staff was contributing. To remedy this state of affairs, first the manager responsible for the office tried to bring clarity to the process by defining individual and team roles and starting to establish visual management. Collectively, the staff mapped processes and set performance objectives. These objectives were shown on a large board, placed so everyone in the office could see it. At the end of each day, process supervisors updated the board with each process' performance for the day. Also indicated on the board were visual representations of various improvement projects being carried out by the teams. Every morning, staff gathered in what was called 'the morning huddle' to discuss the previous day's performance, identify how it could be improved, review the progress of ongoing improvement projects and plan for the upcoming day's work.

The above example illustrates the three main functions of visual management:

 to act as a communication mechanism;

 to encourage commitment to agreed goals;

 to facilitate cooperation between team members.

An important technique used to ensure flow visibility is the use of simple but highly visual signals to indicate that a problem has occurred, together with operational authority to stop the process. For example, on an assembly line, if an employee detects some kind of quality problem, he or she could activate a signal that illuminates a light (called an 'andon' light) above the work station and stops the line. Although this may seem to reduce the efficiency of the line, the idea is that this loss of efficiency in the short term is less than the accumulated losses of allowing defects to continue on in the process. Unless problems are tackled immediately, they may never be corrected.

USING SMALL-SCALE SIMPLE PROCESS TECHNOLOGY

There may also be possibilities to encourage smooth, streamlined flow through the use of small-scale technologies. That is, using several small units of process technology (for example, machines), rather than one large unit. Small machines have several advantages over large ones. First, they can process different products and services simultaneously. For example, in Figure 10.8 one large machine produces a batch of A, followed by a batch of B and followed by a batch of C. However, if three smaller machines are used, they can each produce A, B and C simultaneously. The system is also more robust. If one large machine breaks down, the whole system ceases to operate. If one of the three smaller machines breaks down, it is still operating at two-thirds effectiveness. Small machines are also easily moved, so that layout flexibility is enhanced, and the risks of making errors in investment decisions are reduced. However, investment in capacity may increase in total because parallel facilities are needed, so utilization may be lower (see the earlier arguments).

Eliminating waste through matching demand and supply exactly

The value of the supply of services or products is always time dependent. Something that is delivered early or late often has less value than something

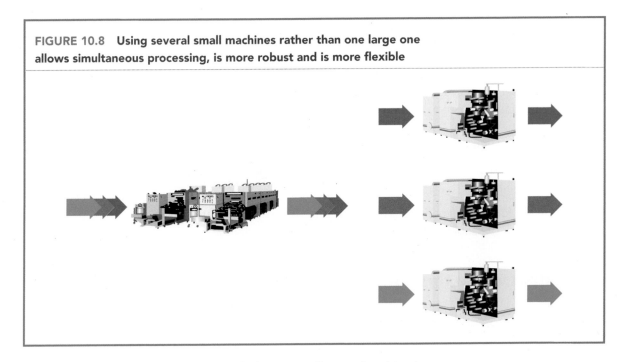

FIGURE 10.8 Using several small machines rather than one large one allows simultaneous processing, is more robust and is more flexible

that is delivered exactly when it is needed. Using pull control and *kanbans* are central to reducing waste by aligning demand and supply. The exact matching of supply and demand is often best served by using 'pull control' wherever possible (discussed in Chapter 9). At its simplest, consider how some fast-food restaurants cook and assemble food and place it in the warm area only when the customer-facing server has sold an item. Production is being triggered only by real customer demand. In another example, an Australian tax office used to receive applications by mail, open the mail and send it through to the relevant department who, after processing it, sent it to the next department. This led to piles of unprocessed applications building up within its processes, causing problems in tracing applications, and losing them, sorting through and prioritizing applications and, worst of all, long throughput times. Now they only open mail when the stages in front can process it. In turn, departments request more work only when they have processed previous work. The essence of pull control is to let the downstream stage in a process, operation or supply network 'pull' items (product, customers or information) through the system, rather than have them 'pushed' to them by the supplying stage.

> **operations principle**
> Delivering only, and exactly, what is needed and when it is needed smooths flow and exposes waste.

USING *KANBANS*

The use of *kanbans* is one method of operationalizing pull control. *Kanban* is the Japanese for 'card' or 'signal'. In its simplest form, it is a card used by a customer stage to instruct its supplier stage to send more items. *Kanbans* can also take other forms. In some Japanese companies, they are solid plastic markers or even coloured ping-pong balls. Whichever kind of *kanban* is being used, the principle is always the same: the receipt of a *kanban* triggers the movement, production or supply of one unit or a standard container of units. If two *kanbans* are received, this triggers the movement, production or supply of two units or standard containers of units, and so on. *Kanbans* are the only means by which movement, production or supply can be authorized. Some companies use 'kanban squares'. These are marked spaces on the shop floor or bench that are drawn to fit one or more work pieces or containers. Only the existence of an empty square triggers production at the stage that supplies the square. Likewise, kanban whiteboards are increasingly used to 'pull' activity through service process (see the Torchbox 'Operations in practice' example). The kanban is seen as serving three purposes:

 It is an instruction for the preceding process to send more.

 It is a visual control tool to show up areas of over-production and lack of synchronization.

 It is a tool for kaizen (continuous improvement). Toyota's rules state that 'the number of kanbans should be reduced over time'.

Eliminating waste through flexible processes

Responding exactly and instantaneously to customer demand implies that operations resources need to be sufficiently flexible to change both what they do and how much they do of it without incurring high cost or long delays. In fact, flexible processes (often with flexible technologies) can significantly enhance smooth and synchronized flow. For example, a firm of lawyers used to take ten days to prepare its bills for customers. This meant that customers were not asked to pay until ten days after the work had been done. Now they use a system that, every day, updates each customer's account. So, when a bill is sent it includes all work up to the day before the billing date. The principle here is that process inflexibility also delays cash flow.

REDUCING CHANGEOVER TIMES

For many processes, increasing flexibility means reducing the time taken to changeover the process from one activity to the next. And changeover time can usually be reduced, sometimes radically. For example, compare the time it takes you to change the tyre on your car with the time taken by a Formula 1 team. Changeover time reduction can be achieved by a variety of methods, such as the following:

Measure and analyze changeover activities   Sometimes simply measuring the current changeover times, recording them and analyzing exactly what activities are performed can help to improve changeover times.

Separate external and internal activities   'External' activities are simply the activities that can be carried out while the process is continuing. For example, processes could be getting ready for the next customer or job while waiting (see the example of aircraft maintenance described earlier). 'Internal' activities are those that cannot be carried out while the process is going on (e.g. interviewing the customer while completing a service request for the previous customer). By identifying and separating internal and external activities, the intention is to do as much as possible while the step/process is continuing.

Operations in practice

| Story | To Do | In Progress | To Verify | Done |

Kanban control at Torchbox web designers[3]

Torchbox is an independently-owned web design and development company based in Oxfordshire (see the 'Operations in practice' box in Chapter 1, 'Torchbox: award-winning web designers', for more details). Just because it is a company that relies on its staff's creative capabilities does not mean that lean techniques have no place in its operations. On the contrary, it makes full use of the *kanban* approach to controlling its work as it progresses through the web-design process. "We know that *kanban* control originated from car manufacturers like Toyota, but our development teams can also benefit from its basic principles", says Edward Kay, the head of production at Torchbox. "It is a way of scheduling work based on what needs to be produced and what resources are available to produce it with. At Torchbox we use a large magnetic whiteboard (called the *kanban* board) to track completed features through each stage of the design process: from discovery through development, design, demo, deployment and on to the finish of the design (called the 'done' stage). Each feature has its own paper slip which physically moves across the board, held in place with a magnet. You can't have more features in progress than the number of magnets you have to hold them in place, so the principle is enforced with a physical limitation. When one feature enters the 'Done' column, another one can be pulled through into discovery. There's a pulling process, where completing work allows you to start on something new."

At the start of every day, the team has a stand-up meeting at the *kanban* board where each member quickly runs through what they did the day before, and what they'll do in the coming day. Each developer has a few tokens that they place on the features they're working on. This helps link up the 'big picture' of how a design's features are developing with the 'little picture' of what each developer is working on each day, and helps teams to make sure that all work being done is being tracked across the board.

"One of the big benefits of using *kanban*", says Edward Kay, "is that because we're visualizing the steps a feature goes through to be completed, we're able to see where the bottlenecks are that work gets held up on. Because we can see where work is being held up, we're then able to continually improve our processes to make sure we're working as efficiently as possible. If we're finding that a project's features keep getting held up in the design stage, we can bring more designers onto the project to widen the bottleneck. Using *kanban* with feature-driven development helps us constantly deliver value to our clients. This more measured and controlled approach to handling and controlling incoming work helps ensure that every hour we work produces an hour's worth of value. Ultimately, it's all about delivering great products on time and to budget, and *kanban* is a great tool to help achieve this." ● ● ●

Operations in practice

All change at Boeing

Fast changeovers are particularly important for airlines because they can't make money from aircraft that are sitting idle on the ground. It is called 'running the aircraft hot' in the industry. For many smaller airlines, the biggest barrier to running hot is that their markets are not large enough to justify passenger flights during the day and night. So, in order to avoid aircraft being idle over night, they must be used in some other way. That was the motive behind Boeing's 737 'Quick Change' (QC) aircraft. With it, airlines have the flexibility to use it for passenger flights during the day and, with less than a one-hour changeover (set-up) time, use it as a cargo airplane throughout the night. Boeing engineers designed frames that hold entire rows of seats that can glide smoothly on and off the aircraft, allowing twelve seats to be rolled into place at once. When used for cargo, the seats are simply rolled out and replaced by special cargo containers designed to fit the curve of the fuselage and prevent damage to the interior. Before reinstalling the seats, the sidewalls are thoroughly cleaned so that, once the seats are in place, passengers cannot tell the difference between a QC aircraft and a normal 737. Some airlines particularly value the aircraft's flexibility. It allows them to provide frequent reliable services in both passenger and cargo markets. So, the aircraft that has been carrying passengers during the day can be used to ship freight during the night. ● ● ●

Convert internal to external activities   The other common approach to changeover time reduction is to convert work that was previously performed during the changeover to work that is performed outside the changeover period. There are three major methods of achieving the transfer of internal set-up work to external work:

   Pre-prepare activities or equipment, instead of having to do it during changeover periods.

   Make the changeover process intrinsically flexible and capable of performing all required activities without any delay.

   Speed up any required changes of equipment, information or staff – for example, by using simple devices.

Practice changeover routines   Not surprisingly, the constant practice of changeover routines and the associated learning-curve effect tends to reduce changeover times.

operations principle
Changeover flexibility reduces waste and smooths flow.

Eliminating waste through minimizing variability

One of the biggest causes of the variability that will disrupt flow and prevent lean synchronization is variation in the quality of products and services. This is why a discussion of lean synchronization should always include an evaluation of how quality conformance is ensured within processes – what was referred to as *mura* earlier. In particular, the principles of statistical process control (SPC) can be used to understand quality variability. (Chapter 12 examines this subject, so in this section we shall focus on other causes of variability.) The first cause of variability we consider is the mix of items moving through processes, operations or supply networks.

LEVELLING PRODUCT OR SERVICE SCHEDULES

Levelled scheduling (or *heijunka*) means keeping the mix and volume of flow between stages at an even rate over time. For example, instead of producing 500 items in one batch, which would cover the needs for the next three months, levelled scheduling would require the process to produce items on a regular basis that satisfied demand. Thus, the principle of levelled scheduling is very straightforward; however, the requirements to put it into practice are quite severe, although the benefits resulting from it can be substantial. The move from conventional to levelled scheduling is illustrated in Figure 10.9. Conventionally, if a mix of items were required in a time period (usually a month), a batch size would be calculated for each item and the batches produced in some sequence. Figure 10.9 (a) shows three items that are produced in a 20-day time period in an operation:

Quantity of item A required = 3000
Quantity of item B required = 1000
Quantity of item C required = 1000
Batch size of item A = 600
Batch size of item B = 200
Batch size of item C = 200

Starting at day 1, the unit commences producing item A. During day 3, the batch of 600 As is finished and dispatched to the next stage. The batch of Bs is started, but is not finished until day 4. The remainder of day 4 is spent making the batch of Cs and both batches are dispatched at the end of that day. The cycle then repeats itself. The consequence of using large batches is, first, that relatively large amounts of inventory accumulate within and between the units and, second, that most days are different from one another in terms of what they are expected to produce (in more complex circumstances, no two days would be the same).

Now suppose that the flexibility of the unit could be increased to the point where the batch sizes for the items were reduced to a quarter of their previous levels without loss of capacity (see Figure 10.9 (b)):

Batch size of item A = 150
Batch size of item B = 50
Batch size of item C = 50

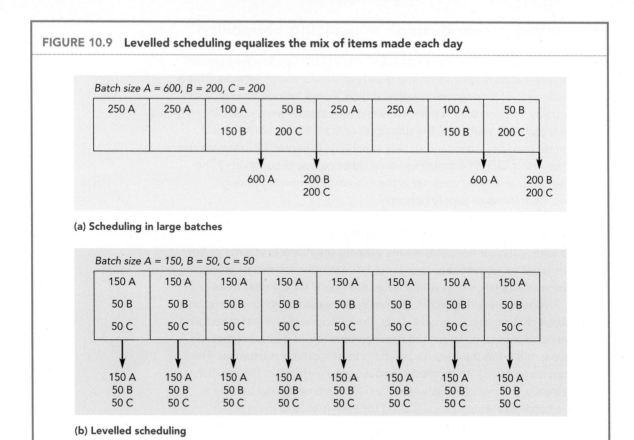

FIGURE 10.9 Levelled scheduling equalizes the mix of items made each day

A batch of each item can now be completed in a single day, at the end of which the three batches are dispatched to their next stage. Smaller batches of inventory are moving between each stage, which will reduce the overall level of work in progress in the operation. Just as significant, however, is the effect on the regularity and rhythm of production at the unit. Now, every day in the month is the same in terms of what needs to be processed. This makes planning and control of each stage in the operation much easier. For example, if on day 1 of the month the daily batch of As was finished by 11.00 am, and all the batches were successfully completed in the day, then the following day the unit will know that, if it again completes all the As by 11.00 am, it is on schedule. When every day is different, the simple question 'Are we on schedule to complete our processing today?' requires some investigation before it can be answered. However, when every day is the same, everyone in the unit can tell whether production is on target by looking at the clock. Control becomes visible and transparent to all, and the advantages of regular, daily schedules can be passed to upstream suppliers.

operations principle
Variability, in product/service quality, or quantity, or timing, acts against smooth flow and waste elimination.

LEVELLING DELIVERY SCHEDULES
A similar concept to levelled scheduling can be applied to many transportation processes. For example, a chain of convenience stores may need to make deliveries of all the different types of products it sells every

week. Traditionally, it may have dispatched a truck loaded with one particular product around all its stores so that each store received the appropriate amount of the product that would last them for one week. This is equivalent to the large batches discussed in the previous example. An alternative would be to dispatch smaller quantities of all products in a single truck more frequently. Then, each store would receive smaller deliveries more frequently, inventory levels would be lower and the system could respond to trends in demand more readily because more deliveries means more opportunity to change the quantity delivered to a store. This is illustrated in Figure 10.10

ADOPTING MIXED MODELLING

The principle of levelled scheduling can be taken further to give a repeated mix of outputs – what is known as 'mixed modelling'. Suppose that processes can be made so flexible that they achieve the ideal of a 'batch' size of one? The sequence of individual items emerging from the process could be reduced progressively, as illustrated in Figure 10.11. This would produce a

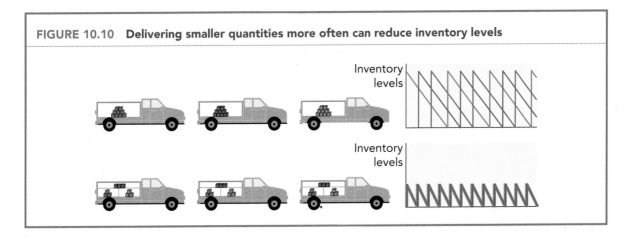

FIGURE 10.10   Delivering smaller quantities more often can reduce inventory levels

FIGURE 10.11   Levelled scheduling and mixed modelling: mixed modelling becomes possible as the batch size approaches one

Low	DEGREE OF LEVELLING	High
High	SET-UP TIMES	Low
Low	SYSTEM FLEXIBILITY	High

Large batches, e.g.	Small batches, e.g.	Mixed modelling, e.g.
200 A 120 B 80 C	5 A 3 B 2 C	A A B A B A B C A B C A

steady stream of each item flowing continuously from the process. However, the sequence of items does not always fall as conveniently as in Figure 10.11. The unit processing times for each item are not usually identical, and the ratios of required volumes are less convenient. For example, if a process is required to process items A, B and C in the ratio 8:5:4, it could produce 800 of A, followed by 500 of B, followed by 400 of C, or 80A, 50B and 40C. But, ideally, to sequence the items as smoothly as possible, it would produce in the order BACABACABACABACAB. . . repeated. . . repeated. . . , etc. Doing this achieves relatively smooth flow (but does rely on significant process flexibility).

Keeping things simple – the 5S method

The 5S terminology comes originally from Japan and can be thought of as a simple housekeeping methodology to organize work areas, which focuses on visual order, organization, cleanliness and standardization. Although the translation into English is approximate, the five are generally taken to represent the following:

  Sort (*Seiri*)   Eliminate what is not needed and keep what is needed.

  Straighten (*Seiton*)   Position things in such a way that they can be easily reached whenever they are needed.

  Shine (*Seiso*)   Keep things clean and tidy; no refuse or dirt in the work area.

  Standardize (*Seiketsu*)   Maintain cleanliness and order – perpetual neatness.

  Sustain (*Shitsuke*)   Develop a commitment and pride in keeping to standards.

How does lean apply throughout the supply network?

Although most of the concepts and techniques discussed in this chapter are devoted to the management of stages *within* processes, and processes *within* an operation, the same principles can apply to the whole supply network. In this context, the stages in a process are the whole businesses, operations or processes between which products flow. And as any business starts to approach lean, it will eventually come up against the network. So, achieving further gains must involve trying to spread lean practice outward to its partners in the network. Ensuring the entire supply networks are lean is clearly a far more demanding task than doing the same within a single process. The nature of the interaction between whole operations is far more complex than between individual stages within a process. A far more complex mix of products and services is likely to be being provided, and the network is likely to be subject to a less predictable set of potentially disruptive events. To make a supply network lean means more than making each operation in the chain lean. A collection of localized lean operations rarely leads to an overall lean network. Rather, one needs to apply the lean philosophy to the network as a whole. Yet the advantages from truly lean chains can be significant.

Essentially the principles of lean are the same for a supply network as they are for a process. Fast throughput throughout the whole supply network is still valuable and will save cost throughout the supply network. Lower levels of inventory will still make it easier to achieve lean. Waste is just as evident (and even larger) at the level of the supply network and reducing waste is still a worthwhile task. Streamlined flow, exact matching of supply and demand, enhanced flexibility and minimizing variability are all still tasks that will benefit the whole network. The principles of pull control can work between whole operations in the same way as they can between stages within a single process. In fact, the principles and the techniques of lean synchronization are essentially the same, no matter what level of analysis is being used.

> **operations principle**
> The advantages of lean synchronization apply at the level of the process, the operation and the supply network.

The concept of the lean supply chain has been likened to an air traffic control system, in that it attempts to provide continuous, 'real-time visibility and control' to all elements in the chain. This is the secret of how the world's busiest airports handle thousands of departures and arrivals daily. All aircraft are given an identification number that shows up on a radar map. Aircraft approaching an airport are detected by the radar and contacted using radio. The control tower precisely positions the aircraft in an approach pattern that it coordinates. The radar detects any small adjustments that are necessary, which are communicated to the aircraft. This real-time visibility and control can optimize airport throughput while maintaining extremely high safety and reliability.

Contrast this to how most supply chains are coordinated. Information is captured only periodically, probably once a day, and any adjustments to logistics and output levels at the various operations in the supply chain are adjusted, and plans rearranged. But imagine what would happen if this was how the airport operated, with only a 'radar snapshot' once a day. Coordinating aircraft with sufficient tolerance to arrange take-offs and landings every two minutes would be out of the question. Aircraft would be jeopardized or, alternatively, if aircraft were spaced further apart to maintain safety, throughput would be drastically reduced. Yet this is how most supply chains have traditionally operated, using a daily 'snapshot' from their ERP systems. This limited visibility means operations must either space their work out to avoid 'collisions' (i.e. missed customer orders) – thereby reducing output, or they must 'fly blind' – thereby jeopardizing reliability.

One of the weaknesses of lean principles is that it is difficult to achieve lean when conditions are subject to unexpected disturbance. This is especially a problem with applying lean synchronization principles in the context of the whole supply network. Whereas unexpected fluctuations and disturbances do occur within operations, local management has a reasonable degree of control that it can exert in order to reduce them. Outside the operation, within the supply network, it is far more difficult. Nevertheless, it is generally held that, although the task is more difficult and the pace of change slower, the benefits of lean implementation across supply networks are proportionally greater.

When just-in-time ideas first started to have an impact on operations practice in the West, some authorities advocated the reduction of between-process inventories to zero. While in the long term this provides the ultimate in motivation for operations managers to ensure the efficiency and reliability of each process stage, it does not admit the possibility of some processes always being intrinsically less than totally reliable. An alternative view is to allow inventories (albeit small ones) around process stages with higher-than-average uncertainty. This at least allows some protection for the rest of the system.

Summary answers to key questions

Each chapter has a 'Summary answers to key questions' section. Use it to check your understanding of the issues covered in the chapter.

WHAT IS LEAN?

★ Lean is an approach to operations that tries to meet demand instantaneously with perfect quality and no waste. It is an approach that differs from traditional operations practices insomuch as it stresses waste elimination and fast throughput, both of which contribute to low inventories.

★ The ability to deliver just-in-time not only saves working capital (through reducing inventory levels) but also has a significant impact on the ability of an operation to improve its intrinsic efficiency.

★ The lean philosophy can be summarized as concerning three overlapping elements: the elimination of waste in all its forms; the inclusion of all staff of the operation in its improvement; and the idea that all improvement should be on a continuous basis.

★ Most of the ideas of lean synchronization are directly applicable to service operations.

HOW DOES LEAN ELIMINATE WASTE?

★ The most significant part of the lean philosophy is its focus on the elimination of all forms of waste – defined as any activity that does not add value.

★ Lean identifies seven types of waste that, together, form four barriers to achieving lean synchronization: waste from irregular (non-streamlined) flow; waste from inexact supply; waste from inflexible response; and waste from variability.

HOW DOES LEAN APPLY THROUGHOUT THE SUPPLY NETWORK?

★ Most of the concepts and techniques of lean synchronization, although usually described as applying to individual processes and operations, also apply to the whole supply networks.

★ The concept of the lean supply chain has been likened to an air traffic control system, in that it attempts to provide continuous, 'real-time visibility and control' to all elements in the chain.

Problems and applications

All chapters have problems and application questions that will help you practice analyzing operations. They can be answered by reading the chapter. Model answers for the first question can be found on the companion website for this text.

➔ Re-examine the description of the Toyota Production System in the 'Operations in practice' box, 'Toyota's lean DNA'.

a) List all the different techniques and practices that Toyota adopts. Which of these would you call just-in-time philosophies and which are just-in-time techniques?

b) How are operations objectives (quality, speed, dependability, flexibility, cost) influenced by the practices that Toyota adopts?

➔ Consider this record of an ordinary flight: "Breakfast was a little rushed but left the house at 6.15. Had to return a few minutes later, forgot my passport. Managed to find it and leave (again) by 6.30. Arrived at the airport 7.00, dropped Angela off with bags at terminal and went to the long-term car park. Eventually found a parking space after 10 minutes. Waited 8 minutes for the courtesy bus. Six-minute journey back to the terminal, we start queuing at the check-in counters by 7.24. Twenty-minute wait. Eventually get to check-in and find that we have been allocated seats at different ends of the plane. Staff helpful but takes 8 minutes to sort it out. Wait in queue for security checks for 10 minutes. Security decide I look suspicious and search bags for 3 minutes. Waiting in lounge by 8.05. Spend 1 hour and 5 minutes in lounge reading computer magazine and looking at small plastic souvenirs. Hurrah, flight is called 9.10, takes 2 minutes to rush to the gate and queue for further 5 minutes at gate. Through the gate and on to air bridge that is continuous queue going onto plane, takes 4 minutes but finally in seats by 9.21. Wait for plane to fill up with other passengers for 14 minutes. Plane starts to taxi to runway at 9.35. Plane queues to take-off for 10 minutes. Plane takes off 9.45. Smooth flight to Amsterdam, 55 minutes. Stacked in queue of planes waiting to land for 10 minutes. Touch down at Schiphol Airport 10.50. Taxi to terminal and wait 15 minutes to disembark. Disembark at 11.05 and walk to luggage collection (calling at lavatory on way), arrive luggage collection 11.15. Wait for luggage 8 minutes. Through customs (not searched by Netherlands security who decide I look trustworthy) and to taxi rank by 11.26. Wait for taxi for 4 minutes. Into taxi by 11.30, 30 minutes ride into Amsterdam. Arrive at hotel 12.00."

a) Analyze the journey in terms of value-added time (actually going somewhere) and non-value-added time (the time spent queuing, etc.).

b) Visit the websites of two or three airlines and examine their business-class and first-class services to look for ideas that reduce the non-value-added time for customers who are willing to pay the premium.

c) Next time you go on a journey, time each part of the journey and perform a similar analysis.

 3 An insurance underwriting process consists of the following separate stages:

Stage	Processing time per application (minutes)	Average work in progress before the stage
Data entry	30	250
Retrieve client details	5	1500
Risk assessment	18	300
Inspection	15	150
Policy assessment	20	100
Dispatch proposal	10	100

What is the value-added percentage for the process? (Hint – use Little's law to work out how long applications have to wait at each stage before they are processed. Little's law is covered in Chapter 5.)

 4 Examine the value-added versus non-value-added times for some other services. For example:

a) When handing an assignment in for marking if you are currently studying for a qualification, what is the typical elapsed time between handing the assignment in and receiving it back with comments? How much of this elapsed time do you think is value-added time?

b) When posting a package – the elapsed time is between posting the package and it being delivered to the recipient.

Want to know more?

Bicheno, J. and Holweg, M. (2010) *The Lean Toolbox: The Essential Guide to Lean Transformation,* 4th edition, Buckingham, UK: PICSIE Books.

➔ A practical guide from two of the European authorities on all matters lean.

Holweg, M. (2007) 'The genealogy of lean production', *Journal of Operations Management,* **25,** pp. 420–437.

➔ An excellent overview of how lean ideas developed.

Mann, D. (2010) *Creating a Lean Culture,* 2nd edition, New York: Productivity Press.

➔ Treats the soft side of lean.

Modig, N. and Ahlstrom, P. (2012) *This is Lean: Resolving the Efficiency Paradox,* Sweden: Rheologica Publishing.

➔ A simple book that provides a very practical overview of lean, covering not only tools and methods but also broader issues of *why* lean is useful.

Womack, J.P. and Jones, D.T. (1996) *Lean Thinking: Banish Waste and Create Wealth in Your Corporation,* New York: Simon and Schuster.

➔ Some of the lessons from *The Machine that Changed the World* (by J.P. Womack – one of the most influential books on lean) but applied in a broader context.

The objective of lean operations is to make sure that items being processed (materials, information, or people) flow between stages smoothly and with as little delay as possible – just like the well-rehearsed changeover in a relay race. This can expose problems and waste in the process.

Operations improvement

11

Introduction

Even when an operation's direction is set, its design finalized and its deliveries planned and controlled, the operations manager's task is not finished. Even the best operation will need to improve and develop, partly because customers' expectations are likely to be rising and partly because the operation's competitors will also be improving. This chapter looks at operations improvement – how managers can make their operation perform better (including reducing the risk of things going wrong) through the use of the many elements of new (and not so new) improvement ideas. Some of these ideas focus on specific techniques and prescriptions, while others look at the underlying philosophy of improvement. Both aspects are covered in this chapter, because both aspects of improvement have their place in effective improvement. Figure 11.1 shows where this topic fits into our overall model of operations management.

Key questions

Why is improvement so important in operations management?

Why is failure management also improvement?

What are the key elements of operations improvement?

What are the broad approaches to improvement?

What techniques can be used for improvement?

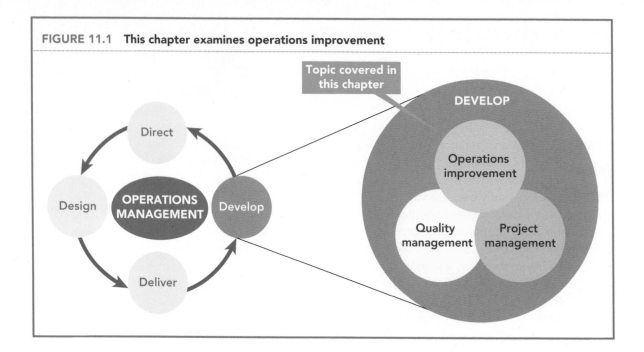

FIGURE 11.1   **This chapter examines operations improvement**

Why is improvement so important in operations management?

mprovement means to make something better. So, why is operations improvement so important? Well, who doesn't want to get better? And businesses are (or should be) just the same as people – they generally want to get better. Not just for the sake of their own excellence, although that may be one factor, but mainly because improving operations performance has such an impact on what any organization is there to do. Emergency services want to reach distressed people faster and treat them better because by doing so they are fulfilling their role more effectively. Package delivery businesses want to deliver more reliably, at lower cost, while reducing emissions because it means happier customers, higher profits and less pollution. Development charities want to target their aid and campaign for improvement in human conditions as wisely and efficiently as possible, because more money will find its way to beneficiaries rather than be wasted or consumed in administration. Not surprising, then, that operations managers are judged not only on how they meet their ongoing responsibilities of producing products and services to acceptable levels of quality, speed, dependability, flexibility and cost, but also on how they improve the performance of the operations function overall.

operations principle
Performance improvement is the ultimate objective of operations and process management.

Operations in practice

Improving Sonae Corporation's retail operations[1]

The retail industry may not seem to be the most likely setting for the use of improvement approaches more usually associated with manufacturing, but Sonae Corporation's retail chain Continente now has 22,500 employees in its 170 stores and two distribution centres – demonstrating that any type of business can benefit. Jaime Maia, Sonae's human resource director, was keen that staff training should be 'on the job' and asked a consulting firm, The Kaizen Institute (KI), to help – first by observing daily operations at several retail stores. The results were surprising, as KI uncovered a significant amount of wasted effort. The findings caused some discomfort; after all, Sonae was the most successful retailer in Portugal. Yet the improvement programme went ahead, despite several managers arguing that lean principles would not work in retail. Several processes were examined. 'Back-office' processes included unloading trucks, routing goods to sales areas or the warehouses, cleaning and shelf replenishment. 'Front-office'

processes included sales areas and their supporting checkout and customer service areas. Key operational goals included the efficient use of space, increasing sales per square metre of store space and customer satisfaction. The first stage of the programme focused on 'goods reception' and 'shelf replenishment'. Simple lean tools such as 5S and visual management (see Chapter 10) were used, as was the idea of 'gemba', or working out improvements in the workplace. Jaime Maia explained: "Improvements were suggested by store managers, top down. But those ideas were immediately enriched and put into action by the teams in the stores, bringing about further improvements in a continuous fashion."

After just one year there had been an "explosion of creativity" in the stores. Productivity had increased, inventory and stock-outs were reduced and customer satisfaction increased. As Jaime Maia put it, "continuous improvement stimulates a good attitude and a constant sense of

critique". A typical improvement project concerned the company's shelf-replenishing policy. Initially, stock was continuously replenished as sales took place during the day. However, this meant that product movements were constrained by customer flows and the need to keep the store clean and tidy. So, a new method was tested. "The store is fully loaded before the morning opening. From then on, we just need to perform minimal stock maintenance during the day. There is a time of the day at which a shelf may appear to be quite empty. However, typically, there is no need to replenish the shelf, but simply bring the products from the back to the front of the shelf, or from the upper shelves to the eye-level shelves", explained Nuno Almeida, regional operations manager. Only a few fast-moving goods needed to be replenished during the day while the store was open.

With the success of the programme, it was expanded to involve all employees in the programme. ●●●

Radical, or breakthrough, change

Radical, 'breakthrough' improvement (or 'innovation-based' improvement, as it is sometimes called) is a philosophy that assumes that the main vehicle of improvement is major and dramatic change in the way the operation works. The total redesign of a computer-based hotel reservation system or the introduction of a novel online degree programme at a university are both examples of breakthrough improvement. The impact of these improvements is relatively sudden, abrupt and represents a step-change in practice (and hopefully performance). Such improvements usually require high levels of investment, often disrupt ongoing operations and may involve changes in technology. The bold line in Figure 11.2 (a) illustrates the pattern of performance with several breakthrough improvements. The improvement pattern illustrated by the dotted line in Figure 11.2 (a) is regarded by some as being more representative of what really occurs when operations rely on pure breakthrough improvement. Breakthrough improvement places a high value on creative solutions. It encourages free thinking and individualism. It is a radical philosophy insomuch as it fosters an approach to improvement that does not accept many constraints on what is possible. 'Starting with a clean sheet of paper', 'going back to first principles' and 'completely rethinking the system' are all typical breakthrough improvement principles.

operations principle
Performance improvement sometimes requires radical change.

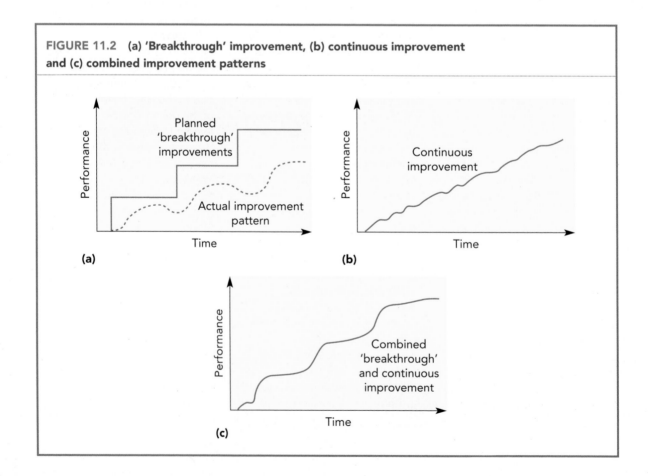

FIGURE 11.2   (a) 'Breakthrough' improvement, (b) continuous improvement and (c) combined improvement patterns

Continuous, or incremental, improvement

Continuous improvement, as the name implies, adopts an approach to improving performance that assumes many small incremental improvement steps. For example, modifying the way a product is fixed to a machine to reduce changeover time, simplifying the question sequence when taking a hotel reservation and rescheduling assignment completion dates on a university course so as to smooth students' workloads are all examples of incremental improvements. While there is no guarantee that such small steps towards better performance will be followed by other steps, the whole philosophy of continuous improvement attempts to ensure that they will be. Continuous improvement is not concerned with promoting small improvements per se. It does view small improvements, however, as having one significant advantage over large ones – they can be followed relatively painlessly by other small improvements (see Figure 11.2 (b)). Continuous improvement is also known as *kaizen*, a Japanese word, the definition of which is given by Masaaki Imai[2] (who has been one of the main proponents of continuous improvement) as follows: "*Kaizen* means improvement. Moreover, it means improvement in personal life, home life, social life and work life. When applied to the work place, *kaizen* means continuing improvement involving everyone – managers and workers alike."

In continuous improvement, it is not the *rate* of improvement that is important – it is the *momentum* of improvement. It does not matter if successive improvements are small; what does matter is that every month (or week, or quarter, or whatever period is appropriate) some kind of improvement has actually taken place.

operations principle
Performance improvement almost always benefits from continuous improvement.

Exploitation or exploration

A closely related distinction to that between continuous and breakthrough improvement, is the one that management theorists draw between what they call 'exploitation' versus 'exploration'. Exploitation is the activity of enhancing processes (and products) that already exist within a firm. The focus of exploitation is on creating efficiencies rather than radically changing resources or processes. Its emphasis is on tight control of the improvement process, standardizing processes, clear organizational structures and organizational stability. The benefits from exploitation tend to be relatively immediate, incremental and predictable. They also are likely to be better understood by the firm and fit into its existing strategic framework. Exploration, by contrast, is concerned with the exploration of new possibilities. It is associated with searching for and recognizing new mind-sets and ways of doing things. It involves experimentation, taking risks, simulation of possible consequences, flexibility and innovation. The benefits from exploration are principally long term, but can be relatively difficult to predict. Moreover, any benefits or discoveries that might come may be so different from what the firm is familiar with that it may not find it easy to take advantage of them.

ORGANIZATIONAL 'AMBIDEXTERITY'

It is clear that the organizational skills and capabilities to be successful at exploitation are likely to be very different from those that are needed for the radical exploration of new ideas. Indeed, the two views of improvement may actively conflict. A focus on thoroughly exploring for totally novel choices may consume managerial time, effort and the financial resources that would otherwise be used for refining existing ways of doing things, thus reducing the effectiveness of improving existing processes. Conversely, if existing processes are improved over time, there may be less motivation to experiment with new ideas. So, although both exploitation and exploration can be beneficial, they may compete both for resources and for management attention. This is where the concept of 'organizational ambidexterity' becomes important. Organizational ambidexterity means the ability of a firm to both exploit and explore as it seeks to improve; to be able to compete in mature markets where efficiency is important, by improving existing resources and processes, while also competing in new technologies and/or markets where novelty, innovation and experimentation are required.

> **operations principle**
> Organizational ambidexterity is the ability to both exploit existing capabilities and explore new ones as an operation seeks to improve.

The structure of improvement ideas

There have been hundreds of ideas relating to operations improvement that have been proposed over the last few decades. To understand how these ideas relate to each other, it is important to distinguish between three aspects of improvement:[3]

 The *elements* contained within improvement approaches   These are the fundamental ideas of what improves operations; they are the 'building blocks' of improvement.

 The broad *approaches* to improvement   These are the underlying sets of beliefs that form a coherent philosophy and shape how improvement should be accomplished. Some improvement approaches (such as total quality management, see next chapter) are well established, others are relatively recent (for example, Six Sigma, explained later). But do not think that approaches to improvement are different in all respects; there are many elements that are common to several approaches.

 The improvement *techniques*   There are many 'step-by-step' techniques, methods and tools that can be used to help find improved ways of doing things; some of these use quantitative modelling and others are more qualitative.

Later in this chapter we will treat each of these aspects of improvement. The best way to understand improvement is to deal with the elements contained within improvement approaches first, then see how they come together to form broad approaches to improvement and finally examine some typical improvement techniques.

Why is failure management also improvement?

No matter how much effort is put into improvement, all operations will face risk and occasionally experience failures. So minimizing these failures, or reducing their impact, is one way of improving performance, compared with what it would otherwise have been. Yet accepting that failure occurs is not the same thing as tolerating or ignoring it. And operations managers have four ways to reduce the effects of failure: identifying things that could go wrong; stopping them going wrong; reducing the consequences when things do go wrong (called failure or risk 'mitigation'); and recovering after things have gone wrong (see Figure 11.3).

operations principle
Resilience is governed by the effectiveness of failure prevention, mitigation and recovery.

Assessing the potential causes and consequences of failure

The first stage of failure management is to understand where failure might occur and what the consequences of failure might be. Each potential cause of failure needs to be assessed in terms of how likely it is to occur and the impact it may have. Only then can measures be taken to prevent or minimize the effect of the more important potential failures. The classic approach to assessing potential failures is to inspect and audit operations activities. Unfortunately, inspection and audit cannot, on their own, provide complete assurance that undesirable events will be avoided. The causes of some failure

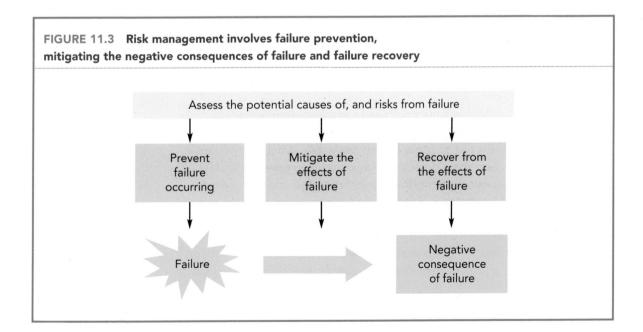

FIGURE 11.3 **Risk management involves failure prevention, mitigating the negative consequences of failure and failure recovery**

are purely random, like lightning strikes, and are difficult, if not impossible, to predict. However, the vast majority of failures are caused by something that could have been avoided. Many operations use simple checklists to try and identify potential causes of failure.

E-SECURITY[4]

Any advance in processes or technology creates risks. No real advance comes without risk, threats and even danger. This applies particularly to e-business. In almost all businesses, information has become critical. So, information security management has become a particularly high priority. But herein lies the problem. The internet is, by design, an open non-secure medium. The original purpose of the internet was not for commercial purposes; it is not designed to handle secure transactions. So there is a trade-off between providing wider access through the internet, and the security concerns it generates. Three developments have amplified e-security concerns. First, increased connectivity (we all rely on internet-based systems) means that everyone has at least the potential to 'see' everyone else. Second, there has been a loss of 'perimeter' security as more people work from home or through mobile communications. Third, for some new, sometimes unregulated, technologies, such as some mobile networks, it takes time to discover all possible sources of risk.

How can failure be prevented?

The obvious method of failure prevention is to systematically examine any processes involved and 'design out' any failure points. In addition, three further approaches of preventing failure can be used:

Redundancy   Building-in redundancy to an operation means having back-up systems or components in case of failure. It can be expensive and is generally used when the breakdown could have a critical impact. Redundancy means doubling or even tripling some parts of a process or system in case one element fails. Nuclear power stations, spacecraft and hospitals all have auxiliary systems in case of an emergency.

Fail-safeing   Sometimes called *poka-yoke* in Japan, from *yokeru* (to prevent) and *poka* (inadvertent errors), the idea is based on the principle that human mistakes are, to some extent, inevitable. What is important is to prevent them becoming defects. *Poka-yokes* are simple (preferably inexpensive) devices or systems that are incorporated into a process to prevent inadvertent mistakes. Examples include trays used in hospitals with indentations shaped to each item needed for a surgical procedure (items not back in place after the procedure might be in the patient), the locks on aircraft lavatory doors that must be turned to switch the light on and height bars on amusement rides to prevent customers ignoring size limitations.

Maintenance   Maintenance is how operations try to avoid failure by taking care of their physical facilities. It is an important part of most operations' activities, particularly in operations dominated by physical facilities such as power stations, hotels, airlines and petrochemical refineries. The benefits of effective maintenance include enhanced safety, increased reliability, higher quality (badly maintained equipment is more likely to cause errors), lower operating costs (because regularly serviced process technology is more efficient) and a longer life for process technology.

How can operations mitigate the effects of failure?

Failure mitigation means isolating a failure from its negative consequences. The nature of the action taken to mitigate failure will obviously depend on the nature of the risk of failure. In most industries, technical experts have established a classification of failure mitigation actions that is appropriate for the types of failure likely to be suffered. In agriculture, for example, government agencies and industry bodies have published mitigation strategies for such risks as the outbreak of crop disease, contagious animal infections and so on. Likewise, governments have different contingency plans in place to deal with the spread of a major health risk, such as the H1N1 and H7Np influenza viruses and the Ebola outbreak in West Africa. Such documents will outline the various mitigation actions that can be taken under different circumstances and detail exactly who is responsible for each action.

How can operations recover from the effects of failure?

Failure recovery is the set of actions that are taken to reduce the impact of failure once the customer has experienced its negative effects. Recovery needs to be planned and procedures put in place that can discover when failures have occurred, guide appropriate action to keep everyone informed, capture the lessons learned from the failure and plan to absorb lessons into any future recovery. All types of operation can benefit from well-planned recovery. For example, a construction company whose mechanical digger breaks down can have plans in place to arrange a replacement from a hire company. Recovery procedures will also shape customers' perceptions of failure. Even where the customer sees a failure, it may not necessarily lead to dissatisfaction. Indeed, in many situations, customers may well accept that things do go wrong. It is not necessarily the failure itself that leads to dissatisfaction but often the organization's response to the breakdown. While mistakes may be inevitable, dissatisfied customers are not. A failure may even be turned into a positive experience. A good recovery can turn angry, frustrated customers into loyal ones.

operations principle
Successful failure recovery can yield more benefits than if the failure had not occurred.

What are the key elements of operations improvement?

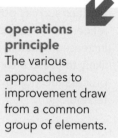

operations principle
The various approaches to improvement draw from a common group of elements.

he elements of improvement are the individual basic fundamental ideas of improvement. Think of these elements of improvement as the building blocks of the various improvement approaches that we shall look at later. Here we explain some, but not all (there are lots), of the more common elements in use today.

Improvement cycles

An important element within some improvement approaches is the use of a literally never-ending process of repeatedly questioning and re-questioning the detailed working of a process or activity, usually summarized by the idea of the 'improvement cycle'. Two are widely used – the PDCA cycle and the DMAIC (pronounced De-Make) cycle, made popular by the Six-Sigma approach (see later). The PDCA cycle model is shown in Figure 11.4 (a). It starts with the P (for plan) stage, which involves an examination of the problem – collecting and analyzing data so as to formulate a plan of action that is intended to improve performance. The next step is the D (for do), which is the implementation stage during which the plan is tried out in the operation. Next comes the C (for check) stage, where the new implemented solution is evaluated. Finally, at least for this cycle, comes the A (for act) stage, when the change is consolidated or standardized if it has been successful. Alternatively, if the change has not been successful, the lessons learned from the 'trial' are formalized before the cycle starts again.

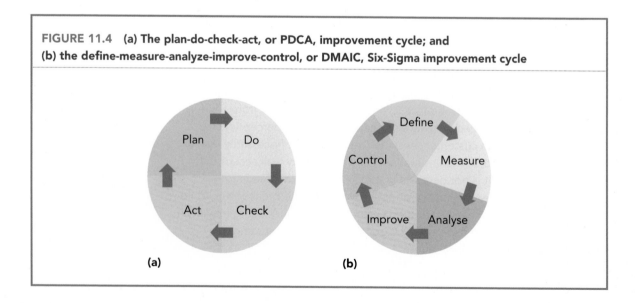

FIGURE 11.4   (a) The plan-do-check-act, or PDCA, improvement cycle; and (b) the define-measure-analyze-improve-control, or DMAIC, Six-Sigma improvement cycle

The DMAIC cycle is in some ways more intuitively obvious than the PDCA cycle in that it follows a more 'experimental' approach (see Figure 11.4 (b)). It starts with (D) – defining the problem or problems, partly to understand the scope of what needs to be done and partly to define exactly the requirements of the process improvement. After definition comes (M), the measurement stage. This stage involves validating the problem to make sure that it really is a problem worth solving. Once these measurements have been established, they can be (A), analyzed. Once the causes of the problem are identified, work can begin on (I), improving the process. The improved process needs then to be continually monitored and (C), controlled to check that the improved level of performance is sustaining. After this point, the cycle starts again and defines the problems that are preventing further improvement. Remember, though, it is the last point about both cycles that is the most important – that the cycle starts again.

A process perspective

Taking a process perspective has two major advantages. First, it means that improvement can be focused on what actually happens in reality. Second, all parts of the business manage processes. This is what we call operations as 'activity' rather than operations as a 'function'. So, if improvement is described in terms of how processes can be made more effective, those messages will have relevance for all the other functions of the business, in addition to the operations function.

End-to-end processes

Some improvement approaches use the idea that operations should be organized around the total process that adds value for customers, rather than the functions or activities that perform the various stages of the value-adding activity. We have already pointed out the difference between conventional processes within a specialist function and an end-to-end business process in Chapter 1. Identified customer needs are entirely fulfilled by an 'end-to-end' business process. In fact, the processes are designed specifically to do this, which is why they will often cut across conventional organizational boundaries. Figure 11.5 illustrates this idea.

Evidence-based problem solving

In recent years there has been a resurgence of the use of quantitative techniques in improvement approaches. However, the statistical methods used in improvement activities do not always reflect conventional academic statistical knowledge as such. They emphasize observational methods of collecting data and the use of experimentation to examine hypotheses. Techniques include graphical methods, analysis of variance and two-level factorial experiment design. Underlying the use of these techniques is an

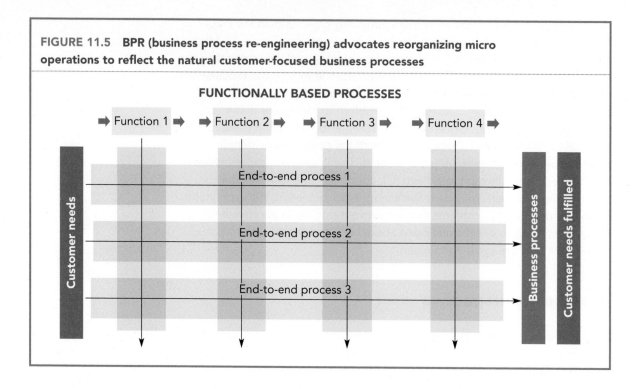

FIGURE 11.5   BPR (business process re-engineering) advocates reorganizing micro operations to reflect the natural customer-focused business processes

emphasis on the scientific method, responding only to hard evidence and using statistical software to facilitate analysis.

Customer-centricity

There is little point in improvement unless it meets the requirements of the customers. However, it can mean more than simply meeting the expectations of customers. It involves the whole organization in understanding the central importance of customers to its success and even to its survival. Customers are seen not as being external to the organization but as the most important part of it. However, customer-centricity does not mean that they must be provided with everything that they want. Operations managers have to strike a balance between what customers would like and what the operation can afford (or wants) to do.

Systems and procedures

A type of system that supports the improvement effort is often used by organizations. An improvement system (sometimes called a 'quality system') is defined as: 'the organizational structure, responsibilities, procedures, processes and resources for implementing quality management.[5] It should. . . define and cover all facets of an organization's operation, from identifying and meeting the needs and requirements of customers, design, planning, purchasing, manufacturing, packaging, storage, delivery and service, together with all relevant activities carried out within these functions. It deals with organization, responsibilities, procedures and processes. Put simply [it] is good management practice.'[6]

Improvement at Heineken[7]

Heineken International produces and sells beer around the world. However, sales growth can put pressure on any company's operations. For example, Heineken's Zoeterwoude facility, a packaging plant that fills bottles and cans in the Netherlands, faced two challenges. First, it needed to improve its operations processes to reduce its costs. Second, because it would have taken a year to build a new packaging line, it needed to improve the efficiency of its existing lines in order to increase its capacity. So, improving line efficiency was vital if the plant was to cut its costs and create the extra capacity it needed to delay investment in a new packaging line.

The objective of the improvement project was to improve the equipment efficiency of the operation by focusing improvement around two themes. First, obtaining accurate operational data that could be converted into useful business information on which improvement decisions could be based. Second, changing the culture of the operation to promote fast and effective decision making. Having access to accurate and up-to-date information helped people in the plant to focus on the *improvement* of how they do their job, rather than just 'doing their job'. Before the improvement, project staff had approached problem solving as an ad hoc activity, only to be done when circumstances made

it unavoidable. Staff also started using problem-solving techniques, such as cause–effect and Pareto diagrams (see later in the chapter). "Until we started using these techniques", says Wilbert Raaijmakers, Heineken Netherlands brewery director, "there was little consent regarding what was causing any problems. There was poor communication between the various departments and job grades. For example, maintenance staff believed that production stops were caused by operating errors, while operators were of the opinion that poor maintenance was the cause." The use of better information, analysis and improvement techniques helped the staff to identify and treat the root causes of problems. ● ● ●

Reduce process variation

Processes change over time, as does their performance. Some aspects of process performance are measured periodically. These are then plotted on a simple time-scale, to check that the performance of the process is, in itself, acceptable. They can also be used to check if process performance is changing over time, and to check on the extent of the variation in process performance. In the next chapter we illustrate how random variation in the performance of any process can obscure what was really happening within the process. So, a potentially useful method of identifying improvement opportunities is to try and identify the sources of random variation in process performance.

Synchronized flow

Synchronized flow means that items in a process, operation or supply network flow smoothly and with even velocity from start to finish (see Chapter 10). This is a function of how inventory accumulates within the operation. Once this smooth synchronization of flow has been achieved, it becomes easier to expose any irregularities of flow that may be the symptoms of more deep-rooted underlying problems.

Emphasize education/training

Several improvement approaches stress the idea that structured training and organization of improvement should be central to improvement. Not only should the techniques of improvement be fully understood by everyone engaged in the improvement process, the business and organizational context of improvement should also be understood. Some improvement approaches in particular place particular emphasis on formal education. For example, Six Sigma (see later) often mandates a minimum level of training deemed necessary before improvement projects should be undertaken.

Perfection is the goal

Almost all organization-wide improvement programmes will have some kind of goal or target that the improvement effort should achieve. And while targets can be set in many different ways, some improvement authorities hold that measuring process performance against some kind of absolute target does most for encouraging improvement. By an 'absolute target', one literally means the theoretical level of perfection – for example, zero errors, instant delivery, delivery absolutely when promised, infinite flexibility, zero waste, etc. Of course, in reality such perfection may never be achievable. That is not the point. What is important is that current performance can be calibrated against this target of perfection in order to indicate how much more improvement is possible.

Waste identification

All improvement approaches aspire to eliminate waste. In fact, any improvement implies that some waste has been eliminated, where waste is any activity that does not add value. But the identification and elimination of waste is sometimes a central feature. For example, as we discussed in Chapter 10, it is arguably the most significant part of the lean philosophy.

Include everybody

Harnessing the skills and enthusiasm of every person and all parts of the organization seems an obvious principle of improvement. The contribution of all individuals in the organization may go beyond understanding their contribution to 'not make mistakes'. Individuals are expected to bring something positive to improving the way they perform their jobs. The principles of 'empowerment' are frequently cited as supporting this aspect of improvement.

Develop internal customer–supplier relationships

One of the best ways to ensure that external customers are satisfied is to establish the idea that every part of the organization contributes to external customer satisfaction by satisfying its own internal customers. It means stressing that each process in an operation has a responsibility to manage these internal customer–supplier relationships.

What are the broad approaches to improvement?

By the 'broad approaches to improvement' we mean the underlying sets of beliefs that form a coherent philosophy and shape how improvement should be accomplished. But do not think that approaches to improvement are different in all respects; there are many elements that are common to several approaches. Some of these approaches have, or will be, described in other chapters – for example, lean operations (in Chapter 10) and TQM (in Chapter 12). So, in this section we will only briefly examine TQM and lean operations, specifically from an improvement perspective, and also add two further approaches – business process re-engineering (BPR) and Six Sigma.

> **operations principle**
> There is no one universal approach to improvement.

Total quality management as an improvement approach

Total quality management (TQM) was one of the earliest management 'fashions'. Its peak of popularity was in the late 1980s and early '90s. As such, it has suffered from something of a backlash in recent years. Yet the general precepts and principles that constitute TQM are still hugely relevant. Few, if any, managers have not heard of TQM and its impact on improvement. Indeed, TQM has come to be seen as an approach to the way operations and processes should be managed and improved generally. It is best thought of as a philosophy of how to approach improvement. This philosophy, above everything, stresses the 'total' of TQM. It is an approach that puts quality (and indeed improvement generally) at the heart of everything that is done by an operation. As a reminder, this totality can be summarized by the way TQM lays particular stress on the following elements (see Chapter 12 for more detail):

 meeting the needs and expectations of customers;

 improvement that covers all parts of the organization (and should be group-based);

 improvement that includes every person in the organization (and success is recognized);

 including all costs of quality;

 getting things 'right first time' – designing-in quality, rather than inspecting it in;

 developing the systems and procedures that support improvement.

Lean as an improvement approach

The idea of 'lean' spread beyond its Japanese roots and became fashionable in the West at about the same time as TQM. And although its popularity has not declined to the same extent as TQM, over 25 years of experience has diminished the excitement once associated with the approach. But, unlike TQM, it was seen initially as an approach to be used exclusively in manufacturing. Now, lean has become fashionable as an approach that can be applied in service operations. As a reminder (see Chapter 10 for more detail), the lean approach aims to meet demand instantaneously, with perfect quality and no waste. The key elements of lean, when used as an improvement approach, are as follows:

 customer-centricity;

 internal customer–supplier relationships;

 perfection as the goal;

 synchronized flow;

 reduced variation;

 including all people;

★ waste elimination.

Business process re-engineering (BPR)

The idea of business process re-engineering originated in the early 1990s, when Michael Hammer proposed that rather than using technology to automate work, it would be better applied to doing away with the need for the work in the first place ('don't automate, obliterate'). In doing this, he was warning against establishing non-value-added work within an information technology system where it would be even more difficult to identify and eliminate. All work, he said, should be examined for whether it adds value for the customer and, if not, processes should be redesigned to eliminate it. It advocates radical rather than incremental changes. It has been defined as: 'the fundamental rethinking and radical redesign of business processes to achieve dramatic improvements in critical, contemporary measures of performance, such as cost, quality, service and speed'.[8] But, it was the potential of information technologies to enable the fundamental redesign of processes that acted as the catalyst in bringing these ideas together. The main principles of BPR can be summarized in the following points:

 Rethink business processes in a cross-functional manner that organizes work around the natural flow of information (or materials or customers).

 Strive for dramatic improvements in performance by radically rethinking and redesigning the process.

 Have those who use the output from a process, perform the process. Check to see if all internal customers can be their own supplier, rather than depending on another function in the business to supply them (which takes longer and separates out the stages in the process).

 Put decision points where the work is performed. Do not separate those who do the work from those who control and manage the work.

EXAMPLE[9]

We can illustrate this idea of reorganizing (or re-engineering) around business processes through the following simple example. Figure 11.6 (a) shows the traditional organization of a trading company that purchases consumer goods from several suppliers, stores them and sells them on to retail outlets. At the heart of the operation is the warehouse that receives the goods, stores them and packs and dispatches them when they are required by customers. Orders for more stock are placed by the purchasing department, which also takes charge of materials planning and stock control. Purchasing buys the goods based on a forecast that is prepared by the marketing team, which takes advice from the sales department that is processing customers' orders. When a customer does place an order, it is the sales department's job to instruct the warehouse to pack and dispatch the order and tell the finance department to invoice the customer for the goods. So, traditionally, five departments (each a micro operation) have between them organized the flow of materials and information within the total operation. But at each interface between the departments there is the possibility of errors and miscommunication arising. Furthermore, *who is responsible for looking after the customer's needs?* Currently, three separate departments all have dealings with the customer. Similarly, *who is responsible for liaising with suppliers?* This time two departments have contact with suppliers.

Eventually, the company reorganized around two essential business processes. The first process (called purchasing operations) dealt with everything concerning relationships with suppliers. It was this process' focused and unambiguous responsibility to develop good working relationships with suppliers. The other business process (called customer

FIGURE 11.6 **Before (a) and after (b) re-engineering a consumer goods trading company**

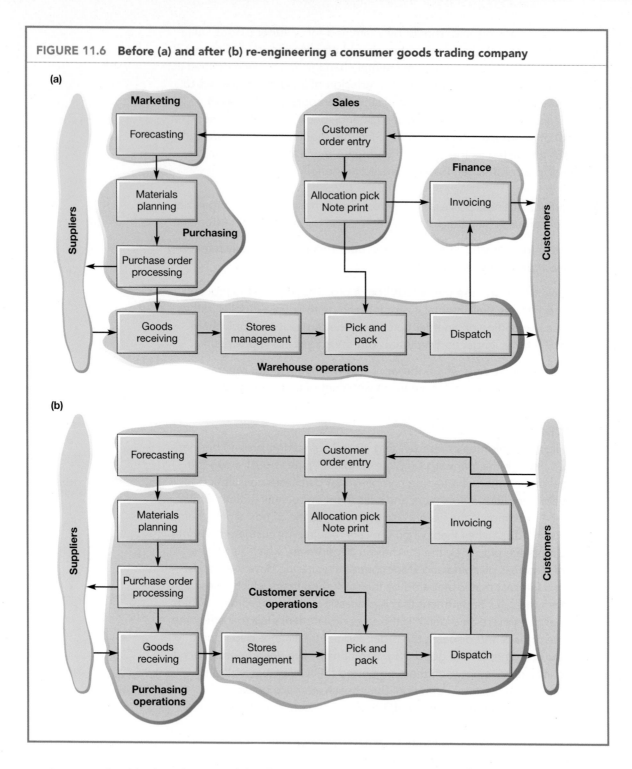

service operations) had total responsibility for satisfying customers' needs. This included speaking 'with one voice' to the customer.

BPR has aroused considerable controversy. Because BPR sometimes looks only at work activities rather than at the people who perform the work, people can become 'cogs in a machine'. Some critics equate BPR with the much earlier principles of scientific management, pejoratively known as 'Taylorism'.

Generally, these critics mean that BPR is overly harsh in the way it views human resources. Certainly, there is evidence that BPR is often accompanied by a significant reduction in staff. Studies at the time when BPR was at its peak often revealed that the majority of BPR projects could reduce staff levels by over 20 per cent. Moreover, a combination of radical redesign together with downsizing could mean that an essential core of experience is lost from the operation.

Six Sigma

The Six-Sigma approach was first popularized by Motorola, the electronics and communications systems company, when it set its quality objective as 'total customer satisfaction'. The Six Sigma concept was so named because it required that the natural variation of processes (± 3 standard deviations) should be half their specification range. In other words, the specification range of any part of a product or service should be ± 6 the standard deviation of the process (see Chapter 12). The Greek letter sigma (σ) is often used to indicate the standard deviation of a process – hence the Six-Sigma label.

Figure 11.7 illustrates the effect of progressively narrowing process variation on the number of defects produced by the process, in terms of defects per million. The 'defects-per-million' measure is used within the Six-Sigma approach to emphasize the drive towards a virtually zero-defect objective.[10] Now the definition of Six Sigma has widened to well beyond this rather narrow statistical perspective. General Electric (GE), who were probably the best known of the early adopters of Six Sigma, defined it as, 'A disciplined methodology of defining, measuring, analysing, improving and controlling the quality in every one of the company's products, processes and transactions – with the ultimate goal of virtually eliminating all defects'. So, now, Six Sigma should be seen as a broad improvement concept rather than a simple examination of process variation.

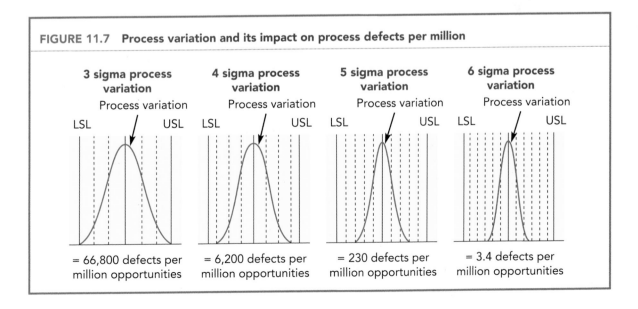

FIGURE 11.7   Process variation and its impact on process defects per million

3 sigma process variation	4 sigma process variation	5 sigma process variation	6 sigma process variation
= 66,800 defects per million opportunities	= 6,200 defects per million opportunities	= 230 defects per million opportunities	= 3.4 defects per million opportunities

Although the scope of Six Sigma is disputed, among elements frequently associated with Six Sigma include the following:

 Customer-driven objectives   Six Sigma is sometimes defined as 'the process of comparing process outputs against customer requirements'. In particular, it expresses performance in terms of defects-per-million-opportunities (DPMO).

 Use of evidence   Although Six Sigma was not the first approach to operations to use statistical methods, it has done a lot to emphasize the use of quantitative evidence.

 Structured improvement cycle   The structured improvement cycle used in Six Sigma is the DMAIC cycle.

 Process capability and control   Not surprisingly, given its origins, process capability and control is important within the Six-Sigma approach.

 Process design   Latterly, Six-Sigma proponents also include process design into the collection of elements that define the Six-Sigma approach.

 Structured training and organization of improvement   The Six-Sigma approach holds that improvement initiatives can only be successful if significant resources and training are devoted to their management.

THE 'MARSHAL ARTS' ANALOGY

The terms that have become associated with Six-Sigma experts (and denote their level of expertise) are Master Black Belt, Black Belt and Green Belt. Master Black Belts are experts in the use of Six-Sigma tools and techniques, as well as how such techniques can be used and implemented. They are seen as teachers who can not only guide improvement projects, but also coach and mentor Black Belts and Green Belts, who are closer to the day-to-day improvement activity. They are expected to have the quantitative analytical skills to help with Six-Sigma techniques and also the organizational and interpersonal skills to teach and mentor. Given their responsibilities, it is expected that Master Black Belts are employed full time on their improvement activities. Black Belts can take a direct hand in organizing improvement teams. Like Master Black Belts, Black Belts are expected to develop their quantitative analytical skills and also act as coaches for Green Belts.

Differences and similarities

In this chapter, we have chosen to explain (very briefly) four improvement approaches. It could have been more. But the four included here constitute a representative sample of the most commonly used approaches. Nor do we have the space to describe them fully. Yet there are some common elements between these approaches – and there are also differences. For example, one important difference relates to whether the approaches emphasize a gradual/ continuous approach to change, or whether they recommend a more radical/'breakthrough' change. Another difference concerns the aim of the approach. What is the balance between whether the approach emphasizes *what* changes should be made, or *how* changes should be made? Some approaches have a firm view of what is the best way to organize the operation's processes and resources. Other approaches hold no particular view on what an operation should do, but rather concentrate on the method of deciding how an operation should decide what to do. Indeed, we can position each of the elements and the approaches that include them. This is illustrated in Figure 11.8. The approaches differ in the extent that they prescribe appropriate operations practice. BPR, for example, is very clear in what it is recommending – namely, that all processes should be organized on an end-to-end basis. Its focus is *what* should happen rather than *how* it should happen. To a slightly lesser extent, lean is the same. It has a definite list of things that processes should or should not be – waste should be eliminated, inventory should be reduced, technology should be flexible and so on. Contrast this with both Six Sigma and TQM, which focus to a far greater extent on *how* operations should be improved. Six Sigma, in particular, has relatively little to say about what is good or bad in the way operations resources are organized (with the possible exception of it emphasizing the negative effects of process variation). Its concern is largely the way improvements should be

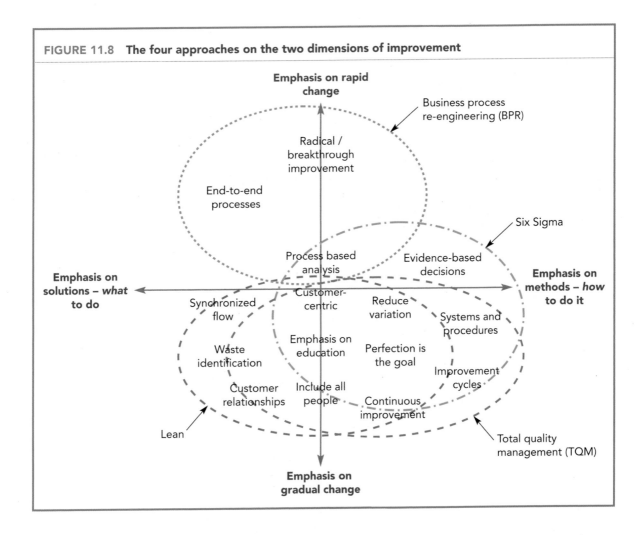

FIGURE 11.8 **The four approaches on the two dimensions of improvement**

made: using evidence, using quantitative analysis, using the DMAIC cycle and so on. They also differ in terms of whether they emphasize gradual or rapid change. BPR is explicit in its radical nature. By contrast, TQM and lean both incorporate ideas of continuous improvement. Six Sigma is relatively neutral on this issue, and can be used for small or very large changes.

operations principle
There is significant overlap between the various approaches to improvement in terms of the improvement elements they contain.

What techniques can be used for improvement?

operations principle
Improvement can be facilitated by relatively simple analytical techniques.

All the techniques described in this book can be regarded as 'improvement' techniques. However, some techniques are particularly useful for improving operations and processes generally. Here, we select some techniques that either have not been described elsewhere, or need to be reintroduced in their role of helping operations improvement in particular.

Scatter diagrams

Scatter diagrams provide a quick and simple method of identifying whether there is evidence of a connection between two sets of data: for example, plotting the same journey on a graph that has departure time on one axis and journey time on the other could give an indication of whether departure time and journey time are related, and if so, how. Scatter diagrams can be treated in a far more sophisticated manner by quantifying how strong the relationship between the sets of data is. But, however sophisticated the approach, this type of graph only identifies the existence of a relationship, not necessarily the existence of a causality.

EXAMPLE: KASTON PYRAL SERVICES LTD (A)
Kaston Pyral Services Ltd (KPS) installs and maintains environmental control, heating and air-conditioning systems. It has set up an improvement team to suggest ways in which it might improve its levels of customer service. The improvement team has completed its first customer-satisfaction survey. The survey asked customers to score the service they received from KPS in several ways. For example, it asked customers to score services on a scale of 1 to 10 on promptness, friendliness, level of advice, etc. Scores were then summed to give a 'total satisfaction score' for each customer – the higher the score, the greater the satisfaction. The spread of satisfaction scores puzzled the team and it considered what factors might be causing such differences in the way its customers viewed KPS. Two factors were put forward to explain the differences.

(a) the number of times in the past year the customer had received a preventive maintenance visit;

(b) the number of times the customer had called for emergency service.

All these data were collected and plotted on scatter diagrams, as shown in Figure 11.9. Figure (a) shows that there seems to be a clear relationship between a customer's satisfaction score and the number of times the customer was visited for regular servicing. The scatter diagram in Figure 11.9 (b) is less clear. Although all customers who had very high satisfaction scores had made very few emergency calls, so had some customers with low satisfaction scores. As a result of this analysis, the team decided to survey customers' views on its emergency service.

Process maps (flow charts)

Process maps (described in Chapter 5, sometimes called flow charts in this context) can be used to give a detailed understanding prior to improvement. Recording each stage in the process can show up poorly organized flows, and can clarify improvement opportunities. Probably most importantly, they highlight problem areas where no procedure exists to cope with a particular set of circumstances.

EXAMPLE: KASTON PYRAL SERVICES LTD (B)

As part of its improvement programme, the team at KPS is concerned that customers are not being served well when they phone in with minor queries over the operation of their heating systems. These queries are not usually concerned with serious problems, but often concern minor irritations that can be equally damaging to the customers' perception of KPS' service. Figure 11.10 shows the process map for this type of customer query. The procedure had never been formally laid out in this way before, and it showed

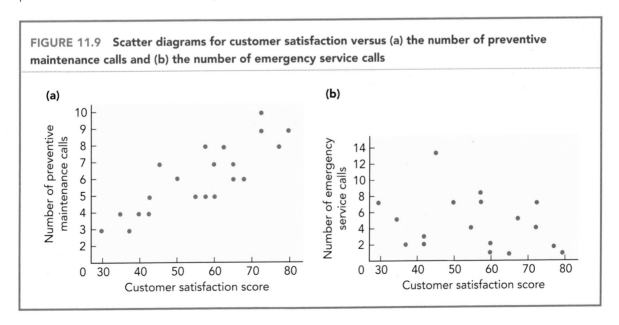

FIGURE 11.9 Scatter diagrams for customer satisfaction versus (a) the number of preventive maintenance calls and (b) the number of emergency service calls

up three areas where information was not being recorded. These are the three points marked with question marks on the process map in Figure 11.10. As a result of this investigation, it was decided to log all customer queries so that analysis could reveal further information on the nature of customer problems.

Cause–effect diagrams

Cause–effect diagrams are a particularly effective method of helping to search for the root causes of problems. They do this by asking what, when, where, how and why questions, but also add some possible 'answers' in an explicit way.

FIGURE 11.10   **Process map for customer query**

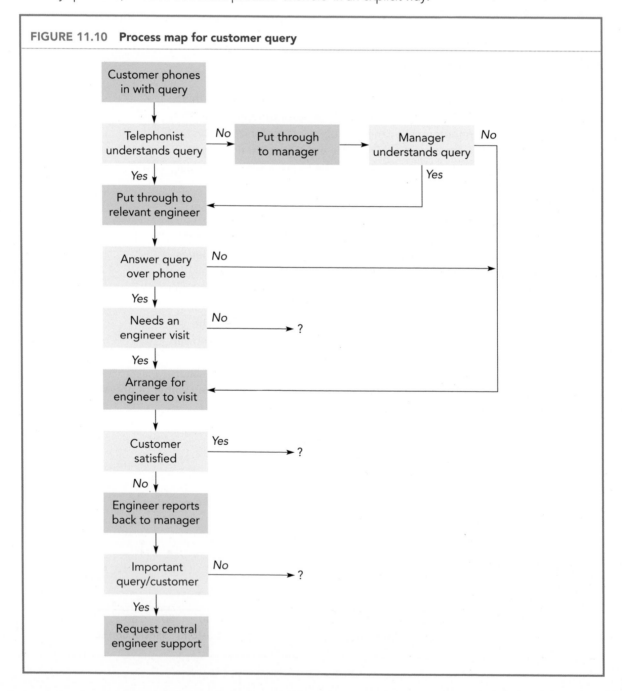

They are used in improvement programmes because they provide a way of structuring group brainstorming sessions. Often the structure involves identifying possible causes under the (rather old-fashioned) headings of machinery, manpower, materials, methods and money. Yet, in practice, any categorization that comprehensively covers all relevant possible causes could be used.

EXAMPLE: KASTON PYRAL SERVICES LTD (C)

The improvement team at KPS was working on a particular problem. Whenever service engineers were called out to perform emergency servicing for a customer, they took with them the spares and equipment that they thought would be necessary to repair the system. Although engineers could never be sure exactly what materials and equipment they would need for a job, they could guess what was likely to be needed and take a range of spares and equipment that would cover most eventualities. Too often, however, the engineers would find that they needed a spare that they had not brought with them. The cause–effect diagram for this particular problem, as drawn by the team, is shown in Figure 11.11.

Pareto diagrams

In any improvement process, it is worthwhile distinguishing what is important and what is less so. The purpose of the Pareto diagram (described in Chapter 8) is to distinguish between the 'vital few' issues and the 'trivial many'. It is a relatively straightforward technique that involves arranging items of information on the types of problem or causes of problem into their order of importance (usually measured by 'frequency of occurrence'). This can be used to highlight areas where further decision making will be useful. Pareto

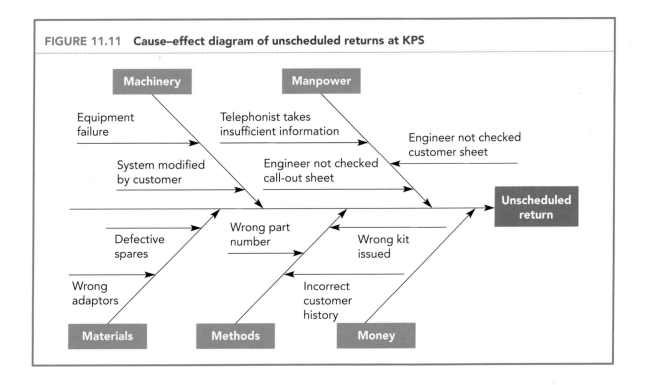

FIGURE 11.11   Cause–effect diagram of unscheduled returns at KPS

analysis is based on the phenomenon of relatively few causes explaining the majority of effects.

EXAMPLE: KASTON PYRAL SERVICES LTD (D)

The KPS improvement team that was investigating unscheduled returns from emergency servicing (described in the cause–effect diagram in Figure 11.11) examined all occasions over the previous 12 months on which an unscheduled return had been made. They categorized the reasons for unscheduled returns as follows:

1   The engineer had incorrectly predicted the nature of the fault.

2   There was insufficient information given when the call was taken.

3   The system had been modified in some way and not recorded on KPS' records.

4   The part had been incorrectly issued to the engineer by stores.

5   The relevant part was out of stock.

6   The wrong equipment had been taken for whatever reason.

7   Any other reason.

The relative frequency of occurrence of these causes is shown in Figure 11.12. About a third of all unscheduled returns were due to the first category, and more than half the returns were accounted for by the first and second categories together. It was decided that the problem could best be tackled by concentrating on how to get more information to the engineers, enabling them to predict the causes of failure more accurately.

Why–why analysis

Why–why analysis starts by stating the problem and asking *why* that problem has occurred. Once the reasons for the problem occurring have been identified, each of the reasons is taken in turn and again the question is asked *why* those reasons have occurred, and so on. This procedure is continued until either a cause seems sufficiently self-contained to be addressed by itself, or no more answers to the question 'Why?' can be generated.

EXAMPLE: KASTON PYRAL SERVICES LTD (E)

The major cause of unscheduled returns at KPS was the incorrect prediction of reasons for the customer's system failure. This is stated as the 'problem' in the why–why analysis in Figure 11.13. The question is then asked, 'why was the failure wrongly predicted?'. Three answers are proposed: first, that the engineers were not trained correctly; second, that they had insufficient knowledge of the particular product installed in the customer's location; and third, that they had insufficient knowledge of the customer's particular system with its modifications. Each of these three reasons is taken in turn, and the questions are asked, 'why is there a lack of training?', 'why is there a lack of product knowledge?', and 'why is there a lack of customer knowledge?' And so on.

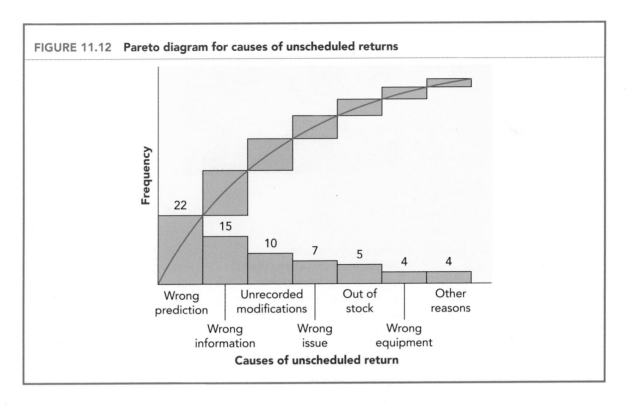

FIGURE 11.12 Pareto diagram for causes of unscheduled returns

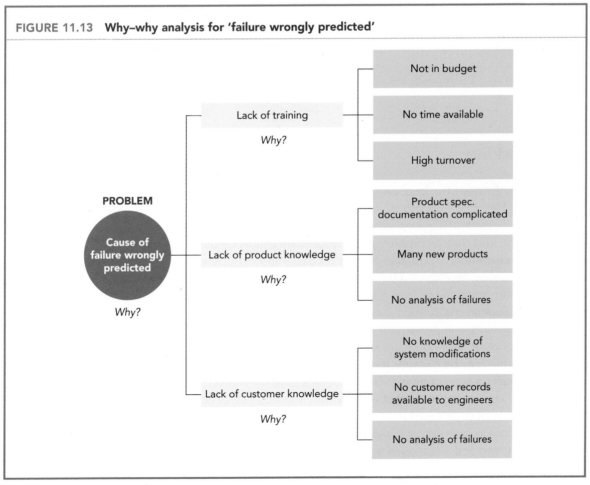

FIGURE 11.13 Why–why analysis for 'failure wrongly predicted'

Operations in practice

Learning from Formula One[11]

As driving jobs go, there could be no bigger difference than that between Formula One racing drivers and a supermarket truck driver. But they have more in common than one would suspect. Both Formula One and truck drivers want to save fuel, either to reduce pit-stops (Formula 1) or keep delivery costs down (heavy goods vehicles). Computer-assisted simulation programs developed by the Williams Formula One team are being deployed to help Sainsbury's (a UK supermarket group) drivers develop the driving skills that could potentially cut their fuel bill by up to 30 per cent. The simulator technology, which allows realistic advanced training to be conducted in a controlled environment, was developed originally for the advanced training of Formula One drivers and can now train drivers to a high level of professional driving skills and road-safety applications. Roger Burnley, Sainsbury's retail and logistics director, said, "We are committed to reducing our environmental impact and, as a result, we are often at the very forefront of technological innovation. By partnering with Williams F1, we can take advantage of some of the world's most advanced automotive technology, making our operations even more efficient and taking us a step closer to meeting our CO_2 reduction targets." ● ● ●

Benchmarking

Benchmarking is more of an improvement philosophy than a technique. It is 'the process of learning from others', and involves comparing one's own performance, or methods, against other comparable operations. Its rationale is based on the idea that: (a) problems in a process are almost certainly shared by processes elsewhere; and (b) that there is probably another operation somewhere that has developed a better way of doing things. For example, a bank might learn some things from a supermarket about how it could cope with demand fluctuations during the day. Benchmarking is essentially about stimulating creativity in improvement practice. But, although benchmarking has become popular, some businesses have failed to derive maximum benefit from it. Partly this may be because there are some misunderstandings as to what benchmarking actually entails. First, it is not a 'one-off' project; it is best practiced as a continuous process of comparison. Second, it does not provide 'solutions'; rather, it provides ideas and information that can lead to solutions. Third, it does not involve simply copying or imitating other operations; it is a process of learning and adapting in a pragmatic manner.

operations principle
Improvement is aided by contextualizing processes and operations performance through some kind of benchmarking.

Summary answers to key questions

Each chapter has a 'Summary answers to key questions' section. Use it to check your understanding of the issues covered in the chapter.

WHY IS IMPROVEMENT SO IMPORTANT IN OPERATIONS MANAGEMENT?

★ Improvement is now seen as the prime responsibility of operations management. Furthermore, all operations management activities are really concerned with improvement in the long term. Also, many companies are having to improve simply to retain their position relative to competitors.

★ A common distinction is between radical, or breakthrough, improvement on one hand, and continuous, or incremental, improvement on the other.

★ This distinction is closely associated with the distinction between the exploitation of existing capabilities versus the exploration of new ones. The ability to do both is called 'organizational ambidexterity'.

WHY IS FAILURE MANAGEMENT ALSO IMPROVEMENT?

★ Failure management is about things going wrong and what operations can do to stop things going wrong. It consists of four broad activities: understanding what failures could occur, preventing failures occurring, minimizing the negative consequences of failure (called 'mitigation') and recovering from failures when they do occur.

WHAT ARE THE KEY ELEMENTS OF OPERATIONS IMPROVEMENT?

★ There are many 'elements' that are the building blocks of improvement approaches. These include: using improvement cycles, having a process perspective, stressing evidence-based problem solving, being customer-centric, using systems and procedures, reducing process variation, synchronizing flow, emphasizing education/training, using perfection as a goal, waste identification, including everybody and developing internal customer-supplier relationships.

WHAT ARE THE BROAD APPROACHES TO IMPROVEMENT?

 What we have called 'the broad approaches to improvement' are relatively coherent collections of some of the 'elements' of improvement. The four most common are: total quality management (TQM), lean, business process re-engineering (BPR) and Six Sigma.

 Total quality management was one of the earliest management 'fashions' and has suffered from a backlash, but the general precepts and principles of TQM are still influential.

 Lean was seen initially as an approach to be used exclusively in manufacturing, but has since become an approach that can also be applied in service operations.

 BPR is a typical example of the radical approach to improvement. It attempts to redesign operations along customer-focused processes, rather than on the traditional functional basis.

 Six Sigma is a disciplined methodology of defining, measuring, analyzing, improving and controlling the quality in every one of an operation's products, processes and transactions – with the ultimate goal of virtually eliminating all defects.

 There are differences between these improvement approaches. Although they use overlapping sets of elements, they each have a different emphasis. They can be positioned on two dimensions: (a) whether the approaches emphasize a gradual, continuous approach to change or a more radical 'breakthrough' change; and (b) whether the approach emphasizes *what* changes should be made or *how* changes should be made.

WHAT TECHNIQUES CAN BE USED FOR IMPROVEMENT?

 Many of the techniques described throughout this text could be considered improvement techniques.

 Techniques often seen as 'improvement techniques' include: scatter diagrams, flow charts, cause–effect diagrams, Pareto diagrams, Why–why analysis and benchmarking.

Problems and applications

All chapters have problems and application questions that will help you practice analyzing operations. They can be answered by reading the chapter. Model answers for the first question can be found on the companion website for this text.

➔ Sophie was sick of her daily commute. "Why", she thought "should I have to spend so much time in the morning stuck in traffic listening to some babbling half-wit on the radio? We can work flexi-time after all. Perhaps I should leave the apartment at some other time?" So resolved, Sophie deliberately varied her time of departure from her usual 8.30. Also, being an organized soul, she recorded her time of departure each day and her journey time. Her records are shown in Table 11.1.

    a) Draw a scatter diagram that will help Sophie decide on the best time to leave her apartment.

    b) How much time per (5-day) week should she expect to be saved from having to listen to a babbling half-wit?

TABLE 11.1 Sophie's journey times (in minutes)

Day	Leaving time	Journey time	Day	Leaving time	Journey time	Day	Leaving time	Journey time
1	7.15	19	6	8.45	40	11	8.35	46
2	8.15	40	7	8.55	32	12	8.40	45
3	7.30	25	8	7.55	31	13	8.20	47
4	7.20	19	9	7.40	22	14	8.00	34
5	8.40	46	10	8.30	49	15	7.45	27

➔ "Everything we do can be broken down into a process", said Lucile, COO of an outsourcing business for the 'back-office' functions of a range of companies. "It may be more straightforward in a manufacturing business, but the concept of process improvement is just as powerful in service operations. Using this approach, our team of Black Belts has achieved 30 per cent productivity improvements in six months. I think Six Sigma is powerful because it is the process of comparing process outputs against customer requirements. To get processes operating at less than 3.4 defects-per-million-opportunities means that you must strive to get closer to perfection and it is the customer that defines the goal. Measuring defects-per-opportunity means that you can actually compare the process of, say, a human-resources operation with a billing and collection operation."

   a)   What are the benefits of being able to compare the amount of defects in a human-resources process with those of collection or billing?

   b)   Why is achieving defects of less than 3.4 per-million-opportunity seen as important by Lucile?

   c)   What do you think are the benefits and problems of training Black Belts and taking them off their present job to run the improvement projects, rather than the project being run by a member of the team that has responsibility for actually operating the process?

3 ➡ Think back to the last product or service failure that caused you some degree of inconvenience. Draw a cause–effect diagram that identifies all the main causes of why the failure could have occurred. Try and identify the frequency with which such causes happened. This could be done by talking with the staff of the operation that provided the service. Draw a Pareto diagram that indicates the relatively frequency of each cause of failure.

Suggest ways in which the operation could reduce the chances of failure in future.

4 ➡ **Step 1**   As a group, identify a 'high-visibility' operation that you all are familiar with. This could be a type of quick-service restaurant, record store, public transport system, library, etc.

Step 2   Once you have identified the broad class of operation, visit a number of them and use your experience as customers to identify:

   a)   the main performance factors that are of importance to you as customers;

   b)   how each store rates against each other in terms of its performance on these same factors.

Step 3   Draw an importance–performance diagram for one of the operations that indicates the priority they should be giving to improving their performance.

Step 4   Discuss the ways in which such an operation might improve its performance and try to discuss your findings with the staff of the operation.

Want to know more?

Ahlstrom, J. (2015) *How to Succeed with Continuous Improvement: A Primer for Becoming the Best in the World*, New York: McGraw-Hill Professional.

➜ This is very much a practical guide. Slightly evangelical, but it gets the message over.

Goldratt, E.M. and Cox, J. (2004), *The Goal: A Process of Ongoing Improvement*, Farnham, UK: Gower Publishing Limited.

➜ Updated version of a classic.

Hendry, L. and Nonthaleerak, P. (2004) 'Six Sigma: Literature review and key future research areas', working paper, Lancaster University Management School, 2005/044: http://www.lums.lancs.ac.uk/publications/

➜ Good overview of the literature on Six Sigma.

Pande, P.S., Neuman, R.P. and Cavanagh, R. (2002) *Six Sigma Way Team Field Book: An Implementation Guide for Project Improvement Teams*, New York: McGraw Hill.

➜ An unashamedly practical guide to the Six-Sigma approach.

Simchi-Levi, D. Schmidt, W. and Wei, Y. (2014) 'From superstorms to factory fires: Managing unpredictable supply-chain disruptions,' *Harvard Business Review*, pp. 97–101.

➜ Another practitioner-focused article, looking at the low-probability, high-impact end of the failure continuum.

Quality management

12

Introduction

Quality management has always been an important part of operations management, but was often seen as an essential but 'routine' activity, preventing errors having an impact on customers. Increasingly, quality management is viewed as also having a part to play in how operations improve. Quality management can contribute to improvement by making the changes to operations processes that lead to better outcomes for customers. In fact, in most organizations, quality management is one of the main drivers of improvement. It is also the only one of the five 'operations performance objectives' to have its own dedicated chapter in this text, and partly this is because of its central role in improvement. Some operations managers believe that, in the long run, quality is the most important single factor affecting an organization's performance, relative to its competitors. Figure 12.1 shows where quality management fits into the model of operations activities.

Key questions

What is quality and why is it so important?

What steps lead towards conformance to specification?

What is total quality management (TQM)?

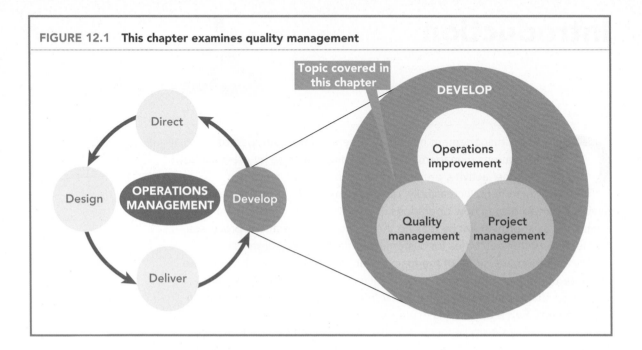

FIGURE 12.1 **This chapter examines quality management**

What is quality and why is it so important?

I t is worth revisiting some of the arguments that were presented in Chapter 2 regarding the benefits of high levels of quality. It will help to explain why quality is seen as being so important by most operations. Figure 12.2 illustrates the various ways in which quality improvements can affect other aspects of operations performance. Revenues can be increased by better sales and enhanced prices in the market. At the same time, costs can be brought down by improved efficiencies, productivity and the use of capital. So, a key task of the operations function must be to ensure that it provides quality goods and services, both to its internal and external customers.

The operation's view of quality

There are many definitions of quality: here, we define it as 'consistent conformance to customers' expectations'. The use of the word 'conformance' implies that there is a need to meet a clear specification. Ensuring a service or product conforms to specification is a key operations task. 'Consistent' implies that conformance to specification is not an ad hoc event, but that the service or product meets the specification because quality requirements are used to design

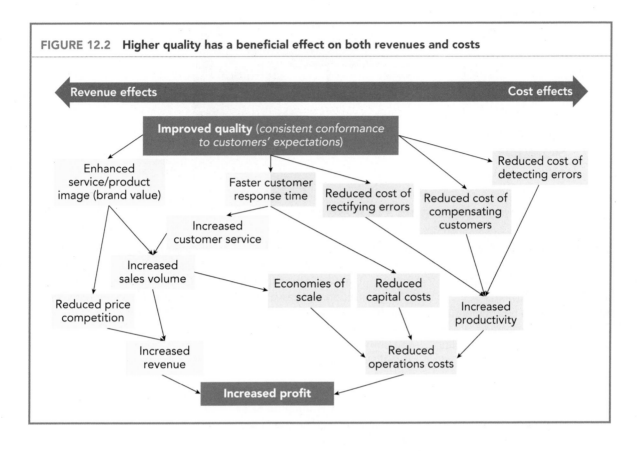

FIGURE 12.2 Higher quality has a beneficial effect on both revenues and costs

and run the processes that produce services or products. The use of 'customers' expectations' recognizes that the service or product must take the views of customers into account, which may be influenced by price. Also note the use of the word 'expectations' in this definition, rather than needs or wants.

Customers' view of quality

Past experiences, individual knowledge and history will all shape customers' expectations. Furthermore, customers may each *perceive* a service or product in different ways. One person may perceive a long-haul flight as an exciting part of a holiday; the person on the next seat may see it as a necessary chore to get to a business meeting. So quality needs to be understood from a customer's point of view because, to the customer, the quality of a particular service or product is whatever he or she perceives it to be. If the passengers on a skiing charter flight perceive it to be of good quality, despite long queues at check-in or cramped seating and poor meals, then the flight really is of good perceived quality.[1] Also, customers may be unable to judge the 'technical' specification of the service or product and so use surrogate measures as a basis for their perception of quality. For example, a customer may find it difficult to judge the technical quality of dental treatment, except that it does not give any more trouble. The customer may therefore perceive quality in terms of the demeanour of the dentist and technician and how they were treated as a patient.

operations principle
Quality is multi-faceted – its individual elements differ for different operations.

Operations in practice

Quality at Victorinox and Four Seasons

Victorinox and the Swiss Army knife[2]

The famous Swiss Army knife is made by the Victorinox Company, which has numerous letters from its customers testifying to its product's quality. For example:"I was installing a new piece of equipment in a sewage treatment plant. The knife slipped out of my hand and fell into the aeration tank. . . that is extremely corrosive to metals. Four years later, I received a small parcel with a note from the supervisor of the

plant. They had emptied the aeration tank and found my knife . . . that was in astonishingly good condition. . . I can assure you that very few products could have survived treatment like this, the components would have dissolved or simply disappeared."

Recently, a major threat to sales is the appearance on the market of fake Swiss Army knives that look similar to the original; they even have the familiar Swiss cross on the handle. So what is

the company's defence against these fakes? "Quality", says CEO Carl Elsener. "We have exhausted all legal means for the brand protection of our popular products. Our best means of protection is quality, which remains unsurpassed and speaks louder than words." It is the 'Victorinox quality-control system' that is at the heart of this defence. This is how it works. First, receiving inspection ensures that incoming materials conform to quality specifications. All alloys are tested for

Reconciling the operation's and the customer's views of quality

The operation's view of quality is concerned with trying to meet customer expectations The customer's view of quality is what he or she *perceives* the service or product to be. To create a unified view, quality can be defined as the degree of fit between customers' expectations and customer perception of the service or product.[4] Using this idea allows us to see the customers' view of quality of (and, therefore, satisfaction with) the service or product as the result of the customers comparing their expectations of the service or product with their perception of how it performs. If the service or product experience was better than expected, then the customer is satisfied and quality is perceived to be high. If the service or product was less than his or her expectations, then quality is low and the customer may be dissatisfied. If the service or product matches expectations then the perceived quality of the service or product is seen to be acceptable. These relationships are summarized in Figure 12.3.

Both customers' expectations and perceptions are influenced by a number of factors, some of which cannot be controlled by the operation and some of composition by means of spectrum analysis. Metallurgical inspection, including an 'edge retention test', uses special equipment to test the ability of the material to retain its edge. During the production of the knives, process control is employed at all stages of the production process. Company employees use it to maintain, implement and improve products and quality procedures, and for continuous, measurable improvement. At the end of the production process, the 'final inspection department' employs 50–60 people who are responsible for ensuring that all products conform to requirements.

Four Seasons, Canary Wharf[3]

The first Four Seasons Hotel opened over 50 years ago and the chain has now grown to 100 properties all over the world. It has won countless awards for the quality of its service, using the same guiding principle: 'to make the quality of our service our competitive advantage'. The company has what it calls its 'Golden Rule': 'Do to others (guests and staff) as you would wish others to do to you'. It is a simple rule, but it guides the whole organization's approach to quality. "Quality service is our distinguishing edge and the company continues to evolve in that direction. We are always looking for better, more creative and innovative ways of serving our guests", says Michael Purtill, the general manager of the Four Seasons Hotel, Canary Wharf, in London. "All employees are empowered to use their creativity and judgment in delivering exceptional service and making their own decisions to enhance our guests' stay. For example, one morning an employee noticed that a guest had a flat tyre on their car and decided on his own accord to change it for them, which was very much appreciated by the guest. At Four Seasons, we believe that our greatest asset and strength are our people. We pay a great deal of attention to selecting the right people with an attitude that takes great pride in delivering exceptional service. Our objective is to exceed guest expectations. We have created an in-house database that is used to record all guest feedback (whether positive or negative). Our 'Guest History' database remains vital in helping us to achieve this. All preferences and specific comments about service experience are logged on the database. Every comment and every preference is discussed and planned for, for every guest, for every visit. It is our culture that sets Four Seasons apart; the drive to deliver the best service in the industry that keeps our guests returning again and again." ● ● ●

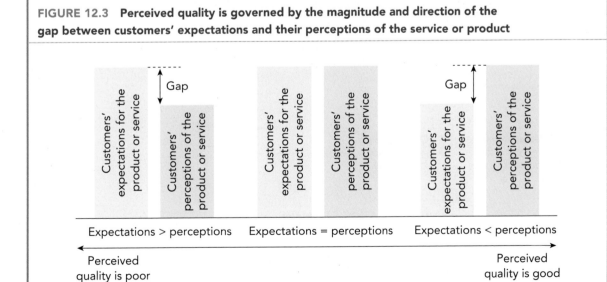

FIGURE 12.3 Perceived quality is governed by the magnitude and direction of the gap between customers' expectations and their perceptions of the service or product

which, to a certain extent, can be managed. Figure 12.4 shows some of the factors that will influence the gap between expectations and perceptions. This model of customer-perceived quality can help us understand how operations can manage quality, and identifies some of the problems in so doing. The bottom part of the diagram represents the operation's 'domain' of quality and the top part the customer's 'domain'. These two domains meet in the actual service or product, which is provided by the organization and experienced by the customer. Within the operation's domain, management is responsible for designing the service or product and providing a specification of the quality to which the service or product has to be created. Within the customer's domain, his or her expectations are shaped by such factors as previous experiences with the particular service or product, the marketing image provided by the organization and word-of-mouth information from other users. These expectations are internalized as a set of quality characteristics.

operations principle
Perceived quality is governed by the magnitude and direction of the gap between customers' expectations and their perceptions of a product or service.

FIGURE 12.4   **The customer's domain and the operation's domain in determining the perceived quality, showing how the gap between customers' expectations and their perception of a service or product could be explained by one or more gaps elsewhere in the model**

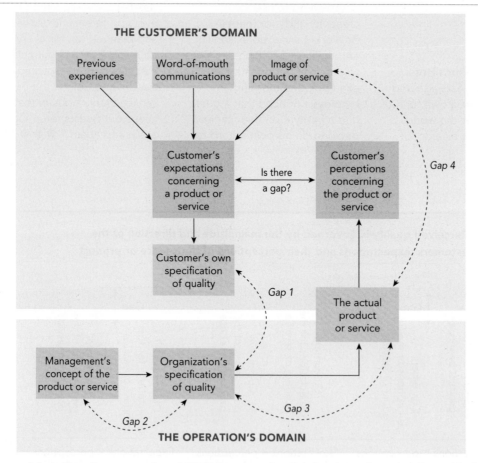

Source: Adapted from Parasuraman, A. et al. (1985) 'A conceptual model of service quality and implications for future research', *Journal of Marketing*, 49, Fall.

Operations in practice

Quality at Magic Moments

Magic Moments is a small but successful wedding photography business. Its owner, Richard Webber, has seen plenty of changes over the last 20 years: "In the past, my job involved taking a few photos during the wedding ceremony and then formal group shots outside. I was rarely at a wedding for more than two hours. Clients would select around 30 photos to go in a standard wedding album. It was important to get the photos right, because that was really the only thing I was judged on. Now it's different. I usually spend all day at a wedding, and sometimes late into the evening as well. This creates a very different dynamic with the wedding party, as you're almost like another guest. Whilst the bride and groom are still my primary concern, other guests at the wedding are also important. The challenge is to find the right balance between getting the best photos possible whilst being as discreet as possible. I could spend hours getting the perfect picture, but annoy everyone in the process. It's difficult, because clients judge you on both the technical quality of your work and the way you interact with everyone on the day. The product has changed too. Clients receive a memory stick with around 500 photos taken during the day. Also I can give them a choice of 10 albums in different sizes, ranging from 30–100 photos. This year, I have started offering photo books, which allow a much greater level of customization and have proved popular with younger couples. For the future, I'm considering offering albums with wedding items such as invitations, confetti and menus; and individual paintings created from photographs. Obviously I would have to outsource the paintings. I'm also going to upgrade our website, so wedding guests can order photos and related products online. This will generate revenue and act as a good marketing tool. My anxiety is that advertising this additional service at the wedding will be seen as being too commercial, even if it's actually of benefit to guests.

One of the biggest problems for the business is the high level of demand in the summer months. Weekends in June, July and August are often booked up two years in advance. One option is to take on additional photographers during busy periods. However, the best ones are busy themselves. The concern is that the quality of the service I offer would deteriorate. A large part of the business is about how one relates to clients and that's hard to replicate. Having been to so many weddings, I often offer clients advice on various aspects of their wedding, such as locations, bands, caterers, and florists. Wedding planning is clearly an area that could be profitable to the business. Of course, another option is to move beyond weddings into other areas, such as school photos, birthdays, celebrations or studio work." ● ● ●

How can quality problems be diagnosed?[5]

Figure 12.4 also shows how quality problems can be diagnosed. If the perceived quality gap is such that customers' perceptions of the service or product fail to match their expectations of it, then the reason (or reasons) must lie in other gaps elsewhere in the model, as follows.

Gap 1: The customer's specification–operation's specification gap   Perceived quality could be poor because there may be a mismatch between the organization's own internal quality specification and the specification that is expected by the customer. For example, a car may be designed to need servicing every 10,000 kilometres, but the customer may expect 15,000-kilometre service intervals.

Gap 2: The concept–specification gap   Perceived quality could be poor because there is a mismatch between the service or product concept (see Chapter 5) and the way the organization has specified quality internally. For example, the concept of a car might have been for an inexpensive, energy-efficient means of transportation, but the inclusion of a climate control system may have both added to its cost and made it less energy-efficient.

Gap 3: The quality specification–actual quality gap   Perceived quality could be poor because there is a mismatch between actual quality and the internal quality specification (often called 'conformance to specification'). For example, the internal quality specification for a car may be that the gap between its doors and body, when closed, must not exceed 7 mm. However, because of inadequate equipment, the gap in reality is 9 mm.

Gap 4: The actual quality–communicated image gap   Perceived quality could be poor because there is a gap between the organization's external communications or market image and the actual quality delivered to the customer. This may be because the marketing function has set unachievable expectations, or because operations is not capable of the level of quality expected by the customer. For example, an advertising campaign for an airline might show a cabin attendant offering to replace a customer's shirt on which food or drink has been spilt, whereas such a service may not in fact be available should this happen.

What steps lead towards conformance to specification?

Conformance to specification means providing a service or producing a product to its design specification. It is usually seen as the most important contribution that operations management can make to the customer's perception of quality. We shall examine how it can be achieved by describing quality management as six sequential steps. Achieving conformance to specification requires the following steps:

Step 1   Define the quality characteristics of the service or product.
Step 2   Decide how to measure each quality characteristic.
Step 3   Set quality standards for each quality characteristic.

Step 4   Control quality against those standards.
Step 5   Find and correct causes of poor quality.
Step 6   Continue to make improvements.

Step 1 – define the quality characteristics

Much of the 'quality' of a service or product will have been specified in its design and can be summarized by a set of quality characteristics. Table 12.1 shows a list of the quality characteristics that are generally useful. Also, many

TABLE 12.1   **Quality characteristics for an automobile, a bank loan and an air journey**

Quality characteristic	Automobile (Material transformation process)	Bank loan (Information transformation process)	Air journey (Customer transformation process)
Functionality – how well the service or product does its job	Speed, acceleration, fuel consumption, ride quality, road-holding, etc.	Interest rate, terms and conditions	Safety and duration of journey, onboard meals and drinks, car and hotel booking services
Appearance – the sensory characteristics of the service or product: its aesthetic appeal, look, feel, etc.	Aesthetics, shape, finish, door gaps, etc.	Aesthetics of information, website, etc.	Decor and cleanliness of aircraft, lounges and crew
Reliability – the consistency of the product's or service's performance over time	Mean time to failure	Keeping promises (implicit and explicit)	Keeping to the published flight times
Durability – the total useful life of the service or product	Useful life (with repair)	Stability of terms and conditions	Keeping up with trends in the industry
Recovery – the ease with which problems with the service or product can be resolved	Ease of repair	Resolution of service failures	Resolution of service failures
Contact – the nature of the person-to-person contact that might take place	Knowledge and courtesy of sales staff	Knowledge and courtesy of branch and call-centre staff	Knowledge, courtesy and sensitivity of airline staff

services have several elements, each with their own quality characteristics, and to understand the quality characteristics of the whole service it is necessary to understand the individual characteristics within and between each element of the whole service.

Step 2 – decide how to measure each characteristic

These characteristics must be defined in such a way as to enable them to be measured and then controlled. This involves taking a very general quality characteristic, such as 'appearance', and breaking it down, as far as one can, into its constituent elements. 'Appearance' is difficult to measure as such, but 'colour match', 'surface finish' and 'number of visible scratches' are all capable of being described in a more objective manner. They may even be quantifiable. Other quality characteristics pose more difficulty. The 'courtesy' of airline staff, for example, has no objective quantified measure. Yet operations with high customer contact, such as airlines, place a great deal of importance on the need to ensure courtesy in their staff. In cases like this, the operation will have to attempt to measure customer *perceptions* of courtesy.

VARIABLES AND ATTRIBUTES

The measures used by operations to describe quality characteristics are of two types: variables and attributes. Variable measures are those that can be measured on a continuously variable scale (for example, length, diameter, weight or time). Attributes are those that are assessed by judgement and are dichotomous – that is, they have two states (for example, right or wrong, works or does not work, looks OK or not OK). Table 12.2 categorizes some of the measures that might be used for the quality characteristics of the automobile and the airline journey.

Step 3 – set quality standards

When operations managers have identified how any quality characteristic can be measured, they need a quality standard against which it can be checked; otherwise they will not know whether it indicates good or bad performance. The quality standard is that level of quality that defines the boundary between acceptable and unacceptable. Such standards may well be constrained by operational factors, such as the state of technology in the factory, and the cost limits of making the product. At the same time, however, they need to be appropriate to the expectations of customers. But quality judgments can be difficult. If one airline passenger out of every 10,000 complains about the food, is that good because 9,999 passengers out of 10,000 are satisfied? Or is it bad because, if one passenger complains, there must be others who, although dissatisfied, did not bother to complain? And if that level of complaint is similar to other airlines, should it regard its quality as satisfactory?

TABLE 12.2 Variable and attribute measures for quality characteristics

Quality characteristic	Automobile		Airline journey	
	Variable	Attribute	Variable	Attribute
▶ **Functionality**	▶ Acceleration and braking characteristics from test bed	▶ Is the ride quality satisfactory?	▶ Number of journeys that actually arrived at the destination (i.e. didn't crash!)	▶ Was the food acceptable?
▶ **Appearance**	▶ Number of blemishes visible on car	▶ Is the colour to specification?	▶ Number of seats not cleaned satisfactorily	▶ Is the crew dressed smartly?
▶ **Reliability**	▶ Average time between faults	▶ Is the reliability satisfactory?	▶ Proportion of journeys that arrived on time	▶ Were there any complaints?
▶ **Durability**	▶ Life of the car	▶ Is the useful life as predicted?	▶ Number of times service innovations lagged competitors	▶ Generally, is the airline updating its services in a satisfactory manner?
▶ **Recovery**	▶ Time from fault discovered to fault repaired	▶ Is the serviceability of the car acceptable?	▶ Proportion of service failures resolved satisfactorily	▶ Do customers feel that staff deal satisfactorily with complaints?
▶ **Contact**	▶ Level of help provided by sales staff (1 to 5 scale)	▶ Did customers feel well served (yes or no)?	▶ The extent to which customers feel well-treated by staff (1 to 5 scale)	▶ Did customers feel that the staff were helpful (yes or no)?

Step 4 – control quality against those standards

After setting up appropriate standards, the operation will then need to check that the products or services conform to those standards; doing things right, first time, every time. This involves three decisions:

1   Where in the operation should they check that it is conforming to standards?

2   Should they check every service or product or take a sample?

3   How should the checks be performed?

WHERE SHOULD THE CHECKS TAKE PLACE?

At the start of the process, incoming resources may be inspected to make sure that they are to the correct specification. For example, a car manufacturer

Operations in practice

Ryanair's reforms its view of service quality[6]

Ryanair is arguably the best-known, and certainly the most successful, budget airline in Europe, but it was not the first to focus its operations strategy on very low operating costs. The idea was born when Southwest Airlines in the USA, organised its airline operations ruthlessly around providing a low-cost 'no frills' service, it could both grow its customer base and do so profitably. To some extent the strategy included trading off certain aspects of quality of service for reduced costs. Complimentary in-flight services were kept to a minimum, secondary and sometimes less convenient airports were used, and one standard class of travel was offered. But, some critics said that Ryanair went too far in their attitude towards service quality. However, the boss of the airline, Michael O'Leary's policy on customer service was both straightforward and clear. *"Our customer service,"* he said *"is about the most well defined in the world. We guarantee to give you the lowest air fare. You get a safe flight. You get a normally on-time flight. That's the package. We don't, and won't, give you anything more. Are we going to say sorry for our lack of customer service? Absolutely not. If a plane is cancelled, will we put you up in a hotel overnight? Absolutely not. If a plane is delayed, will we give you a voucher for a restaurant? Absolutely not."* And Ryanair's customer satisfaction ratings were high, with over 90% of customers surveyed expressing satisfaction with their overall flight experience, according to the airline. Also, in 2018 also announced their Environmental plan which included a commitment to eliminate all non-recyclable plastics from their operations over a five year period. Yet, said Ryanair, 'while we continue to innovate, the one thing that won't change will be our low fares'.

However, one attempt by Ryanair to cut costs prompted something of a backlash when it was criticised by the UK's Office of Fair Trading (OFT). John Fingleton. The OFT's boss criticized the company for adding extra fees when customers use any but a MasterCard prepaid card to pay for flights. Although within the law, Mr Fingleton was reported as saying that the company were using a legal loophole to justify charging the extra fee., Stephen McNamara, Ryanair's Head of Communications retorted that, *"What the OFT must realise is that passengers prefer Ryanair's model as it allows them to avoid costs, such as baggage charges, which are still included in the high fares of high cost, fuel surcharging.... airlines."* But the backlash against Ryanair's policy continued, perhaps encouraged by the airline's reluctance to apologise, or sometimes even comment. Then, after a drop in their hitherto rapid profit growth and some shareholders voicing concern, Ryanair announced that it was to reform its "abrupt culture, and try to eliminate things that unnecessarily annoy customers". Included in these annoying practices were fines for small luggage size transgressions and an unpopular €70 fee for issuing boarding passes at the airport rather than printing it out at home (it was lowered to €10). Ryanair did insist that such charges had not been money-spinning schemes, but were designed to encourage the type of operational efficiency that kept fairs low, in fact fewer than ten passengers a day had to pay for forgotten boarding passes. ●●●

will check that components are of the right specification. A university will screen applicants to try to ensure that they have a high chance of getting through the programme. During the process, checks may take place before a particularly costly process, prior to 'difficult to check', immediately after a process with a high defective rate, before potential damage or distress might be caused, and so on. Checks may also take place after the process itself, to ensure that customers do not experience non-conformance.

CHECK EVERY PRODUCT AND SERVICE, OR TAKE A SAMPLE?

While it might seem ideal to check every single service or product, a sample may be more practical for a number of reasons:

 It might be dangerous to inspect everything. A doctor, for example, checks just a small sample of blood rather than taking all of a patient's blood! The characteristics of this sample are taken to represent those of the rest of the patient's blood.

 Checking everything might destroy the product or interfere with the service. Not every light bulb is checked for how long it lasts as it would destroy every bulb. Waiters do not check that customers are enjoying the meal every 30 seconds.

 Checking everything can be time-consuming and costly. It may not be feasible to check all output from a high-volume machine or to check the feelings of every bus commuter every day.

Also, 100 per cent checking may not guarantee that all defects will be identified. Sometimes it is intrinsically difficult. For example, although a physician may undertake the correct testing procedure, he or she may not necessarily diagnose a (real) disease. Nor is it easy to notice everything. For example, try counting the number of 'e's on this page. Count them again and see if you get the same score.

TYPE I AND TYPE II ERRORS

Although it reduces checking time, using a sample to make a decision about quality does have its own inherent problems. Like any decision activity, we may get the decision wrong. Take the example of a pedestrian waiting to cross a street. He or she has two main decisions: whether to continue waiting, or to cross. If there is a satisfactory break in the traffic and the pedestrian crosses, then a correct decision has been made. Similarly, if that person continues to wait because the traffic is too dense, then he or she has again made a correct decision. There are two types of incorrect decisions or errors, however. One incorrect decision would be if he or she decides to cross when there is not an adequate break in the traffic, resulting in an accident – this is referred to as a type I error. Another incorrect decision would occur if he or she decides not to cross, even though there was an adequate gap in the traffic – this is called a type II error. In crossing the road, therefore, there are four outcomes, which are summarized in Table 12.3.

TABLE 12.3   **Type I and type II errors for a pedestrian crossing the road**

| Decision | Road conditions | |
	Unsafe	Safe
▶ **Cross**	▶ Type I error	▶ Correct decision
▶ **Wait**	▶ Correct decision	▶ Type II error

Type I errors are those that occur when a decision is made to do something and the situation did not warrant it. Type II errors are those that occur when nothing was done, yet a decision to do something should have been taken as the situation did indeed warrant it. For example, if a school's inspector checks the work of a sample of 20 out of 1,000 pupils and all 20 of the pupils in the sample have failed, the inspector might draw the conclusion that all the pupils in the school have failed. In fact, the sample just happened to contain 20 out of the 50 students who had failed the course. The inspector, by assuming a high fail rate, would be making a type I error. Alternatively, if the inspector checked 20 pieces of work, all of which were of a high standard, he or she might conclude that all the pupils' work was good despite having been given, or having chosen, the only pieces of good work in the whole school. This would be a type II error. Although these situations are not likely, they are possible. Therefore, any sampling procedure has to be aware of these risks.

HOW SHOULD THE CHECKS BE PERFORMED?

In practice, most operations will use some form of sampling to check the quality of their services or products. The most common approach for checking the quality of a sample service or product so as to make inferences about all the output from an operation is called statistical process control (SPC). SPC is concerned with sampling the process during the production of the goods or the delivery of service. Based on this sample, decisions are made as to whether the process is 'in control' – that is, operating as it should be. The value of the SPC is not just to make checks of a single sample, but to monitor quality over a period of time. It does this by using 'control charts' to see if the process seems to be performing as it should, or alternatively if it is 'out of control'. If the process does seem to be going 'out of control' then steps can be taken *before* there is a problem. Figure 12.5, or something like it, could be found in almost any operation. The chart could, for example, represent the percentage of customers, within a sample of a thousand, who each month were dissatisfied with a restaurant service. While the amount of dissatisfaction may be acceptably small, management should be concerned that it has been increasing over time, and may wish to investigate why this is so. In this case, the control chart is plotting an attribute measure of quality (satisfied or not). Looking for trends is an important use of control charts. If the trend suggests the process is getting steadily worse, then it will be worth investigating the process. Even if the trend is improving, it may still be worth investigating to try and identify why.

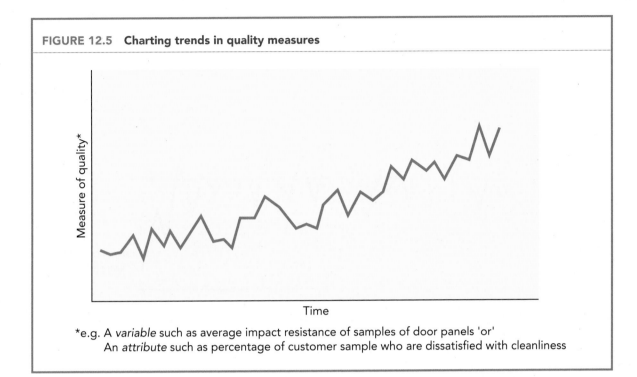

FIGURE 12.5 Charting trends in quality measures

*e.g. A *variable* such as average impact resistance of samples of door panels 'or'
An *attribute* such as percentage of customer sample who are dissatisfied with cleanliness

COMMON CAUSES OF VARIABILITY

In addition to looking at trends in quality performance, a key aspect of SPC is that it looks at the variability in performance. Look again at Figure 12.5; it showed an upwards trend, but the trend was neither steady nor smooth – it varied, sometimes up, sometimes down. All processes vary to some extent, so it is not surprising that measures of quality will also vary. So-called 'natural' variations, which derive from *common causes,* can never be entirely eliminated (although they can be reduced). For example, if a machine is filling boxes with rice, it will not place *exactly* the same weight of rice in every box it fills. When the filling machine is in a stable condition (that is, no exceptional factors are influencing its behaviour), each box could be weighed and a histogram of the weights could be built up. Usually this type of variation can be described by normal distribution, with 99.7 per cent of the variation lying within ±3 standard deviations. The obvious question for any operations manager would be: 'is this variation in the process performance acceptable?' The answer will depend on the acceptable range of weights that can be tolerated by the operation. The range is called the *specification range.* If the weight of rice in the boxes is too small then the organization might infringe labelling regulations; if it is too large, the organization is giving away too much of its product for free.

operations principle
A key objective of statistical process control is to check whether the process is operating as it should do (known as the process being 'in control').

ASSIGNABLE CAUSES OF VARIABILITY

Not all variation in processes is the result of common causes. There may be something wrong with the process that is assignable to a particular and preventable cause: equipment may have been set up badly, or an untrained

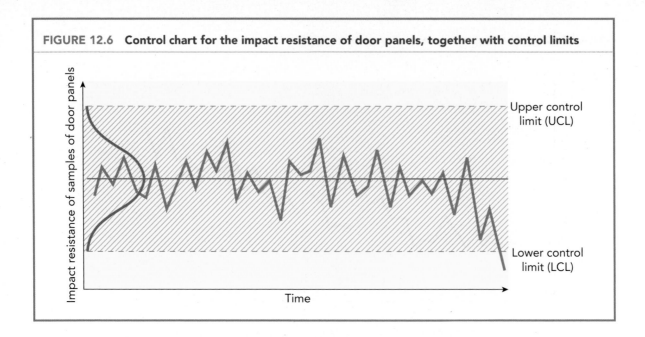

FIGURE 12.6   Control chart for the impact resistance of door panels, together with control limits

person may not be following prescribed procedures. The causes of such variation are called *assignable causes*. The question is whether the results from any particular sample, when plotted on the control chart, simply represent the variation due to common causes or due to some specific, and correctable, *assignable* cause. Figure 12.6, for example, shows the control chart for the average impact resistance of samples of door panels taken over time. Like any process, the results vary, but the last three points seem to be lower than usual. So, is this is natural (common cause) variation, or the symptom of some more serious (assignable) cause?

To help make this decision, control limits can be added to the control chart (the red dotted lines) that indicate the expected extent of 'common-cause' variation. If any points lie outside these control limits (the shaded zone), then the process can be deemed 'out of control' in the sense that variation is likely to be due to assignable causes. These control limits could be set intuitively, but they can also be set in a more statistically revealing manner. For example, if the process that tests door panels had been measured to determine the normal distribution that represents its common-cause variation, then control limits can be based on this distribution. Figure 12.6 also shows how control limits can be added; here, put at ± 3 standard deviations (of the population of sample means) away from the mean of sample averages. It shows that the probability of the final point on the chart being influenced by an assignable cause is very high indeed. When the process is exhibiting behaviour that is outside its normal 'common-cause' range, it is said to be 'out of control'. Yet there is a small but finite chance that the (seemingly out-of-limits) point is just one of the rare but natural results at the tail of the distribution that describes perfectly normal behaviour. Stopping the process under these circumstances would represent a type I error, because the process is actually in control. Alternatively, ignoring a result that in reality is due to an assignable cause is a type II error.

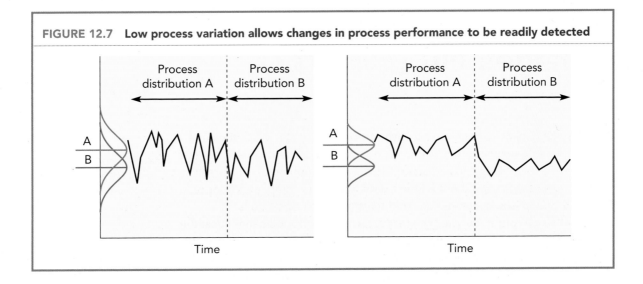

FIGURE 12.7 Low process variation allows changes in process performance to be readily detected

WHY VARIABILITY IS A BAD THING

Assignable variation is a signal that something has changed in the process, which therefore must be investigated. But normal variation is itself a problem because it masks any changes in process behaviour. Figure 12.7 shows the performance of two processes, both of which are subjected to a change in their process behaviour at the same time. The process on the left has such a wide natural variation that it is not immediately apparent that any change has taken place. Eventually, it will become apparent because the likelihood of process performance violating the lower (in this case) control limit has increased, but this may take some time. By contrast, the process on the right has a far narrower band of natural variation. Because of this, the same change in average performance is more easily noticed (both visually and statistically). So, the narrower the natural variation of a process, the more obvious are changes in the behaviour of that process. And the more obvious are process changes, the easier it is to understand how and why the process is behaving in a particular way. Accepting any variation in any process is, to some degree, admitting to ignorance of how that process works.

operations principle
High levels of variation reduce the ability to detect changes in process performance.

Steps 5 and 6 – find and correct causes of poor quality and continue to make improvements

The final two steps in our list of quality management activities are, in some ways, the most important, yet also the most difficult. They also blend into the general area of operations improvement, covered in the previous chapter. Nevertheless, there is an aspect of quality management that has been particularly important in shaping how quality is improved and the improvement activity made self-sustaining. This is total quality management (TQM). The remainder of the main body of this chapter is devoted to TQM.

What is total quality management (TQM)?

Total quality management (TQM) was one of the earliest of the current wave of management 'fashions'. Its peak of popularity was in the late 1980s and early '90s. It has suffered from something of a backlash in recent years and there is little doubt that many companies adopted TQM in the simplistic belief that it would transform their operations performance overnight. Yet the general precepts and principles that constitute TQM are still the dominant mode of organizing operations improvement. The approach we take here is to stress the importance of the 'total' in total quality management and how it can guide the agenda for improvement.

TQM as an extension of previous practice

TQM can be viewed as a logical extension of the way in which quality-related practice has progressed (see Figure 12.8). Originally, quality was achieved by inspection – screening-out defects before they were noticed by customers.

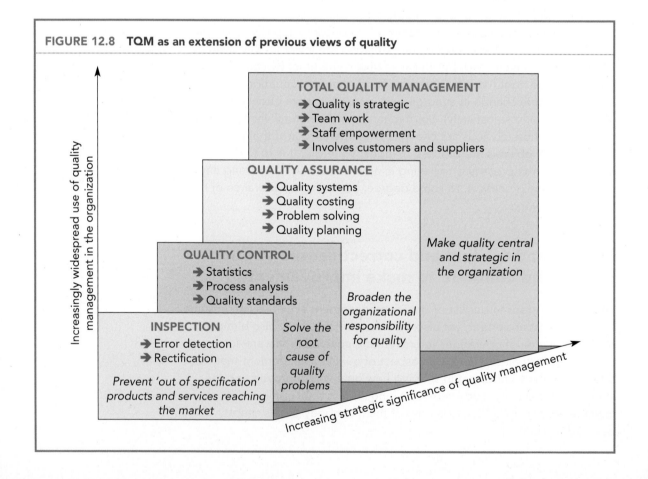

FIGURE 12.8   TQM as an extension of previous views of quality

The quality control (QC) concept developed a more systematic approach to not only detecting but also treating quality problems. Quality assurance (QA) widened the responsibility for quality to include functions other than direct operations. It also made increasing use of more sophisticated statistical quality techniques. TQM included much of what went before, but developed its own distinctive themes to make quality both more strategic and more widespread in the organization. We will use some of these themes to describe how TQM represents a clear shift from traditional approaches to quality.

The principles of TQM

TQM is 'an effective system for integrating the quality development, quality maintenance and quality improvement efforts of the various groups in an organization so as to enable production and service at the most economical levels which allow for full customer satisfaction'.[7] However, it was the Japanese who first made the concept work on a wide scale, and subsequently popularized the approach and the term 'TQM'. It was then developed further by several so-called 'quality gurus'. Each 'guru' stressed a different set of issues, from which emerged the TQM approach. It is best thought of as a philosophy of how to approach quality improvement. This philosophy, above everything, stresses the 'total' of TQM. It is an approach that puts quality at the heart of everything that is done by an operation and includes all activities within an operation. This totality can be summarized by the way TQM lays particular stress on the following:

 meeting the needs and expectations of customers;

 covering all parts of the organization;

 including every person in the organization;

 examining all costs that are related to quality, especially failure costs, and getting things 'right first time';

 developing the systems and procedures that support quality and improvement;

 developing a continuous process of improvement.

Not surprisingly, several researchers have tried to establish how much of a relationship there is between adopting total quality management and the performance of the organization. One of the best known studies[8] found that there was a positive relationship between the extent to which companies implement TQM and their overall performance. It found that TQM practices did indeed have a direct effect on operating performance, but managers should implement TQM as a whole set of ideas rather than simply picking a few techniques to implement. The same study also suggests that where TQM does not prove successful in improving performance, the problems could be the result of poor implementation rather than in the TQM practices themselves, and that a serious commitment on the part of top management to TQM is a prerequisite for success.

TQM means meeting the needs and expectations of customers

Earlier in this chapter, we defined quality as 'consistent conformance to customers' expectations'. Therefore, any approach to quality management must necessarily include the customer perspective. In TQM, this customer perspective is particularly important. It may be referred to as 'customer-centricity' (discussed briefly in Chapter 11) or the 'voice of the customer'. However it is called, TQM stresses the importance of starting with an insight into customer needs, wants, perceptions and preferences. This can then be translated into quality objectives and used to drive quality improvement.

TQM means covering all parts of the organization

For an organization to be truly effective, every single part of it, each department, each activity and each person at each level, must work properly together, because every person and every activity affects and in turn is affected by others. One of the most powerful concepts that has emerged from various improvement approaches is the concept of the internal customer/supplier. This is recognition that everyone is a customer within the organization and consumes goods or services provided by other internal suppliers, and everyone is also an internal supplier of goods and services for other internal customers. The implication of this is that errors in the service provided within an organization will eventually affect the service or product that reaches the external customer.

> **operations principle**
> An appreciation of, involvement in and commitment to quality should permeate the entire organization.

SERVICE-LEVEL AGREEMENTS

Some organizations bring a degree of formality to the internal customer concept by encouraging (or requiring) different parts of the operation to agree service-level agreements (SLAs) with each other. SLAs are formal definitions of the dimensions of service and the relationship between two parts of an organization. The type of issues that would be covered by such an agreement could include response times, the range of services, dependability of service supply and so on. Boundaries of responsibility and appropriate performance measures could also be agreed. For example, an SLA between an information systems support unit and a research unit in the laboratories of a large company could define such performance measures as:

 the types of information network services that may be provided as 'standard';

 the range of special information services that may be available at different periods of the day;

 the minimum 'up time' – that is, the proportion of time the system will be available at different periods of the day;

 the maximum response time and average response time to get the system fully operational should it fail;

 the maximum response time to provide 'special' services.

Operations in practice

Fat finger syndrome[9]

Feeling sleepy one day, a German bank worker briefly fell asleep on his keyboard when processing a €64 debit (withdrawal) from a pensioner's account, repeatedly pressing the number 2. The result was that the pensioner's account had €222 million withdrawn from it instead of the intended €64. Fortunately, the bank spotted the error before too much damage was done (and before the account-holder noticed). More seriously, the supervisor who should have checked his junior colleague's work was sacked for failing to notice the blunder (unfairly, a German labour tribunal later ruled). It is known as 'fat finger syndrome' – used to describe a person who makes keyboard errors when chatting, tired or overstressed. For some people, such as traders working in fast-moving electronic financial markets, if they press the wrong button on their keyboard it means a potential fortune could be lost.

Fat-finger trading mistakes are not uncommon. In 2009, Swiss bank UBS mistakenly ordered 3 trillion yen (instead of 30 million yen) of bonds in a Japanese video games firm. In 2005 a Japanese trader tried to sell one share of a recruitment company at 610,000 yen per share. But he accidentally sold 610,000 shares at one yen each, despite this being 41 times the number of shares available. Unlike the German example, the error was not noticed and the Tokyo Stock Exchange processed the order. It resulted in Mizuho Securities losing 27 billion yen. The head of the Exchange later resigned. But what is believed to be the biggest fat-finger error on record occurred in 2014, when share trades worth more than the size of Sweden's economy had to be cancelled in Tokyo. The error briefly sparked panic after a trader accidentally entered a trade worth nearly 68 trillion yen in several of the Asian country's largest blue-chip companies. The Japan Securities Dealers Association said the trader had, in error, put together the volume and price of a series of transactions instead of the volume alone. However, the transactions were cancelled 17 minutes after they were made and no permanent (financial) damage was done. ● ● ●

TQM means including every person in the organization

Every person in the organization has the potential to contribute to quality, and TQM was among the first approaches to stress the centrality of harnessing everyone's potential contribution to quality. There is scope for creativity and innovation, even in relatively routine activities, claim TQM proponents. The shift in attitude that is needed to view employees as the most valuable intellectual and creative resource that the organization possesses can still prove difficult for some organizations. Yet most advanced organizations do recognize that quality problems are almost always the result of human error.

TQM means all costs of quality are considered

The costs of controlling quality may not be small, whether the responsibility lies with each individual or a dedicated quality-control department. It is therefore necessary to examine all the costs and benefits associated with quality (in fact, 'cost of quality' is usually taken to refer to both costs and benefits of quality). These costs of quality are usually categorized as prevention costs, appraisal costs, internal failure costs and external failure costs.

Prevention costs are those costs incurred in trying to prevent problems, failures and errors from occurring in the first place. They include such things as:
- identifying potential problems and putting the process right before poor quality occurs;
- designing and improving the design of products and services and processes to reduce quality problems;
- training and development of personnel in the best way to perform their jobs;
- process control through SPC.

Appraisal costs are those costs associated with controlling quality to check to see if problems or errors have occurred during and after the creation of the service or product. They might include such things as:
- the setting up of statistical acceptance sampling plans;
- the time and effort required to inspect inputs, processes and outputs;
- obtaining processing inspection and test data;
- investigating quality problems and providing quality reports;
- conducting customer surveys and quality audits.

Internal failure costs are failure costs associated with errors that are dealt with inside the operation. These costs might include such things as:
- the cost of scrapped parts and materials;
- reworked parts and materials;
- the lost production time as a result of coping with errors;
- lack of concentration due to time spent troubleshooting rather than improvement.

External failure costs are those that are associated with an error going out of the operation to a customer. These costs include such things as:
- loss of customer goodwill affecting future business;
- aggrieved customers who may take up time;
- litigation (or payments to avoid litigation);
- guarantee and warranty costs;
- the cost to the company of providing excessive capability (too much coffee in the pack, or too much information to a client).

THE RELATIONSHIP BETWEEN QUALITY COSTS

In traditional quality management, it was assumed that failure costs reduce as the money spent on appraisal and prevention increases. Furthermore, it was assumed that there is an *optimum* amount of quality effort to be applied in

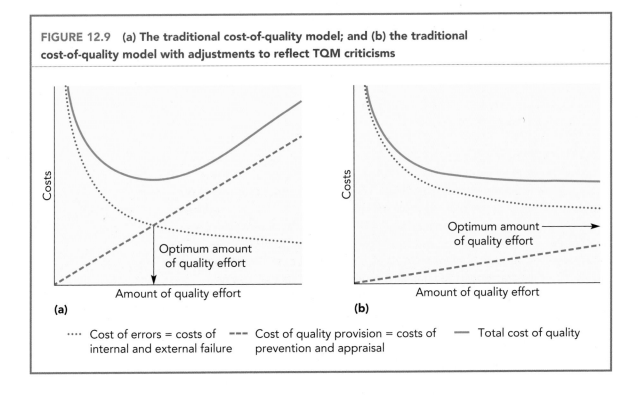

FIGURE 12.9 (a) The traditional cost-of-quality model; and (b) the traditional cost-of-quality model with adjustments to reflect TQM criticisms

(a)

(b)

Costs

Optimum amount of quality effort

Amount of quality effort

Optimum amount of quality effort

Amount of quality effort

···· Cost of errors = costs of internal and external failure   --- Cost of quality provision = costs of prevention and appraisal   — Total cost of quality

any situation, which minimizes the total costs of quality. The argument is that there must be a point beyond which diminishing returns set in – that is, the cost of improving quality gets larger than the benefits that it brings. Figure 12.9 (a) sums up this idea. As quality effort is increased, the costs of providing the effort – through extra quality controllers, inspection procedures and so on – increases proportionally. At the same time, however, the cost of errors, faulty products and so on decreases because there are fewer of them. However, TQM proponents believe that this logic is flawed. First, it implies that failure and poor quality are acceptable. Why, TQM proponents argue, should any operation accept the *inevitability* of errors? Some occupations seem to be able to accept a zero-defect standard. No one accepts that pilots are allowed to crash a certain proportion of their aircraft, or that nurses will drop a certain proportion of the babies they deliver. Second, it assumes that costs are known and measurable. In fact, putting realistic figures to the cost of quality is not a straightforward matter. Third, it is argued that failure costs in the traditional model are greatly underestimated. In particular, all the management time wasted by failures and the loss of concentration it causes are rarely accounted for. Fourth, it implies that prevention costs are inevitably high because it involves expensive inspection. But why should not quality be an integral part of everyone's work, rather than employing extra people to inspect? Finally, the 'optimum-quality level' approach, by accepting compromise, does little to challenge operations managers and staff to find ways of improving quality. Put these corrections into the optimum-quality effort calculation and the picture looks very different (see Figure 12.9 b). If there is an 'optimum', it is a lot further to the right, in the direction of putting more effort (but not necessarily cost) into quality.

operations principle
Effective investment in preventing quality errors can significantly reduce appraisal and failure costs.

THE TQM QUALITY-COST MODEL

TQM rejects the optimum-quality level concept and strives to reduce all known and unknown failure costs by preventing errors and failure taking place. Rather than looking for 'optimum' levels of quality effort, TQM stresses the relative balance between different types of quality cost. Of the four cost categories, two (costs of prevention and costs of appraisal) are open to managerial influence, while the other two (internal costs of failure and external costs of failure) show the consequences of changes in the first two. Rather than placing most emphasis on appraisal (so that 'bad products and service don't get through to the customer'), TQM emphasizes prevention (to stop errors happening in the first place). That is because the more effort that is put into error prevention, the more internal and external failure costs are reduced. Then, once confidence has been firmly established, appraisal costs can also be reduced. Eventually, even prevention costs can be stepped down in absolute terms, though prevention remains a significant cost in relative terms. Figure 12.10 illustrates this idea. Initially, total quality costs may rise as investment in some aspects of prevention – mainly training – is increased. However, a reduction in total costs can quickly follow.

GETTING THINGS 'RIGHT FIRST TIME'

Accepting the relationships between categories of quality cost, as illustrated in Figure 12.10, has a particularly important implication for how quality is managed. It shifts the emphasis from *reactive* (waiting for something to happen) to *proactive* (doing something before anything happens). This change in the view of quality costs has come about with a movement from an inspect-in (appraisal-driven) approach to a design-in (getting it right first time) approach.

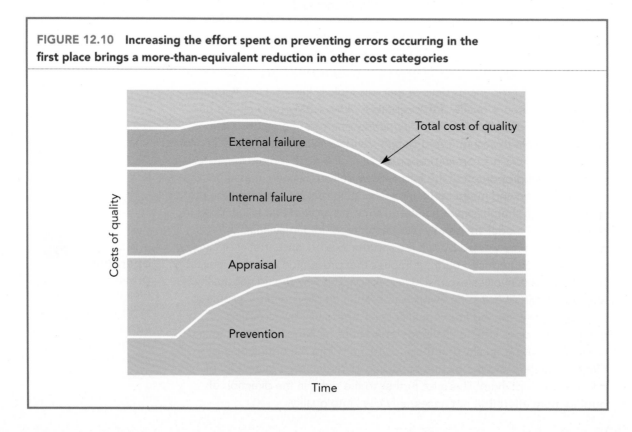

FIGURE 12.10   **Increasing the effort spent on preventing errors occurring in the first place brings a more-than-equivalent reduction in other cost categories**

TQM means developing the systems and procedures that support quality and improvement

The emphasis on highly formalized systems and procedures to support TQM has declined in recent years, yet one aspect is still active for many companies. This is the adoption of the ISO 9000 standard. And although, ISO 9000 can be regarded as a stand-alone issue, it is very closely associated with TQM.

THE ISO 9000 APPROACH

The ISO 9000 series is a family of standards compiled by the International Organization for Standardization (ISO), which is the world's largest developer and publisher of international standards, based in Geneva, Switzerland. According to the ISO, 'the standards represent an international consensus on good quality management practices. It consists of standards and guidelines relating to quality management systems and related supporting standards.'

The ISO illustrates the benefits of the standard as follows: 'Without satisfied customers, an organization is in peril! To keep customers satisfied, the organization needs to meet their requirements. The ISO 9001:2008 standard provides a tried-and-tested framework for taking a systematic approach to managing the organization's processes so that they consistently turn out product that satisfies customers' expectations.'[10] In addition, it is also seen as providing benefits both to the organizations adopting it (because it gives them detailed guidance on how to design their control procedures) and especially to customers (who have the assurance of knowing that the products and services they purchase are produced by an operation working to a defined standard). Further, it may also provide a useful discipline to stick to 'sensible', process-orientated procedures, which lead to error reduction, reduced customer complaints and reduced costs of quality, and may even identify existing procedures that are not necessary and can be eliminated. Moreover, gaining the certificate demonstrates that the company takes quality seriously; it therefore has a marketing benefit.

THE EFQM EXCELLENCE MODEL

Over 20 years ago, Western European companies formed the European Foundation for Quality Management (EFQM). Since then, the importance of quality excellence has become far more accepted. According to the EFQM, 'Whilst there are numerous management tools and techniques commonly used, the EFQM Excellence Model provides a holistic view of the organization and it can be used to determine how these different methods fit together and complement each other. The Model. . . [is] . . . an overarching framework for developing sustainable excellence. Excellent organizations achieve and sustain outstanding levels of performance that meet or exceed the expectations of all their stakeholders. The EFQM Excellence Model allows people to understand the cause-and-effect relationships between what their organization does and the results it achieves.'[11]

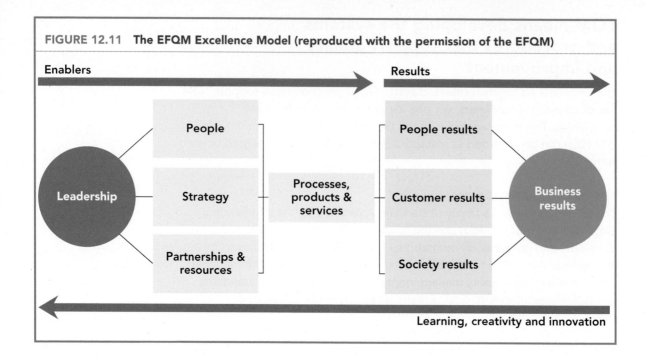

FIGURE 12.11   **The EFQM Excellence Model (reproduced with the permission of the EFQM)**

The model is based on the idea that it is important to understand the cause-and-effect relationships between what an organization does (what it terms 'the Enablers'), and the 'Results' it achieves. The EFQM Excellence Model is shown in Figure 12.11. There are five enablers:

1   **Leadership** that looks to the future, acts as a role model for values and ethics, inspires trust, is flexible, enables anticipation and so can react in a timely manner.

2   **Strategy** that implements the organization's mission and vision by developing and deploying a stakeholder-focused strategy.

3   **People** who should be valued by their organizations, creating a culture that allows mutually beneficial achievement of both organizational and personal goals, develops the capabilities of people, promotes fairness and equality, cares for, communicates, rewards and recognizes people, in a way that motivates and builds commitment.

4   **Partnership and resources** such as external partnerships, suppliers and internal resources that organizations should plan and manage in order to support strategy and policies and the effective operation of processes.

5   **Processes, products and services** that organizations should design, manage and improve to ensure value for customers and other stakeholders.

Results are assessed using four criteria. They are:

1   **Customer results** meeting or exceeding the needs and expectations of customers.

2   **People results** meeting or exceeding the needs and expectations of employees.

3   **Society results** achieving and sustaining results that meet or exceed the needs and expectations of the relevant stakeholders within society.

4   **Business results** achieving and sustaining results that meet or exceed the needs and expectations of business stakeholders.

Summary answers to key questions

Each chapter has a 'Summary answers to key questions' section. Use it to check your understanding of the issues covered in the chapter.

WHAT IS QUALITY AND WHY IS IT SO IMPORTANT?

★ Quality is defined here as 'consistent conformance to customers' expectations'. It is important because it has a significant impact on profitability.

★ Quality can be modelled as the gap between customers' expectations concerning the service or product and their perceptions of it. This allows the gap to be explained by four other gaps (customer's specification vs operation's specification; concept vs specification; quality specification vs actual quality; and actual quality vs communicated image).

WHAT STEPS LEAD TOWARDS CONFORMANCE TO SPECIFICATION?

★ There are six steps: define quality characteristics; decide how to measure each of the quality characteristics; set quality standards for each characteristic; control quality against these standards; find and correct the causes of poor quality; and continue to make improvements.

★ Most quality planning and control involves sampling performance, but sampling can give rise to errors, classed as either type I or type II errors. Type I errors involve making corrections where none are needed. Type II errors involve not making corrections where they are, in fact, needed.

★ Statistical process control (SPC) involves using control charts to track the performance of quality characteristics. The power of SPC lies in its ability to set control limits derived from the statistics of the natural variation of processes.

★ Process control charts allow operations managers to distinguish between the 'normal' variation inherent in any process and the variations that could be caused by the process going 'out of control'.

WHAT IS TOTAL QUALITY MANAGEMENT (TQM)?

 TQM is 'an effective system for integrating the quality development, quality maintenance and quality improvement efforts of the various groups in an organization so as to enable production and service at the most economical levels which allow for full customer satisfaction'.

 It is best thought of as a philosophy that stresses the 'total' of TQM and puts quality at the heart of everything that is done by an operation.

 'Total' in TQM means: meeting all the needs and expectations of customers; covering all parts of the organization, including every person in the organization; examining all costs that are related to quality; getting things 'right first time'; and developing the systems and procedures that support quality and improvement.

Problems and applications

All chapters have problems and application questions that will help you practice analyzing operations. They can be answered by reading the chapter. Model answers for the first question can be found on the companion website for this text.

1   → Human error is a significant source of quality problems. Think through the times that you have (with hindsight) made an error, and answer the following questions.

   a)   How do you think that human error causes quality problems?
   b)   What could one do to minimize human error?

2   → Re-read the 'Operations in practice' box, 'Quality at Magic Moments'.

   a)   How has the business changed over time?
   b)   What do you think are the key quality challenges facing the business?
   c)   What do you think should be done to ensure the business maintains quality levels in the future?

3   → Re-read the 'Operations in practice box', 'Ryanair reforms its view of service quality'. What does this example tell us about the trade-off between service quality and cost?

4   → Understanding type I and type II errors is essential for a surgeon's quality planning. In appendectomy operations, for example, removal of the appendix is necessary because of the risk of it bursting, causing potentially fatal poisoning of the blood. The surgical procedure is a relatively simple operation, but there is always a small risk with any invasive surgery. It is also expensive; in the USA it costs around $4,500 per operation. Unfortunately, appendicitis is difficult to identify, and diagnosis is only 10 per cent accurate. However, a new technique claims to be able to identify 100 per cent of true appendicitis cases prior to surgery. The new technique costs less than $250, which means that one single avoided surgery pays for around 20 of these tests.

   a)   How does this new test change the likelihood of type I and type II errors?
   b)   Why is this important?

Want to know more?

ASQ Quality Press (2010) *Seven Basic Quality Tools*, Milwaukee, WI: ASQ Quality Press.

➜ Very much a 'how to do it' handbook.

Dale, B.G., van der Wiele, T. and van Iwaarden, J. (2007) *Managing Quality*, 5th edition, Hoboken, NJ: Wiley-Blackwell.

➜ This is the latest version of a long-established, comprehensive and authoritative text.

Garvin, D.A. (1988) *Managing Quality*, New York: Free Press.

➜ Somewhat dated now, but relates to our discussion at the beginning of this chapter.

Goetsch, D.L. and Davis, S. (2013) *Quality Management for Organizational Excellence: Introduction to Total Quality*, 7th edition, Harlow, UK: Pearson Education.

➜ Up-to-date account of the topic.

Oakland, J.S. (2014) *Total Quality Management and Operational Excellence: Text with Cases*, 4th edition, London: Routledge.

➜ A classic text from one of the founders of TQM in Europe.

Webber, L. (2007) *Quality Control For Dummies*, Hoboken, NJ: John Wiley & Sons.

➜ Not just for dummies (though they might like it too).

Project management

13

Introduction

In this chapter, we are concerned with the management of 'projects'. Projects occupy the low-volume/high-variety end of the continuum of processes that we introduced in Chapter 4. They are typical of the kind of improvement initiatives that often are a part of an operation's development activities. These 'project' processes come in all shapes and sizes but, in many respects, share key characteristics that make their management tasks broadly universal. First, managers must understand the fundamental characteristics of a project and the likely implications of these characteristics for management. Second, they must be able to understand the project environment and manage key project stakeholders. Third, they must be able to define, plan and control projects through their life cycle, while balancing competing performance objectives and competing (internal and external) stakeholder requirements. Figure 13.1 shows where this chapter fits in with the overall activities of operations management.

Key questions

What is project management?

What is a project's 'environment'?

How can projects be planned?

How can projects be controlled?

FIGURE 13.1 **This chapter examines managing projects**

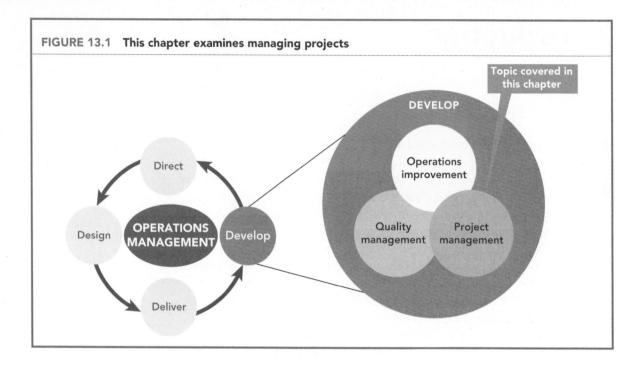

What is project management?

irst, what is a project? A project is a set of activities with a defined start point and a defined end state, which pursues a defined goal and uses a defined set of resources. Technically, many small-scale operations management endeavours, taking minutes or hours, conform to this definition of a project. However, in this chapter we will also be examining the management of relatively larger-scale projects, often taking days, months or years. Most operations improvement (even continuous improvement) can be seen as a series of overlapping 'mini-projects' that cumulatively contribute to a never-ending development effort. Some projects, such as infrastructure projects, new buildings, railways, sports stadia and airports, do contribute to a larger social purpose (such as 'improving communications'), but can be so large that they seem to stand alone. By contrast, other projects really are relatively stand-alone in the sense that they are a 'one-off' end in themselves. These are often projects that are focused on delivering a specific event, such as the Olympics or a soccer World Cup.

What do projects have in common?

While projects vary a great deal, they share a number of common features. All projects are mission focused – that is, they are dedicated to achieving a specific goal that should be delivered within a set timeframe, to certain

operations principle
A project is a set of activities with a defined start point and a defined end state, which pursues a defined goal and uses a defined set of resources.

specifications, using a defined group of resources. The result is that project outcomes are unique, or at least highly customized, involve many non-routine and complex tasks and therefore face relatively high levels of risk and uncertainty when contrasted with higher-volume and lower-variety operations. This is why so many projects fail in some way, with changed specifications (quality), severe delays (time), cost escalation (cost) and major disputes between key stakeholders being commonplace.

Operations in practice

Imagineering projects at Disney[1]

Ever since the creation of famous characters such as Mickey Mouse and Snow White, the Disney Corporation has been synonymous with innovative quality entertainment. At the Walt Disney Studios and Parks, persuasive stories come alive with technology and artistry coming together to delight visitors and audiences. This is particularly true for Walt Disney's 'Imagineering' operation ('imagineering' is a word that combines 'imagination' and 'engineering'), which, in effect, is the research and development arm of Walt Disney Parks and Resorts. It is responsible for creating many of the attractions, shows, firework displays and parades at the Disney theme parks. These complex and often innovative attractions will be closely scrutinised by thousands or millions of Disney's 'guests', so it is vital to pay attention to details, which means that professional project management is particularly important. Walt Disney World's Imagineering department's project managers work with the interactive technologies, the park staff, special-effects wizards, digital designers and others to create an interactive experience for the guests. Although many of the projects are technical in nature, project managers work with a wide range of different disciplines, from construction to marketing.

David Van Wyk is the vice president of project management for Walt Disney Imagineering and he fully understands the importance of effective project management. "Without it", he says, "how can we be as relevant tomorrow as we are today? How can we meet and exceed guest expectations in a changing world? We have somewhere between 140 and 150 different skill sets in Imagineering, including engineers, creative staff, artists, architects, accountants, writers, theme and new media specialists and more. A culture of interdisciplinary coordination with diverse stakeholders aims to interact and socialize to understand issues and problems. We have developed and keep working on a culture of collaboration. We do not have an NIH ('not invented here') culture." The Imagineering group is very much aware that, over the life of a project, cost increases while the ability to change decreases. So, it is important to solve issues early on in the design process, when it's more economical to make changes – especially those involving equipment. Which is why, says David Van Wyk, "we seek to incorporate more peer review earlier in the engineering–design process. We also look for on-time delivery, getting it right before it gets to the field, with a strong start, strong finish and careful resource allocation." ● ● ●

What is project management exactly?

Project management is the activity of defining, planning, controlling and learning from projects of any type. It is concerned with balancing what the project delivers, the time it takes and its cost within the so-called 'iron triangle' (quality, time and cost). Project management is a very broad activity in that it can encompass almost all the operations management tasks described in this text. We have chosen to place it in the context of operations development because the majority of projects that managers will be engaged in are essentially improvement projects. Often, there are many related projects involved in operations improvement. Which is why it is worth pointing out the distinction between 'projects' and 'programmes'. A programme, such as a continuous improvement programme, has no defined end point. Rather, it is an ongoing process of change. Individual projects may be individual sub-sections of an overall programme, but 'programme management' will overlay and integrate the individual projects. Generally, it is a more difficult task in the sense that it requires sometimes complex resource coordination – for example, when several projects within a programme share common resources.

In order to coordinate the efforts of many people in different parts of the organization (and often outside it as well), all projects need a project manager. The people working in the project team need a clear understanding of their roles in the (very often, temporary) organization. Controlling an uncertain project environment requires the rapid exchange of relevant information with the project stakeholders, both within and outside the organization. Which means that much of a project manager's activities are concerned with managing human resources. People, equipment and other resources must be identified and allocated to the various tasks. Undertaking these tasks successfully makes the management of a project a particularly challenging operations activity.

Not all projects are the same

So far, we have shown what projects have in *common* – temporary activities, with specific and highly customized goals, within time, cost and quality requirements, involving many non-routine and complex tasks. However, it is also critical to understand *differences* between projects. Key things for a project manager to consider are volume and variety characteristics – its scale and its complexity.

DIFFERENTIATING BY PROJECTS' VOLUME AND VARIETY CHARACTERISTICS

At a simple level, we can use the 'product–process' matrix (already explored in Chapter 6 of this text) to distinguish between projects based on their volume and variety characteristics. This is shown in Figure 13.2. Of course, all project processes are, by definition, in the top-left corner of the matrix. But within that end of the 'natural diagonal', projects do vary. At the very top

Operations in practice

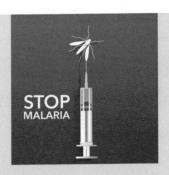

STOP MALARIA

Halting the growth of malaria[2]

In 2000 the World Health Organization (WHO) set a challenging objective – to halt the growth of malaria. At the time, there were an estimated 300–500 million cases of malaria each year, with between 1.1 and 2.7 million deaths, and the largest proportion of these being children under 5 years old. The WHO faced a hugely complex project management climate, with major political, economic, climatic and cultural impediments to success. And yet, by 2013 the reported number of malaria cases was down to 198 million and the number of deaths down to 580,000. At the heart of its success was a clear overriding vision that gained buy-in from the project's diverse set of stakeholders. Building on this, the WHO spent significant time understanding the project environment – the internal and external factors that might influence the success or failure of its various malaria projects worldwide. They also committed significant resources to objective setting, scoping and planning of their projects. Finally, in technically executing different malaria-related projects (focused on both preventing incidence of malaria and on curing those infected), the WHO and its partners relied heavily on careful project monitoring, milestones and continuing stakeholder engagement to ensure that they were on track. The fight against malaria is far from over, but at least this preventable and curable disease is in decline. ● ● ●

left-hand part of the matrix are projects that are genuinely 'first timers', with a very high degree of uniqueness, a volume of one and infinite variety. With less uniqueness, higher volume and less variety ('as before, but. . . ') projects may share some of the attributes of previous projects, but may have new features where project managers have little or no previous experience to help guide them. With higher volume (therefore a greater degree of repetition) and lower variety, so called 'paint by numbers' projects are relatively routine and predictable, and therefore (generally) more straightforward to manage.

operations principle
Although all projects are relatively low volume and high variety, their volume and variety can differ.

DIFFERENTIATING BY PROJECTS' SCALE, COMPLEXITY AND UNCERTAINTY CHARACTERISTICS

An alternative approach to distinguishing between projects is by considering their scale, complexity and uncertainty. This is shown in Figure 13.3. For example, a wedding planning project has (relatively) low levels of scale, complexity and uncertainty. The effect is that the management challenges of

FIGURE 13.2   Differentiating projects using their volume and variety characteristics

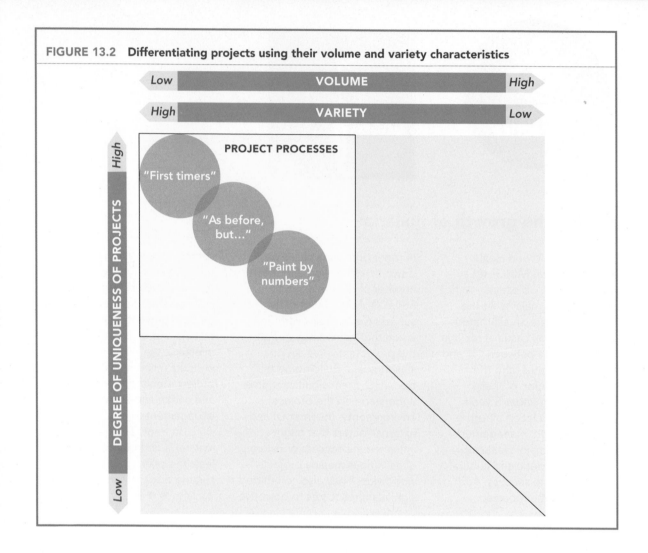

FIGURE 13.3   Differentiating projects by scale, complexity and uncertainty

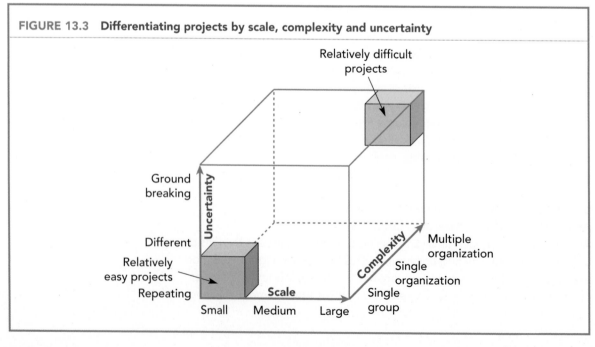

such a project are significantly different to developing the Airbus A380, which exhibited much higher levels of all three dimensions. The scale, complexity and uncertainty of such 'ground-breaking' projects demand far more sophisticated planning, greater and more flexible resources and careful control if they are to be successful.

operations principle
The difficulty of managing a project is a function of its scale, complexity and uncertainty.

The stages of project management

Figure 13.4 shows the stages that are necessary for effective project management:

Stage 1   Understanding the project environment – internal and external factors that may influence the project.
Stage 2   Defining the project – setting the objectives, scope and strategy for the project.
Stage 3   Project planning – deciding how the project will be executed.
Stage 4   Technical execution – performing the technical aspects of the project.
Stage 5   Project control – ensuring that the project is carried out according to plan.

In this chapter we examine stages 1, 2, 3 and 5. Stage 4, the technical execution of the project, is determined by the specific technicalities of individual projects, so we don't examine it. However, it is important to

---

FIGURE 13.4   **The five stages of the project management model**

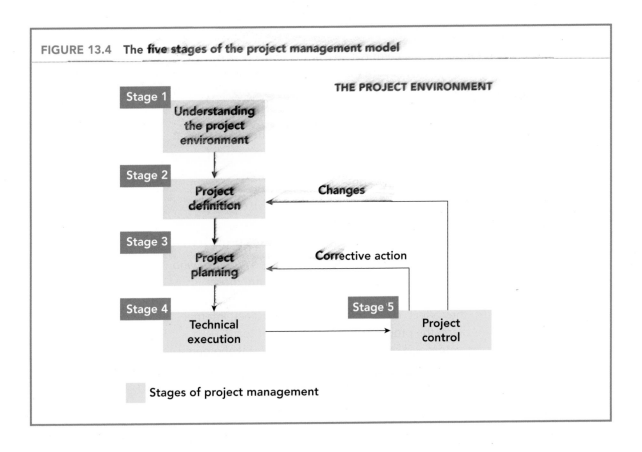

Stages of project management

understand that these stages are not a simple sequential chain of steps. Project management is essentially an *iterative* process. Problems or changes that become evident in the control stage may require re-planning and may even cause modifications to the original project definition.

What is a project's 'environment'?

The project environment comprises all the factors that may affect the project during its life. It is the context and circumstances in which the project takes place. It is important because the environment affects the way in which a project will need to be managed and (just as important) the possible dangers that may cause the project to fail. Environmental factors are often considered under the following four headings:

1 **Geo-social environment** geographical, climatic and cultural factors that may affect the project.

2 **Econo-political environment** economic, governmental and regulatory factors in which the project takes place.

3 **Business environment** industrial, competitive, supply network and customer expectation factors that shape the likely objectives of the project.

3 **Internal environment** individual company's or group's strategy and culture, the resources available and the interaction with other projects that will influence the project.

The role of stakeholders in projects

One way of operationalizing the importance of understanding a project's environment is to consider the various 'stakeholders' (also called 'agents') who have some kind of interest in the project. Project stakeholders are those individuals, groups or entities that have an interest in the project process or outcome. In other words, they affect, or are affected by, the project. Internal stakeholders include the client, the project sponsor, the project team, functional managers, contractors and project support. External stakeholders (i.e., those outside of the core project, rather than necessarily outside of the organization) include end users, suppliers, competitors, lobby groups, shareholders, government agencies and employees.

Complex projects can have many stakeholders, who can have sometimes conflicting views on a project's objectives. At the very least, different stakeholders are likely to stress different aspects of a project. So, as well as an ethical imperative to consider the views of as many people as possible from an early stage, it is often useful to do this in order to prevent objections and problems later. Moreover, there can be significant direct benefits from using a stakeholder-based approach. Project managers can use the opinions of powerful stakeholders to shape the project, making it more likely that they will support it, and even improve it. Communicating with stakeholders early and frequently can ensure that they fully understand the project and understand potential benefits. Stakeholder support may even help to win additional resources, increasing the likelihood that the project will be successful. Perhaps most important, one can anticipate stakeholder reaction to various aspects of the project and plan the actions that could prevent opposition, or that could build support.

operations principle
All projects have stakeholders with different interests and priorities.

MANAGING STAKEHOLDERS

Managing stakeholders can be a subtle and delicate task, requiring significant social and, sometimes, political skills. This is because stakeholders often have different interests in a project, and must be managed in different ways. One approach to discriminating between different stakeholders, is to distinguish between their power to influence the project and their interest in doing so. Stakeholders who have the power to exercise a major influence over the project should never be ignored. At the very least, the nature of their interest, and their motivation, should be well understood. But not all stakeholders who have the power to exercise influence over a project will be interested in doing so, and not everyone who is interested in the project has the power to influence it. The power–interest grid, shown in Figure 13.5, classifies stakeholders simply in terms of these two dimensions.

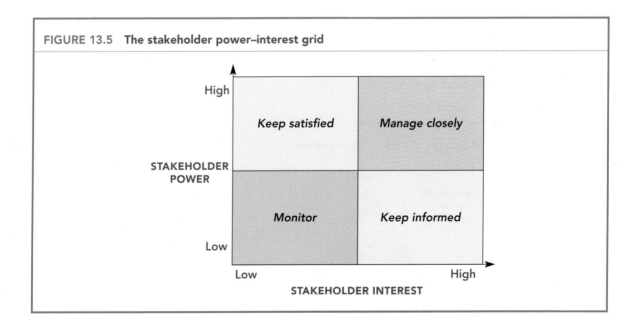

FIGURE 13.5 **The stakeholder power–interest grid**

Although there will be graduations between them, the two dimensions are useful in providing an indication of how stakeholders can be managed in terms of four categories. High-power, interested groups must be fully engaged, with the greatest efforts made to satisfy them. High-power, less-interested groups require enough effort to keep them satisfied, but not so much that they become bored or irritated with the message. Low-power, interested groups need to be kept adequately informed, with checks to ensure that no major issues are arising. These groups may be very helpful with the detail of the project. Low-power, less-interested groups need monitoring, though without excessive communication.

operations principle
Different stakeholder groups will need managing differently.

Project definition

Before starting the complex task of planning and executing a project, it is necessary to be clear about exactly what the project is – its definition. This is not always straightforward, especially in projects with many stakeholders. Three different elements define a project:

 its objectives – the end state that project management is trying to achieve;

 its scope – the exact range of the responsibilities taken on by project management;

 its strategy – how project management is going to meet its objectives.

PROJECT OBJECTIVES

Objectives help to provide a definition of the end point, which can be used to monitor progress and identify when success has been achieved. They can be judged in terms of the five performance objectives – quality, speed, dependability, flexibility and cost. However, flexibility is regarded as a 'given' in most projects, which, by definition, are to some extent one-offs, and speed and dependability are typically compressed to one composite objective – 'time'. This results in what is known as the 'iron triangle of project management' – cost, time and quality. Figure 13.6 shows the 'project objectives triangle', with three types of project marked.

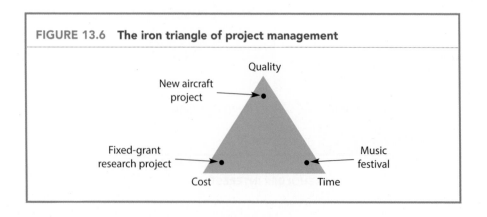

FIGURE 13.6   **The iron triangle of project management**

The relative importance of each objective will differ for different projects. Some aerospace projects, such as the development of a new aircraft, which impact on passenger safety, will place a very high emphasis on quality objectives. With other projects, for example a research project that is being funded by a fixed government grant, cost might predominate. Other projects emphasize time: for example, the organization of an open-air music festival has to happen on a particular date if the project is to meet its objectives. In each of these projects, although one objective might be particularly important, the other objectives can never be totally forgotten.

Good objectives are those that are clear, measurable and, preferably, quantifiable. Clarifying objectives involves breaking down project objectives into three categories – the purpose, the end results and the success criteria. For example, a project that is expressed in general terms as 'improve the budgeting process' could be broken down into:

 Purpose to allow budgets to be agreed and confirmed prior to the annual financial meeting.

 End result a report that identifies the causes of budget delay, and which recommends new budgeting processes and systems.

 Success criteria the report should be completed by 30 June, meet all departments' needs and enable integrated and dependable delivery of agreed budget statements. Cost of the recommendations should not exceed $200,000.

PROJECT SCOPE

The scope of a project identifies its work content and its products or outcomes. It is a boundary-setting exercise that attempts to define the dividing line between what each part of the project will do and what it won't do. Project scoping is critical, and failure to scope appropriately or constantly changing scopes are two of the key reasons projects fail. Defining scope is particularly important when part of a project is being outsourced. A supplier's scope of supply will identify the legal boundaries within which the work must be done. Sometimes the scope of the project is articulated in a formal 'project specification'. This is the written, pictorial and graphical information used to define the output, and the accompanying terms and conditions. The project scope will also outline limits or exclusions to the project. This is critical, because perceptions of project success or failure often originate from the extent to which deliverables, limits and exclusions have been clearly stated and understood by all parties during the scoping phase.

PROJECT STRATEGY

The third part of a project's definition is the project strategy, which defines, in a general rather than a specific way, how the project is going to meets its objectives. It does this in two ways: by defining the phases of the project, and by setting milestones and/or 'stagegates'. Milestones are important events during the project's life. Stagegates are the decision points that allow the project to move on to its next phase. A stagegate often launches further activities and therefore commits the project to additional costs, etc. 'Milestone' is a more passive term, which may herald the review of a part-complete project or mark the completion of a stage, but does not necessarily have more significance than a measure of achievement or completeness. At this point, the actual dates for each milestone are not necessarily determined. It is useful, however, to at least identify the significant milestones and stagegates – either to define the boundary between phases, or to help in discussions with the project's customer.

How can projects be planned?

 ll projects, even the smallest, need some degree of planning. The planning process fulfils four distinct purposes:

 It determines the cost and duration of the project. This enables major decisions to be made – such as the decision whether to go ahead with the project at the start.

 It determines the level of resources that will be needed.

 It helps to allocate work and to monitor progress. Planning must include the identification of who is responsible for what.

 It helps to assess the impact of any changes to the project.

Planning is not a one-off process. It may be repeated several times during the project's life as circumstances change; nor is replanning a sign of project failure or mismanagement. As discussed earlier, projects can and should be differentiated based on their characteristics – in our case, we examined the three alternative approaches of volume–variety, uncertainty–complexity–scale and novelty–technology–complexity–pace. And when managing particularly difficult projects, it is a normal occurrence to repeat planning throughout the project's life. The process of project planning involves five steps (see Figure 13.7).

Identify activities – the work breakdown structure

Most projects are too complex to be planned and controlled effectively unless they are first broken down into manageable portions. This is achieved by structuring the project into a 'family tree' that specifies major tasks or sub-projects. These, in turn, are divided up into smaller tasks until

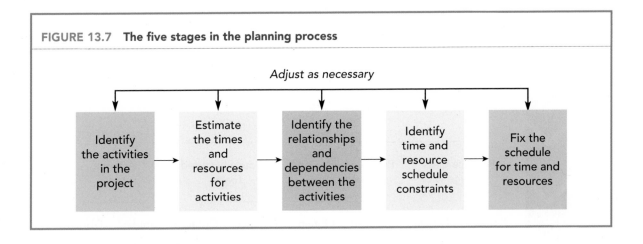

FIGURE 13.7　**The five stages in the planning process**

a defined, manageable series of tasks, called a *work package,* is arrived at. Each work package can be allocated its own objectives in terms of time, cost and quality. Typically, work packages do not exceed 10 days, should be independent from each other, should belong to one sub-deliverable and should constantly be monitored. The output from this is called the 'work breakdown structure' (WBS). The WBS brings clarity and definition to the project planning process. It shows 'how the jigsaw fits together'. It also provides a framework for building up information for reporting purposes.

EXAMPLE PROJECT

As a simple example to illustrate the application of each stage of the planning process, let us examine the following domestic project. The project definition is:

 purpose to make breakfast in bed;

 end result breakfast in bed of boiled egg, toast and orange juice;

 success criteria plan uses minimum staff resources and time, and product is high quality (egg freshly boiled, warm toast, etc.);

 scope project starts in kitchen at 6.00 am and finishes in bedroom; needs one operator and normal kitchen equipment.

The work breakdown structure is based on the above definition and can be constructed as shown in Figure 13.8.

Estimate times and resources

The second stage in project planning is to identify the time and resource requirements of the work packages. Without some idea of how long each part of a project will take and how many resources it will need, it is impossible to define what should be happening at any time during the execution of the project. Estimates are just that, however – a systematic best guess, not a perfect forecast of reality. Estimates may never be perfect, but they can be made with some idea of how accurate they might be.

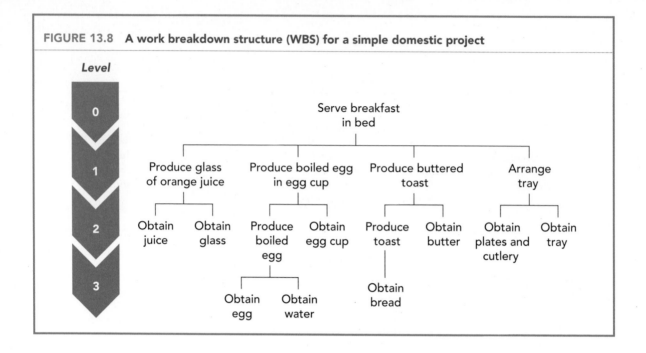

FIGURE 13.8   **A work breakdown structure (WBS) for a simple domestic project**

EXAMPLE PROJECT

Returning to our very simple example of the 'breakfast-in-bed' project, the activities were identified and times have been estimated, as in Table 13.1. While some of the estimates may appear generous, they take into account the time of day and the state of the operator.

PROBABILISTIC ESTIMATES

The amount of uncertainty in a project has a major bearing on the level of confidence that can be placed on an estimate. The impact of uncertainty on estimating times leads some project managers to use a probability curve to describe the estimate. In practice, this is usually a positively skewed distribution, as in Figure 13.9. The greater the risk, the greater the range of the distribution. The natural tendency of some people is to produce *optimistic* estimates, but these will have a relatively low probability of being correct because they represent the time that would be taken if *everything* went well. *Most likely* estimates have the highest probability of proving correct. Finally, *pessimistic* estimates assume that almost everything that could go wrong does go wrong. Because of the skewed nature of the distribution, the expected time for the activity will not be the same as the most likely time.

> **operations principle**
> Probabilistic activity-time estimates facilitate the assessment of a project being completed on time.

Identify relationships and dependencies

The third stage of planning is to understand the interactions between different project work packages. All the work packages (or activities) that are identified will have some relationship with one another that will depend on the logic of the project. Some activities will, by necessity, need to be executed in a particular order. For example, in the construction of a house, the foundations

TABLE 13.1 Time and resources estimates for a 'breakfast-in-bed' project

Activity	Effort (person-min)	Duration (min)
▶ Butter toast	▶ 1	▶ 1
▶ Pour orange juice	▶ 1	▶ 1
▶ Boil egg	▶ 0	▶ 4
▶ Slice bread	▶ 1	▶ 1
▶ Fill pan with water	▶ 1	▶ 1
▶ Bring water to boil	▶ 0	▶ 3
▶ Toast bread	▶ 0	▶ 2
▶ Take loaded tray to bedroom	▶ 1	▶ 1
▶ Fetch tray, plates, cutlery	▶ 1	▶ 1

FIGURE 13.9 Probability distribution of time estimates

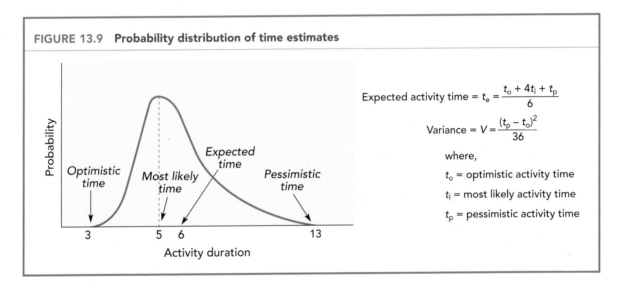

$$\text{Expected activity time} = t_e = \frac{t_o + 4t_l + t_p}{6}$$

$$\text{Variance} = V = \frac{(t_p - t_o)^2}{36}$$

where,

t_o = optimistic activity time

t_l = most likely activity time

t_p = pessimistic activity time

must be prepared before the walls are built, which in turn must be completed before the roof is put in place. These activities have a *dependent* or *series* relationship. Other activities do not have any such dependence on each other. The rear garden of the house could probably be prepared totally independently of the garage being built. These two activities have an *independent* or *parallel* relationship.

Project planning is greatly aided by the use of techniques that help to handle time, resource and relationships complexity. The simplest of these techniques is the Gantt, or bar, chart (which we introduced in Chapter 10). Gantt charts are the simplest way to exhibit an overall project plan, because they have excellent visual impact and are easy to understand. They are also useful for communicating project plans and status to senior managers, as well as for day-to-day project control.

Operations in practice

The Scottish Parliament Building³

The Scottish Parliament Building, opened in 2004, divides opinions like few other projects in the world. To some, it is an architectual masterstroke that is without parallel in 100 years, described by one crtiic as 'A Celtic–Spanish cocktail to blow both minds and budgets [. . .] energetically mining a new seam of National Romanticism refined and reinterpreted for the twenty-first century'. To others, it is an example of appalling cost estimation and lack of control. The project timeline makes for interesting reading:

- July 1997: a budget range of £10–40m is set;

- Sept 1997: indicative estimates are between £54m and £71m;

- June 1998: five designers submit bids ranging from £58m to £90m;

- July 1998: the bid of Enric Miralles, the Spanish architect, is chosen, with a cost in the range of £50–55m, not including VAT or site acquisition costs;

- June 1999: provisional cost estimated at £109m including consultancy fees, site costs, demolition, VAT, archaeology work, risk and contingencies;

- Nov 2001: cost estimate rises to £241m due to increase in space and major design change;

- Dec 2002: cost estimate rises to £295m due to increased security needs and 'hidden extras' in the construction process;

- June 2003: cost estimate rises to £374m due to higher-than-expected consultancy fees, which now top £50m;

- Feb 2004: cost estimate rises to £430m due to construction problems.

At one level, the Scottish Parliament is still a success story, with around 400,000 visitors every year coming to a building that pushed the boundaries of architecture. Yet, from a project management perspective, it should be viewed as a failure. Ultimately, the project was delivered at cost of £414.6m,

10–40 times the original budget of £10–40m, and instead of launching in 2001 it wasn't opened until 2004. Several causes have been identified for the failure of the project, including: the approved design being more complex than envisaged at the feasibility stage; increases in construction cost estimates, almost half of which were attributable to a 47 per cent increase in the total area of the building; additional costs for landscaping and road re-alignment work; poor cost reporting; and inadequate risk allowance. Yet, the Scottish Parliament project is not alone in failing to accurately predict or effectively manage its costs. Building the Wembley Stadium in London cost £900m, compared to the original forecast of £757m, and was delivered a year late, while the hosting of the 2014 football World Cup in Brazil was originally estimated at $2.05bn and had a final approximate cost of $4.25bn. ●●●

EXAMPLE PROJECT

Table 13.1 identified the activities for the breakfast preparation project. The list shows that some of the activities must necessarily follow others. For example, 'boil egg' cannot be carried out until 'fill pan with water' and 'bring water to boil' have been completed. Further logical analysis of the activities in the list shows that there are two major 'chains', where activities must be carried out in a definite sequence:

Slice bread – Toast bread – Butter toast
Fill pan with water – Bring water to boil – Boil egg

Both of these sequences must be completed before the activity 'take loaded tray to bedroom'. The remaining activities ('pour orange juice' and 'fetch tray, plates, cutlery') can be done at any time, provided that they are completed before 'take loaded tray to bedroom'. An initial project plan might be as shown in Figure 13.10. Here, the activities have been represented as blocks of time in proportion to their estimated durations. From this, we can see that the 'project' can be completed in nine minutes. Some of the activities have spare time (called float), indicated by the dotted line. The sequence 'Fill pan – Boil water – Boil egg – Bedroom' has no float, and is called the *critical path* of the project. By implication, any activity that runs late in this sequence would cause the whole project to be delayed accordingly.

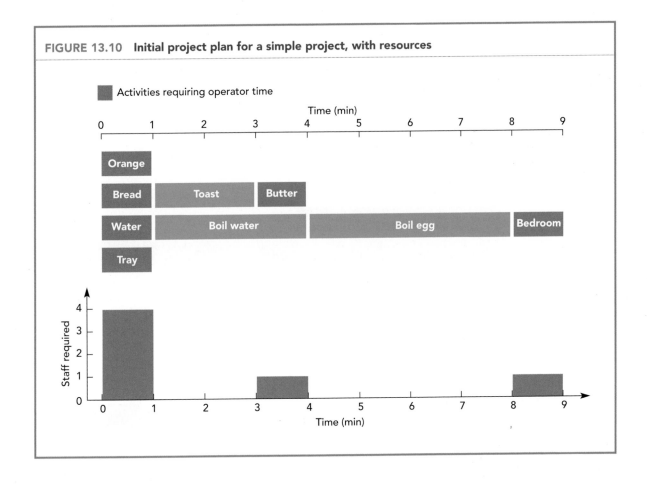

FIGURE 13.10 **Initial project plan for a simple project, with resources**

Identify schedule constraints

Once estimates have been made of the time and effort involved in each activity, and their dependencies identified, it is possible to compare project requirements with the available resources. The finite nature of critical resources – such as special skills – means that they should be taken into account in the planning process. This often has the effect of highlighting the need for more detailed re-planning. There are essentially two fundamental approaches:

 Resource-constrained   Only the available resource levels are used in resource scheduling, and are never exceeded. As a result, the project completion may slip. Resource-constrained scheduling is used, for example, when a project company has its own highly specialized assembly and test facilities.

 Time-constrained   The overriding priority is to complete the project within a given time. Once normally available resources have been used up, alternative ('threshold') resources are scheduled.

EXAMPLE PROJECT

Returning to the breakfast-in-bed project, we can now consider the resource implications of the plan in Figure 13.11. Each of the four activities scheduled at the start (pour orange, cut bread, fill pan, fetch tray) consumes staff resources. There is clearly a resource-loading problem, because the project

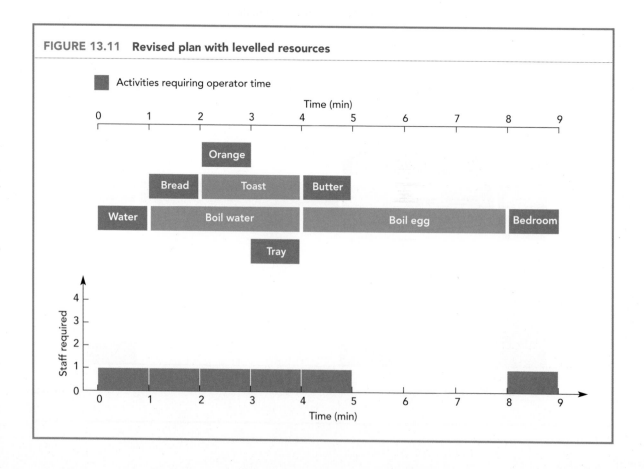

FIGURE 13.11   Revised plan with levelled resources

definition states that only one person is available. This is not an insuperable difficulty, however, because there is sufficient float to move some of the activities. A plan with levelled resources can be produced, as shown in Figure 13.11. All that has been necessary is to delay the toast preparation by one minute, and to use the elapsed time during the toasting and water-boiling processes to pour orange and fetch the tray.

Fix the schedule

Project planners should ideally have a number of alternatives to choose from. The one that best fits project objectives can then be chosen or developed. While it can be challenging to examine several alternative schedules, especially in very large or very uncertain projects, computer-based software packages such as Bitrix24, Trello, 2-Plan PMS, Asana, MS project and Producteev make critical-path optimization more feasible.

operations principle
A prerequisite for project planning is some knowledge of times, resources and relationships between activities.

EXAMPLE PROJECT
A further improvement to the breakfast plan can be made. Looking again at the project definition, the success criteria state that the product should be 'high quality'. In the plan shown in Figure 13.11, although the egg is freshly boiled, the toast might be cold. An 'optimized' plan that would provide hot toast would be to prepare the toast during the 'boil egg' activity. This plan is shown in Figure 13.12.

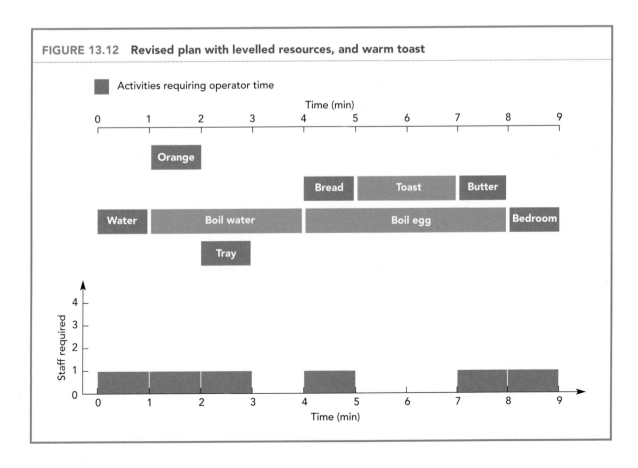

FIGURE 13.12   Revised plan with levelled resources, and warm toast

Network analysis

As project complexity increases, it becomes more necessary to identify clearly the relationships between activities and show the logical sequence in which activities must take place. This is typically done using the 'critical-path method' (CPM), to clarify the relationships between activities diagrammatically. Though there are alternative methods of carrying out critical-path analysis, by far the most common, and also the one used in most project management software packages, is the 'activity-on-node' (AoN) method. For example, Table 13.2 shows the activities, time estimates, precedence relationships and resources needed (in terms of the number of IT developers) for one phase of a new sales knowledge management system that is being installed in an insurance company. The project is a cooperation between the company's IT systems department and its sales organization.

Figure 13.13 shows the critical-path analysis for the new sales knowledge management system. Some of the conventions of the AoN representation of project network need explaining. Activities are drawn as boxes, and arrows are used to define the relationships between them. In the centre of each box is the description of the activity (in this case. 'Activity a', 'Activity b' and so on). Above the description is the duration (D) of the activity (or work package), the earliest start time (EST) and earliest finish time (EFT). Below the description is the latest start time (LST), the latest finish time (LFT) and the 'float' (F) – the number of extra days that the activity could take without slowing down the overall project. The diagram shows that there are a number of chains of events that must be completed before the project can be considered as finished (event 5). In this case, activity chains a – c – f, and a – d – e – f, and b – e – f must all be completed before the project can be considered as finished. The longest (in duration) of these chains of activities is called the 'critical path' because it represents the shortest time in which the project can be finished, and therefore dictates the project timing. In this case b – e – f is the longest path, and the earliest the project can finish is after 57 days.

Activities that lie on the critical path will have the same earliest and latest start times and earliest and latest finish times. That is why these activities are critical.

TABLE 13.2 **Time, resource and relationships for the sales system interface design project**

Code	Activity	Immediate Predecessor(s)	Duration (Days)	Resources (Developers)
a	Form and train user group	none	10	3
b	Install systems	none	17	5
c	Specify sales training	a	5	2
d	Design initial screen interface	a	5	3
e	Test interface in pilot area	b, d	25	2
f	Modify interface	c, e	15	3

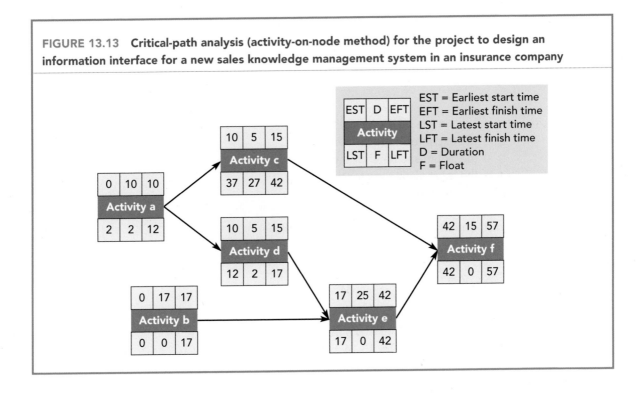

FIGURE 13.13 Critical-path analysis (activity-on-node method) for the project to design an information interface for a new sales knowledge management system in an insurance company

Non-critical activities, however, have some flexibility as to when they start and finish. This flexibility is quantified into a figure that is known either as 'float' or 'slack'. So, activity c, for example, is only of 5 days duration and it can start any time after day 10 (when activity a is completed) and must finish any time before day 42 (when activities a, b, c, and d are completed). Its 'float' is therefore $(42 - 10) - 5 = 27$ days (i.e. latest finish time minus earliest start time minus activity duration). Obviously, activities on the critical path have no float; any change or delay in these activities would immediately affect the whole project.

The rather tedious computation necessary in network planning can relatively easily be performed by project planning models. All they need are the basic relationships between activities, together with timing and resource requirements for each activity. Earliest and latest event times, float and other characteristics of a network can be presented, often in the form of a Gantt chart (see Chapter 10). More significantly, the speed of computation allows for frequent updates to project plans. Similarly, if updated information is both accurate and frequent, such computer-based systems can also provide effective project-control data.

Program evaluation and review technique (PERT)

The program evaluation and review technique, or PERT as it is universally known, is a technique that recognizes that activity durations and costs in project management cannot be forecast perfectly, so probability theory should be used. In this type of network, the duration of each activity is estimated on an optimistic, a most-likely and a pessimistic basis, as shown in Figure 13.14. If it is assumed that these time estimates are consistent with a beta probability distribution, the mean and variance of the distribution can be estimated as follows:

$$t_e = \frac{t_o + 4t_l + t_p}{6}$$

Where

t_e = the expected time for the activity
t_o = the optimistic time for the activity
t_l = the most likely time for the activity
t_p = the pessimistic time for the activity

The variance of the distribution (V) can be calculated as follows:

$$V = \frac{(t_p - t_o)^2}{6^2} = \frac{(t_p - t_o)^2}{36}$$

The time distribution of any path through a network will have a mean, which is the sum of the means of the activities that make up the path, and a variance, which is a sum of their variances. In Figure 13.14:

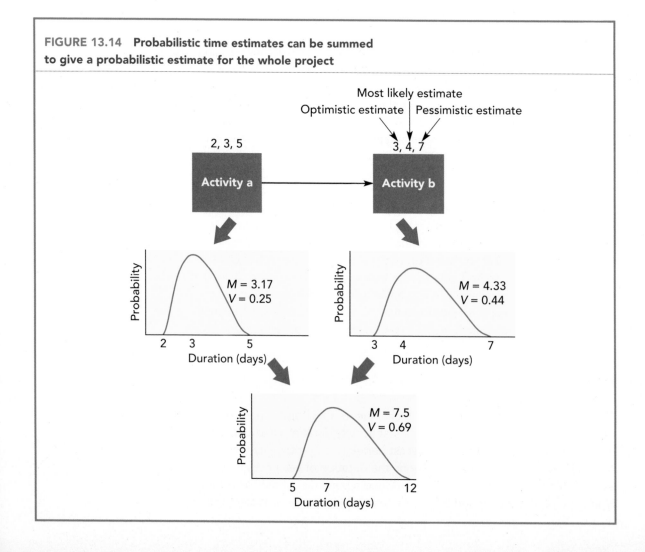

FIGURE 13.14   Probabilistic time estimates can be summed to give a probabilistic estimate for the whole project

The mean of the first activity (a) $= \dfrac{2 + (4 \times 3) + 5}{6} = 3.17$

The variance of the first activity (a) $= \dfrac{(5 - 2)^2}{36} = 0.25$

The mean of the second activity $= (b) \dfrac{3 + (4 \times 4) + 7}{6} = 4.33$

The variance of the second activity (b) $= \dfrac{(7 - 3)^2}{36} = 0.44$

The mean of the network distribution $= 3.17 + 4.33 = 7.5$

The variance of the network distribution $= 0.25 + 0.44 = 0.69$

It is generally assumed that the whole path will be normally distributed. The advantage of this extra information is that we can examine the 'riskiness' of each path through a network, as well as its duration. Given the increased attention on risk management within project management over recent years, this is essential. For example, Figure 13.15 shows a simple two-path network. The top path is the critical one; the distribution of its duration has a mean of 14.5 with a

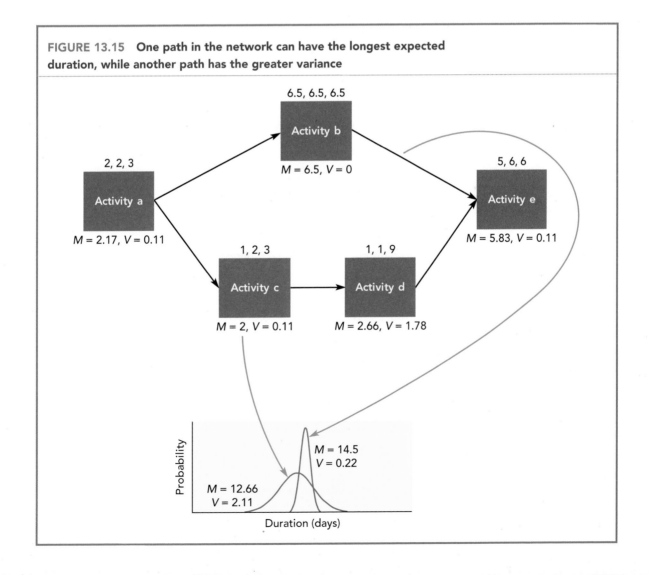

FIGURE 13.15   One path in the network can have the longest expected duration, while another path has the greater variance

variance of 0.22. The distribution of the non-critical path has a lower mean of 12.66 but a far higher variance of 2.11. The implication of this is that there is a chance that the non-critical path could, in reality, be critical. Although we will not discuss the probability calculations here, it is possible to determine the probability of any sub-critical path turning out to be critical when the project actually takes place. However, on a practical level, even if the probability calculations are judged not to be worth the effort involved, it is useful to be able to make an approximate assessment of the riskiness of each part of a network.

How can projects be controlled?

Understanding the project environment, project definition and project planning stages of project management largely takes place before the actual project begins. Project control, on the other hand, deals with the management activities that take place during the execution of the project. As such, project control is the essential link between planning and doing. It involves four key challenges:

 how to monitor the project in order to check on its progress;

 how to assess the performance of the project by comparing monitored observations of the project with the project plan;

 how to intervene in the project in order to make the changes that will bring it back to plan;

 how to manage matrix tensions in the project in order to reconcile the interests of both the project and different organizational functions.

Project monitoring

Project managers have first to decide what they should be looking for as the project progresses. Usually a variety of measures are monitored. To some extent, the measures used will depend on the nature of the project. However, common measures include current expenditure to date, supplier price changes, amount of overtime authorized, technical changes to project, inspection failures, number and length of delays, activities not started on time, missed milestone, etc. Some of these monitored measures affect mainly cost, some mainly time. However, when something affects the quality of the project, there are also time and cost implications. This is because quality problems in project planning and control usually have to be solved in a limited amount of time.

Assessing project performance

The monitored measures of project performance at any point in time need to be assessed so that project management can make a judgment concerning overall performance. A typical planned cost profile of a project through its life is shown in Figure 13.16. At the beginning of a project some activities can be started, but most activities will be dependent on finishing. Eventually, only a few activities will remain to be completed. This pattern of a slow start followed by a faster pace, with an eventual tail-off of activity, holds true for almost all projects, which is why the rate of total expenditure follows an S-shaped pattern, even when the cost curves for the individual activities are linear. It is against this curve that actual costs can be compared in order to check whether the project's costs are being incurred to plan. Figure 13.16 shows the planned and actual cost figures compared in this way. It shows that the project is incurring costs, on a cumulative basis, ahead of what was planned.

Intervening to change the project

If the project is obviously out of control in the sense that its costs, quality levels or times are significantly different from those planned, then some kind of intervention is almost certainly likely to be required. The exact nature of the intervention will depend on the technical characteristics of the project, but it is likely to need the advice of all the people who would be affected. Given the interconnected nature of projects – a change to one part of the project will have knock-on effects elsewhere – this means that interventions often require wide consultation. Sometimes intervention is needed even if the project looks

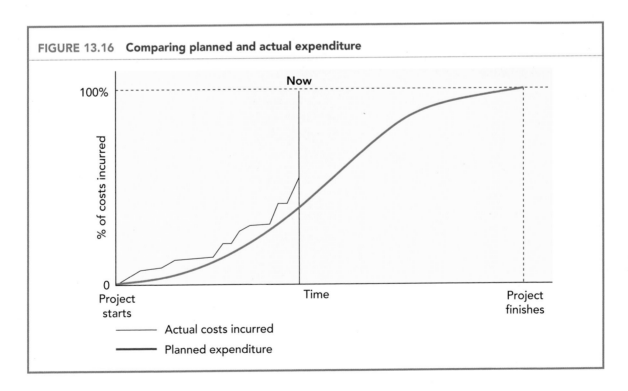

FIGURE 13.16   Comparing planned and actual expenditure

to be proceeding according to plan. For example, the schedule and cost for a project may seem to be 'to plan', but when the project managers project activities and cost into the future, they see that problems are very likely to arise. In this case it is the *trend* of performance that is being used to trigger intervention.

Managing matrix tensions

In all but the simplest projects, project managers usually need to reconcile the interests of both the project itself and the departments contributing resources to the project. When calling on a variety of resources from various departments, projects are operating in a 'matrix management' environment, where projects cut across organizational boundaries and involve staff who are required to report to their own line manager as well as to the project manager. This is why matrix management requires a high degree of cooperation and communication between all individuals and departments. Although decision-making authority will rest formally with either the project or departmental manager, most major decisions will need some degree of consensus. Arrangements need to be made that reconcile potential differences between project managers and departmental managers. To function effectively, matrix management structures should have the following characteristics:

 There should be effective channels of communication between all managers involved, with relevant departmental managers contributing to project planning and resourcing decisions.

 There should be formal procedures in place for resolving the management conflicts that do arise.

 Project staff should be encouraged to feel committed to their projects, as well as to their own department.

 Project management should be seen as the central coordinating role, with sufficient time devoted to planning the project and securing the agreement of the line managers to deliver on time and within budget.

Summary answers to key questions

Each chapter has a 'Summary answers to key questions' section. Use it to check your understanding of the issues covered in the chapter.

WHAT IS PROJECT MANAGEMENT?

★ A project is a set of activities with a defined start point and a defined end state, which pursues a defined goal and uses a defined set of resources. Project management is the activity of defining, planning, controlling and learning from projects.

★ While projects share similarities, they can also be differentiated by volume and variety characteristics, and by their scale, complexity and degree of uncertainty.

★ Project management involves three particularly important activities: understanding the project environment, defining and planning the project.

WHAT IS A PROJECT'S 'ENVIRONMENT'?

★ It is important to understand the environment because it influences the way a project is carried out, often through stakeholder activity, and is the main determinant of the uncertainty surrounding the project.

★ Project definition involves determining objectives (the end state that project management is trying to achieve), scoping (the exact range of the responsibilities taken on by project management) and strategy (how project management is going to meet the project objectives).

HOW CAN PROJECTS BE PLANNED?

★ Project planning involves five stages: (1) identifying the activities within a project; (2) estimating times and resources for the activities; (3) identifying the relationship and dependencies between the activities; (4) identifying the schedule constraints; and (5) fixing the schedule.

★ Gantt charts and network planning are the most common project-planning techniques. Network planning, typically using the 'activity-on-node' method, is a useful way to assess the total duration of a project and the degree of flexibility or float of the individual activities within the project.

HOW CAN PROJECTS BE CONTROLLED?

 Project control deals with the management activities that take place during the execution of the project and involves deciding how to *monitor* the project in order to check on its progress, how to *assess the performance* of the project by comparing monitored observations of the project with the project plan, how to *intervene* in the project in order to make the changes that will bring it back to plan and how to *manage matrix tensions* within a project to reconcile the interests of both the project and different organizational functions.

Problems and applications

All chapters have problems and application questions that will help you practice analyzing operations. They can be answered by reading the chapter. Model answers for the first question can be found on the companion website for this text.

1 ➜ Revisit the 'Operations in practice' example in the chapter describing the type of projects undertaken by Disney Imagineering.
Using the two methods of distinguishing between projects that are described in the chapter (their volume and variety characteristics, and their scale, complexity and degree of uncertainty), compare Disney's project management with that necessary for a major civil-engineering project, such as the construction of a mass rapid-transport system.

2 ➜ The activities, their durations and precedences for designing, writing and installing a bespoke computer database are shown in the table below. Draw a network diagram (activity-on-node) for the project, and calculate the fastest time in which the operation might be completed.

Bespoke computer database activities

Activity	Duration (weeks)	Activities that must be completed before it can start
1 Contract negotiation	1	-
2 Discussions with main users	2	1
3 Review of current documentation	5	1
4 Review of current systems	6	2
5 Systems analysis (A)	4	3,4
6 Systems analysis (B)	7	5
7 Programming	12	5
8 Testing (prelim)	2	7
9 Existing system review report	1	3,4
10 System proposal report	2	5,9
11 Documentation preparation	19	5,8
12 Implementation	7	7,11
13 System test	3	12
14 Debugging	4	12
15 Manual preparation	5	11

3

→ "Funding comes from a variety of sources; to restore the literally irreplaceable buildings we work on. We try to reconcile historical integrity with commercial viability, and rely on the support of volunteers. So, we need to involve all stakeholders all the way through the project." (Janine Walker, chief project manager of Happy Heritage – a not-for-profit restoration organization.) Her latest project was the restoration of a 200-year-old 'poorhouse', originally built to house local poor, as a new visitor attraction. Janine's team drew up a list of stakeholders and set out to win them over with their enthusiasm for the project. They invited local people to attend meetings, explained the vision and took them to look round the site. Also, before work started Janine took all the building staff on the same tour of the site as they had taken other groups and the VIPs who provided the funding. "Involving the builders in the project sparked a real interest in the project and the archaeological history of the site. Often, they would come across something interesting, tell the foreman who would involve an archaeologist and so preserve an artefact that might otherwise have been destroyed. They took a real interest in their work, they felt involved."

a)   Who do you think would be the main stakeholders for this project?
b)   How might not involving them damage the project, and how would involving them benefit the project?

4

→ In the oil industry, project teams are increasingly using virtual reality and visualization models of offshore structures, which allows them to check out not only the original design but any modifications that have to be made during construction.

a)   Why do you think a realistic picture of a completed project helps the process of project management?
b)   Why are such visualizations becoming more important?

Want to know more?

There are hundreds of books on project management. They range from the introductory to the very detailed, and from the managerial to the highly mathematical. Here are three general (as opposed to mathematical) books that are worth a look:

Cole, R. and Scotcher, E. (2015) *Brilliant Agile Project Management: A Practical Guide to Using Agile, Scrum and Kanban,* Harlow, UK: Pearson Business.
  → A practical and modern take on project management.

Lock, D. (2013) *Project Management,* London: Routledge.
  → A classic text.

Maylor, H. (2018) *Project Management,* 5th edition, Harlow, UK: Pearson.
  → A good basic text on the subject.

Notes

CHAPTER 1

1 Goodman, M. (2011) 'Prêt Smile, it will pay for everyone', *Sunday Times*, 6 March; Prêt A Manger website: http://www.pret.com/

2 Discussions with Tom Dyson and Olly Willans of Torchbox, to whom we are grateful for their advice and assistance.

3 MSF website (2015): http://www.msf.org.uk; Beaumont, P. (2011) 'Médecins sans Frontières book reveals aid agencies' ugly compromises', the *Guardian*, 20 November.

4 The phrase 'triple bottom line' was first used in 1994 by John Elkington, the founder of a British consultancy called SustainAbility. Read Elkington, J. (1997) *Cannibals with Forks: The Triple Bottom Line of 21st Century Business*, Mankato, MN: Capstone. Also good is Savitz, A.W. and Weber, K. (2006) *The Triple Bottom Line: How Today's Best-Run Companies Are Achieving Economic, Social and Environmental Success – and How You Can Too*, Hoboken, NJ: Jossey-Bass.

5 Trangbæk, R. R. (2015) 'Lego group among five most reputable companies in the world', LEGO Group Press Office, 21 April; Diaz, J. (2014) 'Exclusive look inside the Lego Factory', Gizmodo.com: http://lego.gizmodo.com/exclusive-look-inside-the-lego-factory-5022769; Terdiman, D. (2011) 'Watching Lego make its world-famous bricks', CNET: http://www.cnet.com/uk/news/watching-lego-make-its-world-famous-bricks/, 15 June; *The Economist* (2014) 'Unpacking Lego – how the Danish firm became the world's hottest toy company', 8 March.

6 Johnston, R. and Staughton, R. (2009) 'Establishing and developing strategic relationships – the role of operations managers', *International Journal of Operations and Production Management*, **29**(6); Wyganowska, J. (2008) 'The Top 10 Skills of Effective Operations Managers', Recreation Management: http://www.recmanagement.com/200802gc04.php; Operationsmanagers.com (2011) 'The 5 Key Personality Traits of Operations Managers': http://careers-in-business.com/omskill.htm

CHAPTER 2

1 Cookson, C. (2015) 'Guildford's SSTL leads world in small satellite supply', *Financial Times*, June 12; *The Economist* (2015) 'The pioneer of small satellites is laying plans for the infrastructure and services needed for travel to other planets', May 30; SSTL (2015) 'Changing the economics of space – SSTL is the world's premier provider of small satellite missions and services', corporate brochure.

2 Hayes, R.H. and Wheelwright, S.C. (1984) *Restoring Our Competitive Edge*, Hoboken, NJ: John Wiley.

3 For a more thorough explanation, *see* Slack, N. and Lewis, M. (2017) *Operations Strategy*, 5th edition, Harlow, UK: Pearson Education.

4 Mintzberg, H. and Waters, J.A. (1995) 'Of strategies: Deliberate and emergent', *Strategic Management Journal*, July/Sept.

5 Poeter, D. (2011) 'Apple stores' secret sauce spilled', PC Mag.com, June 15; Lipschutz, K. (2011) 'Apple's retail philosophy: employees reveal calculated culture', *Adweek*, June 15; Johnson, R. (2011) 'What I learned building the Apple store', HBR Blog network, November 21.

6 Hill, A. and Hill, T. (2009) *Manufacturing Operations Strategy*, Basingstoke, UK: Palgrave Macmillan.

7 There is a vast amount of literature describing the resource-based view of the firm. For example, Barney, J. (1991) 'The resource-based model of the firm: Origins, implications and prospect', *Journal of Management,* **17**(1); Teece, D.J. and Pisano, G. (1994) 'The dynamic capabilities of firms: An introduction', *Industrial and Corporate Change*, **3**(3).

8 Barney, J. (1991) 'The resource-based model of the firm: Origins, implications and prospect', *Journal of Management,* **17**(1).

9 Definition from: http://searchcio.techtarget.com/definition/outsourcing

10 Burton, G. (2013) 'ARM vs Intel: A battle of business models', *Computing*, May 29; Turley, J. (2014) 'Intel vs. ARM: Two titans' tangled fate', InfoWorld.com, created February 27.

11 Satariano, A. and Burrows, P. (2011) 'Apple's supply-chain secret? Hoard lasers', *Bloomberg Businessweek,* November 3; Elmer-DeWitt, P. (2011) 'How Apple became a monopsonist', CNN News, July 5; Lariviere, M. (2011) 'Operations: Apple's secret sauce?', *The Operations Room,* November 4.

12 Adapted from Slack, N. and Lewis, M.A. (2017) *Operations Strategy,* 5th edition, Harlow, UK: Pearson Education.

13 Weick, K.E. (1990) 'Cartographic myths in organizations', in A. Huff (ed.) *Managing Strategic Thought,* London: Wiley.

14 Definition from techtarget.com: searchdatacenter. techtarget.com/

CHAPTER 3

1 Heisler, Y. (2013) 'Apple's iPhone: The untold story', *Network World,* September 1; Vogelstein, F. (2013) 'And then Steve said,"Let there be an iPhone"', *New York Times Magazine,* October 4; Ahmed, M. (2012) 'Apple nearly ditched the iPhone, designer admits', *The Times,* July 31; Breillatt, A. (2012) 'You can't innovate like Apple', http://www.pragmaticmarketing.com

2 Jervell, E. (2013) 'The long, slow process of IKEA design', *Wall Street Journal,* October 14.

3 Goodwin, L. (2015) 'How to bust the biggest myths about the circular economy', the *Guardian,* March 12; Clegg, A. (2015) 'Sustainable innovation: Shaped for the circular economy', *Financial Times,* August 26; company website, Newlife Paints: www.newlifepaints.com

CHAPTER 4

1 Knowles, T. (2017) 'Berkeley can see its prefabs sprouting up everywhere', *The Times,* January 23; Davey, J. (2010) 'Today we built a house every hour', *The Sunday Times,* January 31; Persimmon company website: www.persimmonhomes.com; Brown, G. (2010), 'Space4 growth gives boost to former car sector workers', *Birmingham Post,* August 27.

2 Carr-Brown, J. (2005) 'French factory surgeon cuts NHS queues', *The Sunday Times,* October 23.

3 Economist (2014) 'The future of jobs: Previous technological innovation has always delivered more long-run employment, not less. But things can change', *The Economist* (print edition) January 18; Economist (2013) 'Schumpeter – the age of smart machines', *The Economist* (print edition), May 25; Finkelstein (2013) 'Machines are becoming cheaper than labour', *The Times,* November 6; Groom, B. (2014) 'Automation and the threat to jobs', *Financial Times,* January 26; Benedikt Frey, C. and Osborne, M.A. (2013) 'The future of employment: How susceptible are jobs to computerisation?', *Oxford Martin School Working Paper,* September 17; Brynjolfsson, E. and McAfee, A. (2014) *The Second Machine Age: Work, Progress, and Prosperity in a Time of Brilliant Technologies,* New York: W.W. Norton & Company.

4 Bone, J., Robertson, D. and Pavia, W. (2010) 'Plane rumpus puts focus on crews' growing revolution in the air', *The Times,* August 12.

CHAPTER 5

1 Board, J. and Kok Fai, L. (2015) 'More airlines, facial recognition technology planned for Changi's Terminal 4', chanelnewsasia.com, July 9; Airport Technology (2014) 'Terminal 4, Changi International Airport, Singapore', airporttechnology.com; SAA Architects (2013) 'South East Asia Aviation Hub Development – design-led Changi Airport Terminal 4, Singapore', saa.com, November 6; Driver, C. (2014) 'And the winners are... Singapore crowned the best airport in the world (and Heathrow scoops top terminal)', *Mail* online, March 28; Talwar, R. (2012) 'Airport 2025 – rethinking the customer experience', futuretravelexperience.com, November 24.

2 Takt time was originated by Toyota the automobile company. It is their adaptation of the German word '*taktzeit*', originally meaning 'clock cycle'.

3 Oches, S. (2015) 'The drive-thru performance study', *QSR* magazine, October; Horovitz, A. (2002) 'Fast-food world says drive-through is the way to go', *USA Today,* April 3.

4 Associated Press (2012) 'Standardised bed chart "could prevent hundreds of hospital deaths"', the *Guardian,* July 27.

5 BBC News website (2014) 'Sainsbury's store in "spend more" poster gaffe', www.bcc.co.uk/news, September 30.

6 The Workflow Management Coalition (2009), www.wfmc.org

7 Schmidt, G. (2005) 'Applicability of the OM triangle to health care', Paper from the David Eccles School of Business, University of Utah; Heskett, J.L. (2003)

'Shouldice Hospital Limited', *Harvard Business Publishing Case*, 9-683-068.

CHAPTER 6

1 Farrell, S. (2014) 'Ocado dismisses fears over Waitrose supply deal', the *Guardian*, September 11: Pratley, N. (2012) 'Ocado: Buy two problems get one free', the *Guardian*, January 23; Tugby, L. (2017) 'Ocado full-year profits spike', *Retail Week*, January 31.

2 The North Face website: http://uk.thenorthface.com/blog/uk/en/sustainability

3 Adapted from Kraljic, P. (1983) 'Purchasing must become supply management', *Harvard Business Review*, **61**(5).

4 Economist (2011) 'Broken links: The disruption to manufacturers worldwide from Japan's disasters will force a rethink of how they manage production', *The Economist* (print edition), March 31; BBC News website (2011) 'Sony considers two-week shutdown due to power shortages: Production at some of Japan's biggest companies has been affected by power shortages', www.bbc.co.uk/news, April 11; BBC News website (2011) 'Toyota motors has suspended production at most of its plants in Japan and also reduced output at its North American and European factories', www.bbc.co.uk/news, April 11.

5 Lee, H.L., Padmanabhan, V. and Whang, S. (1997) 'The bullwhip effect in supply chains', *Sloan Management Review*, Spring.

6 Thanks to Stephen Disney at Cardiff Business School, UK, for help with this section.

CHAPTER 7

1 Blakely, R. (2010) 'Britain can learn from India's assembly-line heart operations, says doctor', *The Times*, May 14; Economist (2011) 'Economies of scale made steel: The economics of very big ships', *The Economist*, Nov 12.

2 Economist (2009) 'A piece of cake: Panettone season arrives', *The Economist*, December 10; Bauli website: http://www.bauligroup.it/en/

3 Horticulture Week (2010) 'Grower guide tackles problem of building sustainable workforces', *Horticulture Week*, May 14; Growing Jobs website: http://growingjobs.org/

4 Kimes, S. (1989) 'Yield management: A tool for capacity-constrained service firms', *Journal of Operations Management*, **8**(4).

5 Flyn, C. (2011) 'Queuing: Pinpointing our happiest moments', *The Sunday Times*, November 6.

CHAPTER 8

1 *The Economist* (2012) 'Energy storage', *Economist Technology Quarterly*, Mar 3.

2 Hipwell, D. (2013) 'Age is no virtue for Treasury Wine Estates, which has a massive American hangover', *The Times*, July 17; Baab-Muguira, C. (2013) 'Treasury Wine down over 10% on writedown news', The Motley Fool, July 15.

3 Duke, S. (2014) 'He knows what you want – before you even want it', *Sunday Times*, February 2; Ahmed, M. (2014) 'Amazon will know what you want before you do', *The Times*, January 27.

CHAPTER 9

1 Interview with Joanne Cheung, Steve Deeley and other staff at Godfrey Hall, BMW Dealership, Coventry.

2 The concept of P:D ratios comes originally from Shingo, S. (1981) *Study of Toyota Production Systems*, Tokyo: Japan Management Association, and was extended by Mather, K. (1988) *Competitive Manufacturing*, Upper Saddle River, NJ: Prentice Hall.

3 Economist (2011) 'Please be seated: A faster way of boarding planes could save time and money', *The Economist*, September 3; Palmer, J. (2011) 'Tests show fastest way to board passenger planes', www.bbc.co.uk/news, August 31.

4 Thanks to Lawrence Wilkins for this example.

5 Goldratt, E.Y. and Cox, J. (1984) *The Goal*, Great Barrington, MA: North River Press.

6 Wight, O. (1984) *Manufacturing Resource Planning: MRP II*, Gloucester, UK: Oliver Wight.

CHAPTER 10

1 Example written and supplied by Janina Aarts and Mattia Bianchi, Department of Management and Organization, Stockholm School of Economics.

2 Corbett, S. (2004) 'Applying lean in offices, hospitals, planes, and trains', presentation at the Lean Service Summit, Amsterdam, June 24.

3 Interview with Edward Kay, Tom Dyson and Olly Willans of Torchbox, January 2012; Torchbox website: http://www.torchbox.com/blog/kanban-project-management; we are grateful to everyone

at Torchbox for their help and allowing us access to their operation.

CHAPTER 11

1 Adapted, with permission, from an original case by Professors Rui Soucasaux Sousa and Sofia Salgado Pinto, Católica Porto Business School, Portugal.

2 Imai, M. (1986) *Kaizen – The Key to Japan's Competitive Success*, New York: McGraw-Hill.

3 Sometimes the 'management of the improvement process' is seen as a fourth aspect of improvement. Space does not permit this aspect to be covered here.

4 Information for this section is based partly on a private communication from Ben Betts, CEO of ht2.com.

5 International Standards Organization, *ISO 8402*, 1986.

6 Dale, B.G. (1994) 'Quality Management Systems', in B.G. Dale (ed.) *Managing Quality*, Upper Saddle River, NJ: Prentice Hall.

7 Company website: http://www.heinekeninternational.com

8 Davenport, T. (1995) 'Re-engineering: The fad that forgot people', *Fast Company*, November.

9 Based on an example in Kruse, G. (1995) 'Fundamental Innovation', *Manufacturing Engineer*, February.

10 Note: These defects-per-million (DPM) figures assume that the mean and/or SD may vary over the long term so the 3 Sigma DPM is actually based on 1.5 Sigma and 6 Sigma on 4.5 Sigma. These distributions are assumed to be 'one-tailed', as the shift is usually one direction.

11 West, K. (2011) 'Formula One trains van drivers', *The Times*, May 1; f1network.net: http://www.f1network.net/main/s107/st164086.htm

CHAPTER 12

1 Parasuraman, A., Zeithaml, V.A. and Berry, L.L. (1985) 'A conceptual model of service quality and implications for future research', *Journal of Marketing*, 49, Fall, pp. 41–50; Gummesson, E. (1987) 'Lip service: A neglected area in services marketing', *Journal of Services Marketing*, **1**(1), pp. 19–23.

2 Vitaliev, V. (2009) 'The much-loved knife', *Engineering and Technology Magazine*, July 21; Zuber, F. (2015) 'The Victorinox Quality System', Victorinox website: www.victorinox.com

3 Interview with Michael Purtill, the general manager of the Four Seasons Hotel, Canary Wharf, in London. We are grateful for Michael's cooperation (and for the great quality of service at his hotel!).

4 Berry, L.L. and Parasuraman, A. (1991) *Marketing Services: Competing Through Quality*, New York: Free Press.

5 Based on Parasuraman, A. *et al.* (1985), *op. cit.*

6 For further information, see for example: The Ryanair corporate website, https://corporate.ryanair.com; Economist (2013) Ryanair's future - Oh really, O'Leary?, The Economist Print Edition.

7 Feigenbaum, A.V. (1986) *Total Quality Control*, New York: McGraw Hill.

8 Kaynak, H. (2003) 'The relationship between total quality management practices and their effects on firm performance', *Journal of Operations Management*, **21,** pp. 405–435.

9 Economist (2013) 'Overtired, and overdrawn', *The Economist* (print edition), June 15; Wilson, H. (2014) 'Fat-fingered trader sets Tokyo alarms ringing', *The Times*, October 2.

10 ISO website: http://www.iso.org/iso/iso_9000_essentials

11 The EFQM website: www.efqm.org

CHAPTER 13

1 Boyes, W. (2011) 'David Van Wyk shares the Disney Imagineering project management process', controlglobal.com, June 29; Hoske, M.T. (2011) 'What do Walt Disney Imagineering and NASA space travel have in common? Engineering inspiration', *Control Engineering*, September 22: http://www.controleng.com/

2 raconteur.net (2015) 'Project management', Raconteur Media Ltd, August 2; World Health Organization malaria programme: http://www.who.int/topics/malaria/en/

3 The Scottish Parliament website (www.scottish.parliament.uk); BBC News (2004) 'Holyrood price tag rise to £430 million', February 24 (retrieved October 29 2014: http://news.bbc.co.uk/1/hi/scotland/3517225.stm; http://www.playthegame.org/news/news-articles/2014/the-lost-legacy-of-brazil%E2%80%99s-world-cup/; http://engineeringsport.co.uk/2010/04/30/whats-wrong-at-wembley/

Index